Military History of Late Rome AD 457–518

For my wife Sini, and children Ari and Nanna

The Military History of Late Rome AD 457–518

Dr. Ilkka Syvänne

© Dr. Ilkka Syvänne 2014

Pen & Sword
MILITARY

First published in Great Britain in 2020 by
Pen & Sword Military
An imprint of
Pen & Sword Books Ltd
Yorkshire – Philadelphia

Copyright © Dr. Ilkka Syvänne 2020

ISBN 978 1 47389 532 4

The right of Dr. Ilkka Syvänne to be identified as Author of this work has
been asserted by him in accordance with the Copyright, Designs and Patents
Act 1988.

Printed and bound in the UK by TJ Books Ltd,
Padstow, Cornwall.

Pen & Sword Books Limited incorporates the imprints of Atlas, Archaeology,
Aviation, Discovery, Family History, Fiction, History, Maritime, Military,
Military Classics, Politics, Select, Transport,
True Crime, Air World, Frontline Publishing, Leo Cooper, Remember
When, Seaforth Publishing, The Praetorian Press, Wharncliffe
Local History, Wharncliffe Transport, Wharncliffe True Crime
and White Owl.

For a complete list of Pen & Sword titles please contact

PEN & SWORD BOOKS LIMITED
47 Church Street, Barnsley, South Yorkshire, S70 2AS, England
E-mail: enquiries@pen-and-sword.co.uk
Website: www.pen-and-sword.co.uk

Or

PEN AND SWORD BOOKS
1950 Lawrence Rd, Havertown, PA 19083, USA
E-mail: Uspen-and-sword@casematepublishers.com
Website: www.penandswordbooks.com

Contents

Acknowledgements

Acknowledgments are due to the very same persons that I mentioned in the first book. I thank both Professor Geoffrey Greatrex for his recommendation and Commissioning Editor Philip Sidnell for accepting my book proposal. Special thanks are also due to Matt Jones, Barnaby Blacker, Tara Moran and other staff of the Pen & Sword for their stellar work and for the outstanding support they give the author.

I thank my family Sini, Ari and Nanna for their patience.

Thanks are due to my father and to my late mother who unknowingly contributed to this volume by bringing back books and photos from Sicily in May 2005. I gave that trip as a gift to my parents but little did I know that I would be able to incorporate material brought back by them exactly nine years later (26 May 2014) after their visit to the city of Agrigento on 26 May 2005 so that the book was basically finished by July of the same year. However, the book has been partially updated after the publication of Ian Hughes' excellent *Patricians and Emperors* in 2015. At the same time, I moved the events taking place in the west after the year 476 to the section dealing with eastern matters, because I felt that the traditional date for the end of West Rome, 476, would be preferable from the narrative point of view. Odoacer/Odovacar did recognize Nepos as his ruler until 480, and then continued to recognize the eastern emperor Zeno at least until 488, but even so it is clear that as a King of Italy he was actually an independent ruler.

I also want to thank in particular Vicus Ultimus, the famous Polish re-enactor group, for their outstanding contribution and support in the form of photos. Without their efforts this book would be a lot less colourful.

List of Plates

Augsburg II helmet. © Vicus Ultimus.
Augsburg II helmet with feathers. © Vicus Ultimus.
Augst helmet. © Vicus Ultimus.
Berkasovo II helmet. © Vicus Ultimus.
A reconstruction of helmet after Ch. Miks. © Vicus Ultimus.
Burgh castle helmet. © Vicus Ultimus.
Christies helmet. © Vicus Ultimus.
Deurne helmet. © Vicus Ultimus.
Deurne helmet from behind. © Vicus Ultimus.
Budapest knife. © Vicus Ultimus.
Bonn-style *spatha*. © Vicus Ultimus.
Burg Castle francisca. © Vicus Ultimus.
Socks, Egypt Tarim stitch. © Vicus Ultimus.
Draco-standard. © Vicus Ultimus.
A Gothic village – Masłomęcz, Poland. © Vicus Ultimus.
Image/mosaic in San Maria Maggiore, Ravenna. (Public Domain).
Members of Vicus Ultimus at Hejmstead, Romo – North Sea coast. © Vicus Ultimus.
A night scene inside a house at the Gothic village – Masłomęcz, Poland. © Vicus Ultimus.
Re-enactors of the Vicus Ultimus group at Hejmstead, Romo – North Sea coast. © Vicus Ultimus.
Male and female re-enactors outside the Gothic village – Masłomęcz, Poland. © Vicus Ultimus.
Decorative gear worn by men. © Vicus Ultimus.
A hunting knife after a British Museum example 4–5th century AD. © Vicus Ultimus.
A bracelet. © Vicus Ultimus.
Musée Parc archéologique des Temps Barbares. © Vicus Ultimus.
Horsemen. Image/mosaic in San Maria Maggiore, Ravenna. (Public Domain).
Re-enactors of the Vicus Ultimus group at Hejmstead, Romo – North Sea coast. © Vicus Ultimus.
Detail from muscle armour. © Vicus Ultimus.
Ejsbol-Sarry subtype 2, variant 2 *spatha*. © Vicus Ultimus.
Manica arm-guard. © Vicus Ultimus.
Soldiers. Image/mosaic in San Maria Maggiore, Ravenna. (Public Domain).
More soldiers. Image/mosaic in San Maria Maggiore, Ravenna. (Public Domain).
Still more soldiers. Image/mosaic in San Maria Maggiore, Ravenna. (Public Domain).
Even more soldiers. Image/mosaic in San Maria Maggiore, Ravenna. (Public Domain).
A coin of Leo I. British Museum. (Photo by author).

List of Maps

Introduction

The intention of this book, the fifth in a series of seven, is to present an overview of all of the principal aspects of Roman military history during the years 457–518. It was then that the Western Empire collapsed while the Eastern Empire started its slow recovery. The structure of the book follows the reigns of the emperors in chronological order, and the events and wars are also usually presented in chronological order. However, for the sake of ease of reading some events that took place in one particular sector of the empire are grouped together. The uneven survival of evidence means that there are huge gaps in our knowledge and that some of my conclusions are only my best educated guesses.

The text follows the same principles as the previous books and includes direct references to sources only when necessary or when my conclusions can be considered controversial or new. Neither have I included descriptions or analyses of the sources used and their problems, because there exists expert literature devoted to this subject. Some general comments, however, are in order. All of the period sources had their limitations. The narrative histories were restricted to dealing with only certain types of information (mainly politics and wars) and followed the literary models set before them. The chronicles usually give only the barest of details. The ecclesiastical histories concentrated mainly on religious events. The panegyrics and orations were also naturally restricted by the genre. All the authors writing within the Roman Empire had to take into account the fact that they wrote under dictators who had the power over life and death. We should also not forget the personal goals of the authors, which naturally varied. The quality of the Armenian, Georgian, Arabic and Persian histories etc vary greatly, and in contrast to the Roman material also present legendary material that has to be sifted through carefully. Nevertheless, in places these sources allow one to shed light on otherwise murky events.

When I refer to some chronicle, for example by Cassiodorus, *Chronica Gallica* (452, 511), Hydatius, Isidore of Seville, Jordanes (*Romana*), Paulus Diaconus, Prosper, etc, the exact point of reference can be found in the annalistic dating even when I do not always state this in the narrative. These sources are conveniently collected in the MGH series, which is available online, for example from Internet Archive.

In this study when I refer to Spain I mean the whole of the Iberian Peninsula including Lusitania (modern Portugal). However, when I refer to Britain, I mean only the portion under Roman control. This solution has been adopted solely for the sake of making references easier.

As far as the language, transliteration, and titles are concerned I have usually adopted the easiest solutions. I have used the transliterations most commonly used except in the case of Greek military terms which I have generally transliterated so that I have maintained the original F of the Greek instead of using the PH. I have also adopted the practice of the Oxford UP and used capital letters for all offices which could be held by only one person at a time. I have also used capital letters for all specific types of troops and military units. However, when I have referred to several office holders simultaneously (e.g. *comites*/counts, *duces*/dukes) I have used small letters.

All illustrations, drawings, maps and diagrams etc have been drawn and prepared by the author unless stated otherwise. I have used the *Barrington Atlas* as the principal source for the maps.

Abbreviations

a.455	year 455/AD 455
BZ	*Byzantinische Zeitschrift*
Cav.	Cavalry
CGall. 452	Chronica Gallica 452 (Chron. Min., Mommsen, Berlin 1892)
CGall. 511	Chronica Gallica 511 (Chron. Min., Mommsen, Berlin 1892)
Com. Dom.	Comes Domesticorum (Count of Domestics)
CRP	Comes Rei Privatae (Count of the Privy Purse)
CSL	Comes Sacrarum Largitionum (Count of the Sacred Largess)
DOP	*Dumbarton Oaks Papers*
GC	Gallic Chronicle
Hydat.	Hydatius
Inf.	Infantry
Isid. HRGVS	Isidorus of Seville, *Historia de regibus Gothorum, Vandalorum et Suevorum*
LHF	Anon. *Liber Historiae Francorum*
LI	Light infantry
Mag. Eq.	Magister Equitum (Master of Horse)
Mag. Eq. et Ped.	Magister Equitum et Peditum (Master of Horse and Foot)
Mag. Mil.	Magister Militum (Master of Soldiers)
Mag. Off.	Magister Officiorum (Master of Office)
Mag. Ped.	Magister Peditum (Master of Foot)
Marc. Com. or Marc.	Marcellinus Comes
MGH	Monumenta Historia Germaniae
MGH AA	Monumenta Historia Germaniae Auctores Antiquitissimonum
MHLR	*Military History of Late Rome*
MVM	Magister Utriusque Militiae (Master of All Arms of Service)
MVM Praes.	Magister Utriusque Militiae Praesentales (Praesental MVM)
Or.	Orations
PLRE1	See Bibliography
PLRE2	See Bibliography
PP	Praefectus Praetorio (Praetorian Prefect)
PPI	Praefectus Praetorio Italiae et Africae (PP of Italy and Africa)
PPIL	Praefectus Praetorio Illyrici
PPG	Praefectus Praetorio Galliarum
PPO	Praefectus Praetorio Orientis
PSC	Praepositus Sacri Cubiculi (Leader of Sacred Bedroom)
PVC	Praefectus Urbis Constantiopolitanae (Urban Prefect of Constantinople)
PVR	Praefectus Urbis Romae
QSP	Quaestor Sacri Palatii (Questor of the Sacred Palace)
REF1	See Bibliography
REF2	See Bibliography

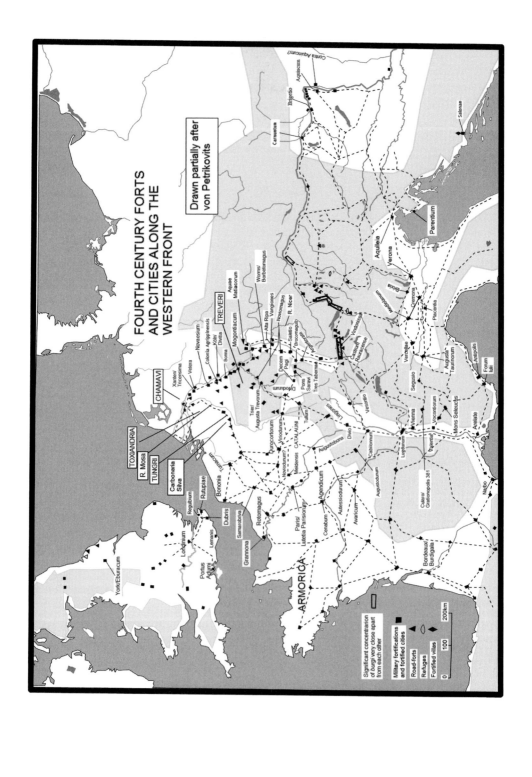

FOURTH CENTURY FORTS
AND CITIES ALONG THE
WESTERN FRONT

Drawn partially after
von Petrikovits

Significant concentration
of *burgi* very close apart
from each other

Military fortifications
and fortified cities

Road-forts

Refuges

Fortified villas

0   100   200km

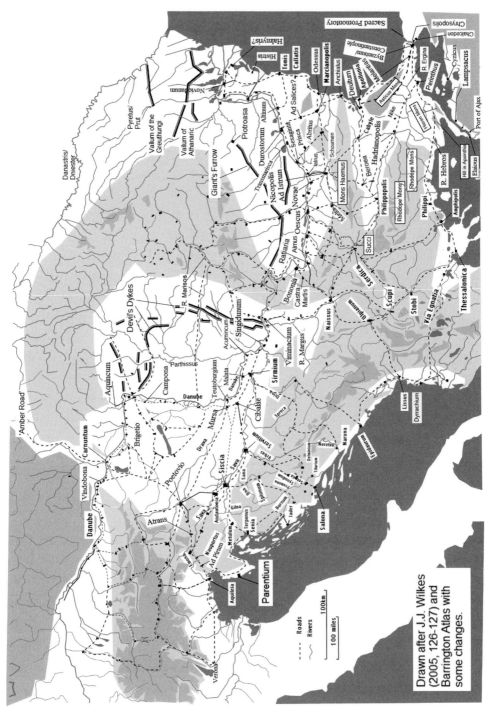

The Balkans

Drawn after J.J. Wilkes (2005, 126-127) and Barrington Atlas with some changes.

Roads
Rivers

100 km
100 miles

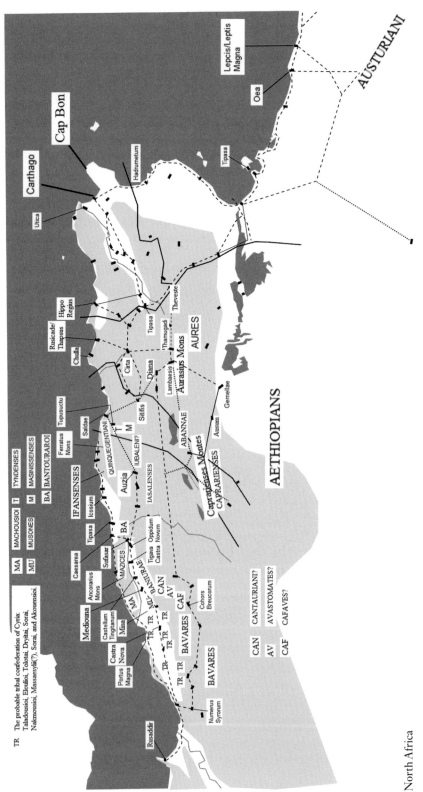

TR   The probable tribal confederation of Cyriu:
     Tabadousioi, Eloultoi, Tolotai, Dryltai, Sorai,
     Nakmousioi, Massaessylii(?), Sorai, and Akouersioi.

MA	MACHOUSIOI	T	TYNIDENSES
MU	MUSONES	M	MASINISSENSES
		BA	BANTOURAROI

IFANSENSES

QUINQUEGENTIANI

IUBALENI?

IASALENSES

ABANNAE

Capraienses Montes

CAPRARIENSES

AETHIOPIANS

CAN   CANTAURIANI?
AV   AVASTOMATES?
CAF   CAFAVES?

Mediouna

BAVARES

BAVARES

AURES

Aurasius Mons

AUSTURIANI

Cap Bon

Carthago

Lepcis/Leptis Magna

Oea

Tipasa

Utica

Hadrumetum

Rusicade/ Thapsus

Hippo Regius

Tipasa

Theveste

Cirta

Diana

Lambaesis

Thamugadi

Chulla

Sitifis

Gemellae

Ausam

Tupusuctu

Saldae

Ferratus Mons

Icosium

Tipasa

Sufasar

Caesarea

Ancorarius Mons

Castellum Tingitanum

Mina

Castra Nova

Portus Magna

Rusaddir

Tigava Oppidum
Castra Novum

Cohors Breucorum

Numerus Syrorum

BA

MAZICES

MA
MU
BANURAE

CAN
AV
CAF

TR
TR
TR
TR
TR
TR
TR
TR
TR
TR

M
T

North Africa

Arabia

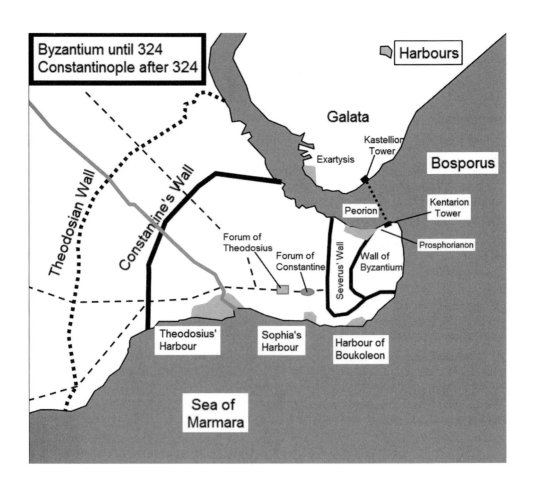

Byzantium until 324
Constantinople after 324

Harbours

Galata

Kastellion
Tower

Exartysis

Bosporus

Theodosian Wall

Constantine's Wall

Peorion

Kentarion
Tower

Prosphorianon

Forum of
Theodosius

Forum of
Constantine

Severus' Wall

Wall of
Byzantium

Theodosius'
Harbour

Sophia's
Harbour

Harbour of
Boukoleon

Sea of
Marmara

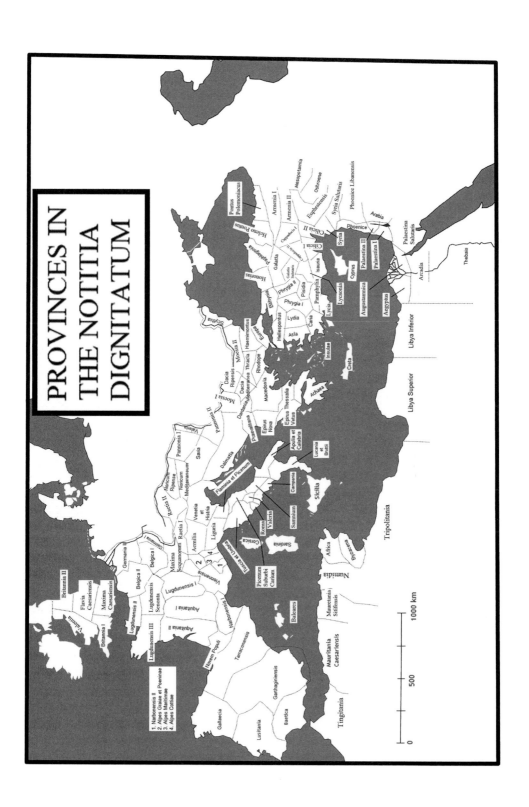

PROVINCES IN
THE NOTITIA
DIGNITATUM

1. Narbonensis II
2. Alpes Graiae et Poeninae
3. Alpes Maritimae
4. Alpes Cottiae

Britannia II
Flavia Caesariensis
Maxima Caesariensis
Britannia I
Valentia

Germania II
Belgica II
Belgica I
Germania I
Maxima Sequanorum
Raetia I
Raetia II
Noricum Mediterraneum
Noricum Ripense
Pannonia I
Savia
Pannonia II
Valeria

Lugdunensis II
Lugdunensis Senonia
Lugdunensis III
Lugdunensis I
Aquitania I
Aquitania II
Novem Populi
Narbonensis I
Viennensis
Acmilia
Venetia et Istria
Liguria
Flaminia et Picenum
Dalmatia

Gallaecia
Lusitania
Tarraconensis
Carthaginiensis
Baetica

Mauretania Caesariensis
Mauretania Sitifensis
Tingitania
Numidia
Byzacena
Africa
Tripolitania

Corsica
Tuscia et Umbria
Picenum Suburbi Carium
Roma
Valeria
Samnium
Campania
Sardinia
Sicilia
Apulia et Calabria
Lucania et Brutii
Balcares

Scythia
Moesia II
Haemimontus
Europa
Rhodope
Thracia
Dacia Ripensis
Dacia Mediterranea
Moesia I
Dardania
Macedonia
Praevalitana
Epirus Nova
Epirus Vetus
Thessalia
Achaea
Creta
Insulae

Pontus Polemoniacus
Heleno Pontus
Paphlagonia
Armenia I
Armenia II
Galatia
Honorias
Bithynia
Phrygia II
Phrygia I
Hellespontus
Lydia
Asia
Caria
Pisidia
Pamphylia
Lycaonia
Lycia
Isauria
Cilicia II
Cilicia I
Cappadocia I
Cappadocia II
Galatia Salutaris

Mesopotamia
Osrhoene
Euphratensis
Syria Salutaris
Phoenice Libanensis
Syria
Phoenice
Cyprus
Augustamnica
Aegyptus
Arabia
Palaestina II
Palaestina I
Palaestina Salutaris
Arcadia
Thebais

Libya Inferior
Libya Superior

1000 km
500
0

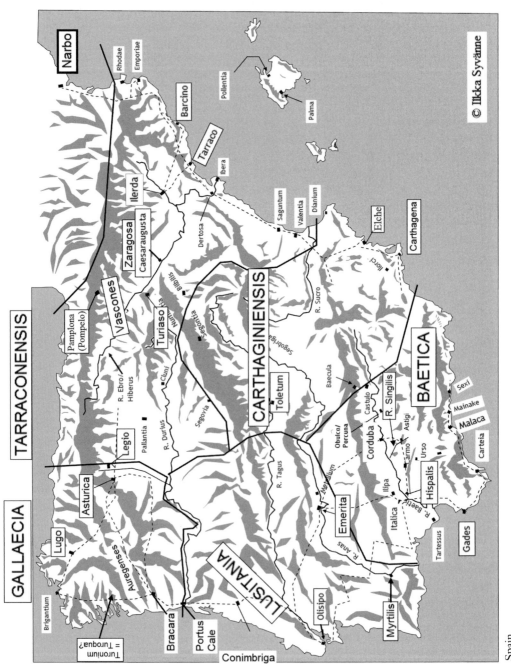

GALLAECIA

TARRACONENSIS

Narbo

Rhodae
Emporiae

Barcino

Tarraco

Ibera

Ilerda

Dertosa

Zaragosa
Caesaraugusta

Saguntum
Valentia
Dianium

Pamplona
(Pompelo)

Vascones

Turiaso

Bilbilis

Numantia

Segontia

Segobriga

Ilorci

R. Sucro

Elche

Carthagena

CARTHAGINIENSIS

Legio

Cluni

Pallantia

R. Durius

Segovia

R. Tagus

Toletum

Baecula

Castulo

Obulco/
Porcuna

Corduba

R. Singilis

BAETICA

Sexi

Astigi

Mainake

Malaca

Carmo

Urso

Carteia

Lugo

Asturica

Auregenses

Metellium

Emerita

Ilipa

Italica

R. Baetis

Hispalis

Brigantium

¿Turonium
= Turoqua?

Bracara

Portus
Cale

LUSITANIA

Olisipo

Myrtilis

R. Anas

Tartessus

Gades

Conimbriga

Spain

© Ilkka Syvänne

R. Ebro/
Hiberus

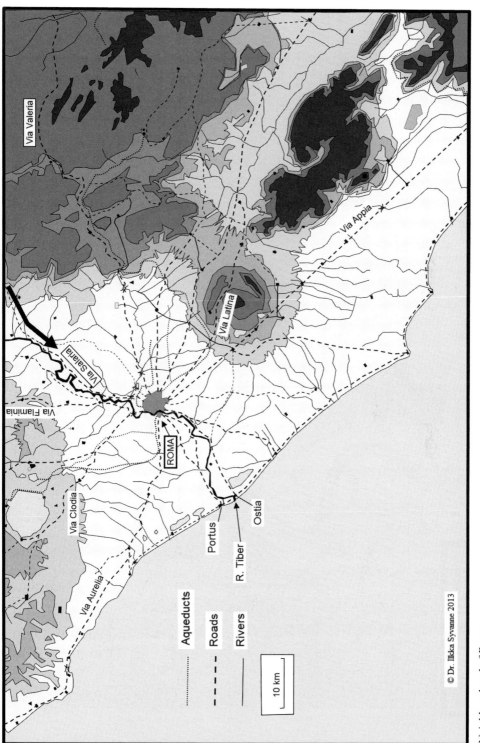

Neighbourhood of Rome

© Dr. Ilkka Syvänne 2013

Via Valeria

Via Appia

Via Latina

Via Flaminia

Via Salaria

Via Clodia

Via Aurelia

ROMA

Portus

R. Tiber

Ostia

Aqueducts

Roads

Rivers

10 km

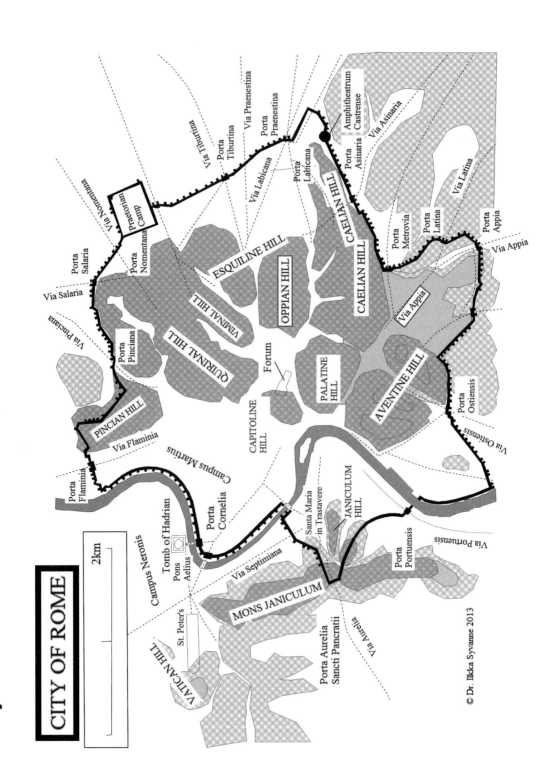

CITY OF ROME

2km

Praetorian Camp

Via Nomentana
Via Tiburtina
Porta Tiburtina
Via Praenestina
Porta Praenestina
Via Labicana
Porta Labicana
Amphitheatrum Castrense
Porta Asinaria
Via Asinaria
Via Latina

CAELIAN HILL
CAELIAN HILL

Porta Metrovia
Porta Latina
Porta Appia
Via Appia

ESQUILINE HILL
OPPIAN HILL
VIMINAL HILL

Porta Salaria
Porta Nomentana
Via Salaria

QUIRINAL HILL

Porta Pinciana
Via Pinciana

Via Appia

PINCIAN HILL

Forum

CAPITOLINE HILL

PALATINE HILL

AVENTINE HILL

Porta Ostiensis
Via Ostiensis

Via Flaminia

Porta Flaminia
Campus Martius

Tomb of Hadrian
Pons Aelius
Campus Neronis

Porta Cornelia

Santa Maria in Trastavere

JANICULUM HILL

Porta Portuensis
Via Portuensis

Via Septimiana

MONS JANICULUM

St. Peter's
VATICAN HILL

Porta Aurelia Sancti Pancratii
Via Aurelia

© Dr. Ilkka Syvänne 2013

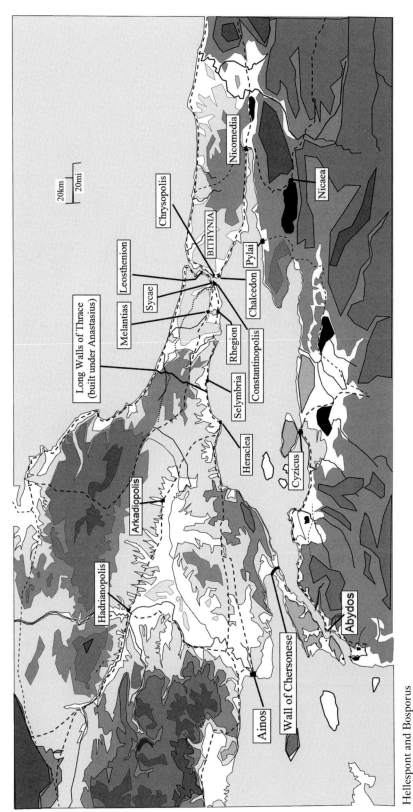

Hellespont and Bosporus

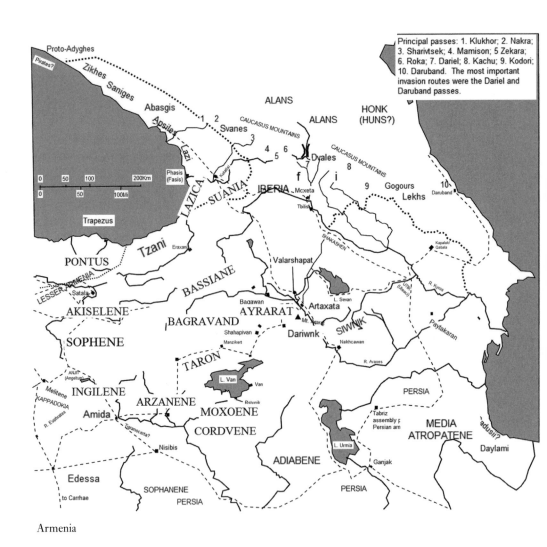

Principal passes: 1. Klukhor; 2. Nakra; 3. Sharivtsek; 4. Mamison; 5 Zekara; 6. Roka; 7. Dariel; 8. Kachu; 9. Kodori; 10. Daruband. The most important invasion routes were the Dariel and Daruband passes.

Proto-Adyghes

Pirates?

Zikhes Saniges

Abasgis

Apsiles

Lazi

ALANS

ALANS

HONK (HUNS?)

Svanes

CAUCASUS MOUNTAINS

CAUCASUS MOUNTAINS

Dvales

Gogours

Lekhs

Daruband

0   50   100   200Km
0   50   100Mi

Phasis (Fasis)

Trapezus

LAZICA

SUANIA

Kutaisi

IBERIA

Mcxeta

Tbilisi

f

i

Kapalak Qabala

Tzani

PONTUS

Eraxani

LESSER ARMENIA

Satala

AKISELENE

BASSIANE

SHAKASHEN

R. Kyros

Valarshapat

Bagawan

AYRARAT

Artaxata

L. Sevan

Mt. Ararat

SIWNIK

Paytakaran

BAGRAVAND

Shahapivan

Dariwnk

SOPHENE

Manzikert

Nakhcawan

R. Araxes

TARON

L. Van

Van

INGILENE

ANUT (Angeltun)

Melitene

KAPPADOKIA

R. Euphrates

ARZANENE

MOXOENE

Rstunik

PERSIA

Amida

Tigranocerta?

CORDVENE

Tabriz
assembly p
Persian arm

MEDIA ATROPATENE

Daylami

Nisibis

L. Urmia

Ganjak

adusii?

Edessa

to Carrhae

SOPHANENE

PERSIA

ADIABENE

PERSIA

Armenia

Chapter One

Introduction: The Roman Empire in 457

The General Situation

Thanks to the fact that Marcian had decided to support the West Romans against the Huns, the Hunnic threat had effectively ended by the end of the reign of Marcian so that all that was left was the mopping up of the remaining scattered Hunnic forces. The Empire was therefore poised to put an end to the second of the major problems, which was the occupation of North Africa by the Vandals.

Despite the fact that much of Spain was controlled by the Suevi, and much of Gaul was controlled by the Visigoths, Franks and Bacaudae, and Dalmatia was the de facto independent domain of Marcellinus, the Vandals were still the principal thorn in the flesh of the Romans. In this situation the principal problem facing the West Romans was that the powerbrokers in the west consisted of figures who lacked the authority to force the senators to pay their fair share of the taxes, including the contribution of native recruits for the army, so that it was not possible to raise a large enough army and navy for the task at hand. This problem concerns in particular the position of Ricimer who, as barbarian, was unacceptable as Emperor and could not force the senators to pay their taxes, but was still powerful enough to act as kingmaker. Ricimer's position depended on his control of the army and on the support he gained from the conservative members of the Senate in return for his support for their demands. This was an impossible equation. It was thanks to this that the West Romans needed East Roman support if they ever hoped to be able to defeat the Vandals and retain control of the rest of their realm.

The second major problem facing the West Romans was the rampant corruption which was the result of the too-powerful position of the Senate and the army vis-à-vis the Emperor. The emperors simply lacked the means to put a stop to the corruption because it was protected by the army which in its turn was supported by the Senate. The contrast between East and West Rome could not have been greater. In the East the emperors retained effective control of the army thanks to the division of the forces among several *magistri*. In addition to this, the East Romans had managed to incorporate the barbarians more tightly into their armed forces and they had also managed to diminish the debilitating effects of corruption better than the West Romans. The principal problem facing the East Romans in 457 was that the position of Aspar had become too dominant for the good of the Empire because he managed to install Leo I, his own man, on the throne. This created a situation in which the barbarian federates formed a power block that relied on Aspar's support and Aspar's position vis-à-vis the Emperor depended on their support. Thus the East Romans faced a power struggle between the native and barbarian factions, which in its turn undid much of the so-far successful integration of the barbarians into East Roman society; and we should not forget that even after this struggle the barbarians were so well integrated into East Roman society that the populace of Constantinople could demand the overthrow of the native Emperor Anastasius and his replacement with the barbarian Areobindus as late as 512.

Roman Society, Administration and Military in 457[1]

At the apex of Roman society stood the emperor with the title of *Augustus*. Actual power, however, could be in the hands of some other important person like a general or administrator or family member. There still existed senates in Rome and Constantinople which could be included in the decision-making process when the emperor (or the power behind the throne) wanted to court the goodwill of the moneyed senators, but this was not usually necessary and could not be done when it was important to make decisions fast. Late-Roman imperial administration was divided into three sections: 1) Military; 2) Palatine; 3) Imperial and Fiscal.

Fifth-century Roman armed forces consisted of the imperial bodyguards, praesental forces (central field armies), *comitatenses* (field armies), *limitanei* (frontier forces), *bucellarii* (private retainers), federates and temporary allies, in addition to which came the civilian paramilitary forces. Basic tactics and military equipment remained much the same as they had been previously. Infantry tactics were based on variations of the phalanx with a clear preference for the use of the hollow square/oblong array, while cavalry tactics were based on variations of cavalry formation with two lines. The Romans possessed a clear advantage over most of their enemies in siege and naval warfare, but as the Vandals had gained possession of the Roman fleet in Carthage they had the advantage over West Roman naval forces. The East Romans, who possessed superior financial and naval resources, still had the advantage, but only when their forces were led by able commanders.

As stated in volumes 3–4, the era from 395 until about 518 saw a massive increase in the size of a typical field army. This process had already started at the turn of the fifth century, but it assumed unprecedented proportions when the rise of Attila the Hun increased the size of the field armies even further, which he did by adding new tribes into his already massive force. The battle of the nations, the battle of the Catalaunian Fields in 451, saw the apogee of this development. This was the result of massing all of the forces of the West against all of the forces of barbarian East Europe, but after this the size of the forces diminished because it was no longer possible to assemble such conglomerations of tribes under single leaders. As I noted in volumes 3–4, the figures recorded in the sources for the Battle of the Catalaunian Fields are actually not as outlandish as usually claimed by the historians. We should remember that both armies consisted of masses of barbarian tribes and tribal confederacies each of which even on their own possessed massive armies. We should also remember that Gaul (mod. France) was a heavily populated area which had once been one of the breadbaskets of the Empire, and that it could therefore support vast armies much akin to the armies of the Revolutionary or Napoleonic-era France.

Roman soldiers were equipped much as they had always been. Martial equipment of the heavy infantry consisted of spears and javelins of various lengths and types, *plumbatae-* darts, swords of various types, typically large round or oval shields (other types of shields were also used), armour (typically chainmail, but scale, plate and segmented armours were also used), and helmet (usually segmented, ridge or plate, but single piece bowls were also used). Some of the heavy-armed were trained to use bows as well, while all of them were trained to use slings. When the purpose was to fight in difficult terrain, the heavy infantry could go without armour (or were equipped with padded coats or leather armour) or helmets and be equipped with smaller and lighter shields, swords and javelins. The light infantry usually wore no armour and were equipped with swords, daggers, javelins, slings or bows. Heavy and light cavalries wore basically the same type of heavy equipment as the heavy and light infantries, but some of its equipment had been modified to suit the needs of the cavalry battle. This concerns in particular the bow, which was weaker than the infantry counterpart. The equipment worn by the rowers/sailors who were required to fight was quite similar to the equipment of the land forces. The same is true for the equipment worn by the marines on board the ships. The only real difference is that the shields used on board were required to be stronger and larger than typically on land. In addition to this, the armed forces possessed specialists for all sorts of needs, the most important of which were the siege specialists with their artillery pieces.

For the equipment worn at this time, see the plates and the images of soldiers included in the text. The following drawings by Mai of the images included in the *Ilias Ambrosiana* (fifth century or turn of the sixth) give a good overall picture of what types of equipment were used by the Romans at this time. These include all of the basic variants: the light infantry, foot archers, heavy infantry, cavalry lancers and mounted archers. See also the excellent reconstructions of equipment by Vicus Ultimus in the Plates section, which give some examples of the types of equipment the Romans used but which are not depicted here.

The following diagrams show the standard land combat formations in use at this time. Those who are interested in analysis of those are advised to consult the previous volumes in this series and also the subsequent volumes (together with my biography of the Emperor Gallienus for earlier instances) which analyze in greater detail the information provided by the *Strategikon*. See also Syvänne, 2004 and forthcoming analysis of combat tactics.

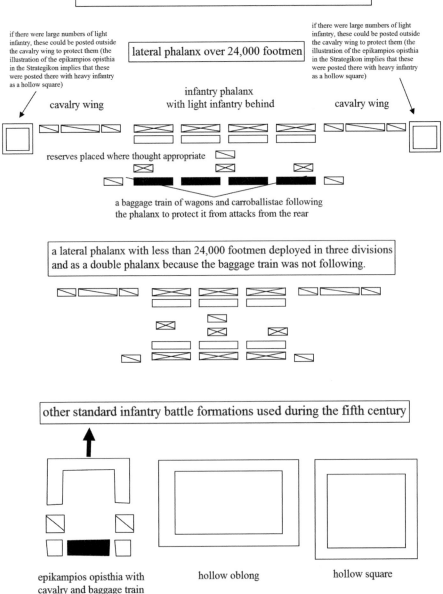

the standard infantry battle formations of the fifth and sixth centuries

if there were large numbers of light infantry, these could be posted outside the cavalry wing to protect them (the illustration of the epikampios opisthia in the Strategikon implies that these were posted there with heavy infantry as a hollow square)

lateral phalanx over 24,000 footmen

if there were large numbers of light infantry, these could be posted outside the cavalry wing to protect them (the illustration of the epikampios opisthia in the Strategikon implies that these were posted there with heavy infantry as a hollow square)

infantry phalanx with light infantry behind

cavalry wing

cavalry wing

reserves placed where thought appropriate

a baggage train of wagons and carroballistae following the phalanx to protect it from attacks from the rear

a lateral phalanx with less than 24,000 footmen deployed in three divisions and as a double phalanx because the baggage train was not following.

other standard infantry battle formations used during the fifth century

epikampios opisthia with cavalry and baggage train

hollow oblong

hollow square

The following diagrams show the standard cavalry battle arrays of this era

The combat formation of a large cavalry army in excess of 10,000-15,000 men:

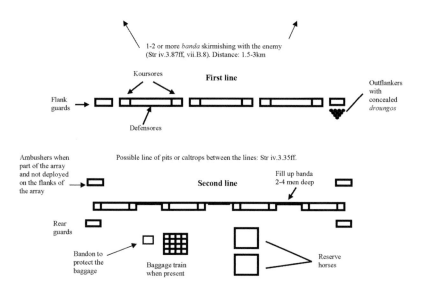

Super large battle array for cavalry armies in excess of ca. 50,000 men:

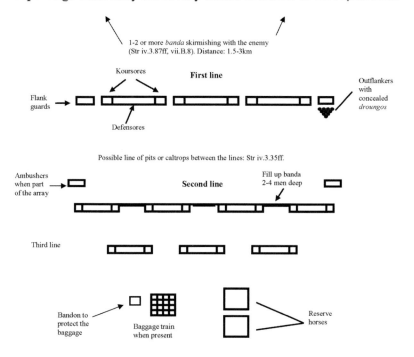

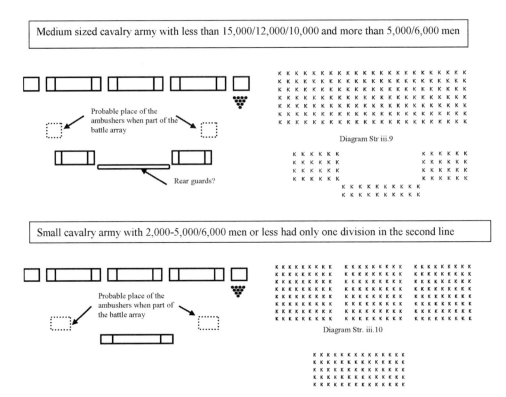

Medium sized cavalry army with less than 15,000/12,000/10,000 and more than 5,000/6,000 men

Probable place of the ambushers when part of the battle array

Rear guards?

Diagram Str iii.9

Small cavalry army with 2,000-5,000/6,000 men or less had only one division in the second line

Probable place of the ambushers when part of the battle array

Diagram Str. iii.10

Naval combat formations were single line abreast with reserves, double line/phalanx with reserves, convex to break through the enemy centre, crescent to outflank, and circle for defence. In advance of these there were two to three ships that acted as scouting ships, but which could also be used to break up the cohesion of the enemy array by leaving them exposed in front. Transport ships were usually placed behind the combat ships. The high quality of Roman seamen, rowers and marines together with better ship designs ensured Roman naval superiority against any foe until the Vandals managed to turn these advantages against them.

Chapter Two

Enemies and Allies

In 457 the enemies of Rome were basically the same as before, with the difference that now some were located inside the Empire, while Britain and Armorica were only nominally part of the Roman Empire as autonomous areas. The Picts and the Irish threatened mainly the Britons, but the Saxons posed a threat to both Britain and Gaul. The Picts and the Irish possessed naval forces while their armies were usually lightly equipped but still capable of fighting in close order formations. Their siege skills were very rudimentary. The Saxon navy was more formidable than the ones used by the Picts, and their land armies were also more numerous and better at close-quarter fighting. Their siege skills were slightly better than that of their neighbours, but still not on par with the Romans.

The Huns and Alans, together with Germanic Franks, Visigoths, Ostrogoths, Burgundians, Vandals, Suevi and other Germanic tribes, formed the principal threats for the Romans in continental Europe. With the exception of the Huns, some scattered Ostrogoths and some other Germanic tribes, most now dwelt inside the Roman Empire. The Huns, however, were no longer a major threat as they had been under Attila. In other words, the principal problem posed by these enemies was strategic. The Romans no longer possessed clear geographical territories which to defend.

The tactical threat remained the same. The Huns and other nomads used mainly mounted archers in combat, but were still prepared to fight at close quarters when needed. The Germanic peoples specialized in the close-quarters fighting with cavalry or infantry, but some of the tribes like the Goths were quite good at long distance fighting with bows too. For a fuller discussion and analysis of tactics, see vols. 1–4.

The principal threats in the east were the Sasanians, but the Caucasian peoples, Alans, Huns and Arabs, could also make trouble. The Sasanian Empire was a particularly fearsome enemy because the Persians possessed a very large and well organized empire with vast reserves of high quality cavalry and equally vast numbers of footmen usable as cannon fodder. Most importantly, the Sasanians possessed expertise in siege warfare and were in some ways even more effective in that than the Romans. The Romans were therefore lucky that the Persians faced similar troubles with the nomads on their northern and Central Asian frontiers. The basic components of Sasanian military methods remained the same as before, but Bahram V Gur had introduced a number of reforms. These included the increased importance of mounted archery among the Sasanians, the introduction of more powerful archery shooting techniques, the introduction of the arrow guide and possibly also the very small *siper*-shield to increase the length of the draw. For these see my article on the reign of Bahram available online at academia.edu. The reign of Peroz saw further development in the abandonment of the two-handed use of the lance in favour of the combination of shield and spear. The idea behind the use of the shield was probably that it gave better protection for its wielder against the arrows of the mounted archers of Central Asia that Peroz faced. The reign of Peroz also saw an end to the use of the lancer charge as a principal tactical doctrine of the Persian cavalry. It was thanks to his failures that the Persians became more methodical in their approach to warfare and largely abandoned the advantage that the mobility of their cavalry forces could have given them.

The enemies facing the Romans in the deserts of Arabia, Egypt and North Africa were also the same as before: Arabs, Yemenite Arabs, Nubians, Ethiopians and Berbers/Moors. These did not pose any major threats until 468, when naval losses enabled the Arabs and Yemenites to threaten the Romans in the Red Sea. In fact, the main threat to the Romans in North Africa were the Vandals, who crossed the Straits of Gibraltar with dire consequences, for the Romans now lost their naval supremacy in the Western Mediterranean, a major source of income, and one of the breadbaskets of the empire.

For a fuller discussion of the enemies of Rome and their tactics, see the *MHLR* vols. 1–4. In the following narrative, I do not necessarily refer to the original sources when I include details of the combat methods used by some particular enemy because I expect that readers are already familiar with these from previous volumes.

Chapter Three

The West 456–461: Majorian and Ricimer[1]

The Interregnum in the West 456–457: Marcian and Leo as sole emperors

The two rebels, Majorian and Ricimer, did not move to take the title of *Augustus* after their victory against the emperor Avitus but sought to obtain acceptance for their deed from the East. See *MHLR* Vol.4. Consequently there was a period during which West Rome was without its own emperor and was ruled by Ricimer and Majorian together. Ricimer was presumably *Comes et Magister Utriusque Militiae* (*Magister Peditum*) and Majorian *Comes Domesticorum*. It is usually assumed that Majorian was the junior partner in this alliance, because Ricimer had a higher rank and the backing of the military behind him, but we should not forget that Majorian was actually a native *Comes Domesticorum* with forces of his own, that he had the backing of the Italian nobility, and that he had been the designated successor of Valentinian III. Therefore I agree with Ian Hughes (2015, 63–64, 70–71) that Majorian was 'his own man' with his own goals. Regardless, it is still clear that Ricimer was militarily in the stronger position because he controlled the mostly barbarian military forces settled in the north of Italy and was also related to the royal barbarian houses. Ricimer's position however was weakened by the fact that he could not usurp power himself.

The process of obtaining acceptance from Constantinople was also complicated by the death of Marcian on 27 January 457. He was succeeded by Leo on 7 February 457. Consequently it is not entirely certain which of the Eastern emperors nominated Majorian as *MVM* (*Mag.Eq.*) and Ricimer as *Patricius* on 28 February 457. What is notable about these is that Ricimer was still recognized as Majorian's superior in the hierarchy of titles.

The toppling of Avitus led to troubles in Spain and in Gaul. The ousting of Avitus was not well received by his Visigothic and Burgundian allies and by his Gallic supporters who all rose against the usurpers and abandoned their campaign against the Suevi. When Theoderic learnt the news of the death of Avitus, he departed from Emerita shortly after Easter (31 March 457) and dispatched part of his allied force against the Romans of Gallaecia. According to Hydatius and Isidore, Theoderic had planned to sack Emerita, but was prevented by the warnings of the martyr Eulalia – the real cause would of course have been the urgent need to march to Gaul. The instructions of the allied force were to act as if they were coming to help the Romans against the Suevi and with this excuse they managed to gain entrance into Asturica. Theoderic's undercover special operatives (*praedontes* = robbers/pirates) spearheaded the operation. The barbarians sated their thirst for blood by initially slaughtering everyone they encountered but then started to take prisoners as booty. They pillaged the valuables, torched the city, and destroyed the churches and some of the surrounding fields. The Burgundian kings would not have felt any remorse about the destruction of the Catholic churches, because after their defeat in 436/7 they apparently first returned to being pagans after which they converted to Arian belief under the Visigothic influence (Escher, 73–78). The wives of the kings, however, appear to have usually been Catholics so that the Burgundians were clearly not as vehement in their beliefs as the Goths.

The nearby city of Palentia/Palencia met with similar fate, but the fort of Coviacum which lay at a distance of thirty miles could no longer be taken by surprise. The Visigoths settled on a prolonged siege, but were forced to abandon it after they had suffered too many casualties. After this the allies continued their march back to Gaul where they were to join the Gallic senators in opposition to Ricimer and Majorian. Hydatius states laconically that Aiolfus died in Portus Cale (Oporto) in June, which I take to mean that the returning Visigoths presumably under Theoderic himself crushed the rebel there.

Some of the Suevi of Gallaecia in their turn opposed Maldras and chose Framtane (or Franta) as their king. Both factions appear to have concluded peace with the Romans to limit the number of enemies they were facing. Maldras, however, broke his word immediately and threacherously invaded Lusitania where his forces entered the city of Olisipo (or Ulixippona, mod. Lisbon) in about 457/8 under the pretext of being allies. The city and the surrounding areas were pillaged.

The exact sequence of events in Gaul is not known with any certainty, but it appears probable that Avitus had kept Agrippinus in office as *MVM per Gallias* with the result that he was now in a position to support the enemies of Ricimer. Agrippinus and the Gallic senators appear to have now formed a faction with Visigothic and Burgundian support, because according to Marius of Avenches (a.456) the Burgundians occupied part of Gaul (parts of Lugdunensis I, Viennensis, Sequania) and divided it with the Gallic senators in 456/7. The Burgundians were ruled by two kings, Gundioc who now established his court at Lyons, and Hilperic whose court was located at Geneva. It seems probable that the Burgundians were settled mostly in those areas which had been vacated through death among Avitus's forces in the battle of Placentia on 17 October 456. It is possible that most of these lands consisted of those given to Alans by Aetius, but it is also possible that these were the areas that had been promised to them from the start by Avitus for their military service.

It is unsurprising that Aegidius accused Agrippinus of having favoured the barbarians and of having planned to surrender Roman provinces to them. Ricimer's men arrested Agrippinus and took him to Italy to be interrogated; he was condemned to death without a hearing. Agrippinus, however, managed to flee from prison and stay in hiding. Aegidius was appointed to succeed Agrippinus (Greg. 2.11), but faced the problem of having not enough available troops in south-eastern Gaul. Consequently Aegidius travelled north to have a meeting with the Salian Franks, his subjects.

According to Gregory of Tours 2.12, the reason for Childeric's downfall was that he had debauched the women of his followers. Childeric's subjects had intended to assassinate Childeric, but he had managed to flee to Thuringia with the help of a loyal subject called Wiomad (Greg. 2.12; Fredegar 3.11). Childeric divided a gold coin with Wiomad and instructed him to send the other half to him when the Franks were prepared to receive Childeric back. The Franks chose as their new king none other than Aegidius. This has been needlessly suspected by several modern historians. It was entirely in keeping with Germanic tribal habits to choose the man they thought most powerful as their king.

A good later example of this phenomenon is the appointment of Belisarius as king of the Goths. It was also not uncommon for the Frankish officers in Roman service to be simultaneously kings of their own tribes. It is also possible that Aegidius could have had some family connection with the Merovingians as suggested by MacGeorge. Regardless of this possible connection, it is still clear that Aegidius belonged to the Roman upper classes and may have belonged to the noble house of Syagrii of Lyon. It is probable that the nomination of Aegidius as King of the Salian Franks took place in about 453/4, presumably with Aetius' approval because Aegidius ruled the Salian Franks for eight years and Childeric I is attested to be among the commanders at the battle of Orleans in 463, so it is likely that Childeric had returned in about 461/2. I would therefore suggest that one of the reasons for the nomination of Aegidius as successor of Agrippinus was that he was not only a Roman but also a king of the Salian Franks.[2]

Reconstruction of the equipment worn by the Frankish king Childeric I (died c. 481/2) on the basis of equipment found from his tomb. For an analysis of the archaeological finds, see Brulet. Note the similarity of equipment with first century AD Germans. The basic Germanic equipment had remained the same. They did not wear armour or helmets, but used shields, spears and swords. The only addition to the older type of equipment is the pointed shield-boss which enabled its user to use 'shield bash' with greater efficiency. Note the simultaneous use of the *scramasax* and *spatha*. Note also the long hair, which signalled to all that he was a member of the royal family. (Drawn after Lebedynsky, 2001, 98 which is based on the reconstruction of P. Pellerin; This drawing was included in *MHLR* vol.1)

While in exile among the Thuringians, Childeric seduced Basina, wife of the local king Bisinus, with whom he was later to have the child called Clovis. The exile lasted for eight years, in the course of which Childeric's friend Wiomad acted as an advisor and sub-king (*regulus*) to *Rex* Aegidius on Frankish matters. Wiomad advised Aegidius to institute a poll tax of one gold coin, which subsequently increased to two coins and then to three. The Franks were prepared to pay the taxes because they hated the womanizing Childeric intensely, but then Wiomad managed to convince Aegidius that the Franks were planning to revolt and had to be cowed into obedience through mindless violence. Aegidius foolishly swallowed the bait and had 100 Franks executed as a warning in about 461. The time was then ripe for the return of Childeric, and Wiomad dispatched the other half of the coin to him. See later.[3]

The fact that the Gallic senators cooperated with the Burgundians meant the loss of south Gaul and whatever remained of its military forces, and we should not forget that these were not the only problems the usurpers were facing. The Vandals were threatening all coastal areas and the Alamanni were attacking Raetia. According to Sidonius, one 900-man detachment of Alamanni that had invaded through Raetia managed to penetrate as far as Campi Canini (near Bilitio[4]), but they were destroyed by a small force (*comitante manu*) under Burco sent by the *MVM* Majorian. This event can be dated to between 28 February and 1 April 457, because Majorian was appointed *MVM* on 28 February 457 and his soldiers proclaimed him *Caesar* on 1 April 457 at the military camp of Columella. Since we find Majorian near the city of Milan while he was *MVM*, it is clear that the defence of north-western Italy was in his hands while Ricimer was in charge of the Danubian campaign.

It is usually thought that Ricimer was behind Majorian's nomination as *Caesar* on 1 April 457 and then as *Augustus* on 28 December 457 because Malalas claims that Ricimer chose him and because Majorian in his own legislation (NMaj. 1 on 11 Jan. 458) calls Ricimer *parens*. The usual view is that Ricimer intended to use the native Roman noble as his puppet ruler. As noted by Ian Hughes, this is not necessarily the case, because Majorian was proclaimed *Caesar* by the troops and Majorian was clearly no puppet. The title of *Caesar* was less offensive than that of *Augustus* to both Leo and Ricimer and suggests some sort of pre-planning. If this is the case, then, as appears quite possible, Majorian spent the rest of 457 trying to obtain Leo's and Ricimer's approval for his measures, which finally came after the campaign season of 457 was over. Leo and Ricimer presumably felt that it was better to accept the situation than fight a civil war in a situation in which the Empire was threatened on all fronts. The fact that Majorian then paid particular respect to Ricimer in his first piece of legislation can be seen as a measure meant to sooth the potential rift between the two men. Majorian's subsequent actions however, suggest that he was acting independently of Ricimer even if he continued to pay his respect to him. If this line of reasoning is correct (which is not certain) then it is probable that Ricimer only waited for the right opportunity to get rid of his disloyal friend. It is possible that Ricimer chose Majorian even if he himself was away fighting against the enemy tribes while Majorian was shouted as *Caesar* by the troops.

One possibility for the final decision to nominate an independent *Caesar* and then *Augustus* for the West by Majorian, Ricimer, Leo, and the Senate, after some initial hesitance, was to prevent the prospect of having to face an independent Emperor nominated and dominated by the Gallic senators as had happened with Avitus. The final straw must have been the Gallic movement in 456/7 to nominate Marcellinus (or Marcellus?) as *Augustus* of the West despite the fact that Marcellinus did not want that. The choice of Marcellinus as Emperor would have been very beneficial for the West because he was undoubtedly the most gifted military commander of his age, the best evidence of which is his ability to defend Dalmatia successfully while still being able to defeat the Vandals and capture Sicily. The great Gaiseric/Gaiseric was no match for him. The principal problem however was that Marcellinus was a devout pagan and therefore unacceptable to the Italians. He could of course have converted superficially but he was apparently unwilling to do that, or even more likely he was just unwilling to initiate a full-scale civil war in a situation in which Majorian had already been nominated. Subsequent events prove that Marcellinus was quite prepared to conclude a peace and alliance with Majorian. He was a patriot first and foremost.

The Reign of Majorian, 28 December 457–2 August 461[5]

Majorian Strikes Back in 458

The year 458 saw several almost simultaneous campaigns: wars against the Gallic senators, Burgundians and Visigoths in Gaul under some unknown commander; the continuation of the Visigothic and Suevic attacks against the Romans in Spain; the defence of Italy against the Vandals under Majorian himself;[6] operations along the Danube under Ricimer.

The person in charge of the 458 campaign in Gaul was some unknown *MVM* praised by Sidonius the next year in 459. The likeliest candidates for this unknown *MVM* are the *MVM* Aegidius, *MVM* Nepotianus, and the *Magister Epistolarium* Petrus.[7] Considering the dearth of soldiers, it is probable that the bulk of the Roman forces during this campaign consisted of Franks under Aegidius, but this does not necessarily mean he would have been the overall commander.

Augustus Flavius Valerius Maiorianus =
emperor Majorian (457-461). Source: Hodgkin

It is unfortunate that we do not possess any details of the actual campaign. One possibility is that the Romans put the Burgundians between two armies so that Nepotianus advanced from Arles to Lyon while Aegidius marched his forces from the north to Lyon; a second is that Aegidius was in possession of south-eastern Gaul with Arles as his HQ where he stayed until reinforcements under Nepotianus arrived from Italy after which the Romans marched together along the Rhone against the Burgundians; a third is that Aegidius as *MVM per Gallias* was the only person in charge of operations.

The Romans appear to have both defeated the Burgundians in battle (the unknown *MVM* excelled Sulla in fighting) and forced them to seek shelter in Lyon through skilful manoeuvres (the *MVM* excelled Fabius in battlecraft). The subsequent siege involved the destruction and torching of the buildings and property outside the city walls. See the Map.

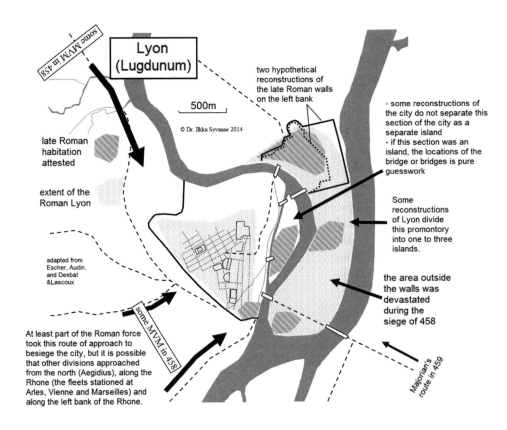

The siege was ended through negotiations conducted by the *Magister Epistolarium* Petrus. The Burgundians handed over hostages and allowed the Romans into the city. I would suggest that the reason for the negotiated settlement was that the Visigoths had mounted a relief operation while the Romans had placed a separate shielding army under Aegidius at Arles (if the bridge directly below the city walls was demolished and another pontoon bridge was located further away) or Valence or Vienne – at least this seems to be the likeliest reason and place for the besieging of Aegidius by some barbarians at some unknown city along the Rhone and Roman victory over the Visigoths in 458. The Visigoths must have attempted to bring help to their allies even if one of their armies was also fighting in Spain. As noted by MacGeorge (85ff.) Paulinus of Perigueux's poem appears to imply that Aegidius charged out of the city gates at the very moment a Roman relief army reached the scene and secured the pontoon bridge over the river. All of the abovementioned cities would fit the bill if one presumes that the Roman relief force advanced from Lyon on the right side of the Rhone River and that Aegidius needed to secure the pontoon bridge so that this relief army could be brought across. See the maps of the cities of Arles, Valence and Vienne in vol.3. The capture of the pontoon bridge also had the benefit of blocking the only route of retreat from the Visigoths, which forced them to negotiate terms of peace. The peace is to be dated to the year 458, because Majorian was expecting to obtain Visigothic allies when he marched to Lyon during the winter of 458/9.[8] The defeat of the Burgundians in Lyon should not be seen as a real victory because Majorian allowed the Burgundians to remain on the lands given to them by the Gallic senators in return for their military service. Therefore the Burgundians had actually enlarged their territory even in defeat.

Framtane, the second of the competing Suevic kings, died of unnamed causes between Easter and Pentecost in 458 which probably means that he was assassinated by Maldras's men. Framtane's men chose Rechimund (or Reccimund/Remismundus) as their leader. The death of Framtane left Maldras as the sole ruler and Rechimund made peace with him (Isid. HRGVS 88). After this Maldras' Suevi, who were returning from Lusitania, pillaged Roman Gallaecia bordering the Durius River (the area south of Bracara and north of Durius). This resurgence of Suevic power brought about a response. I would suggest that in spite of the order of the references in Hydatius's *Chronicle* that Theoderic and the Vandals both dispatched envoys to Maldras (presumably to discuss terms of alliance) before Theoderic dispatched his army into Baetica in July. The order of the references in Hydatius' text merely reflects the order in which he received news of the events. Subsequent operations in Baetica suggest that the Vandals managed to convince the Suevi to become their ally and attack Baetica. Theoderic also sent an army under *dux* Cyrila to Baetica in July 458, but we do not know whether he did this in his own name or on behalf of the Romans. Hydatius notes the peace between Majorian and Theoderic as the last note for the year 459, but Sidonius' text makes it certain that peace was already agreed in 458. Consequently it is not impossible that Theoderic's army was operating against the Suevi in Baetica in an effort to secure it for the forthcoming invasion of Mauretania by Majorian's army. It is possible that the return of the Bishop of Hispalis, Sabinus, from Gaul back to his see in Hispalis, which was located in Baetica (Hyd. a.458), is connected with this Visigothic campaign.

While the generals were fighting in Gaul or in the Balkans, Majorian conducted the defence of Italy in person and once again proved himself a gifted cavalry commander. Sidonius reports that the Vandals invaded Campania, but it seems probable that they had already invaded Sicily before that. Therefore I suggest that the Vandals invaded Sicily in 457/8 in an effort to prevent the Romans from using it as a launching pad for an attack against Carthage and then used Sicily as a base for further attacks on the Italian mainland and that the support of Marcellinus was needed against them. According to Sidonius (5.440–446), Majorian had already launched a project to build a huge fleet on the Upper and Lower Sea (the Adriatic and Tyrrhenian Seas) so that 'every' forest of the Apennines had been 'felled' into the water. Later, in 459 after the Burgundians and Visigoths had been subdued, this project was expanded by making both Gaul and Spain pay additional ships as tax (Sid. 5.446–448; Hyd. a. 460). Majorian's response to the Vandal invasion was to lead the Italian armies in person against the Vandal force that had landed in Campania.[9]

The exact location of the Vandal landing is not known. The only clues are: 1) it was in Campania; 2) it was a natural harbour; 3) there was a river beside the landing site that made a backward curve; 4) in front of the landing there was a plain and behind the plain there were hills; 5) the plain was well-suited to cavalry fighting; 6) there were no large cities in the immediate vicinity because the Moors accompanying the Vandals attacked husbandmen; 7) it was possible for Majorian to place his cavalry army in an ambush which was not located near the hills.

The fact that Majorian was able to react to the Vandal landing in timely fashion proves that his intelligence apparatus was functioning well. We do not know what types of intelligence gathering network Majorian employed, but one may make the educated guess that it included some of the following: 1) military intelligence on land (scouts and guard towers); 2) naval scouting ships along the coast; 3) civilian paramilitary intelligence on land (towers, patrols). We do not know whether there were any Roman intelligence operatives among the Vandal army, which is a real possibility because it included native Romans and Moors. It is possible that the Roman cavalry army actually shadowed the Vandal navy at a distance from the shore with the help of scouts. What is clear is that the Vandals were unaware of the presence of the Roman army just as the peasants close to the landing site were unaware of the presence of the Vandals. The Romans clearly maintained really tight security. It is notable that Majorian did not at the time possess enough ships in the Tyrrhenian Sea to attack the Vandal vessels at anchor.

When the Vandals landed their vessels they dispatched their lightly-equipped Moorish auxiliaries to spearhead the landing. The Berber warriors were able to surprise the peasants completely and started taking captives. It was at this moment that the Romans launched their attack. The cavalry charged into the space between the Moors and Vandals and forced the Moors to flee to the safety of the mountains. Majorian sent a part of his force in pursuit and deployed the rest to face the Vandals who disembarked their cavalry. The Vandals deployed the most sophisticated landing craft (hollow skiffs, '*lintre cavata*') in existence which enabled them to land their horsemen straight onto the beach. Their horsemen were equipped with chain-mail armour, bows, and poisoned arrows. This suggests that most of the Vandals had also become mounted archers just like the Alans accompanying them. Both cavalry forces followed the dragon standards. The Romans charged when the tuba sounded the attack. It is worth quoting poetic translation of Sidonius's text by Anderson (97–99): '*From everywhere a shower of steel comes down, but from our side it comes down on the throats of the foe; a hurtling javelin lays one man in the dust ...; another man is sent spinning by a thrust of a pike; one gashed by a harpoon, another by a lance, falls headlong from his horse; yet another, flung down by a flying shaft, lies there, ... again a warrior sweeps off part of a foeman's brain and part of his helmet together, cleaving the hapless skull with a two-edged sword wielded by a strong arm. Soon as the Vandal began to turn and flee, carnage took the place of battle.*' The Vandal cavalry were forced to flee headlong into the sea and try to swim to their ships. The commander of the Vandals, the husband of Gaiseric's daughter, was pierced by numerous pikes during the flight and died. This was a major victory for the Romans.

Majorian's Campanian campaign can be dated approximately on the basis of his *novellae*. As Majorian also needed to quell a military revolt in northern Italy in 458 (see below) the likeliest dates are: 1) between 11 March and 8 May; 2) between 8 May and 11 July; 3) between July 11 and 4 September.[10]

After the Vandals had been thoroughly trashed, Majorian returned to his previous duties which were the correction of problems through legislation (see below) and preparation necessary for the reconquest of Africa from the Vandals.

Ricimer and Majorian needed to find a new source of recruits, which on the basis of Sidonius's list of nations (*Pan. Maj.* 470ff.) accompanying Majorian in the winter of 458/9 can be guessed to have consisted of the tribes settled mainly along the Danube. These tribes were: Bastarnians, Suebians (one branch of the Alamanni), Pannonians (presumably local populations), Neurians ('Scythians', Slavs or Celts), Huns, Getans (presumably nomads settled in Dacia), Dacians (natives of the area), Alans (settlements in northern Italy and along the Danube), Bellonotians (Sarmatians?), Rugians, Alites (a tribe living close to Aletes/Elek in modern Hungary?), Bisaltae (Thracians), Ostrogoths, Procrustians (bandits?), Sarmatians (settlements in Italy and along the Danube), and Moschans.

It is probable that some of these forces were recruited through warfare rather than by peaceful means, because Sidonius states (*Pan. Maj.* 363–6) that Majorian's strategy was to add new tribal forces into his army through warfare. The person in charge of these operations would have been none other than Ricimer because we find Majorian fighting against the Vandals (Sid. *Pan. Maj.* 383ff.) in 458.[11] It is not known with certainty whether the East Romans cooperated with Ricimer, but this is likely because these areas were under de facto Eastern control. My own educated guess is that both Ricimer and the East Romans were now fighting against the Ostrogoths and their allies in Pannonia and that it was thanks to this cooperation that the new eastern emperor, Leo I, refused to continue the payment of subsidies to the Ostrogoths. One may assume that Marcellinus was cooperating with Ricimer against the Ostrogoths. See also the chapters dealing with Eastern affairs. The names of the tribes suggest that Ricimer was fighting a prolonged campaign in which he advanced along the Danube from Raetia (the Suevi) to Noricum and Pannonia (Sarmatians, Pannonians, Ostrogoths). The Bisaltae (Thracians), Procrustians (bandits?), Moschans, Alites, Sarmatians and others were presumably cooperating with the Ostrogoths and were defeated together.

These newly recruited federate forces (Bastarnians, Suevi, Pannonians, Neurans, Huns, Getans, Dacians, Alans, Bellonoti, Rugians, Alites, Bisalta, Ostrogoths, Procrustians, Sarmatians, Moschans) drawn from the Danube region were to form the vast majority of the forces that Majorian intended to use against the Vandals. Ricimer was rewarded with consulship for the year 459 for these services and as a form of thanks for his continued loyalty towards Majorian. The assembly of these forces appear to have been accomplished barely before Majorian had returned from Campania (Sid. 5.489). One of the tribes brought to Italy, usually presumed to be the Huns, had revolted under Tuldila (Sid. 5.483ff). This time, presumably after some fruitless campaigning, Majorian resorted to a ruse. He offered a pardon, which Tuldila foolishly accepted. Sidonius claims that the soldiers did not accept the pardon and that they killed all rebels against Majorian's wishes. The truth must be that Majorian *had* given the order to kill the rebels, because the spoils were then distributed among the loyal troops and because Sidonius acknowleges that henceforth all barbarians followed Majorian blindly out of fear. This was first rate military leadership, which resembles the treacherous methods used by for example Caracalla. No need to fight needlessly. However, if Majorian was not behind the order to massacre the surrendered enemies, then this instance should be seen as a sign of his weakness vis-à-vis his soldiers and Ricimer, but as stated, it is likelier that the former is the case.

Procopius (*Wars* 3.7.4–14) includes interesting comments regarding Majorian, which would be all too easy to dismiss as legendary except that they come from his pen, which means that there was probably at least a germ of truth behind them. According to Procopius, Majorian (Maiorinos) surpassed in all virtues all of the previous emperors, which is a really flattering statement to make. As an example of this he mentioned that Majorian was not willing to accept the loss of Libya (North Africa) to the Vandals. So he collected a very large army against them and marched to Liguria to take command of this army in person, because he never hesitated to put his own life on the line when he faced the dangers of war. To find out what type of enemy he faced, he decided to pretend to be an envoy of the Emperor dispatched to the court of Gaiseric, dyed his famously fair golden hair dark and went to meet Gaiseric. Procopius claims that during this trip there was a miracle that resembled an earthquake and which must have been a real earthquake if true, but he follows this with an account which is untrue, namely he claims that Majorian then returned to Liguria to lead his army after which he marched to the Pillars of Heracles with the intention of crossing to Africa, but then died of dysentery before being able to accomplish the task. These semi-legendary materials are clear evidence of Majorian's good reputation in the East even if the Western senators appear not to have liked him because of the taxes he forced them to pay. According to Procopius, Majorian was a man who had shown himself moderate towards his subjects, and an object of fear to his enemies – the senatorial class in Italy clearly did not share this view. If Majorian conducted this sort of intelligence-gathering trip, it must have taken place some time before February/March 459. The fact that Majorian led his forces across the Alps in 459 when they were still snow-covered can be used as evidence that his trip to the court of Gaiseric had taken so long that his campaign to Gaul was delayed and was therefore undertaken during the winter. The results of the intelligence gathering trip, however, were meaningless because Majorian was unable to take advantage of his assessment of Gaiseric's character and his forces. The presence of traitors in the Roman ranks made all these efforts futile.

Majorian was now ready to begin final preparations for the war against the Vandals, the first stages of which were: 1) The increasing of the size of the already built fleets possibly as a result of his intelligence gathering trip; 2) The securing of Baetica and Spain together with Sicily for the invasion of North Africa. On the basis of the locations of the military commanders and fleets, the plan appears to have consisted of two parts: the shipping of the army from Spain to Mauretania under Majorian himself with the fleet being built in Italy, Spain, and Gaul while Marcellinus would ship his forces into Sicily (Marcellinus is attested to be in Sicily in 461, but is likely to have been sent there in 460) with his own ships. The Ostrogoths of Valamir sacked the city of Dyrrachium in 459 (*Prosper, Addimenta 4, Auctarium Epitomae Vaticanea 3.11*) at the same time as he defeated the East Roman *dux*, but apparently did not attack West Roman territory proper. This suggests two alternatives: 1) Valamir wanted to avoid simultaneous conflict with both halves of the Empire; 2) Dalmatia under Marcellinus was so well defended that the Ostrogoths wanted to bypass it (but this would have certainly kept Marcellinus in Dalmatia). We do not know whether Majorian's aim was to launch a double invasion of North Africa from Spain and Sicily, or whether the purpose was to attempt to force most of the Vandal fleet to remain opposite Sicily so that it would be easier for Majorian to disembark his troops in Mauretania.

Majorian and his inner circle recognized that they could not win the wars through warfare alone; they also needed to win the hearts and minds of their subjects and ensure that the state received enough taxes to support the administration, army and navy. In light of this, it is not surprising that Majorian intended to conduct the land operations against the Vandals with barbarian federates. It was quite enough that the native Roman populace built and manned the ships. Consequently, Majorian spent a large part of the year 458 issuing a series of legislation meant to correct many existing problems (11 March–6 November 458: *NMaj 1–7*). These *novellae* give a good picture of what was wrong with the West Roman Empire and how far the decay had advanced.

Novella 2 is particularly important because it shows that the apparitors of the prefects and palatine office had fleeced the taxpayers so badly that it was necessary to remit all delinquent taxes up to 457 (excepting the swine meant for the city of Rome) and to reinstate the old system of tax-gathering which was based on governors of the provinces and local city councils. In other words, the government had attempted to secure taxes for the state and to correct the abuses by taking taxation away from the decurions and putting it into the hands of the imperial administrators, but with the result that the situation had only got worse. The greedy apparitors had taken double the amount or even more than they had gathered in taxes for the state with the result that they had ruined both the landholders and decurions. Ian Hughes (2015, 71–72, 95) is probably right when he states that the cancelling of the tax debts together with the *Novellae* 5 and 7, that were meant to lower the level of corruption and to correct the problems facing the decurions, were all meant to enable the taxpayers to pay their current taxes. This in turn would enable Majorian to finance his campaign against the Vandals. The building of the ships and the raising of the mercenary army required money.

Novella 3 noted that the municipalities had become deserted when people were fleeing from them to avoid the tax collectors with the result that the municipilaties no longer possessed defenders. Consequently, the *Novella* required that the system of defenders was to be restored and that upright men were to be selected so that they could protect the plebeians in their own municipilaties against tax collectors. At the same time as Majorian (*NMaj 7.16*) attempted to remove the abuse, he also raised taxes on land from 2 *solidi* to 3.5 *solidi* per measurement because the taxpayers were now supposedly able to pay more because the corrupt practices followed by the imperial tax gatherers had been removed. Majorian needed money.

Novella 4 noted the decay of public buildings in Rome which had been exploited by private individuals who had used them for building materials. The *Novella* forbade this practice and stated that only those public buildings that could not be repaired were to be used for such purpose. This was a particularly pleasing decision to the traditionalist senators who had detested the actions undertaken under Avitus to collect money.

Novella 6 addressed the lack of population growth by stating that all nuns under 40 were to be allowed to marry, and widows without children were required to remarry. The *Novella* also corrected some details dealing with inheritance rights in order to encourage population growth. The West Roman Empire was in a state of advanced decay and needed loyal taxpayers and population growth.

We do not know when and where Majorian issued his *NMaj. 8* The Restoration of the Right to Use Weapons, because the text is lost, but it must have had the same goal as the *Novella* issued to restore the system of Defenders into the towns and cities. Majorian attempted to increase the numbers of paramilitary native civilian forces just as Valentinian III had done before. Since there is no extant evidence for the re-issuing of the ban on civilians carrying weapons after ca 440, this *Novella* was presumably meant to encourage men to carry weapons for self-defence against the barbarians.

The Year 459: the Preparations for the Final Showdown with the Vandals

Majorian marched his army of federates through the snowy Alps to Lyon during the winter of 458/9 – the likeliest date being the early winter of 459. When he reached the city, Sidonius delivered his panegyric. We are not told why Majorian chose so difficult a time to cross the Alps with the federates, but it must have had something to do with a need to ensure that the local nobles and the Burgundians left in charge of Lyon would not exploit the absence of the army that had been marched to relieve Aegidius from the Visigoths. See above. According to Sidonius, the federates complained that they were required to climb the snowy and frozen faces of the mountains only to be reprimanded by the brave young 'king' that it was idlessness that caused the cold. When Majorian then marched his army into Lyon, he apparently added a Burgundian contingent to his army and then marched his army into Arles where he is attested to be by 1 April 459. Majorian appears to have spent most of 459 at Arles presumably in an effort to reorganize the administration and defence of Gaul while making preparations for the forthcoming war against the Vandals. The delay was necessary because the building of ships in Gaul and Spain took time to accomplish and he also needed to secure Baetica so that he could launch the invasion from a secure base (e.g. from Gades/Gadiz, Baelo Claudia, Carteia, Malaca) close to Mauretania Tingitana.

The operation to secure Baetica against the Suevi was left in the hands of the Visigoths. According to Hydatius, MVM Nepotianus and *comes/dux* Sunriericus came to the Gallaecians early in the spring of 459 to announce that Majorian and Theoderic had agreed a peace (after the Visigoths had been defeated in a certain battle). However, Sidonius's text makes it certain that the peace with the Visigoths was signed in 458. Consequently, it is evident that when Theoderic sent reinforcements to Baetica under *dux/comes* Sunriericus and at the same time recalled Cyrila in 459 that it was done on behalf of Majorian. The sending of reinforcements to Baetica did not prevent the Suevi under their king Maldras from pillaging Lusitania while another Suevic contingent under Rechimund pillaged parts of Gallaecia.

At the same time as this happened, a fleet of Heruls on their way to Baetica brutally ravaged several places in the *conventus* of Lucus/Lugo (the north-west corner of Gallaecia). It is unfortunate that Hydatius fails to state the reason for the sailing of the Heruls to Baetica. It is possible that they did this as allies of the Suevi and Vandals or as allies of the Visigoths, but it is equally possible that they were just acting as pirates sailing along the coast. The fact that Maldras killed his brother and then attacked the port fort of Portus Cale (Oporto) at the same time as the Heruls were operating in Gallaecia suggests that Maldras could have asked the Heruls to come to assist him.

Year 460–461: The Final Showdown with the Vandals that Never Came

At the end of February 460, Maldras was assassinated by his own men after which the Suevi became divided into supporters of Frumarius and Rechimund (Hyd., Isid. HRGVS). The likeliest reason for the murder is that Maldras was not considered to be a good military leader. The rival kings sought to gain the loyalty of their men through warfare. Frumarius sacked the neighbourhood of the city of Flavia while Rechimund ravaged the area of Auragenses and the coastal areas of Lugo. The Suevi who lived close to the city of Lugo surprised a number of local notables outside the city because they foolishly believed that the Suevi would respect Easter.

The abovementioned events were not of great concern for the Emperor Majorian who entered Spain in May 460 to begin the much awaited campaign against the Vandals, but then disaster struck. It is probable that Majorian's navy consisted of native Romans (Italians, Gauls and Spaniards), but that his land forces consisted almost entirely of the federates: the Bastarnians, Suebians (Suevi, one branch of the Alamanni), Pannonians, Neurians, Huns, Getans, Dacians, Alans, Bellonotians, Rugians, Alites, Bisaltae, Ostrogoths, Procrustians, Sarmatians, Moschans, Burgundians and Visigoths. This is symptomatic of the West Roman state of affairs. They were forced to rely almost entirely on foreign federates if they intended to conduct offensive wars. The West Roman state was effectively bankrupt and the emperors lacked the will or military might to force the senators to pay their fair share of the costs. In these circumstances the state could not enrol enough costly natives into their professional army and the emperors feared to instigate a return to the citizen army consisting of levies of armed citizens that had been taught to use weapons from their early childhood. It was supposedly less risky and less costly to employ foreigners. It is possible to speculate that the abovementioned law of Majorian (*NMaj. 8 The Restoration of the Right to Use Weapons*) was precisely meant to do this, but since the text is lost we do not know this for certain. If the *Novella* was indeed meant to reintroduce the universal conscription of natives for a national army of legions, then it is easy to understand why the senators and Ricimer were eager to see the end of Majorian. Armed and trained citizens were dangerous to the utterly corrupt upper classes in a situation in which their actions were not acceptable to the populace at large. However, just rulers like Majorian could expect that a conscript army would be loyal to him in the same manner as barbarian warrior citizens were loyal to their kings.

According to Priscus and John of Antioch, Majorian had collected a fleet of 300 ships in readiness for the war. Gaiseric had attempted to negotiate a settlement, but when this had failed he had laid waste all the lands in Mauretania and poisoned all the wells that Majorian would have to use when marching to Carthage. Considering Majorian had assembled a major army, it seems probable that the 300 ships referred to above were probably warships and that the soldiers would have been shipped in civilian transports. However, if one presumes that the figure included some huge transports intended to carry about 400–500 men aboard, then it is possible to think that the figure encompassed the entire fleet of ships. However, when Majorian was approaching the province of Carthaginiensis, a disaster struck. Thanks to information provided by traitors the Vandals managed to capture most of the Roman ships stationed at anchor in Elice/Elche near Carthage (Carthagena) on the Bay of Alicante (Lucentum) before Majorian even reached his fleet. Ian Hughes is likely correct when he suspects that the Vandals had sailed either from Majorca or Ibiza to Elche because the Romans had not been warned, but in my opinion he had needlessly suspected Hydatius' statement that the Romans were betrayed by traitors. Hughes suggests that it is likelier that the traitors were actually only merchants or fishermen or similar who had just told the Vandals where the Roman fleet was located and in what strength, but in my opinion it is likelier in light of what period Spanish author Hydatius states that there were actual traitors amongst the Roman armed forces who then really helped the Vandals to capture the fleet at anchor. On the basis of Hydatius' account of the immediately following events in Spain, it is clear that there were very real traitors among the Romans who sabotaged the efforts of their fellow countrymen against the barbarian enemies. The destruction of the fleet put an end to the project, and Majorian returned to Gaul and disbanded his mercenary army.[12]

After this, the Vandals again dispatched envoys to negotiate terms of peace and this time Majorian was ready to accept them. The exact terms are not known but he appears to have handed over to the Vandals the Mauretanias and Tripolitania in return for peace in late 460 and so that he could then return to Italy in 461. Ian Hughes (2015, 93) is probably correct when he speculates that the terms of peace included the handing over of the imperial captives held by the Vandals even if it took place only in about 462 (in my opinion either in 461 or 462). This was probably the safest course to take in the circumstances, but as noted by Ian Hughes (2015, 92–6), this was not acceptable to the vast majority of the conservatively thinking members of the Senate. However, unlike these dinosaurs, who had their heads in the clouds, Majorian was a realist enough to know that the state was bankrupt and that he needed time to restore the finances and its armed forces before attempting to renew hostilities. Had he had enough money, he would not have needed to disband his barbarian mercenaries.

In the meantime, the war against the Suevi continued unabated. Majorian ordered the 'comites' Suniericus and Nepotianus to continue their campaign against the Suevi in Gallaecia. The generals obliged and dispatched part of the Visigothic army against the Suevi living close to Lugo. They defeated the Suevi and pillaged the area, but were then once again betrayed. This time the traitors were Roman informers Dictynius, Spinio and Ascanius, who managed to convince the army to return to its base without finishing their job. The fact that the Romans were ready to betray their country to the Suevi says much about the situation, but the fact that the Visigoths had inflicted considerable damage to the area in the name of the Emperor just a few years ago must have affected their decision. Frumarius exploited the situation by attacking Aquae Flaviae on 26 July 460. He took Bishop Hydatius (the chronicler of these events) prisoner and pillaged the surrounding territory. Rechimund in his turn attacked Auregenses and the coastal areas of Lugo. After this the Gallaeci managed to conclude peace with the Suevi and the Suevi returned Hydatius to his see in November. These Gallaeci presumably consisted of those who had previously turned the Visigoths back from their territory. Theoderic also dispatched his own envoys to the Suevi. Hydatius fails to mention the results of this embassy, but since he notes that Suniericus managed to capture the city of Scallabis (Santarem) in Lusitania, it is clear that the Visigoths, who were operating on behalf of Majorian, continued their war against the Suevi. On the basis of Isidore's (*HRGVS* 33) account, it is possible that while Suniericus and Nepotianus ravaged the neighbourhood of Lugo in Gallaecia, Cyrila (Ceurila) secured Baetica.

After peace with the Vandals had been achieved, Majorian dismissed his allies, presumably to save money, and then returned to Italy. The shameful peace with the Vandals had tarnished Majorian's reputation as a military leader which Ricimer was not slow to exploit. There was a significant block among the Italian senators who were extremely angry with Majorian for his inability to bring about the reconquest of North Africa, and for his readiness to conclude a humiliating peace after all the money the Italians had spent on the building of the fleet and army. These men urged Ricimer to act against Majorian. Consequently Ricimer and his friends formed a plot against Majorian. They intercepted him and his small entourage at Dertona, forced him to give up his throne on 2 August 461, and he was executed on the 7th. Majorian had clearly not suspected anything because he had disbanded his barbarian troops.[13] The motivation for the sudden change of heart by Ricimer is not known. It is possible that he was just an ambitious plotter and/or that he could not accept the shameful peace with the Vandals because he had a long term family/blood feud with Gaiseric. Ricimer's grandfather Vallia had fought and defeated Gaiseric's father. Jordanes's (Get. 236) account of the death of Majorian may shed additional light on the circumstances of Majorian's death, because he claims that Majorian was on his way to fight against Alans in Gaul. This suggests a possibility in which the Alans of south-east or elsewhere in Gaul (possibly a part of the forces Majorian had just disbanded) had revolted and needed to be crushed. It also suggests a possibility that the war against these Alans continued until 464 – a date for which the sources record a battle between Ricimer and Beorgor at Bergamo. See later. One may even speculate that the information regarding the Alans had been a ruse so that Majorian could be surprised where Ricimer wanted, but in the light of the circumstantial evidence it still appears likely that the revolt was a real one and that the remaining Alans in Gaul were not satisfied with their current situation.

The plot against Majorian was clearly well planned because the sources also mention that it was in 461 that Ricimer managed to bribe the Scythian forces (presumably mainly Huns) to desert Marcellinus in Sicily with the result that Marcellinus was forced to embark his remaining men on the ships and sail the last 'Italian' fleet back to Dalmatia. The reason for Marcellinus's departure was that he could not compete with the wealth possessed by Ricimer. It seems probable that Ricimer instigated this operation at about the same time as he initiated his plot against Majorian, because Ricimer must have known that Marcellinus would not accept the overthrow and killing of Majorian. The fact that Marcellinus was able to take the fleet with him ensured that Italy and the islands lacked any defence against the Vandals.

Chapter Four

Ricimer the Kingmaker: 2 August 461–12 April 467

The Reign of Severus on 19 November 461–14 November 465[1]

Augustus Libius Severus (461-465). Source: Hodgkin

R icimer apparently did not nominate an Emperor immediately because he hoped that he could reconcile his own actions with Leo as he had previously been able to do when he had ousted Avitus. Leo, however, was unwilling to accept this situation. Equally importantly, Ricimer was opposed by the two greatest West Roman warlords of the time, Marcellinus and Aegidius (e.g. Priscus Blockley ed. fr.39.1). In addition to this, Ricimer had to deal with the revolt of the Alans in Gaul on top of which the recently signed peace treaty between Majorian and Gaiseric was now void. Ian Hughes (2015, 104–5) is likely to be correct in suggesting that Majorian's appointment of Nepotianus in Spain could also be considered to have been a potential source of trouble that needed to be dealt with somehow. Consequently, Ricimer was immediately facing the prospect of having to fight a civil war and a foreign war. In addition to this, he could not hope to obtain any naval assistance against the Vandals from the East. He no longer possessed any siginificant naval resources of his own because the Vandals had destroyed or captured it at Elche and whatever else was left of the Western fleet Marcellinus had taken back to Dalmatia. Ricimer's only supporters consisted of the troops in Italy and of his relatives within the royal houses of the Visigoths and Burgundians (his sister had married Gundioc) and even their loyalty needed to be bought with concessions and bribes.

Ricimer's position was very difficult. Aegidius threatened Italy from the west and north-west, the Alans threatened Gaul and Italy, Marcellinus and the East Romans threatened Italy from the east, and the Vandals from the south. When it became apparent that Leo could not be conciliated, Ricimer started a search for a suitable puppet emperor. His choice fell on Lucanian Libius Severus, who lacked a military background and ambitions and was therefore ideally suited to act as a figurehead ruler for Ricimer. Ricimer proclaimed him *Augustus* at Ravenna on 19 November 461. To secure their positions both men needed to placate the powerful senators, and Ian Hughes (2015, 109) is certainly correct in stating this.

Ricimer sought to neutralize Aegidius and his sizable army by replacing him with his personal enemy Agrippinus, who was now duly pardoned and accepted back into favour. This, however, was not sufficient because Aegidius refused to give up his command and Agrippinus lacked a regular army. It is probable that the only forces at Ricimer's and Agrippinus' disposal were the Burgundians of Gundioc, because Gundioc was married to Ricimer's sister, but these forces were needed against the Alans who had revolted in Gaul (Jord. Get. 236). Consequently, Ricimer appears to have instructed Agrippinus to seek the support of the Visigoths because Hydatius and Isidore (HRGVS 33) both state that Agrippinus, a rival of Aegidius, handed the city of Narbo/Narbonne to the Visigoths in 462. This had the short term benefit of giving Agrippinus and Ricimer access to some troops that they could use against Aegidius, but in the long term it was a disaster for the Romans for it gave the Visigoths access to the Mediterranean while cutting off the land route from Roman Gaul to Spain/Hispania. Ian Hughes (2015, 105) has also suggested that one of the possible reasons for the handing of the city to the Visigoths was to isolate Nepotianus in Spain. This is by no means impossible, but I would still suggest that the principal reason for the handing of the city to the Visigoths was that the Visigoths demanded it in return for their support against Aegidius and it is also probable that they demanded other concessions, as will be made clear below. It is not known whether Agrippinus's deal with the Visigoths took place during the interregnum or after Severus's nomination as Emperor. The use of the Visigoths kept Aegidius at bay so that he was unable to advance against Italy. According to Priscus (Blockley ed. fr. 39.1), Aegidius fought hard and bravely against the Goths.

At this time in late 461 or in 462 Theoderic appears to have usurped the right to nominate Roman commanders in Spain. This must have been done with Ricimer's tacit approval because we hear no complaints about it and this concession must have been made at the same time as Narbo had been handed over to the Visigoths. Theoderic recalled his own *comes* Suniericus and the *MVM* Nepotianus from Spain and replaced the latter with Arborius. In my opinion, in this case Ian Hughes (2015, 105–6) is certainly incorrect in suggesting that the nomination of Arborius was an independent action taken by Severus against the wishes of Ricimer and that this would have made Theoderic the equal of Ricimer which Severus could have used to counter Ricimer's influence. As a nonentity Severus was clearly Ricimer's puppet. This means that from 461 onwards Theoderic ruled at least Baetica and Lusitania, and parts of Gallaecia and Tarraconensis in the name of Rome so that the commander of the Visigothic armies in Spain was nominally a Roman *MVM*. Arborius was probably succeeded by Vincentius in 465, who was another Roman in Visigothic service. Ricimer did many great favours to his fellow countrymen and relatives to get their support when it was needed.

After the loss of the West Roman Fleet at Elche and the evacuation of Marcellinus' fleet, the coasts of Sicily and Italy lay defenceless. This in turn caused both Ricimer and Leo to react by sending envoys to Gaiseric. The former's ambassadors demanded that Gaiseric respect the treaty he had just made with the now dead Majorian, while the latter's envoys demanded that Gaiseric stay away from Italy and Sicily and that he should hand over the imperial women. Gaiseric waited until his son Huneric had been married to Eudocia, after which he dispatched the other two women, Eudoxia, the mother, and Placidia, the elder daughter, to Constantinople either in later 461 or in 462. The pleas against the raiding of Sicily and Italy were not listened to because Gaiseric wanted to make Olybrius, the husband of Placidia, Emperor of Rome because this would have made his son Huneric related to the Emperor through marriage. In fact Gaiseric intensified his pillaging of Sicily and Italy in an effort to force Ricimer and Leo to accept his will. His official reason for the ravaging was that he had not been given the property of Valentian III and Aetius despite the fact that his son was married to Eudocia and Aetius' son Gaudentius was living with him, but the underlying reason was what the period sources claim it to have been, namely to put pressure on Ricimer to declare Olybrius the next ruler – obviously Gaiseric could not publicly declare his support for Olybrius because this would have made Olybrius' position impossible. Thanks to the peace treaty with Leo, Gaiseric was free to attack Ricimer. The treaty was also advantageous to Leo, because he was able to put pressure on Ricimer through the Vandals.[2]

According to Priscus (fr. 39.1), while this was going on Ricimer became fearful of Marcellinus because his strength was increasing, which must mean that he was assembling a new army in Dalmatia. Ricimer decided to resort to diplomacy. He lacked the resources to fight all the enemies he was facing. He sent envoys to Constantinople to beg them to use their influence to bring about peace with Marcellinus and the Vandals. The exact date is not known, but this must have happened between 462 and 464. In the name of the greater good Leo agreed to dispatch Phylarchus as his envoy to Marcellinus and the Vandals. In the case of Marcellinus, Phylarchus was successful, but Gaiseric refused to cease hostilities because he already had a peace treaty with Leo. Gaiseric stated that he would not agree to conclude peace with West Rome unless Ricimer gave him the properties of Aetius and Valentinian III. He actually had the law on his side because his son Huneric had married Eudocia and Gaudentius (Aetius's son) lived in Carthage, but Gaiseric's intention was probably to present such humiliating terms that Ricimer could not agree to fulfil them. It is possible that Leo managed to convince Marcellinus to transfer his loyalty to him by making him Eastern commander with the title *Magister Militum Dalmatiae* (attested for his successor Nepos) and by adding Epirus at least up to Dyrrachium to his territories.[3] This had the added benefit for Leo that the agreement made the defence of Dyrrachium and Epirus the duty of Marcellinus.[4]

In the coming years the Vandals made a habit of invading Sicily and Italy with several fleets every spring. They avoided garrisoned cities and attacked only those places that lacked adequate defence. They pillaged and destroyed everything they could, took everyone they could prisoner, and then sailed away before the Romans could bring a force to bear upon them. The West Romans were unable to effectively respond to this because they lacked a fleet and because they could not post forces to guard the entire coastline. So they kept on asking Leo to interfere, but since he had a peace agreement with the

Vandals all he did was to send envoys to Gaiseric, who refused to stop his ravages because he wanted to see Olybrius on the Western throne.[5]

It is a pity we do not know what Aegidius, Agrippinus, the Visigoths and the Burgundians did in Gaul during 462, but since no defeats are recorded for Aegidius he appears to have been able to defend his domains effectively against the Goths, which is no great surprise because according to Priscus (fr.39.1) he had a very large force at his disposal. Furthermore, there is the question of what the Alans did in Gaul during this time. We know that Ricimer replaced Agrippinus in about 462 or 463 because Gundioc (Gundiocus), the husband of Ricimer's sister, is attested to be the *MVM per Gallias* in 463. Does this mean that Agrippinus had been ineffective against the Alans so that this job was given to Gundioc, or does it mean that Gundioc had distinguished himself in combat against the Alans in 462, or does it simply mean that Ricimer was promoting the career of his barbarian relatives?

What is certain is that when the Visigoths and the remaining Roman forces in Spain were fighting under the *comes et magister utriusque militiae* Arborius (in office 461–5) against the Suevi, the remaining Roman forces under Agrippinus together with the Visigoths must have been fighting either against the Alans or Aegidius, or against both if the Alans had allied themselves with Aegidius as has been suggested by Ian Hughes (2015, 106, 109), but it is actually possible that we are dealing with separate groups of Alans in this case so that Aegidius was allied with those who were located in the north while those in revolt were in the south.

Furthermore, it is not known with any certainty when Childeric I was restored to the throne of the Salian Franks (Gregory of Tours 2.12, 2.18). Ian Hughes (2015, 98–99, 109) has suggested that this happened in about 461 because Childeric was later present at the battle of Orleans in 463. This is probably the best guess we have, because the situation facing Aegidius after the death of Majorian was such that he definitely needed the support of the Franks if he wanted to defend himself against the Visigoths. Consequently it is probable that Wiomad, the friend and supporter of Childeric, recalled Childeric I immediately after the death of Majorian in 461, and it is probable that there was also some fighting between the forces of the two which convinced Aegidius to accept the fact.

My own educated guess is that the reason for the readiness of Childeric to accept the alliance with Aegidius was the arrival of Basina, the wife of the Thuringian king Bisinus, into Childeric's court which would have caused the withdrawal of the Thuringian support from Childeric. According to Gregory of Tours (2.12), Childeric had seduced Basina while he had been a refugee in the Thuringian court, and when Childeric once again became king Basina deserted her husband and joined her lover. Childeric supposedly questioned why she had come so far away to marry him, which she answered by saying that she recognized Childeric to be a strong man and she wanted to live with the strongest man around. Childeric was clearly a LUSTY MAN with capital letters, and this was to have long-reaching consequences: Basina was to bear Childeric Clovis, who was destined to unite Gaul under the Franks. In the short term however, it meant peace between Aegidius and Childeric which meant that Aegidius could concentrate his attention against the Visigoths.

I do not accept Hughes' suggestion that Adovaricus, mentioned by Gregory of Tours at 2.18, would not have been Odoacer, because the case for this is in my opinion better than the other alternative because Gregory (2.19) then goes on to state that Odovaricus allied himself with Childeric I. However, I am inclined to accept his view that it is probable that this Adovaricus/Odoacer and the Saxons under him were hired by Aegidius. Nevertheless, it is still possible that he was just an independent leader of a mercenary band of piratical Saxons who were roaming the seas and the Atlantic Ocean at this time, or that he had been hired by the Visigoths. These alternatives receive support from the fact that the Romans under Paulus and the Franks under Childeric I fought against him after the death of Aegidius. To counter this one can use the argument that these two fought against Odoacer only after Aegidius had died and that the war between them would therefore have resulted from the fact that Aegidius' death had made the previous treaties void. For an analysis of the role played by Saxons and the remnants of the Hunnish Empire in the west, see my *Britain in the Age of Arthur* which analyzes the events in this region in greater detail than is possible here.

The Battle of Orleans, or the Battle of the Loire and Loiret in 463

In 463 Aegidius then faced Frederic, the brother of Theoderic, in pitched battle between the Loire and Loiret near Orleans (Marius a.463). Frederic was killed and his followers defeated (Marius a.463; Hyd. a.463). The information given by Marius of Avenches regarding the location is valuable because it enables the making of several educated guesses, and readers are advised that the following is based on conjecture of mine. Firstly, Orleans was located near Armorica[6] and the settlements of Alans and Sarmatians, which makes it very probable that Aegidius's army included contingents from both, as has been suggested also by Ian Hughes. In addition to this, Aegidius would obviously have fielded regular units of the Gallic Army (*comitatenses, limitanei, laeti*), the tribal contingents of the Salian Franks, and possibly some other *foederati*. On the basis of the events of 465 it is possible that the Saxons could have sent some reinforcements to Aegidius, but I would suggest that this was not done because the Visigoths possessed a navy and the Franks in 465 did not. It is likelier that Aegidius used the Saxons to prevent the Visigoths from sailing their fleet up the Loire. The islands of the Loire which were in Saxon hands were ideally suited for this purpose.

Since most of Aegidius's forces consisted of infantry, the location between the Loire and Loiret was ideal, but it is possible that his army was initially deployed along the river to prevent the Visigoths from crossing and was deployed between the rivers only after the Visigoths had outflanked him from the right. The two rivers enabled Aegidius to protect both flanks of his infantry phalanx and place his cavalry contingents behind as reserves.[7]

It is probable that he placed his infantry phalanx just in front of the bridge crossing the Loire from Orleans because this would have enabled him to bring supplies across the river for his army. It is also probable that his army was deployed just in front of the Roman road for the same purpose, because the presence of the paved road behind his forces would have enabled him to transport supplies (food, drink, weapons) in wagons with relative ease while also enabling him to evacuate the wounded from combat. This location was also well-suited because the Loiret was still deep and wide enough at that point to prevent the Visigoths from attempting to swim across the river. It is thanks to this information that we can make a rough estimate of the forces put into the field by the two sides.

The length of Aegidius's infantry phalanx from river to river was ca. 3 km. However, it is probable that Aegidius placed a separate force to guard the bridge on his right flank so that the overall length of the infantry line would have been about 3.5 km. The cavalry would have been posted behind the infantry. It is also probable that Aegidius posted some infantry reserves behind his phalanx as required by late Roman combat doctrine. Additional cavalry units would in all probability have been posted to guard the length of the Loiret to make certain that the Visigoths would not have been able to swim across unnoticed.

The sources do not provide any details on how the battle was fought, but one can make the educated guess that the Franks and Romans would have used the phalanx formation so that the units adopted the kneeling *testudo/foulkon* formation with spears or javelins pointed towards the enemy for the purpose of receiving the Visigothic cavalry charge. The rear rankers would have peppered the advancing Visigoths with arrows, stones, javelins, darts or throwing *Francisca* axes depending on the equipment carried.

We do not know whether Aegidius used any field fortifications, caltrops or hidden trenches to bolster the defences, but it would have been quite sufficient to oppose the cavalry charge with a disciplined infantry formation, and if Frederic fell on the first charge or on one of the subsequent charges then the morale of the Visigothic army would have collapsed right away – the latter is more likely because morale would have been weaker if several charges had already failed when Frederic died. The infantry phalanx could also have been used in another way which was to open sections of the phalanx for the enemy cavalry to pass through after which these enemy cavalry units would have been engaged by the reserves placed behind.

If this tactic was used then the openings in the phalanx would have been closed and the rear halves of the phalanx would have been sent against the isolated enemy cavalry units so that they could be attacked from all sides simultaneously. All of these were standard tactics used by disciplined Roman infantry forces against cavalry forces. The Franks were quite capable of performing these manoeuvres as the Battle of Mursa in 351 so well attests (see Vol. 1).

It is a shame that we do not know which of these tactics were actually used, because the depth of Aegidius's infantry formation depended on the number of men he had and the tactics he had chosen for the battle. If he let isolated units of Visigoths charge through, it is probable that the depth of the phalanx was 16 ranks of heavy infantry and 8 ranks of light infantry, but if the intention was merely to stop the enemy, the depth of 8 ranks of heavies and 4 ranks of light would have sufficed even if this less secure depth would have enabled him to use the former tactic too.

The probable reason for Frederic's decision to fight in the location chosen by Aegidius was that he felt he would be able to crush his foe there and that his victory would be complete because Aegidius's forces lacked good avenues of escape.

Allowing 500 metres for the intervals between the units, the infantry phalanx with a depth of 24 ranks (16 HI, 8 LI) would have consisted of (width per file 90 cm x 3,300 m, figures rounded down) 52,200 HI and 26,400 LI for a total of 78,600 men, while with a depth of 12 ranks (8 HI, 4 LI) it would have consisted of 26,100 HI and 13,200 LI for a total of 39,300. In addition to this one would have to include at least 15,000–20,000 cavalry and 6,000 reserve infantry for a grand total of 60,300/65,300 or 99,600/104,600. On the basis of Procopius's figures for the Frankish field armies of the sixth century, both of these firgures would be quite possible.

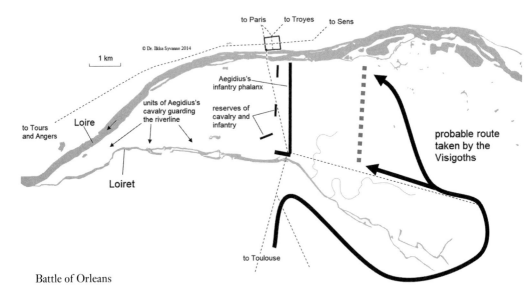

to Paris   to Troyes   to Sens

© Dr. Ilkka Syvänne 2014

1 km

Aegidius's infantry phalanx

units of Aegidius's cavalry guarding the riverline

reserves of cavalry and infantry

Loire

to Tours and Angers

Loiret

to Toulouse

probable route taken by the Visigoths

Battle of Orleans

The Visigoths would probably have followed their standard combat doctrine, which means that most of their forces consisted of cavalry and that in combat their infantry contingent would have been left behind to act as a protective bulwark. Thanks to the fact that the Visigoths possessed superior numbers of cavalry, they would not have needed to have as many troops as Aegidius. Consequently, one can make the educated guess that Frederic's army consisted of 40,000–50,000 cavalry and perhaps 20,000–40,000 infantry. It should be stressed however that all of the above is based on the educated guess that Aegidius had as many troops at his disposal as one third of the Frankish realm had in the sixth century and on the width of the battlefield which would have been suited to this number of troops.

It is unfortunate that we do not know how Aegidius exploited his victory over the Visigoths, but his gains cannot have been great because as cavalry most of the Visigoths would have been able to retreat to their own realm and because the royal army under Theoderic was still intact. One of the results of this defeat appears to have been a desire to withdraw Visigothic forces from Spain to fight against Aegidius, because, according to Hydatius (a.463), Theoderic sent Cyrila together with the Gallacian Palogorius as envoys to Rechimund, the king of the Suevi, apparently to negotiate on behalf of the Gallaecian Romans. The Suevi failed to live up to their promises and once again pillaged Gallaecia after Cyrila had left. As a result, Theoderic dispatched Cyrila and Remismund back to Gallaecia with the Visigothic army that had previously been in Gallaecia. These Visigoths were presumably the army that had previously served in the area, because Remismund was soon after that recalled with the result that the state of war between the Gallaecians and Suevi continued. My interpretation is that Remismund together with the bulk of the forces was recalled as a result of the defeat of Frederic and were then used to defend the Visigothic state against Aegidius.

I would also suggest that Aegidius's victory over the Visigoths near Orleans in 463 had another consequence not mentioned by the extant sources. It is probable that since none of the sources mention the crushing of the revolt of the Alans by Ricimer or by any other commander that Ricimer had used the Burgundians against the Alans during the years 461–3, and when Aegidius then defeated the Visigoths, the Burgundians were forced to abandon their operations against the Alans so that they could transfer their forces against Aegidius with the result that the Alans were able to march to Italy in 464.

Ricimer vs. Beorgor in 464

The next reference in the sources for the western realm is the battle on 6 February 464 between the 'king' Ricimer and Beorgor, king of the Alans, at Bergamo at the foot of the mountains. Of note is the fact that Marcellinus Comes calls Ricimer king. It is possible that this is a mistake, but it is equally possible that Ricimer had indeed assumed the title to be able to lead his mostly barbarian army better. It is unfortunate that we do not know the circumstances in which the battle was fought, which leaves open the question who these Alans were. As noted by MacGeorge, on the basis of the sources that record this battle it is possible that the Alans were a splinter group who had been released to move west thanks to the breakup of the Hunnic Empire and who had then invaded through Raetia or Noricum and then marched through the Brenner or Septimier Pass to Italy; or that Aegidius had sent these Alans from Gaul; or that the Alans in question consisted of the Alan settlers of north Italy who had therefore simply revolted against Ricimer for some unknown reason.[8] However, on the basis of the reasons stated above I would suggest that the Alans were those who had revolted against Majorian in Gaul in 461. In the aftermath of the battle of Orleans it is probable that Gundioc and Ricimer would have transferred the Burgundian forces against Aegidius, which in turn could have left the Alpine passes undefended with the result that Beorgor marched his forces to Italy in 464. It is possible that the Alans and Sarmatians who still remained in Italy joined his forces when he arrived. Regardless of who the Alans were, it is clear that they were completely wiped out by Ricimer's forces at the foot of Bergamo.

The Year 465

The Death of Aegidius
Aegidius had by early 465 come to the decision that he needed to seek new allies against Ricimer. His choice fell on the Vandals. The above account proves that Aegidius's military power was almost entirely based on his position as King of the Salian Franks and when he had lost it he was in trouble. It is plainly obvious that without their support, Aegidius would not have been able to hold onto his position against the Burgundians and Visigoths. Roman military weakness in north Gaul was to be brutally exposed when Clovis turned against them. Aegidius's envoys sailed to Carthage in May 465 and returned in September,

but before these plans could come to fruition a momentuous event took place in Gaul. According to the *Liber Historiae Francorum 8*, some group of Franks attacked Cologne and massacred those who supported Aegidius; Aegidius fled. The location suggests that the Franks may have been assisted by the Thuringians. After this, the Franks marched to Trier which they sacked and burnt. Could it be that it was then that Arbogastes (see below), who was of Frankish origins, became its *Comes Trevirorum*? Following this, Aegidius was either ambushed, killed by poison, or died from pestilence. He was succeeded by his son Syagrius (Hyd. a.465; Greg. 2.18). The death of Aegidius seems to have given control of the region back to the 'legitimate' Roman authorities because we find the Romans under *Comes* Paulus and Childeric I cooperating against the Saxons of Odoacer in ca. 469. It is therefore probable that Childeric I had ambushed or poisoned Aegidius on behalf of Ricimer, and may even have been the leader of the Franks who attacked Cologne and Trier, which would then have enabled him to regain official recognition from Rome.

According to Gregory of Tours (2.18), Odoacer took hostages from Angers and other places after the death of Aegidius, which presumably means a declaration of independence. He follows this with a statement that the Goths expelled the Bretons from Bourges and that many were killed at Bourg-de-Déols, which would suggest that the Goths were attacking the allies of Aegidius. The problem with this is that these events should be connected with the events of 469 and the campaign of Riothamus-Arthur which he describes immediately after this. I would therefore suggest that the Roman authorities in Gaul (presumably *Comes* Paulus), Childeric, Syagrius and the Visigoths, concluded some sort of truce or agreement with Odoacer and his Saxons at this time, which lasted until ca. 468–9. It remains clear that the Visigoths did attack the supporters of Aegidius immediately after he had died, because Hydatius (a.464–5) specifically refers to this. In short, the Visigoths invaded the territories previously held by Aegidius, but in light of what is known of the situation a few years later in 469, it appears probable that they did not achieve much probably because Childeric and Syagrius were reconciled with Ricimer. Furthermore, the subsequent murder of Theoderic by his brother Euric in 466 would have paralyzed the Visigothic realm for a while. It is therefore practically certain that the Romans gained official control of north Gaul after the death of Aegidius so that the principal Roman authority in the area was *comes* Paulus possibly with the title of *MVM per Gallias*, while Syagrius and Childeric had some sort of *foedus* with the Empire.

It is possible that Arbogastes, the descendant of the famous Arbogastes and therefore of Frankish origins, was already on the scene. Sidonius refers to him as *Comes Trevirorum* (Count of Trier) in 477 so that he served in that capacity for the Franks. It is therefore possible that in 465/6 he was *Comes Trevirorum* either as its independent allied ruler like Syagrius was for Soissons, or that he was *Comes Trevirorum* for the Emperor, or that he was already a subject of the Franks.

The Suevi vs. Visigoths in Spain in 465

The Suevi exploited the absence of Visigothic forces by continuing their pillage of Roman Spain. Hydatius (a.465) mentions the pillage of Conimbriga, which the Suevi entered treacherously (thanks to a Roman traitor?). The Suevi kidnapped the mother and sons of the local noble family of Cantaber/Cantabri presumably in an effort to obtain a ransom from the father. It was probably thanks to this that Theoderic recalled the *MVM*

Arborius to Toulouse and replaced him with Vincentius. Theoderic was still clearly acting on behalf of Ricimer's regime. The Suevi sent envoys twice to Toulouse to negotiate in the course of the year 465. The last set of envoys informed the Suevic king that Severus had died (see below) with the result that he resumed hostilities with even greater vigour.

The Troubled Noricum in ca.460–465[9]

Troubles with barbarians also started to mount up in Noricum in the early 460s. According to Alföldy, the march of Huns and their allies through Noricum to Gaul in 451 destroyed many of the defensive structures. This had been followed by the collapse of the Hunnic Empire which released its subject tribes to seek their fortunes elsewhere. These peoples included the Rugii who settled just beyond the north-eastern corner of Noricum. As we have seen, Ricimer managed to stem the barbarian tide temporarily during 458–61, but soon after this the troubles started again and this time Ricimer was unable to send any reinforcements to Noricum because he needed all the men he could muster against the Vandals, Alans and Aegidius.

We know what happened next mainly thanks to the fact that St. Severinus arrived in Noricum taking residence in Faviana (Mautern) shortly after 460. I date his arrival roughly to 463. At the time St. Severinus arrived, the main centre of *Noricum Ripense* along the Danube was Lauriacum, but even this city had suffered from repeated attacks before Severinus' arrival. The Rugii had also forced Faviana and other settlements directly opposite them to pay tribute and made their presence felt in north-western Noricum.

Southern Noricum had already been completely ruined when Radagaisus and Alaric operated in the area so that the city of Solva was ruined in 405, Aguntum partly destroyed in 407 and even Virunum, the capital of *Noricum Mediterraneum*, had been abandoned by its citizens who had fled to mountain hideouts/holdouts while its administrative organs appear to have been transferred to Teurnia at the beginning of the fifth century. Teurnia lay further away from the invasion routes and possessed better natural and manmade defences. According to Alföldy, it seems probable that regular imperial administrators resided there until c. 500. Consequently, despite having suffered very serious damage at the beginning of the fifth century, *Noricum Mediterraneum* managed to survive as a viable province thanks to its closeness to Italy. The southern areas of Noricum appear to have been protected by troops subject to the control of *comes rei militaris Italiae* or *comes limitis Italiae* who was in charge of the defence of the *clausura Alpium Iuliarum* north of Istria (the walls and fortifactions blocking the route[10]) and probably also of the small garrisons of the Norican *burgi*. The *Notitia Dignitatum* doesn't specify any troops for the *Comes Italiae*, but it is possible that the core of his forces consisted of the legions designated as Alpine (three in Italy and one in Illyricum), which seems to have been completely insufficient for the task.

In contrast to southern Noricum, the imperial administration of *Noricum Ripense* had totally collapsed by about 463 (Alföldy suggests by about 460), presumably because of the previous invasions through it, so that when St. Severinus arrived he had to take the administration and defence of the area into his own hands. The only areas that were safe from enemy ravages were the hill forts and fortified hideouts in the mountains which were built in great numbers from 400 onwards. Some of these served as places of refuge, but most were built as new permanent residences for the threatened inhabitants. *Noricum*

Ripense lacked any organized defence to oppose the freely moving barbarian forces, which caused St. Severinus to instruct the inhabitants that when the Rugii appeared they were to seek refuge in their fortified hideouts until the enemy were forced to retreat due to lack of supplies. The same instructions were also given to the inhabitants of Lauriacum who were to collect everything they owned and place them inside the walls for protection when the enemy appeared. The only defence the inhabitants had against the roaming Rugii was its walls.

The Rugii occupied *Commagena* (Tulln) some time in the early 460s and were forced to abandon it only through 'miracle'. The 'barbarians' (i.e. the Rugians) had also destroyed *Astura* (Zeiselmaur) at about the same time and the existing forts upstream from Lauriacum were under continuous attack until their fall in the same decade after which the signal stations further into the interior were also abandoned. After the collapse of the river forts, the defence of the North was entirely in the hands of the local civilians. Without any outside help, the situation was hopeless because the economy was in ruins and the people were suffering from famine when they had been forced to abandon the better agricultural land in favour of the mountain hideouts, which weakened their ability to withstand sieges. The Rugii and Alamanni were roaming the countryside and carried away everything outside the fortified places, including the inhabitants who were taken as slaves together with their cattle and other possessions.

The Death of Severus on 14 November 465

The Emperor Severus died on 14 November 465. According to the official version stated by Sidonius, he died of natural causes, but according to Cassiodorus (*Chron.* a.464) Ricimer poisoned him. In this case Cassiodorus's version is to be preferred because he wrote after the death of Ricimer. He did not have to fear for his life if he told the truth.

We do not know why Ricimer chose to murder Severus, but the likeliest reason would have been that he felt that he was unable to face the Vandals without Eastern help. My own educated guess is that the removal of Severus was Leo's precondition for the reconciliation of the two halves of the Empire, and that the recorded presence of Marcellinus on the island of Sicily in 465 formed part of the deal. According to Hydatius (a 465), Marcellinus defeated the Vandals and expelled them from the island in 465.

The likeliest timetable for the events is that before agreeing to kill Severus, Ricimer required some kind of demonstration of Leo's willingness to act against the Vandals, which was the reconciliation between Marcellinus and Ricimer and the sending of Marcellinus to Sicily. This enabled Leo to keep up the pretence of having abided by the peace agreement with the Vandals because Dalmatia was still officially part of the Western Empire while still demonstrating his willingness to attack the Vandals. As we shall see Gaiseric was not fooled. The dispatching of Marcellinus to Sicily was to become the official *casus belli* for Gaiseric, but only at the time of his choosing.

Interregnum: Ricimer 465–467[11]

Marcellinus, Sicily and Dalmatia 465–467
If my above speculations regarding Ricimer's negotiations with Leo are correct, then the resulting interregnum during which there was no Emperor in the West resulted from

the actions of Gaiseric who sent his fleet to ravage Illyricum, Peloponnesus, Greece and all the islands in 466. The absence of Marcellinus in Sicily enabled Gaiseric's fleet to do this at their leisure with the result that Marcellinus returned to Dalmatia in 466 where he stayed until 467.[12] If the presence of Marcellinus in Sicily had been a precondition for the acceptance of Eastern dominion over Italy, the retreat of Marcellinus from Sicily to Dalmatia would have made this void. Ricimer and Leo both would appear to have thought that it would not be a good thing to elect Olybrius, the favourite of Gaiseric, as the next Emperor because this would have created a situation in which Gaiseric was related to the imperial house. If Ricimer's precondition was support from the East against the Vandals, then the hiatus could also have resulted from the fact that the East Romans were fighting against a series of enemies in the Balkans meaning they could not spare enough men for the Western campaign before Anthemius had finally defeated the Huns at Serdica in about 466. See the reign of Leo.

The Suevic Ravages in 465–67 and Visigothic Reactions

Hydatius' text proves that the death of Severus encouraged the Suevi under Remismund to act with even greater vigour in Spain. Remismund had been chosen as a successor to the deceased King of the Suevi, Frumarius, at the suggestion of Theoderic, King of the Visigoths, in 465. This united the Suevi under a single leader/king once again. Theoderic had even provided weapons and money for Remismund. Remismund must have realized that Visigothic loyalty towards their Roman overlords had to be renegotiated and exploited the situation. Ajax, who was a Greek apostate and now the leading figure among the Arians, was used to unite the Suevi behind their king and cause dissent among the natives. The Suevi were then sent to ravage Aunona, presumably in 466. The only feeble response Theoderic was able to make was to send Salla as envoy to Remismund to protest, but without any result. It is no wonder that Euric, the fanatic brother of Theoderic, murdered him in the same year. As suggested by Ian Hughes (2015, 119), it is possible that the principal reason for the murder was that Euric had expected to succeed his brother Frederic as a 'sub-king' when the latter had been killed at Orleans and when Theoderic then failed to deliver Euric decided to get rid of his brother. On the basis of the silence of the sources, it appears probable that the murder of Theoderic paralyzed the Visigothic realm for a while because Euric needed to secure his own position among the Visigoths. Euric dispatched envoys immediately to the Ostrogoths, Remismund and Emperor (Hydatius a.466–7, but this is a mistake for Ricimer), while Remismund sent the envoys back and dispatched envoys of his own to Euric, the Emperor (Ricimer), and the Vandals. Hydatius fails to state what the aims of the embassies were, but in the case of Euric it must have been to obtain recognition for his position, while Remismund would probably have sought alliances or just aimed to create confusion among his enemies. It is also possible that he had been in contact with his brethren in the Danube just like Euric was with his and that he and these were cooperating with the Vandals for the purpose of keeping the Easterners and Marcellinus away from the Western Mediterranean. What is known is that Hunimund, the chief of the Suevi on the other side of the Danube, exploited Marcellinus' absence later by invading Dalmatia in about 468/9, but this time the Ostrogoths acted as expected and attacked the invaders on behalf of Rome.[13]

Chapter Five

Anthemius the Hellene (467–472) and Ricimer

A coin of Augustus Anthemius (467-472).
Sources: Above Hodgkin; Below Beger 1693.

Anthemius Chosen as Emperor

The long diplomatic exchanges between Ricimer and Leo finally produced a result during late 466 or the winter of 466/7. Leo and his advisors chose Anthemius as Emperor of the West and this choice was accepted by Ricimer. Leo undoubtedly had two goals. The first was to get rid of his potential competitor, because Anthemius was an accomplished general who had a very distinguished family tree and who was also married to the daughter of Marcian. The second would have been to provide the Western

Empire with a native Emperor who was also a skilled general. Ricimer's support for the deal was secured by marrying Anthemius's daughter Alypia to him, which made Ricimer a member of the imperial family, which had only been dreamed of by Stilicho and Aetius. This was an affront to Gaiseric who was attempting to place Olybrius, his relative through marriage, on the throne, but it did not matter because the goal of Leo and Ricimer was to destroy the Vandals once and for all.

Anthemius Arrives with a Large Eastern Army

In the late autumn of 466 or spring of 467 Leo dispatched Anthemius, Marcellinus, selected *comites* and a very large army to Italy. The aim was to launch a naval expedition against the Vandals in 467. Anthemius was then duly proclaimed emperor at Brontotas, three or eight miles from Rome, on 12 April 467. Ian Hughes is likely to be correct that this place was a military camp just like Columellas where Majorian had been acclaimed as Emperor. The aim of this was to secure the loyalty of the Italian army for the new Emperor. Leo and Anthemius did not plan to play second fiddle to Ricimer. Anthemius was a military man and he was accompanied by a huge well-equipped army. Furthermore, Anthemius nominated Marcellinus, who was accompanying him, as *Patricius*, which made him equal to Ricimer in the hierarchy.[1]

The arrival of Anthemius and his forces in Italy was not auspicious. According to a number of sources, which unfortunately are also tendentious in the case of Anthemius, his entry was accompanied by natural disasters or evil omens, which are listed by Ian Hughes (2015, 122). They included an earthquake at Ravenna in 467, famine and pestilence in Campania, strange celestial phenomena, and an outbreak of cattle disease. These quite natural phenomena can of course affect the minds of the superstitious.

On a more serious note, however, there were more important matters that made it difficult for Anthemius to gather adequate support from the locals. His enemies in Italy accused him of a collusion with the famously pagan Flavius Messius Phoebus Severus who had accompanied Anthemius to Rome. The accusation was that they aimed to restore the worship of gods on the Capitol, which was easy enough to believe because Anthemius was known for his Hellenic learning and he was also a 'Hellene/Greek'. It is impossible to know what the truth was and it may have been mere calumny as stated by Hodgkin, but one cannot escape the fact that Anthemius may have had strong pagan sympathies – at least it is clear that both Severus and Marcellinus, who were accompanying Anthemius, were both well-known pagans. What is certain is that Anthemius was also accompanied by Philotheus who was a follower of the so-called Macedonian heresy which denied the divinity of the Holy Ghost. It was then thanks to the influence of Philotheus that Anthemius proposed full religious tolerance towards all Christian sects in Rome. This in itself would have been quite enough to upset the bigoted Roman clergy even without the suspicion of Hellene/pagan sympathies. Christians of the time were quite unable to tolerate any deviant views, indeed they could not even comprehend the concept of religious tolerance, which in itself is an indication of how far Christians had deviated from the actual teachings of the real life Jesus Christ. As one of his last actions as a Pope, Hilarius, who died in September 467, fulminated furiously against such intolerable tolerance with the result that Anthemius was forced to abandon the plan and to promise on oath to the Pope that he would not attempt to introduce it again.[2]

Anthemius' plans in the religious sphere can therefore be considered to have been quite out of place in Italy, which naturally weakened his grip on power among the bigoted Christians of Italy. It was probably partially because of this that Anthemius gave the Urban Prefecture to Sidonius Apollinaris and promoted other Gauls to positions of power. He may have sought support from the Gauls against the Italians. In addition to this, he sought to establish good relations with the Goths, Suevi, Salian Franks, Bretons and even with the Britons of Britannia as we shall see. It is likely that at this stage he did all these moves in conjunction with Ricimer, who had a better grasp of local realities than he as easterner, as suggested by Ian Hughes.[3] Anthemius' aim was undoubtedly to secure his rear so that he could concentrate his war efforts solely against the Vandals, which would then enable him to restore West Roman fortunes with the grain and money of North Africa.

Anthemius' diplomatic efforts proved unsuccessful in Spain. The Suevi under their king Remismund/Remismundus, who had succeeded Frumarius in 465, raided Lusitania. He had been supported and given weapons by Theoderic, King of Visigoths, but his relations with Euric were unfriendly, and the city of Conimbrica was sacked.[4]

A Storm Prevents an Invasion of North Africa in 467

Anthemius's very first act as Emperor was to send Marcellinus again to Sicily from which he was to launch an expedition against the Vandals. The situation was actually very opportune, because Gaiseric had dispatched at least part of his fleet against the East Romans which had raided the whole land of the Eastern Emperor including the island of Rhodes. This had caused fear both in Alexandria and Constantinople and had undoubtedly made Leo's resolve to solve the Vandal question even stronger. However, this was not to be, because the naval attack was recalled because of bad weather. This means that the assembling of the forces for the final campaign had probably taken so long that the autumn storms had arrived. It was thanks to this that once-in-a-lifetime opportunity was lost.[5]

The Great Vandal war of 468

The Vandal invasion of East Roman territory in 467 convinced Leo to send additional forces against the Vandals in 468. Vandal actions had brought home the lesson that it was better for the Eastern Empire to take charge of the campaign rather than leave it solely to Anthemius and Marcellinus who had not invaded North Africa in 467 as had been planned. Leo's plan was truly grandiose and it is analyzed in detail in the chapter dealing with his reign. I will provide here only a summary of the events.

The campaign consisted of two elements so that the attack against the Vandals was three-pronged. Firstly, Leo dispatched Marcellinus with his forces against the Vandals in Sardinia and Heraclius with another fleet from Constantinople to Tripolis in Libya. Both of these commanders achieved their objectives. Heraclius left his ships at Tripolis and advanced on land towards Carthage. The idea was to destroy the Vandals in these outlying areas and to frighten Gaiseric so that and he would dispatch reinforcements to

these areas. The intention was that the main force under Basiliscus would advance straight
to Carthage and inflict the decisive blow. Gaiseric, however, appears to have been aware of
the plan and concentrated his forces against Basiliscus. Basiliscus' fleet inflicted a series of
defeats on the Vandals before they made a landing at Cap Bon in North Africa. Gaiseric
proposed a truce so that he would be able to put into effect the demands of the Emperor
Leo, which Basiliscus accepted for two reasons. Firstly, he was certain that the Vandals had
been defeated and Gaiseric was prepared to accept the terms of peace put forth by Leo.
Secondly, by saving the Vandals, he was doing a favour to Aspar whose support he was
seeking to obtain the throne. Basically, Gaiseric fooled Basiliscus with promises that played
into his hopes, and when the wind had become favourable to the Vandals he launched a
naval attack against the Roman fleet at anchor which was spearheaded by fireships. The
Roman fleet and army were annihilated. The Roman war effort collapsed completely when
an officer of Marcellinus then murdered him in Sicily. The sources fail to mention who
was behind the assassination, but it is clear that the culprit was Ricimer who had the
most to benefit from the death of his personal enemy and competitor. The relationship
between Anthemius and Ricimer had already soured before this to the point of shouting
and accusations so that this action can be considered understandable in the circumstances.
It is very unfortunate that we do not know if there was some collusion and cooperation
between the barbarian *magistri* Aspar and Ricimer because this is entirely plausible.

Euric Invades Spain in 468

The Roman campaign against the Vandals gave Euric a chance to expand his territories
in Spain. According to Isidore of Seville, he invaded and pillaged Lusitania and then sent
another army which conquered Pamplona, and Zaragoza/Saragossa (Caesaraugusta).
According to Gallic Chronicle 511 (651), which dates the event to the year 473, the
commander of the Visigothic army was *Comes* Gauterit, but the dating in Isidore is to be
preferred in this case. This presumably means that Euric invaded first Lusitania as an ally
of the Romans and forced the Suevi back to their strongholds in the north-west corner
of Spain, but then after he had returned to Gaul, he launched another invasion against
Roman-held Tarraconensis where his forces occupied Pamplona and Zaragosa with the
result that the Visigoths brought this province under their rule. After this he defeated a
counter-attack by the Roman nobles who opposed this. This proves that the local Roman
nobility maintained loyalty towards the Roman Empire and were quite prepared to fight
for it. The occupation of the Roman province was a declaration of war against Anthemius
Even if the sources fail to state so, it is possible to think that there was some collusion
between Ricimer and the Visigoths against Anthemius at this stage.[6]

War Against the Visigoths in 469–470[7]

Anthemius's next military goal was to squash the Visigoths. He planned to accomplish
this through a grand alliance which included at least the British forces under their king
Riothamus, the Burgundians under Gundioc, the regulars of Gaul under *Comes* Paulus,
the Salian Franks under Childeric, and the expeditionary force sent from Italy under
Anthemius's son Anthemiolus.

I agree with Geoffrey Ashe that we should equate Riothamus (High-King) of Jordanes and Sidonius Apollinaris with King Arthur and I have discussed this matter in great detail in my monograph *Britain in the Age of Arthur*, but in this book I will not include a detailed discussion of how this identification affects the analysis of what happened in the north of Gaul. I just advise readers to read my analysis of the exploits of Riothamus/Arthur in the *Britain in the Age of Arthur*, because it is practically certain that his exploits on the continent contributed decisively to the downfall of Anthemius and West Rome. The campaign of Riothamus can be dated to roughly 469/70.

Riothamus (Riothamus/Riotimus means great king = *rigo tamos*) appears to have started his campaign against the Visigoths prematurely. He sailed from Britain[8] and disembarked his 12,000-strong army in the state of Bituriges (presumably somewhere close to Tours). This means he sailed his ships along the Loire to a suitable landing site and then advanced to Bourges. I would suggest that Riothamus' men were at this stage reinforced by their Armorican brethren so that the overall size of the force under him cannot have been much smaller than ca. 22,000–24,000. The aim was to unite this force with the Roman army under Paulus, which had been dispatched by Anthemius. However, the Visigoths under their able new king Euric acted before Riothamus and the Romans could unite their forces. Riothamus evacuated Bourges after the Visigoths had inflicted a serious defeat on his army at Bourg-de-Déols/Déols. The location of the battle suggests that Riothamus had advanced from Bourges to meet the Romans, but was then intercepted by the enemy. Riothamus and the remnants of his army retreated to Burgundy where their king and Roman *MVM* Gundioc offered them a place of refuge.

Ashe (1981, 2013) has suggested that possibly the Romans failed to make contact with Riothamus' army in time because of the betrayal of the Praetorian Prefect of Gaul, Arvandus, mentioned by Sidonius (vol.1.371–2). Arvandus apparently urged Euric not to make peace with *the 'Greek Emperor'* [Anthemius] and *insisted that he should attack the Britanni settled to the north of the Liger* [these would be the Bretons of Armorica and/or the army of Riothamus] so that he Euric would divide Gaul with the Burgundians. It is therefore probable that as Praetorian Prefect of Gaul, Arvandus was aware of the imminent arrival of Riothamus and that he informed Euric of this and advised him to attack the Britons immediately and that it was this that enabled Euric to destroy Riothamus's army as suggested by Ashe.[9]

Soon after this, the Roman army consisting of regulars under *Comes* Paulus (presumably the *MVM*) and the Franks under their king Childeric crushed the Visigoths. Meanwhile, the Saxons under Adovacrius/Odovacar/Odoacer had besieged Angers which forced both commanders to abandon their campaign against the Visigoths. The Saxons were clearly allied with the Visigoths against their arch-rivals the Britons. The Roman army arrived too late. The Saxons had captured the city the day before the arrival of the relief army. The Romans attacked immediately. They were victorious despite the death of their commander Paulus, because Childeric still managed to recapture the city. The Romans pursued the fleeing Saxons while Childeric's Franks captured the islands of the Loire from the Saxons. Adovacrius/Odovacar saw no other way out but to surrender. The Romans were ready to grant him terms because the Alamanni had invaded Italy in the meantime. Odoacer/Odovacar and Childeric were now both dispatched against these invaders, and the Alamanni were duly crushed probably when they were already on their way back home somewhere in Raetia-Noricum. The victory over the Saxons presumably enabled the Romans to take full control of Armorica for a while.

The Visigoths and the Final Showdown between Anthemius and Ricimer in 470–472[10]

At this time there was a parallel development in the relationship between the barbarian generalissimos and the Emperor in the east and west. In both cases the barbarian commander appears to have attempted to get rid of the Emperor because they had a will of their own and were not ready to follow the advice of their barbarian general. It was thanks to this development that there was quiet on the Gallic and Spanish fronts. The defeat the Visigoths had suffered at the hands of *Comes* Paulus and Childeric ensured that the Visigoths would lick their wounds in 470 while the state of cold war between Antemius and Ricimer ensured that the West Romans would not initiate new hostilies just like the East Romans because of their own troubles.

John of Antioch (fr. 207, Roberto ed. fr.299) informs us that Anthemius became seriously ill as a result of sorcery in 470 and that Anthemius suspected a plot to kill him. Indeed in my mind there is no doubt that the sorcery was an attempted poisoning and Anthemius acted accordingly.[11] He executed several people who were involved in the plot the most important of whom was *Magister Officiorum* and *Patricius* Romanus who was a close friend of Ricimer. Cassiodorus (Chron. a.470) claims that Romanus was punished because he attempted to usurp power. This is indeed the likeliest alternative, because Ricimer would have needed someone to act as his figurehead emperor.

Ricimer duly fled from Rome, gathered 6,000 men who had been assembled under him for the war against the Vandals, and sought a place of refuge in Milan which was close to the forces of his Burgundian supporters. On the basis of the above, it is probable that the Vandals had raided Sicily and Italy in 469 and that the defence had been conducted by Ricimer and that the intention was that Ricimer would once again take charge of the defence of Italy in 470. We should consider these 6,000 men to be Ricimer's *bucellarii* rather than the remnants of the former praesental army because it is clear that Ricimer was a wealthy individual who had been able to bribe even the Scythians in Marcellinus' service to join him. We should also add to the figure of 6,000 men their squires and servants, which in the case of a wealthy individual like Ricimer would have been numerous perhaps one squire per warrior.

It is not known whether Gundobad, who was the *MVM per Gallias* in 472, had already succeeded his father Gundioc into this position at this time. Katalin Escher (90ff.) suggests that the Burgundian King Gundioc died between 463 and 469 and was succeeded by his brother Chilperic/Hilperic as *MVM per Gallias*, but I would suggest it is likelier that Gundobad was nominated *MVM per Gallias* as a consolation while his uncle became King of the Burgundians, because Gundobad occupied that position in 472. However, the evidence is so poor that we do not know any of this with any certainty and it is because of this that Escher's datings are entirely different to those in the PLRE2.

The situation between Anthemius and Ricimer did not come to fighting because during the winter of 470/1 a delegation of Ligurian nobles managed to convince Ricimer to attempt a reconciliation, and the mutually agreed envoy, the Bishop of Ticinum

(Pavia) Epiphanius, managed to convince the two men to agree to a temporary truce, but the hostilities restarted and erupted into open war in 472 when Ricimer revolted against Anthemius. It is easy to see why the Ligurian nobles were worried. The Alamanni had invaded Italy in 469/70, but thankfully for the Romans, Childeric I and Odoacer had come to the rescue and defeated them presumably somewhere in Raetia-Noricum when they were retreating (Greg. 2.19). It was then that Odoacer presumably met St. Severinus in Noricum. The Visigoths were threatening Gaul even if they remained quiet thanks to their previous defeat during 470. The probable reason for Ricimer's readiness to postpone the conflict was that Anthemius still possessed significant numbers of loyal forces that he could dispatch against him. Furthermore, it was in 471 that Anthemius' son Marcian married Leo's daughter Leontia (now freed from her marriage with Patricius; see the reign of Leo), which signalled a clear Eastern support for Anthemius. In these circumstances it is not surprising that Ricimer thought it advantageous to agree to a truce. In return for this, he may also have obtained as a concession the nomination of Flavius Theodovius Valila as *comes et magister utrisque militiae* as suggested by Ian Hughes (2015, 150) because it is clear that Anthemius must have given him something in return for the truce, but it is of course still possible that his nomination to that post in 471 had nothing to do with Ricimer's wishes.

By the spring of 471 the Visigoths had assembled a sizable force which Euric led against the Romans. Euric dispatched one force against Auvergne/Arverni and the city of Clermont, while he took personal charge of the division which advanced to Provence. Thanks to the truce between himself and Ricimer, Anthemius was able to dispatch an army to relieve the besieged Arles commanded by his young son Anthemiolus with Thorisarius (East Germanic), Evergindus and Hermianus. Euric annihilated this army somewhere east of the Rhône in 471 and killed all of its commanders (PLRE 2, *Chron. Gall.* 511 no. 649 s.a. 471). Euric was therefore able to capture both Arles and Marseilles in 473 (*Chron Gall. 511* 657, ca. a.473). It is possible, as has often been claimed, that the Goths Ricimer and Euric both cooperated in this and that Ricimer had a role in the destruction of the forces of his rival. If my speculation regarding the exploits of King Arthur on the basis of the account of Geoffrey of Monmouth is correct, then King Arthur has also a role in the destruction of the forces of Anthemius in Gaul so that when Euric destroyed the abovementioned forces posted in the south of Gaul, Arthur destroyed the Roman army that had been posted in the north of Gaul. I urge readers to read the reasoning behind this speculation, but I leave it to them to decide whether King Arthur did indeed do the deeds mentioned by Geoffrey and which can definitely be dated to this same period. Those who do not accept this should then think that Euric destroyed almost all of the forces that were loyal to Anthemius so that Ricimer was in a position to start his revolt in 472.

The Visigoths began the siege of the city of Clermont in 471 at the same time as they started their conquest of Auvergne/Arverni. Since the Arverni could not expect any help from the Emperor, the Arvernians took the defence into their own hands so that the local magnates took a leading role in organizing it. The progress of the siege/blockade is described by Sidonius Apollinaris in his letters, which have usefully been collected together by FRMG (233ff.).

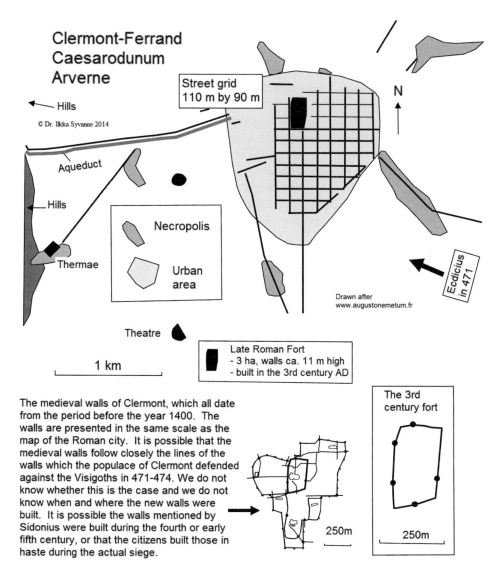

Clermont-Ferrand
Caesarodunum
Arverne

← Hills

© Dr. Ilkka Syvänne 2014

Street grid
110 m by 90 m

N ↑

Aqueduct

← Hills

Necropolis

Thermae

Urban area

Ecdicius in 471

Drawn after
www.augustonemetum.fr

Theatre

1 km

Late Roman Fort
- 3 ha, walls ca. 11 m high
- built in the 3rd century AD

The 3rd
century fort

The medieval walls of Clermont, which all date from the period before the year 1400. The walls are presented in the same scale as the map of the Roman city. It is possible that the medieval walls follow closely the lines of the walls which the populace of Clermont defended against the Visigoths in 471-474. We do not know whether this is the case and we do not know when and where the new walls were built. It is possible the walls mentioned by Sidonius were built during the fourth or early fifth century, or that the citizens built those in haste during the actual siege.

250m

250m

The city of Clermont had a small third-century fort, but it was insufficient to protect the populace. We do not know whether the Romans had built new walls in the fourth or early fifth century, but we know that the citizens manned and protected some walls which cannot have been the walls of the small fort. The city had a population of perhaps about 80,000–90,000 or more. This makes it clear that the walls were added to the defences at the latest at the time when the Visigoths attacked. In my opinion it is probable that the walls were built only in 471 as a response to the Visigothic threat. The initial walls would in all probability have consisted of packed earth, a wooden palisade and a trench, because Sidonius constantly refers to half scorched walls. This is not conclusive however, because fire could also be used to weaken stone and brick walls. It is probable that the citizens would have improved the walls by building stone/brick walls immediately after the Visigoths had returned to their winter quarters in the autumn of 471. It is possible that these new stone/brick walls would have followed approximately the same lines as the medieval walls (see the map), but this is not known with any certainty because they have not been studied from this perspective.

The Visigoths began the siege in the summer of 471, but made very little progress despite the fact that their opposition consisted only of local civilians both men and women. Even though Sidonius fails to mention this, it is possible that Sidonius himself as Bishop of Clermont was in charge of the defence until the arrival of a more experienced military commander. Indeed, at some unknown point in time during the siege, the senator Ecdicius, son of Avitus, returned to his native city to take charge of its defence. According to Sidonius, the ramparts were already half ruined when Ecdicius, accompanied by barely 18 horsemen (10 according to Greg. 2.24), attacked the Visigothic rearguard in the open plain in the middle of the day with the result that the enemy commanders were so badly surprised and frightened that they withdrew all their thousands of warriors to the top of a steep hill. This means that Ecdicius approached either from the south-east or from the east and that the Visigoths withdrew to the hills west of the city. See the map. This account has not unnaturally raised suspicions among modern historians that the 18 horsemen could have been officers in charge of a far greater number of men. However, in my opinion there is no reason to suspect the version given by Sidonius and Gregory. They both relate it precisely because it was so incredible. It was the boldness of the attack that panicked the Visigothic commanders because they were uncertain what would happen next. They thought that nobody would dare to commit such an attack in broad daylight in open terrain unless he had far greater numbers of men following after. Ecdicius was clearly a bold, energetic and daring cavalry commander – a real life hero for readers of Sidonius to emulate!

When Ecdicius reached the city, he reorganized its defence and then raised an army out of his own pockets to resist the Visigoths. The use of the *bucellarii* was the order of the day. There were no regular forces available for Ecdicius to use. After this, Ecdicius conducted so effective a defensive guerrilla campaign against the attackers that his services to the country as a private individual were considered so great that the Emperor Anthemius promised to grant him the title of *Patricius*, but Anthemius died on 11 July 472 before he could fulfil his promise. His successors Olybrius (April 472 – 2 November 472) and Glycerius (3 March 473 – June 474) failed to honour Anthemius's promise, but their successor Iulius Nepos (19/24 June 474 – 9 May 480) corrected the situation in 474.

Ricimer exploited the destruction of Anthemius' army by Euric by calling to his assistance Gundobad, the *MVM per Gallias*, and other barbarian allies or mercenaries, after which he marched to Rome which he put under a siege so that he controlled traffic into the city and outside it. His idea may have been to convince the Romans to hand over Anthemius without a fight as suggested by Ian Hughes (2015, 153ff.) because Anthemius as a Greek was not universally liked and had also angered the Catholic Church. This, however, proved a mistake. The populace appears to have rallied behind their Roman ruler, even if he was from Greece. The threat of the barbarian occupation was quite sufficient for this.

The extant sources claim that it was then in about 471, presumably before the siege began, that Leo formed a plot to kill Ricimer while he publicly still claimed to seek reconciliation between Anthemius and Ricimer. According to Malalas (14.45), Leo dispatched Olybrius to the West with orders to mediate because he was a senator from the west and therefore a person who could be put in charge of such a delicate mission. Leo also ordered Olybrius to continue his journey to Carthage where he was to convince Gaiseric to become an ally of Leo. Olybrius was an ideal candidate for that mission because he was married to Placidia who was a sister of Huneric's wife Eudocia. However, according to Malalas, Leo's real intention was to have both Ricimer and Olybrius assassinated. In order to make his own plans believable, Leo therefore kept Olybrius' wife and daughter at Constantinople presumably as hostages. He then dispatched *magistrianos* (i.e. *agens in rebus*) Modestus with a letter to Anthemius. The letter stated that Anthemius should kill Ricimer like Leo had killed Aspar and that Anthemius should also kill Olybrius. However, Ricimer had posted his loyal Goths at every gate of the city of Rome and also at the harbour to control movement with the result that Modestus was searched and the letters were found. Ricimer showed the letters to Olybrius and asked his sister's son Gundobad (Gundobadus) to bring his forces to Rome. It would be nice to know whether the original letter of Leo had orders to kill Olybrius or whether this was added to it by Ricimer. It is also possible to think that Leo had dispatched this letter with the intention of having both Anthemius (his former rival) and Olybrius (his potential rival) killed by Ricimer and his henchmen. Whatever the case, Olybrius was duly incensed and readily agreed to be appointed as the new Emperor, probably in April 472.

According to John of Antioch (fr. 209.1; Roberto ed. fr. 301), Ricimer fought against Anthemius inside Rome for five months, which dates the beginning of the revolt to February/March 472. The magistrates (authorities) and populace sided with Anthemius, while the barbarian masses sided with Ricimer. The barbarians included the Scirian Odoacer/Odovacar, the son of Edeco and the brother of Onulf, the bodyguard and killer of Armatus.[12] Anthemius lived in the Palace while Ricimer cut off the districts by the Tiber so that the defenders went hungry. Anthemius apparently appointed Bilimer (*Galliarum rector*) as successor of Gundobad in the office *MVM per Gallias* when Gundobad joined Ricimer with the mission to bring relief to Rome against the rebels. On the basis of Paulus Diaconus (*Hist. Rom.* 15.4), Bilimer appears to have managed to bring his forces inside the city so that he protected the bridge beside Castel Sant'Angelo (the Mausoleum of Hadrian) against the forces of Ricimer. We do not know the size of the force under Bilimer, but in the aftermath of the defeats suffered in Gaul and the defection of Gundobad, they cannot have been large. Consequently it is not surprising that Bilimer lost and died heroically in the defence of the bridge and that Ricimer's forces managed to penetrate into the city proper. However, Anthemius and his men were not yet prepared to surrender, so the fight continued.

According to John of Antioch (fr. 209.1; Roberto ed. 301), Ricimer defeated the rest of the defenders through treachery and appointed Olybrius as a ruler with the result that the remaining defenders abandoned Anthemius who mingled with those who begged alms and went with them to the church now known as Santa Maria in Trastavere, but some of the sources claim that it was Saint Peter's Church. Regardless of which church it was, both were located across the Tiber which means that Anthemius was attempting to flee the city in disguise by fleeing towards the barbarian army which he undoubtedly thought was a wiser course than attempting to flee away from them. See the map of Rome. The above account suggests that the final collapse of the defence came about because Ricimer and Olybrius used their senatorial contacts inside the city so that they hailed Olybrius as emperor and that it was this that convinced the rest to give up their arms. It was then in one of the churches mentioned that Gundobad found Anthemius lurking. Gundobad appears to have beheaded Anthemius by himself.

The Roman war against the Vandals and the civil war were not only exploited by the barbarians bordering Gaul, but also by those who bordered the Danube. According to Alföldy,[13] the Ostrogoths of Pannonia conquered parts of eastern Noricum in 468. In my opinion the Ostrogoths probably already had de facto control of this region from the beginning of their settlement in Pannonia by Marcian in about 454–57. This meant that they now controlled the approaches to Italy, and when Flaccitheus King of the Rugi (453–82) asked to be allowed to march into Italy, they were able to deny this. In 472 the Ostrogoths advanced even further and marched along the Drau valley into Teurnia and besieged it. The Ostrogoths failed to take the city with the result that they withdrew after having reached an agreement with the inhabitants. A few years later the Alamanni in their turn attacked from the north-west and ravaged the territory up to the region around Teurnia, but failed to take any of the strongholds.

The situation in *Noricum Ripense* north of the Alps was even worse and the entire administration of this area was in the hands of St. Severinus whose authority over the region was recognized by the people of south Noricum, Rugii, Alamanni and even by Odoacer in Italy. He worked tirelessly against pagans and heretics and attempted to keep the barbarian raiders away from his flock through diplomacy, and when this failed he sought to obtain the release of captured provincials. He was also in charge of the defensive arrangements of the province and dealt with problems of provisioning and social order. He was a realist and recognized that the northern areas would eventually have to be abandoned to the barbarians because the surviving forces were too few to oppose the neighbours. The remnants of the old garrisons were not paid with the result that the few existing soldiers left the ranks. The often quoted example of the fate of the garrison of Passau is illustrative. When men from this garrison went to Italy to collect their pay, they were killed en route by barbarians. It is probable that Raetia was also lost to the Alamanni at this time.

The Rugii subjected the existing forts upstream from Lauriacum to a continuous attack until their fall in the 470s after which the signal stations further into the interior were also abandoned. After the collapse of the river forts, the defence of the North was entirely in the hands of local civilians. Without any outside help, the situation was hopeless because the economy was in ruins and the people were suffering from famine which weakened their ability to withstand sieges. The Rugii and Alamanni were roaming the countryside and carried away everything outside the fortified places, which meant the inhabitants, cattle and other possessions.

The Reign of Anthemius: the Last Chance Wasted

The reign of Anthemius was the last chance for West Roman survival, as it was under him that the East Romans breathed new life into the corpse by sending adequate reinforcements to support the tottering realm. But this was to be in vain, for seven reasons: 1) As an easterner Anthemius was out of touch with West Roman realities, and by his behaviour or intended policies alienated the Catholic Church and many important Italian senators; 2) The first attempt at the reconquest of North Africa under Marcellinus in 467 did not take place due to stormy weather; 3) The naval campaign under Basiliscus ended in disaster; 4) Marcellinus was murdered in Sicily in 468 (probably at the behest of Ricimer); 5) The last viable field army obeying Anthemius was destroyed by Euric in 471; 6) Anthemius failed to assassinate Ricimer when he could have, which was to seal his own fate and the fate of the Empire; 7) Despite being an experienced general Anthemius did not lead the armies in person.

Had Anthemius taken personal charge of military operations, it is possible that he could have defeated the enemies with the result that he could have endeared himself with the troops to such an extent that it would have been impossible for Ricimer to even contemplate his killing. Indeed his greatest blunder was not to assassinate Ricimer at the very beginning of his rule, but it is possible that this had been forbidden by Leo because the intention was to lead a united force against the Vandals and the killing of Ricimer would have undoubtedly caused a civil war.

The rulers following Anthemius no longer possessed adequate resources to stem the barbarian onslaught. One can in fact claim that the barbarians were already in charge because the army in Italy was composed almost solely of barbarian mercenaries.

Chapter Six

Ricimer, Gundobad, Olybrius, Glycerius 11 July 472–June 474

Augustus Anicius Olybrius (472). Source: Hodgkin

The victors of the Roman civil war did not have long to celebrate their victory. Ricimer died forty days after Anthemius's murder on 18 August 472, while Olybrius was attacked by dropsy and died on 2 November 472. It is possible, even if unprovable, that either or both were poisoned. After this followed a short interregnum during which the surviving strongman in the scene, Gundobad, the newly appointed *comes et magister militum et patricius*, presumably negotiated with Leo. However, when it became apparent that Leo did not welcome the death of Anthemius, or at least could not officially do so because his son had married the daughter of Leo in 471, Gundobad raised *comes domesticorum* Glycerius as new Emperor on 3 March 473. It would indeed be nice to know whether Ricimer and Olybrius had been poisoned, as their deaths were so convenient from the point of view of Gundobad, Glycerius and Leo. Their deaths left Gundobad as the only strongman in Italy and he was a man with ambitions. Whatever the case, the appointment of Glycerius was opposed by Leo, and he duly appointed Nepos as *Caesar* and prepared to send a fleet under Nepos to oust Glycerius. Fortunately for the East Romans, Gundobad was forced to return to Gaul before the arrival of Nepos possibly because he had to defend his realm against the Franks and Syagrius, and/or against the Visigoths and/or because his father or uncle had died so that the realm was divided between him and his brothers Gundobad, Godigisel, Chilperic and Godomar in about 473/4. Gundobad ruled together with one or more of his brothers until he managed to kill the last of them in 500 to become the sole ruler.

Ricimer's Poisoned Legacy

As has been recognized by most modern historians, Ricimer is the man who bears the greatest responsibility for the fall of West Rome. The support that Ricimer had given to the conservative Italian senators had meant that the projects undertaken by Avitus and Majorian failed and resulted in the strengthening of the position of the Senate. This in turn made it next to impossible to collect a native Italian/Roman army, which in fact was not in Ricimer's interest because as a barbarian he relied on the support given to him by his *bucellarii* and praesental army of barbarian mercenaries. Therefore it was largely thanks to him that the West Roman Empire was forced to rely on foreign mercenaries and these were loyal only to their leaders of whom Ricimer was one. When the remaining native forces under Anthemiolus, son of Anthemius, were then destroyed by Euric in 471, all that was left were the bodyguard units in the capital with its citizens and some scattered units here and there defending their own locales. It was these and the last remnants of the Gallic Field Army that Anthemius mobilized against the barbarians led by Ricimer.

In short, Ricimer was the man who overthrew all of the able native Roman emperors and commanders that could have saved the situation and in some cases he may even have cooperated with the barbarian invaders to gain advantage for himself. Most of his actions were undoubtedly accepted by the conservative elements within the Senate to their own detriment so that Ricimer could claim to act in its name, but it is still clear that it was Ricimer's personal ambition that drove him to do all these reprehensible actions that led to the terminal illness of the West Roman Empire. His actions were also unforgivable because they did not strengthen the Empire – on the contrary. Had he managed to retake North Africa or had he managed to crush the Visigoths, then it could be claimed that his actions were justifiable, but he achieved none of these. All that he achieved was his own survival at the cost of the Roman Empire. He was a despicable man who certainly deserved his end when he died vomiting blood.

A coin of Glycerius (473-474)
Source: Cohen

The Visigoths Continue Their Ravages

In the meantime, the Visigoths had not been idle. According to the *Gallic Chronicle*,[1] Heldefredus and *dux* Vincentius, possibly with the title *magister militum* and possibly as a successor of Astyrius, besieged Tarraco and captured other coastal cities for Euric. As noted above, the sieges of Arles and Marseilles probably ended in their surrender to the Visigoths in 473. On top of this Euric received assistance from an unexpected corner. According to Jordanes (Get. 283–4), in 473 the Ostrogoths were suffering from hunger in Pannonia owing to their vast numbers. They decided that they would rather seek their fortunes somewhere else with a sword than face the prospect of death through hunger. The ruling Amal brothers drew lots and Vidimer was given Italy. He duly advanced there, but died en route and was succeeded by his son of the same name, Vidimer. The Emperor Glycerius convinced them with a large bribe to continue their journey to Gaul where they joined their Visigothic brethren to rule together both Gaul and Spain. Even if this is not mentioned by any source, it is possible that Gundobad had initially defended Italy against these Ostrogoths and that when they had proved too strong he had asked Glycerius to allow them to march to Gaul, and that it was because of this that Gundobad retreated to his domains to protect them against the newest arrivals and the Visigoths. The arrival of the Ostrogoths strengthened the Visigoths to such an extent that it was now next to impossible for the Romans, Franks or Burgundians to even think of defeating them militarily. It is therefore no wonder that Euric was able to keep what he had conquered and to acquire even more territory at the expense of the others. According to Sidonius's letter to Lambridius (8.9) in 476, the Visigoths had defeated the Saxons, Sygambrians (Franks), Herulians and Burgundians. The arrival of the Ostrogoths clearly tilted the balance in their favour. One may indeed assume that the principal reason for the withdrawl of Gundobad from Italy to his own domains was the ongoing war against the Visigoths.

Despite the impotence of the main enemies at this time, the Visigoths were still vulnerable to one particular type of enemy against which they needed the help of Gallo-Romans. This was the Saxons. Sidonius's letter to his friend Namatius, which is variously dated to shortly before 478 (PLRE2) or considerably earlier than 477 (FRMG 216–17), proves nicely that the Saxons raided the west coast of Gaul during this period, and that the Visigoths maintained a fleet that was operated by Romans under Roman leadership against them. It is probable that this raiding was not limited to areas under Visigothic rule but included the entire Atlantic coastline from the Channel at least up to Gibraltar. According to Sidonius, the Saxon oarsmen in their curved skiffs attacked the unwary during stormy seas and then carried the booty and captives back to their ships. When they were then ready to unfurl their sails for the voyage back home, they sacrificed by drowning every tenth of their captives as a form of thanks to their bloodthirsty gods. The Saxons had earned their fearsome reputation as arch-pirates, but on the basis of the abovementioned letter of Sidonius, the Visigoths managed to defeat them at least occasionally with the help of the Gallo-Roman navy led by Gallo-Roman nobles.

The Visigoths of Euric however, were no longer the well-behaved conquerors of yore. Euric was a fanatic Arian and thought that he had achieved his numerous military successes as a result of this. Consequently, after he had purged the Catholics from his own realm and had closed all Catholic churches, he followed the same policies in the newly conquered areas. When he allowed his warriors to pillage the churches and monasteries, he also rewarded his men with loot. There is another rational explanation for the policy followed by Euric: that he realized that the Roman government used the Catholic Church as its tool of control which meant that removal of the Catholic clergy from the newly conquered areas eased the conquest and control.

In about 473 the Visigoths started a widespread scorched earth policy in Arvernia/ Auvergne to force the Arvernians to surrender through famine.[2] It is probably because of this that Ecdicius withdrew to his Burgundian estates with the result that Sidonius sent a letter to Ecdicius in which he urged him to return at once. However, since Ecdicius was using his private resources to fight the war, he could not. Instead he chose to alleviate the hunger of the Arvernian civilians by transferring as many as possible to his Burgundian estates. His resources sufficed to feed 4,000 civilians and an unknown number of private troopers as long as the famine lasted. Ecdicius was not the only person who sought to feed the hungry. The Bishop of Lyon sent provisions through the Saône and Rhône and then by road to the city of Clermont while Sidonius and other wealthy individuals bought supplies from merchants for those in need. So the Visigothic scorched earth policy failed. The Visigothic practice was to besiege a city every summer and torch all the fields to create famine among the defenders after which they withdrew to their winter quarters. It was this winter break in hostilities that gave the defenders welcome respite from fighting and the opportunity to buy supplies from elsewhere. Nevertheless, the situation in Clermont was still desperate and required constant vigilance. The civilians were constantly rotated between rest and guard duty on the walls.

Chapter Seven

The Fall of West Rome:
Nepos, Orestes and Romulus Augustulus
19 or 24 June 474–ca. 4 September 476

Augustus Iulius Nepos, emperor 474-475(480)
Sources: Above Hodgkin; Below Beger 1693

Meanwhile, the East Romans were once again ready to interfere in the affairs of the West. It is unfortunate that we do not know when Leo dispatched the naval expedition under Nepos against Glycerius, which landed at Portus near Rome. The problematic part of this is that John of Antioch (Roberto ed. frg. 301.21–27) states that the expedition was sent by Leo while all of the other sources claim that Nepos landed at Portus in 474 and was proclaimed Emperor at Rome on 19 or 24 June 474 or at Portus on 19 June.[1] The latter version would imply that the expedition sailed to Portus only after the death of Leo, and indeed this is the likeliest alternative. It is also possible that Nepos' expedition took place at the same time as Vidimer and his Ostrogoths were still in Italy[2] because Jordanes merely dates the event to take place when Glycerius was in power. In that case one can think that the simultaneous presence of the Ostrogoths in the north and the army of Nepos at Rome convinced Glycerius to surrender without a fight. It would otherwise be possible to think that Vidimer's Ostrogoths cooperated with Nepos, but this would be difficult to reconcile with the simultaneous invasion of East Roman territory by his brother. Therefore, it is possible that Nepos did not attack Glycerius in 474 because that would have helped the Goths, and that the two men negotiated and agreed to settle their conflict only after the Ostrogothic problem had been solved. As noted above, it is not too far fetched to think that Gundobad had withdrawn from Italy to protect his domains against the Visigoths and their newest allies the Ostrogoths, which had left Glycerius defenceless against Nepos. It is also clear that the Eastern nominee Nepos brought with him forces from the East and that it was this that convinced Glycerius to surrender. Whatever the truth, it is certain that Roman resources were thinly spread both in the East and West, but more so in the West. It was because of this that Glycerius surrendered and was then exiled and nominated as Bishop of Salona which lay in the domains of Nepos.

Once securely in power, the initial reaction of Nepos appears to have been to fight against both Euric and the Burgundians because the latter had sided with Olybrius and Glycerius and were therefore his enemies. His only reaction to the ongoing Vandal raids appears to have been to defend the coasts as well as he could while attempting to seek peace through Eastern intervention. The impotence of Western naval resources meant that the Vandals were able to obtain possession of significant parts of Sicily which were later to become subjects of bargaining.

However, the Visigoths struck first. Euric wanted to protect his newly acquired possessions in Provence with a pre-emptive strike. On the basis of the Gallic Chronicle (653), Euric had recalled his Roman *magister militum* Vincentius from Spain who was then dispatched to Italy in 474 presumably with the intention of crushing Nepos. Nepos, however, had appointed Alla and Sindila, both of Germanic origin, in charge of the forces in the north of Italy, and these two men defeated and killed Vincentius. The situation was absurd. The Roman army, presumably mostly consisting of barbarian mercenaries,[3] defending Italy, was commanded by two officers of Germanic origin, while the Visigothic army invading Italy was commanded by a native Roman. It is also probable that the Visigothic army included native Roman units and not only officers. There was not much difference in the forces fighting against each other.

This victory strengthened Nepos' hand so that he planned to go on the offensive against both the Visigoths and Burgundians in Gaul. He appointed Ecdicius as *magister militum praesentalis* in 474 and thereby presumably removed Gundobad from office. After this Nepos attempted to undermine the position of the four Burgundian kings, the tetrarchs, in the cities under their rule, because according to the letters of Sidonius (5.6.2, 5.7.1) in the autumn of 474 some Gallo-Romans in the Burgundian domains had plotted to hand over their cities to the new Emperor who must have been Nepos. The Burgundian kings appear to have maintained the pretence of being Roman officers because Sidonius' letter confirms that Chilperic, one of the tetrarchs, held the title of *magister militum* (possibly *per Gallias*). On the basis of the fact that Ecdicius was subsequently operating in Auvergne and there are no references to any hostilities between Gundobad and the Romans and Gundobad held the title of *magister militum* even later, it is probable that Nepos and the Burgundians reached some sort of agreement according to which Gundobad and his brothers were still recognized as Roman commanders.

Meanwhile the ravaging of Arvernia continued unabated, but in the end the Visigoths still proved unable to crush the Arvernian resistance, while the Romans lacked the means to assist the local populace.[4] Nepos sent Ecdicius against Euric. According to Jordanes (Get. 240–1), Euric captured the city of Arverna (Clermont), where the Roman general Ecdicius was in command. He claims that Ecdicius fought for a long time against the Visigoths, but did not possess the power to prevail with the result that he left the country and the city of Arverna to the enemy and then retreated to safer regions. When Emperor Nepos then heard of this, he ordered Ecdicius to leave Gaul and come to him so that he replaced Ecdigius with Orestes. It was then that the defeat took place that sealed the fate of Auvergne, but Jordanes has telescoped the events. Ecdicius may indeed have been defeated and forced to flee, if that does not mean the previous retreat from the city thanks to the famine, but the city of Arverna (Clermont) was not taken as a result of this but as a result of peace negotiations between Nepos and Euric. Both men were apparently ready to conclude a peace at this time to secure their current domains. However, there is another alternative interpretation to this text, which is that Jordanes has actually presented the departure of Ecdicius as military defeat whereas in reality the whole event could have been the result of negotiations. The reason for this conclusion is that it is probable that the title of *patricius* was given to Ecdicius at the same time as he was nominated *praesental magister*, and it is clear that he received this title at a time when Nepos had already started the peace negotiations with Euric as a result of which Auvergne was handed over to the Visigoths in return for Provence.

The initial negotiations were conducted by Quaestor Licinianus with Euric in late 474. Licinianus was apparently among the very few incorruptible Roman officials, but this did not save Auvergne. The Emperor had decided to seek peace at any cost. Notably, according to Sidonius, it was typical for the imperial authorities to be both pompous and ready to sell secret information to the barbarians in return for private advantage. It is not surprising that Roman fortunes were collapsing. A considerable number of civilians preferred to be ruled by the barbarians and the imperial magistrates were eager to be bribed.

Licinianus brought with him the title of *Patricius* for Ecdicius presumably as a signal of his promotion to the position of *MVM Praesentalis*. The final negotiations were conducted on behalf of the Emperor by four bishops, Basilius of Aix, Graecus of Marseilles, Faustus of Riex, and Leontius of Arles. They appear to have been bribed by some wealthy individuals to negotiate with Euric on their behalf because Sidonius makes a complaint regarding this. He was not among those who were granted asylum in Roman territory or whose property and position would remain intact under the Visigoths. Consequently, when Clermont together with Auvergne/Arvenia was handed over to the Visigoths in 475, Sidonius' property was confiscated and he was exiled to the fortress of Livia between Carcassone and Narbonne. In short, while the civilians of Clermont and Auvergne had bravely defended their territories against the Visigoths, the imperial administration abandoned them. However, in return for Auvergne, Nepos got back Provence with its principal cities Arles and Marseilles. The reason for the exchange of possessions must have been, as stated by Ian Hughes, that Italian senators had properties in the south of Gaul and this influenced Nepos, but it is of course possible that the closeness of Provence to Italy was what was decisive in this case as it protected the principal route of approach to Italy. The readiness of Euric to concede these conquests must have been that he also needed peace to secure what he had already obtained while giving him the chance to fight against his other enemies without the fear of having to face West Roman counter-attack. Furthermore, in practice the treaty recognized Euric as equal to the Emperor.

Then, after the conclusion of this peace in 475, Nepos recalled Ecdicius from Gaul and appointed Orestes, a native of Pannonia and former secretary of Attila, as *patricius et magister militum* in his place in the south of Gaul. It is probable, as Ian Hughes (2015, 180) suggests, that Ecdicius was recalled to Italy so that he would not be in possession of an army when the terms of the treaty were implemented because it is clear that he was against the handing of Auvergne to the Visigoths. However, it is still possible that the idea of appointing Orestes to lead the army to the south of Gaul, just obtained from Euric, was to betray the promises made to the Visigoths. But if that was the case, it was not to be, because Orestes had other ideas.

Romulus Augustulus (475-476)
Source: Cohen

Ian Hughes (2015, 185) has rightly stressed the role of the Roman Senate in the events that followed. The senators clearly did not accept the humiliating peace with the barbarian leader even if they got back estates in the south of Gaul. Hughes has noted on the basis of *Auctuarii Hauniensis ordo prior* (p.307), Jordanes (*Get.* 241) and Anonymous Valesianus (2.7.36) that Orestes was sent against Nepos when Nepos was residing in the city (i.e. at Rome), which implies that Orestes was acting on behalf of the Senate. Nepos then fled to Ravenna with Orestes in pursuit. Nepos in his turn boarded a ship and led his fleet back to Dalmatia on 28 August 475 with the result that Orestes nominated his own son Romulus Augustulus as Emperor on 31 October. Romulus's official title was of course *Augustus*, but since the actual ruler was his father the people called him 'Little Augustus' and this name has stuck. Then things turned from bad to worse. The barbarian federates (the Sciri, Heruli, Torcilingi and others) demanded land and Orestes refused to give it. This was a grave mistake. The Federates declared Odoacer, brother of Onulf, their king on 23 August 476 when he promised to give them the land they demanded. This was quite easy to do because the East Romans were in the middle of a civil war of their own. Odoacer marched against Orestes, occupied the military base of Ticinum, and then killed Orestes at Placentia on 28 August 476, after which he marched against Orestes' brother Paulus who was at Ravenna. Paulus was killed on 4 September 476 and Romulus Augustulus was deposed but allowed to live as a private citizen.

The usurpation of Orestes and his son made all treaties with the barbarians void with the result that Euric invaded Provence again in 476 and occupied it with its cities Arles and Marseilles (*Chron. Gall.* 511, 657) and this time permanently. It is not entirely certain whether this took place when Orestes was in power or after his downfall, but what is certain is that this problem was on the table of his successor Odoacer when he in turn usurped power. According to Candidus (Blockley ed. fr.1.84ff.), the Gauls of the West revolted against Odoacer in 476 and then dispatched an embassy to Zeno to ask his support against Odoacer. It is therefore possible that the Gauls actually handed over their territories to Euric at this stage, but it is equally possible that this was a reaction to Euric's invasion in a situation in which Odoacer failed to protect the Gallo-Romans. Regardless of which version is true, Odoacer was forced to recognize Euric's conquests when Zeno was unable to send any help in a situation in which he had just returned to power. Euric was now the most powerful man in the Western Mediterranean and received envoys from all over Western Europe, even as far as from Persia. By the time of his death in 484, he had conquered all of Spain with the exception of the north-west corner which was still in Suevic hands.

At this point in time in 476 all that was left of the West Roman Empire were Italy, some areas in Gaul that had revolted against Odoacer and were about to be lost, whatever was left of Raetia most of which was definitely in Burgundian hands, the western section of *Noricum Ripense* and some parts of the south of Spain, *Noricum Mediterranean*, and a separate independent Roman kingdom under Syagrius in the north of Gaul. The Franks and Burgundians still officially recognized the Roman Empire, but were in practice independent from it. South of Spain was eventually conquered by the Visigoths and the Kingdom of Syagrius was annihilated by the Franks in 481. The Rugians, Heruls and Alamanni carved up the western section of *Noricum Ripense* between ca. 472 and 480. The final end of *Noricum Ripense* came only after the death of St. Severinus on 8 January 482 and one may speculate that his death removed the only man who could have had any real influence on the course of the events. The end of *Noricum Ripense* finally came in 488 when Odoacer decided that the situation in *Noricum Ripense* was hopeless (see later). *Noricum Mediterranean* was not destroyed by the barbarians because it was in 'Italian hands' until the early sixth century.[5]

The year 476 has traditionally been seen as the end of West Rome, and in a sense this is because Romulus Augustulus was the last native Roman Emperor accepted by the Roman Senate and who resided in Italy, but strictly speaking this was not yet the end of the Roman Empire in Italy because Odoacer recognized Nepos as his Emperor until 480, and after Nepos' death he recognized Zeno as his Emperor until 488. After this, the new conquerors of Italy, the Ostrogoths of Theoderic the Great, initially sought acceptance from the East. Regardless of these complications, I have here decided to put an end of the West Roman Empire where it has traditionally been placed and discuss the later developments in the context of East Rome.

Chapter Eight

Leo I (7 February 457–18 January 474)

Augustus Leo (457-474). Source: Hodgkin

Coins of Leo I
(drawings by Beger, 1696)

Accession

When Marcian died at the age of 65 in January or 30 April (Theophanes) 457 officially of gangrene of the feet, his son-in-law Anthemius would have been the natural candidate to take the throne, but the choice fell on the 60-year-old Leo, *tribunus militimum* of the *Mattiarii Seniores*, who was also *domesticus* of Aspar.

According to the *Chronicon Paschale* (457) Leo was proclaimed Emperor on 7 February, but on the basis of Theophanes' text this is uncertain. According to Sidonius (2.210ff.), the reason for this been that Anthemius was unwilling to don the purple, but the likeliest reason is that Anthemius feared Aspar's reaction and chose to opt for the course of lesser evil while Aspar sought to secure the throne for someone of lesser status that he thought he could control. At the time of his nomination, Leo was *comes et tribunus* of the *Mattiarii* and *domesticus* of Aspar. Even though the sources fail to mention this, it is probable that Leo had originally belonged to the corps of the *Protectores Domestici* from which he had been detached to serve as a domestic of Aspar, from which position he was promoted to become a tribune of the *Mattiarii*. The *Mattiarii* were in charge of the Selymbrian Gate of Constantinople (also known as the Golden Gate) with headquarters at Selymbria/Eudoxiopolis. This means that the *Mattiarii* protected one of the main roads that passed through Selymbria to the capital.[1]

In return for the nomination Leo promised Aspar to name his son Ardabur/Ardaburius as *Caesar* and to marry him to one of his daughters. However, thanks to the fact that both of Leo's daughters were underage he was able to delay the actual nomination and betrothal to a later date, and use the intervening time to gather himself loyal supporters, which he sorely needed in a situation in which he lacked a personal powerbase. In the initial stages, Leo was therefore forced to follow Aspar's advice quite closely and use Anthemius, the Senate and the civilian administration as a sort of counterbalance against Aspar and his Gothic faction.

The Troubled Eastern Church in 457–459

The religious community had been in a state of confusion ever since the Council of Chalcedon because the so-called Monophysites were vehemently opposed to its decisions. The situation was at its worst in the city of Alexandria thanks to the corrupt practices of its Orthodox Bishop Proterius, which was very unhelpful from the point of view of the Orthodox Church and Emperor. Marcian had tried to force his will through John the Chief of the *Silentiarii*, but when John heard of the corruption he did not push the case but returned to Constantinople with a detailed report of Proterius' misconduct. This is how the situation stood at the time of Marcian's death. In addition, there were riots in Egypt and also in Palestine in the beginning of Leo's reign. On top of this, the entry of the Orthodox Bishop John into Ephesus had led to great slaughter after the Monophysite Bishop Bassianus had fled.[2]

When the Monophysites of Alexandria heard of the death of Marcian they took matters into their own hands and nominated their own bishop, Timothy Aelurus/Ailouros better known as Timothy the Weasel or Cat, because the *strategos* (*Comes Aegypti*) Dionysius was absent in Upper Egypt. When Dionysius learnt of this, he marched back on the double and imprisoned Timothy. In the process his soldiers killed many of those who opposed. Dionysius ordered the prisoner to be taken to the Tomb of Osiris, and when this took place the citizens attacked the soldiers violently. After this there were daily fights between the citizens and soldiers with the result that Dionysius was forced to ask for funds from the Church to encourage the men. Zachariah mentions that Dionysius incited and urged on particular soldiers, who were called *Cartadon*[3] and who were passionate Arians, to fight against the people. However, according to Zachariah the people managed to kill large numbers of soldiers and their wives, on top of which the soldiers became divided in their loyalties and started to fight against each other and so the chaos that had lasted for days became even worse. The desperate Dionysius, who had now lost control of his men, decided to put the matter into the hands of a famous monk called Longinus. He gave Timothy to Longinus, telling him to restore Timothy to his see on condition that the fighting would stop. This he did and returned Timothy to the Great Church while Proterius occupied the Quirinian Church. However, then came Easter and the followers of Timothy drove Proterius out of the Church of Quirinus with great slaughter. It was then that Proterius threatened the soldiers by noting that they were ready to take his gold but did not attack his enemies. Basically, Proterius threatened to expose the corruption of the army, but his threats did not work the way he thought. A dead Proterius was less dangerous to the soldiers than a live one. One of the soldiers then asked Proterius to witness how many enemies he had killed on his behalf and when Proterius then went to see the corpses, the soldier and his accomplices drew their swords and stabbed him to death after which they dragged his corpse to Tetrapylum where they left him and shouted 'This is Proterius'. When the people saw this they dragged the corpse to the Hippodrome and burned it.[4]

Now that Timothy was the only Bishop of Alexandria he immediately changed the policies of Proterius and no longer paid the soldiers anything. Instead he gave the money to the poor and needy, and several rich men gave him more money to distribute. The Proterian Party, the Orthodox, were not happy. This group included many wealthy figures and on the basis of Zachariah's account it seems probable that they had attempted to bribe Timothy so that he would receive their petition against alleged abuse by the Monophysites. When the Monophysites then prevented reception of the petition, the Orthodox took their case to Pope Leo in Rome and Emperor Leo I in Constantinople. Timothy defended himself in a letter to the Emperor and according to Zachariah Leo would have convened a new Council had not Bishop Anatolius of Constantinople intervened. It was thanks to this that in about 458/9 Leo sent an encyclical letter to the bishops in which he asked whether they were satisfied with the results of Chalcedon and whether Timothy should remain in office. All of them replied in the affirmative while they expressed their dissatisfaction towards Timothy. Only Amphilochius of Side censured the transactions of Chalcedon, but even he was opposed to Timothy. Amphilochus escaped punishment only thanks to the intervention of *stratêlatês* (*praesental MVM*) Aspar, which stands as a good example of his influence over Leo at the beginning his reign.[5] In 459 Leo ordered *stratêgos* Stilas to arrest Timothy so that he could be banished to Gangra. When the bishop had been captured, the supporters of Proterius thought that they now had the opportunity to exact vengeance on the bishop. The frightened Stilas and Timothy sought a place of refuge in the baptistery of the Great Church, but the Orthodox Proterian clergy and monks attacked them with armed force and captured Timothy. This led to further violence when the Monophysites learned what had happened and, according to Zachariah, the Monophysites killed more than 10,000 enemies to free the bishop. Zachariah unfortunately fails to state on which side the Roman soldiers stood and merely notes that they killed many Alexandrians and then recaptured Timothy. This should probably be interpreted to mean that the soldiers did not take sides but killed indiscriminately anyone who opposed them including those Proterians who had captured Timothy. After this Timothy was exiled to Gangra. But even in Gangra Timothy proved a problem because he began to hold rival assemblies, so Leo exiled him to Cherson. Timothy's successor as Bishop of Alexandria was also called Timothy, but his nickname was White and he was an Orthodox Christian.[6]

The East Romans and the Vandals in 457–467

In his relations with the Vandals Leo initially followed the policy of Marcian by intervening only diplomatically, probably because this appears to have been the preferred policy of Aspar. His principal objective was to obtain the release of Eudoxia and her daughters Placidia and Eudocia through diplomacy. Consequently, he supported the West by using Marcellinus of Dalmatia as his proxy which enabled him to maintain deniability. It was then in 461/2 that Gaiseric returned the widow Eudoxia and Placidia to Constantinople in return for the recognition of the marriage between Eudocia and Huneric, son of Gaiseric, and the release of some of the lands in the east to Eudocia that had belonged to Valentinian III, and for the conclusion of some agreement the details of which we do not know. Blockley (1992, 72) has speculated that one of the terms must have been the official support of Olybrius, the husband of the released Placidia, to the throne of West Rome instead of the current Emperor Libius Severus. Whatever the terms, it is clear that the East Romans did not recognize Severus and they did not give the Westerners military support when the Vandals broke the treaty that they had concluded with Majorian and continued their attacks against West Rome. This time their official reason was the demand that the West Romans would hand over the property of Valentinian III and Aetius because the daughter of the former was married to Huneric, and the latter's son resided in North Africa. The real reason, however, was to attempt to force the West Romans to install Olybrius on the throne because he was now related to Huneric.[7]

According to Procopius (3.5.5ff.), after Gaiseric had released the women, he tore down the walls of all the cities with the exception of Carthage. His idea was to make certain that the locals could not begin revolts in the protection of their walls and likewise that the invading Romans could not hope to occupy them with the idea of causing trouble to the Vandals. Procopius notes that this may have seemed like a good idea at the time, but when Belisarius then invaded it made it all the easier for him, so the idea actually looked foolish. In fact this idea proved to be foolish even before this because it enabled the Moors to raid Vandal possessions with impunity after the death of Gaiseric. Under him the Moors were still united with the Vandals and served aboard their raiding fleets. It is possible that it was this that had kept them from raiding Vandal lands and which changed after the Vandals stopped raiding Roman territory.

Leo dispatched two embassies to Carthage on behalf of West Rome in an effort to stop the attacks, but to no avail. The second of these embassies in 464/5 was led by *patricius* Tatianus, who was a member of the party opposing Aspar's policy of peace with the Vandals. This was a first sign of the policy change to come, and it is therefore not surprising that Gaiseric refused to even receive the envoy, especially if Marcellinus had already been dispatched to retake Sicily from the Vandals in 465 as appears probable.[8]

The use of Marcellinus enabled the East Romans to claim that they had not broken the treaty. Geiseric was not fooled, and in 466–7 raided East Roman territory. According to Procopius, Gaiseric raided Illyricum, most of Peloponnessus and Greece, and all of the islands that were near those places, after which he raided Sicily and Italy en route back home. It is therefore clear that he had by then come to the conclusion that a war would be inevitable and it was better to start it himself. The raiding caused such panic that it was rumoured in the capital that Gaiseric intended to attack Alexandria.

According to the *Life of St. Daniel the Stylite* (56), the Emperor then planned to dispatch an army to Egypt, and with this in mind sent eunuch *spatharius* Hylasius to inform Daniel of his plans. The idea was presumably to obtain St. Daniel's blessing for the operation. Daniel's answer shows his wisdom. He said that neither Gaiseric nor any of his followers would be able to see Alexandria, that if the Emperor wished to send an army it was a matter for him to decide, and that God would strengthen the Emperor and his soldiers against the enemies of Rome. In other words, Leo got the blessing for his campaign that he desired. It is easy to see that the Vandal attack gave the East Romans the righteous excuse that they needed. Now they could claim God was on their side, and this was confirmed by none other than Saint Daniel the Stylite.

The Gothic War ca. 458–461/2

According to Sidonius (*Pan. Anth.*, 2.223ff.), some time during the reign of Leo, Valamir, king of the Ostrogoths, severely defeated an incompetent Roman *dux* and killed his soldiers with the result that the Ostrogoths were free to devastate Illyricum at will. In response to this disaster, Leo dispatched Anthemius to take charge of the operations. Anthemius is claimed to have advanced his eagles against the dragons with the result that the enemy was crushed and forced to beg for mercy. The eagles obviously refers to the legionary standards and the dragons to the cavalry standards of the enemy. This evidence should be interpreted symbolically because the Romans had been using dragons for at least three centuries by now. There is every reason to believe that the Romans relied primarily on their infantry forces as they did during the next war against the Huns (see below) while the Ostrogoths relied primarily on their cavalry. This war is usually connected with the war that is claimed to have taken place against the Ostrogoths in about 459–461 (my dating 458–461), which had probably resulted from Leo's refusal to continue to pay them their subsidies, but this seems very unlikely because if Anthemius had defeated the Ostrogoths so severely as claimed by Sidonius, Leo would not have needed to agree to the demands put forth by the Ostrogoths. In short, this commonly accepted view is utterly wrong.

As noted above, it is inherently more likely that the war in which the East Romans restored the subsidies to the Ostrogoths took place earlier, under Marcian. Therefore, it is more than likely that we are here dealing with a separate war that was fought between the East Romans and Ostrogoths, and it is also probable that it was during this war Valamir sacked the city of Dyrrachium, mentioned by Prosper for the year 459 (*Prosper, Addimenta 4, Auctarium Epitomae Vaticanea 3.11, MGH AA, Chron. Min. 1, p.492*), which also means that the *dux* who had been defeated in Illyricum (Sid. *Pan. Anth.*, 223–6) had probably been the *MVM per Illyricum*, with the implication that Anthemius cannot have been *MVM per Illyricum* as suggested by the PLRE2 (p.1291), but either *MVM* without permanent command or *MVM per Thracias* (unattested for the period 447–c.464) or *Magister Praesentales 1* (unattested for the period 451–468). The reason for the war is not known. The likeliest reason remains the refusal to pay the subsidy promised by Marcian, but since it is clear that Jordanes has purposely mixed the two different wars it is impossible to say for sure. The war was not quite as easy as Sidonius makes it look, as it appears to have taken a full four years for Anthemius to defeat the Ostrogoths. Anthemius' forces consisted of both infantry and cavalry, which included Hunnic cavalry, but it was the infantry that played the decisive role.

The war appears to have started with a joint campaign by Ricimer and Anthemius against the Ostrogoths and others in Pannonia so that Ricimer was able to recruit really large numbers of recruits for the forthcoming Vandal war. See the reign of Majorian. The war, however, was not over when Ricimer returned to Italy in 458, because the Ostrogoths then went on to defeat the unknown *MVM per Illyricum* in 459 and to sack Dyrrachium in Epirus. This kept Marcellinus in place in Dalmatia so that he was able to begin his campaign against the Vandals in Sicily only in 460. Anthemius' counter-attack in about 459/60 must therefore have been successful because it enabled Marcellinus to start his operations. Furthermore, the fact that Theoderic the Amal was handed as a hostage in about 461/2 proves that Anthemius had inflicted a severe defeat on the Ostrogoths in about 459–61, but as we shall see, the Ostrogoths were not yet pacified. This was to be a truce.

The Troubled Balkans in 463–467: Wars against the Ostrogoths and Huns

The background

The movement of Turkic peoples westwards against the Avars caused a domino effect against the Roman frontiers. By about 460 the Avars had defeated the Sabiri and they were pushed westwards. The Sabiri in their turn forced the Saraguri, Urogi and Onoguri away from their lands. The Saraguri then defeated and drove away the Akatiri, who dwelled presumably north of the Sea of Azov. It was then in about 463/4 that the Saraguri, Urogi and Onoguri sent envoys to the Romans to ask for an alliance. The reception was friendly, but the fragment of Priscus fails to make it clear whether they concluded an alliance – in my opinion they probably did. The following fragments of Priscus (Blockley fr. 40.1–2, 46) refer to troubles with the fugitive peoples and with the sons of Attila.[9]

I would suggest that we should connect the above with Sidonius' description of the Hunnic war in which Anthemius distinguished himself (Sid. 2.269–306), with the wars of the Ostrogoths against the Sadagir in Pannonia (Jord. Get. 272–3) and the Sciri 'north' of the Danube (Priscus, Blockley fr. 45, in which the Romans sided with the Sciri), and with the war of Huns under Dengizich/Dinzig, son of Attila (Jord. Get. 273). There is no certainty regarding the following reconstruction of events; it is based on my educated guess of how the above pieces of evidence should be pieced together, but in my opinion it is the most likely explanation based on various degrees of probability.

Firstly, it is possible that the East Romans fought two separate wars against the nomadic peoples of the north, the first of which was against the fugitive peoples that the sons of Attila had allowed to pass through their territory and which was then crushed by

Anthemius in about 464/5, and the second of which was the war fought between the East Romans and sons of Attila in about 466–469, and that the Ostrogoths joined the mayhem when the Romans allied themselves with the Sciri in 465 so that they fought a separate war against the Romans that lasted from 465 until 467. In this case the Hunnic attack against the Ostrogoths was taken on their own initiative.

Secondly, and I consider this to be the likeliest alternative, it is possible that the Ostrogoths put in motion the whole process by attacking the Sciri (Priscus, Blockley fr. 45). The war appears to have ended in a stalemate so that both sides sent their envoys to Leo to ask for his support in about 464. Aspar was of the opinion that the Romans should not ally with either side, but Leo decided to help the Sciri and ordered the *MVM per Illyricum* to assist them.[10] I would suggest that it was already in 464 that Basiliscus, brother of the *Augusta* Verina, achieved the first of his many successes as *MVM per Thracias* against the Scythians (Goths) in Thrace mentioned by Theophanes (AM 5956 and 5961) because Basiliscus was nominated as a consul for the year 465. I would also suggest that Leo's policy of siding with the Sciri against the Ostrogoths was planned to put pressure against the Western Government of Ricimer whose puppet *Augustus* at the time was Libius Severus (Nov. 461–14 Nov. 465). Severus was not recognized by Leo. I would also suggest that the Ostrogoths had once again decided to recognize both halves of the Roman Empire in an effort to obtain money from both and that it was this that had angered Leo. Another possible reason or even likely reason for Leo's willingness to support the Sciri against the Pannonian Ostrogoths was that Aspar relied on the support of the Thracian Ostrogoths under Theoderic Strabo and it would therefore have been in Leo's interest to sow further discord between the two groups of Ostrogoths and also to make certain that the Thracian Ostrogoths would not obtain new arrivals from the ranks of the Pannonian Ostrogoths.[11]

The discord between the two halves of the Empire was also probably the reason for the dispatch of Marcellinus to retake Sicily in 465 – the main aim was to demonstrate the comparative naval weakness of the Western Governent so that Ricimer would have to comply with the wishes of Leo. If the West Romans wanted naval support from the East, they would have to obey their wishes. It is likely that the reconquest of Sicily took place before the murder of Severus, because Severus died in November. It is also quite possible or even probable that Ricimer could have asked for some demonstration of military support from the East before agreeing to kill Severus. This means that it was this action and the action taken against the Ostrogoths that brought about the murder of Severus by Ricimer. Leo's secondary aim was undoubtedly to put additional pressure also against the Vandals. However, we know that the Vandals continued to ravage Sicily even after this because there is a fragment of Priscus (Blockley fr.52) which refers to a demand presented by Leo in 467 for Gaiseric to evacuate Sicily and Italy – which certainly refers primarily to piratical raiding rather than to actual permanent conquest even if it is still likely that the Vandals did indeed occupy some fortresses along the coasts. It is clear that it was the combined pressure of the Eastern Government together with the other problems that forced Ricimer to poison Severus so that he could find a way for reconciliation with Leo. This proved difficult and the West did not have any Emperor for almost two years. The impasse ended finally when Ricimer asked Anthemius to become Emperor of the West in 467.[12]

At about the same time as the above envoys arrived at Constantinople, the envoys of the sons of Attila also reached the capital with the idea of removing the causes of their disagreements. They demanded that the Romans establish a market and that a peace treaty should be agreed. Leo refused because he thought the Huns had caused much damage to the Romans and should not therefore have access to Roman trade. If there were two wars in the 460s then this could refer to the first of them, but it could equally refer to any of the previous damage. Dengizich wanted to invade, but Hernach/Ernach opposed this because he was preoccupied with wars presumably fought against the tribes pushed westward by the Sabiri.[13]

Dengizich advanced close to the bank of the Danube and threatened war. Anagastes, son of Arnegisclus (presumably the one mentioned later in this chapter),[14] was in charge of the defences in this part of Thrace presumably as a *dux*, but his forces failed to command the respect of Dengizich. Dengizich threatened war unless he and his army were given land and money. The Emperor stated that he was prepared to comply if they would form an alliance with him. Blockley (1992, 73) dates this to the year 467, which is possible, but I would suggest 465/6.[15] This suggests that Leo did give Dengizich both land and money and that he used him in some military capacity, and I would suggest that he intended to use Dengizich/Dintzic against the Ostrogoths in 466. The following fragments of Priscus (Blockley frgs 48.2–49) suggest that it was indeed immediately after this that the East Romans fought a war against the Ostrogoths, which I date to 466/7 because it took place just before Anthemius was dispatched to the west in 467 (Priscus Blockley fr. 50), but at such a time that Anthemius was no longer in charge of operations.

Of particular note is the reference by Theophanes AM 5961 (with AM5956) to the many victories of Basiliscus (brother of *Augusta* Verina) against the Scythians (probably Goths) in Thrace during his period as *MVM per Thracias* in 464–467/8. This suggests that Basiliscus had achieved more successes against the Goths than are described in the extant fragment 49 (Blockley) of Priscus which describes events of 467.

The Hunnic Invasion in about 465/6–466/7

There are two possible reasons for the Hunnic invasion. Firstly, that it was in the winter of 465/6 or 466/7 that Dinzig/Dengizich, son of Attila, together with the Ulzinzures, the Angisciri (clearly somehow related to the Sciri), the Bittugures and the Bardones attacked the Ostrogoths as stated by Jordanes (*Get.* 272–3) and that they did this as allies of Rome. In light of events in the west, it is more likely that this invasion took place during the winter of 465/6. When the Huns reached Bassiana, a city in Pannonia, they besieged it and pillaged the surrounding territory. The Ostrogoths naturally abandoned their plans to attack the Sadagir-Huns in Pannonia and attacked the invading Huns and drove them away once again. In this alternative the Huns then probably thought that the Romans had betrayed them to the Ostrogoths with the result that they attacked Roman territory. The other possibility is of course that the Huns did not act as allies of the Romans at all, but betrayed them immediately and invaded both the Roman and Ostrogothic lands once they had been allowed across the frozen Danube and thereby overextended their resources. In this case the Huns who attacked the Ostrogoths were under Dengizich and the Huns who attacked Serdica were under Hernach, if Hormidac means him. Whatever the truth, it is clear that Anthemius then defeated those Huns who had advanced against the city of Serdica, and that this took place definitely before the spring of 467 (probably during the fall of 466 or during the winter of 466/7), and that the generals who were left in charge of the war after Anthemius had already travelled to Constantinople defeated the Ostrogoths in the spring of 467 (Priscus Blockley frgs. 49–50) and the Huns of Dengizich permanently by 468/9. The head of Dengizich was brought to Constantinople in 468 according to *Chronicon Pachale* and in 468–9 according to Marcellinus Comes.

Of note also is the great economic resilience of the Eastern Empire at this time. They were able to fight successful wars in the Balkans despite the fact that large areas of Thrace, the Hellespont, Ionia and the Cyclades were hit by an earthquake, and torrential rains had caused troubles at Constantinople and Bithynia at about the same time as the 'Scythian war' began. These troubles and the reconstruction of large sections of Constantinople which had been destroyed in a fire in 464 did not cause any significant financial difficulties for the regime.[16]

Sidonius Apollinaris (2.235ff.) describes the Hunnic invasion as follows. Of note is also Sidonius's reference (246ff.), not included below, to the use of skull-binding so that the top of Hunnic skulls were pointed and to the flattening of their noses so that they could use the visored helmets with greater ease – the last-mentioned part can actually be taken as a mistaken description of a face with Mongolian features.

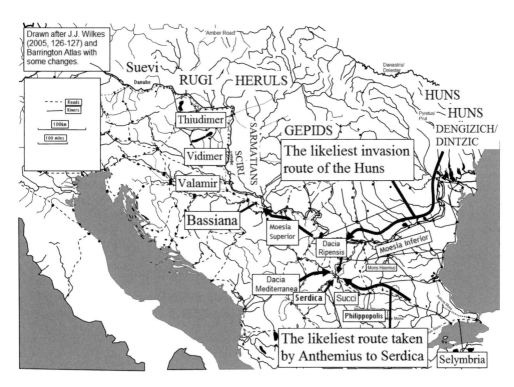

This quote is taken from the translation of Anderson (pp.29, 31–35 with comments added in parentheses):

… a race whose leader [*dux*] was Hormidac [*It is possible that Hormidac was actually the commander of Federate forces that betrayed Anthemius if Sidonius has confused the names, but he could also be a Hunnic general serving under Dengizich or even his brother Hernach who disappears from the sources at this time even before his brother who was captured in 468/9. The last version is probably the most likely.*], … This people [*Huns*] had burst forth in a sudden invasion; they had come crossing with wheels the solid Danube, … Straight against them didst thou go, as they roamed through the Dacian fields; thou didst attack and vanguish and hem them in [*There are two alternative routes Anthemius could have taken: Firstly, he could have cut off the enemy's route of retreat and approached them from the direction they had come; Secondly, he could have marched from the south-east through the Succi Pass. The latter is likelier. The text clearly implies that Anthemius was able to defeat the enemy force that had blocked his route, presumably at the Succi Pass, which is not surprising in light of the fact that his army consisted mainly of infantry, and then force the enemy inside Serdica*]; as soon as Serdica beheld thee with thine encampment [*agger*] laid out, thou didst straitly besiege them. The town marvelled at thee as thou didst tarry thus for long within the rampart, because thy soldiers went not forth into the field in regular or stealthy raids. Though oft they lacked corn and always wine [*Note that his army did not seek courage from wine; notably the sixth century Strategikon recommended the use of water before battle so that the senses would remain intact for fighting. However, water was still less safe to use than wine and it is clear that the Romans did not carry enough for the whole length of the siege. The text also implies that the Romans relied solely on the provisions that they had brought with them and that the Huns were not completely blockaded inside the city so that the Romans stayed inside their fortifications.*], they lacked not discipline [*Note the superb discipline of the Eastern armies! This army was of the same calibre as Julius Caesar's elite forces had been when fighting against Pompey*]; hence though the foe was nigh they feared their general more. So at length it came to pass that he who chanced to be thine ally then but straightaway played thee false gained nothing when he retreated before the foe at the first onset [*i.e. the Sarmatian, see below. It is possible that the ally refers to a Sarmatian, but it is equally possible that the Sarmatian was in this case a Hun and it is also possible that this is a dual reference to the Hunnic betrayal and the desertion of a dux in the middle of a combat*]; for when he had begun to flee, turning aside and laying bare the wings, thou didst stand thy ground, a host in thyself; to thee did those warriors rally whom their captain's [*ductor's*] flight had scattered, back to thee came cavalry as thou didst toil and sweat, fighting on foot [*This means that the betrayal of the cavalry dux caused the rest of the cavalry to rout after which they retreated to their infantry support as required by standard combat doctrine for defeated cavalry. It is unfortunate that Sidonius fails to state what infantry formation was used because if the infantry was deployed as a single phalanx with wagons following or as a double phalanx the cavalry regrouped between these while part of the cavalry dismounted to fight as infantry. On the other hand if the infantry was formed either as a hollow square/oblong or as hollow squares/oblongs, then the cavalry retreated through the intervals on the flanks and/or behind the formations to regroup. It is also unfortunate that Sidonius fails to state clearly whether he meant a battle that was fought before the siege of Serdica or possibly after it if the enemy had managed to fight their way through the siege. However, on the basis of the contents it appears likelier that this referred to the battle that had taken place before the siege of Serdica*]; and following thy standards [*signa*] the soldiers felt that they were not deserted in the fray.

… The captain [*dux – this person must now be the commander of the Huns, Hormidac, because the following refers to the enemy force as a whole*] flees; thou dost pursue; he renews the fray; thou conquerest; he shuts himself in; thou dost storm his entrenchment; he slips away [*Sidonius uses: 'dux fugit: insequeris; renovat certamina; vincis; clauditur; expugnas; elabitur'. It is unfortunate that he fails to specify the location at which the enemy was blockaded and then stormed. It is possible that it was an encampment of the Huns near Philippopolis or in front of Serdica or Serdica itself, or that the Huns had already fled Serdica and were encamped somewhere north of it. If it was Serdica itself, then the storming of it took place only after a considerable period of time and the subsequent negotiations referred to the situation after the Huns had fled from it. If it was an encampment in front of Serdica, then the following demand to hand over the traitor in return for peace was presented to the enemy in the course of the siege of Serdica. The last is the likeliest*]; thou dost overwhelm him, and dost demand his life as the price of peace with the Sarmatians [*I would suggest that the person whose head Anthemius demanded was actually the head of Hernach/Hormidac, son of Attila, and that Sidonius has probably confused the two possibly purposely if Anthemius was behind the policy of using the Huns against the Ostrogoths. As noted above, the dux of Sidonius from line 294 onwards referred to the commander of the entire enemy host. The Huns inside Serdica were clearly forced to accept Anthemius' terms because they must have suffered even more from hunger and thirst than Anthemius' own men..*]. Thy will is done, and straightaway the deserter has suffered the death decreed and … slain by a foreign sword. … but the man that deserted thee was cut off by a death that had been commanded.'

There are many uncertainties and problems with the reconstruction of the likely course of the wars that took place at this time, but the following presents my best effort to untangle the above mess of evidence. In short, it is probable that the Huns either invaded the Ostrogothic lands as Roman allies and then turned against them after they thought the Romans had betrayed them, or that they betrayed the Romans immediately and invaded Roman and Ostrogothic lands simultaneously. My educated guess is that we should identify Hormidac with Hernach, son of Attila, who disappears from the sources at this time, so that he attacked Serdica while his brother Dengizich attacked Bassiana.

It is unfortunate that we do not know the sizes of the invading Hunnic forces, but what is certain is that their size was nowhere close to what they had been under Attila. My best educated guess is that both brothers had probably about 30,000–40,000 veteran warriors plus their families carried in the wagons. The size of the city of Serdica can be used as a clue to how many soldiers the Huns would have needed to take it. On the basis of its size, it housed about 20,000 civilians and soldiers plus an unknown number of refugees from

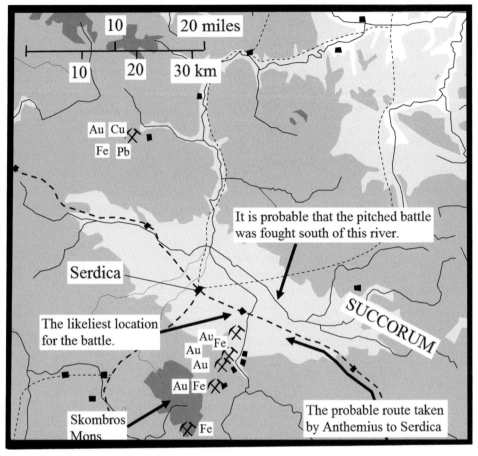

Battle of Sercida 1

the countryside. There is obviously no proof for this but my guess is that the above figure of 30,000–40,000 would have sufficed to take the city. It is probable that the army that Anthemius marched against the Huns consisted of approximately the same number of men so that it would have consisted of one praesental field army bolstered with Federates and detachments from the Thracian field army for a total of about 20,000–30,000 footmen and at least about 12,000 horsemen plus the personal retainers of Anthemius. It is also possible or even probable that Basiliscus, Anagast/Anagastes and Ostrys served as his subordinates during this campaign because these generals served in the Balkans at this time.[17]

It is unfortunate that we cannot be certain which half of the praesental forces Anthemius is likely to have taken with him as *MVM* because Aspar seems to have been the commander of the forces that were garrisoned on the European side of the Bosporus[18] and it is unlikely that Aspar would have given Anthemius command of all of those even in such a situation in which he would have retained most of the Gothic Federates near Constantinople to secure his own position vis-à-vis Leo. This may mean that Anthemius took with him the praesental forces posted in Asia Minor because he was their commander.

In light of the extant evidence this appears to be the most likely alternative.[19] However, it is also possible that Anthemius used a mix of forces that he drew from both praesental forces and from the Army of Thrace and the Federates posted in Thrace.

There are also many possibilities regarding the place of the battle, because on the basis of an inscription commemorating the victories of Basiliscus at Philippopolis (it was on the route to Serdica) it is possible that the pitched battle took place near it and that the pursuit of the Huns continued up to Serdica. My educated guess is that the battle took place near Serdica and that the Hun cavalry did not attempt to block the Succi Pass, because Sidonius clearly refers to a battle in which the Romans had placed their cavalry on the wings, or if they had, then it had proved insufficient to block the pass against the disciplined Roman infantry. In other words, I suggest that the Huns allowed the Romans to deploy their army in the open terrain in front of Serdica and that they had not placed their entire force inside Serdica because it could not house their families and wagons. Rather, on the basis of the account, the Huns appear to have formed a wagon laager in front of the city from which they then approached the Romans.

In the following reconstruction of the battle I have deployed the Roman infantry as a single phalanx 24 deep (16 heavies with 8 light infantry so that it retained the ability to form a double phalanx) with wagons following to protect the rear so that most of the cavalry forces are deployed in the frontline and smaller numbers as reserve forces. Readers are still advised to keep their minds open to the possibility that the Romans could have been deployed as a double phalanx or as hollow oblongs so that the wagons were left behind in the previous marching camp, or as a single hollow oblong with wagons placed inside. This would not have made a great difference to the outcome even if the hollow oblong, hollow oblongs and double phalanx were slightly more secure against outflanking than the single phalanx with the wagons following. The sixth century *Strategikon* makes it clear that the single phalanx with wagons was also secure against threats from the rear because the wagons with their *carroballistae* formed an adequate defensive barrier against attacks from behind, and that it was also quite possible for the cavalry to regroup securely between the phalanx and wagons. The reference to the cavalry wings can be taken to imply that the likeliest array meant by Sidonius was either the single or double phalanx. I have opted for the former because it was in this array that the wagons followed the army during marching. I have assumed that the phalanx followed standard military theory so that it would have had a 24,000-strong infantry phalanx (16,384 heavies, 8,192 light) with reserves of perhaps 4,000 footmen deployed in the middle and wings and on wagons. The wagons would have had armed servants, drivers, ca. 1,800 soldiers (two extra men per eight-man infantry file), artillerymen and engineers not included in the above figures. This would have given the phalanx a frontline of approximately 1,400–1,500 metres with all intervals included. Considering the easy availability of Federate cavalry in Thrace, I have assumed that Anthemius would have had at least 12,000 horsemen, so it would have been deployed ten deep as required by military doctrine when there were large numbers of horsemen available (i.e. over 12,000).[20] I have assumed that he placed 2,000 of them as wing reserves (1,000 per wing), and the rest on the wings of the frontline. It is also probable that Anthemius had so-called *bucellarii* as bodyguards and that these formed the cavalry reserve of the centre. It is impossible to know how many he would have had, but as a rich aristocrat he certainly would have had a sizable contingent, possibly something like

1,000 horsemen or even more. Each of the cavalry wings in close order ten deep would have occupied roughly about 700–800 metres so that the entire length of the Roman frontline was about 2,800–3,000 metres. However, if some of the Federate cavalry units were deployed in open or irregular order and with wide intervals between the units at the beginning of the battle contrary to combat doctrine, then it is possible that the frontage could have been about 3,500 to 4,000 metres. The former, however, is more likely.

With the assumption that the Huns had left an occupying force behind in the city of Serdica and another force in their wagon laager possibly as a third ambushing force, one may estimate that they deployed at most 30,000 horsemen (assuming that the young and old were left to protect camp and city) against the Romans with the implication that they may have had less or an equal number of men. If we assume that the Huns deployed most of their men in front and only about a quarter to a third as a reserve (25,000 in front, 5,000 in reserve) and that they followed up their standard combat doctrine of deploying their units either as wedges or as oblongs in close order at the very beginning of the battle so as to be ready for close quarters combat, they would have had a frontage of about 2,800–3,000 metres; even if they deployed all their units with wider intervals in wedges or deep arrays their frontage would not have been more than 4,000 metres at the beginning of the battle. The former, however, is more likely. Therefore, it is clear that the Huns sought to confuse and outflank the Romans immediately by using the so-called Scythian manoeuvre which widened their frontage, or just by outflanking the Roman array in a simpler manner by widening the frontage by sending flank units to outflank the enemy wings while the Romans sought to prevent this by attacking the outer edges of the Hunnic formation with their cavalry wings.

I would suggest that the pitched battle between the Huns and Romans progressed as described by Sidonius because it conforms very closely to the different stages of battle described by numerous military treatises and in this case most importantly by the late Roman *Strategikon* which summarises Roman and late Roman practices. The first stage of the battle was the deployment of both sides for combat. The information provided by the *Strategikon* regarding the Hunnic battle formation suggests strongly that it was initially compact with the result that the Romans preferred to attack them before they had a chance to spread out to harrass the Romans. The information given by Sidonius is in agreement with this. He states that the Roman cavalry attacked first but was defeated thanks to the desertion of a Sarmatian *dux*.

The defeated Roman cavalry then performed the standard retreating manoeuvre and retreated to the safety of their infantry support. The infantry then received the charge of the enemy cavalry with perfect discipline with the result that the enemy turned and fled. This was followed with another text-book move, the sending of the regrouped cavalry in pursuit while the infantry followed. According to Sidonius, the Huns renewed the fight against their pursuers, which probably happened when the Huns reached their ambushing reserve. It is unfortunate that Sidonius fails to state how the Romans then defeated the regrouped Huns, which leaves three alternatives: Firstly, it is possible that the pursuing cavalry defeated the regrouped Huns with a charge; second, it is possible that the regrouped Huns forced the cavalry back to its reserves, which turned the tables once again; third, it is possible that the Roman cavalry once again retreated back to the infantry, which forced the Huns to renew their flight when the infantry reached it. The

Battle of Serdica in ca. 466

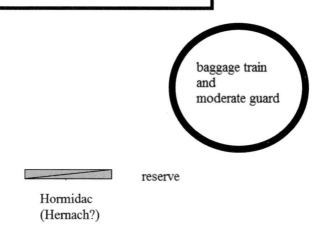

baggage train
and
moderate guard

reserve

Hormidac
(Hernach?)

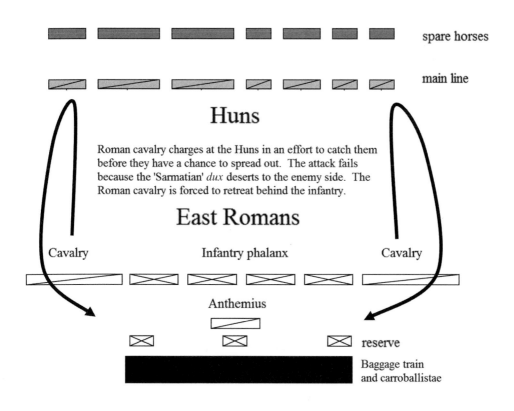

spare horses

main line

Huns

Roman cavalry charges at the Huns in an effort to catch them
before they have a chance to spread out. The attack fails
because the 'Sarmatian' *dux* deserts to the enemy side. The
Roman cavalry is forced to retreat behind the infantry.

East Romans

Cavalry   Infantry phalanx   Cavalry

Anthemius

reserve

Baggage train
and carroballistae

Romans then pursued the defeated foe up to their wagon laager/camp and stormed it. The storming was probably performed primarily by infantry thanks to the presence of the enemy wagons. However, unluckily for the Romans the enemy leader still managed to flee with a significant number of his followers. After this follows the key problem: Did this battle take place before the siege of Serdica or after it? If it took place before,

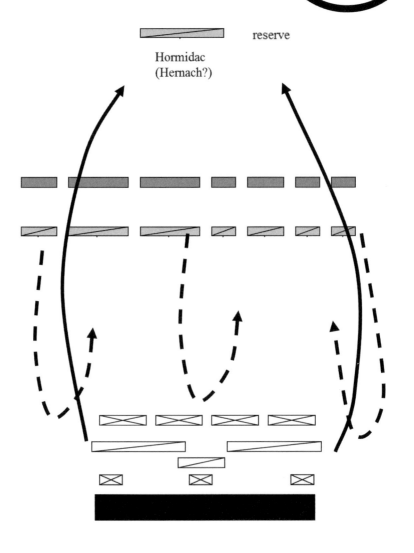

The Roman infantry and the dismounted cavalry on the flanks receive the Hun attack and force them to retreat. The Roman horsemen mount their horses again and give a pursuit. The Huns regroup when they reach their reserve and renew the fight. The Roman cavalry defeats them again or they do that with the help of their infantry when it reaches the scene after which the Romans storm the enemy wagon laager.

baggage train and moderate guard

reserve

Hormidac (Hernach?)

which is likelier, then the Huns fled to Serdica where they were hemmed in and forced to surrender. If it took place after the siege so that the Huns fled from the city and were then pursued by Anthemius, then the Huns would have taken a place of refuge somewhere in the surrounding mountains where the Romans would have blockaded them until their surrender.

This campaign was a great success for East Rome. All that was left of the Hunnic threat were the Huns of Dengizich and their strength had already been seriously weakened by a series of defeats the last of which was their defeat close to Bassiana by the Ostrogoths. This campaign, however, was left to others because it was now presumably in the spring of 467 that Anthemius was recalled to Constantinople so that he could be sent to the West as their new Emperor. The two halves of the Empire were once again united in common cause and this time the principal target was Gaiseric who had ravaged Illyricum, Greece, Peloponnessus and all the islands in 466.

Civilian and Military Hierarchy in the 460s

Luckily for us the Justinian Constitutes have preserved an Edict which lists the civilian and military dignitaries dating from the year 466. This is a very valuable piece of evidence because it which gives us a glimpse into how the Eastern Empire had organized its civilian and military hierarchy, which can also be used to shed light on the areas controlled by the Empire at the time. See below:

CJ 12.60.10 Notitia:
'Civilian Admininstration':
1) Praefecti praetorio Orientis et Illyrici et Urbis
2) Proconsules Asiae et Achaiae
3) Praefecti Augustalis (in Egypt)
4) Comes Orientis
5) Comes diuinarum domorum
6) Vicarii of Thracia, Pontus, Asia, Macedonia, and thesauriensium classis (treasure fleet)

'Military Administration':
1) magistri militum utriusque militiae in praesenti, Orientis (per Orientem) et Illyrici (per Illyricum). *Magister militum per Thracias* is missing, but can be attested to have existed at the time the edict was written, which means that its absence is a clerical error or an error made by a later copyist.
2) *duces* Palestinae, Mesopotamiae, noui limitis Phoenices, Oshroenae, Syriae et Augustae Euphratensis, Arabiae et Thebaidis, Libyae, Pentapoleos, utriusque Armeniae, utriusque Ponti, Scythiae, Mysiae primae, secundae, Daciae, Pannoniae.
3) *comites* Aegypti, Pamphyliae, Isauriae, Lycaoniae et Pisidae

This list proves that by 466 the Eastern Empire had managed to incorporate into its civilian and military administration all of the areas that were still contested in 457. Of particular note is the inclusion of the *duces* of Pannonia. One wonders whether this means regular forces that would have been billeted in the same areas as the Ostrogoths or whether all three Ostrogothic brothers held this title. I am personally of the opinion that the latter alternative is more likely so that Valamir, Vidimer and Thiudimer received regular pay and *annonae* as *duces* for the upkeep of their federate forces, but which appears to have been insufficient to meet the demands posed by the large numbers of warriors and their dependants that needed to be fed. It was probably because of this that the brothers sought money from the West or occasionally revolted or attacked their neighbours.

The Gothic Phase of the War in the Balkans in 467

The fragment (Blockley fr. 49, *Exc. de Leg. Gent.* 21) of Priscus describes the decisive event of the war that was fought between the East Romans and Goths (also called Scythians) which took place just before Anthemius was dispatched to take the throne of West Rome (Priscus Blockley fr.50). It is unfortunate that we do not know anything about its background beyond what is stated above, namely that it must have resulted from the Roman support to the Sciri. It is also unfortunate that we do not know where the following incident took place, but on the basis of the list of commanders, who were all located in Thrace, I would suggest that the event took place either in Thrace proper, or in Dacia, or in Moesia Inferior possibly at a time when the Ostrogoths were pursuing Dengizich. However, there is another possibility, which is that Basiliscus was already named as praesental *MVM* immediately after Anthemius went to Constantinople so that Anagast/Anagastes would already have been nominated as *MVM per Thracias*. It is of note that it was one of the generals mentioned here, namely Anagastes, who then engaged and killed Dengizich next year in 468. It is a pity that we do not know what had been the many victories of Basiliscus against the Scythians in Thrace mentioned by Theophanes (AM 5956 and 5961). We possess an inscription at Philippopolis quoted in the PLRE2 that commemorates one of the victories of Basiliscus in Thrace that took place between 465 and 467. Since Philippopolis lies on the likely route taken by Anthemius from the capital[21] to Serdica it is possible that Basiliscus had defeated the Huns rather than the Goths here. It is possible that a pitched battle between the Romans under Anthemius and the Huns took place close to Philippopolis and that they were pursued all the way up to Serdica, but it is probably even likelier that Basiliscus defeated the Gothic army there, after which he forced it to the hollow place mentioned below. It is also possible that he achieved some victories against the Goths in 464 so that he was nominated consul in 465, about which we know nothing.

The translation of the following fragment is taken from Maenchen-Helfen pp.167–8 with my comments added:

Anagastes [*According to the PLRE2, a Gothic comes rei militaris in Thrace in 466/7 and MVM per Thracias in 469–470, but in my opinion he may already have been nominated to the latter post by now.*], Basiliscus [*According to the PLRE2, brother of the empress Verina and MVM per Thracias 464–467/8, but in my opinion he may already have been nominated to succeed Anthemius as praesental MVM in 467*], Ostryis [*Ostrys was a Gothic comes rei militaris and a very loyal retainer of Aspar*], and other generals ['*stratêgôn Rhômaiôn*': *these would have been hypostrategoi*] ... blockaded the Goths in a hollow place. [*I would suggest it is probable that the three men mentioned were commanders of the left wing, centre and right and that Basiliscus was the overall commander*] The Scythians [*i.e. Goths*], hard pressed by starvation and lack of necessities, sent an embassy to the Romans. They said they were ready to surrender, once they were given land. The Romans answered that they would forward their requests to the emperor. ... The Roman generals ... promised to supply food until the decision of the emperor came, provided the Scythians would split themselves into just as many groups as the Roman army was divided into. In this way the Roman generals could better care for them. The Scythians accepted ... Chelchal, a man of Hunnic race, the lieutenant general [*hypostrategos*] in Aspar's *tagmata* [*I have here changed the translation to something that I consider more accurate; Chelchal was therefore Ostrys' second-in-command*], came to the barbarian horde... He summoned the prominent Goths, who were more numerous than the others [*i.e. most of the army penned in the valley, consisting of the Goths*] and began a speech .... The emperor would give land ... to the Huns among them. ... They themselves, the Goths, were treated like slaves and forced to feed the Huns ... He, Chelchal, was a Hun and proud of it, but he was saying these things to the Goths from a desire of justice ... The Goths were greatly disturbed by this and, ... attacked the Huns in their midst and killed them. When Aspar [*Maenchen-Helfen n.835 corrects this to read Anagastes, but in my opinion the text should be corrected to read commander in charge of Aspar's forces, meaning Ostrys*[22]*] learned of this, he [*in my opinion Ostrys*] and the commanders of the other camps drew up their troops and killed the barbarians they came upon. When the Scythians perceived the ... treachery, they gathered together and turned against the Romans. Aspar's men anticipated them and killed the barbarian horde allotted to them to the last man. But the fight was not without danger for the other generals, as the barbarians fought courageously. Those who survived broke through the Roman formations and escaped the blockade [*This account implies that Ostrys and Chelchal had purposely incited the conflict probably because Aspar had instructed them to do so and that they had not informed the other commanders or even the overall commander Basiliscus of their plans with the result that the barbarians were more successful against them. By this time Aspar was certainly afraid for his own position which was reliant on the support of the Gothic forces under Theoderic Strabo in Thrace. Aspar clearly wanted to destroy the Amali Ostrogoths as far as was possible so that Leo could not use them as a counterbalance against him.*].

I would suggest that the abovementioned defeat ended the war between the Goths and the Romans, because the next time the Ostrogoths are mentioned by Jordanes (Get. 273ff., see below) they clearly fight to defend Roman territory in Dalmatia, when the two halves cooperated closely. This would have presumably taken place in about 467/8. It was probably thanks to his great successes against the 'Scythians' in Thrace that Basiliscus was appointed to lead the huge naval expedition against the Vandals. It is also possible that if Basiliscus had previously served under Anthemius, which is very likely, that this contributed to the decision to employ him, because their previous cooperation could be seen as advantageous in a situation in which the two halves were to cooperate. The above account also suggests the possibility that there existed serious divisions among the

Roman high command at this time that influenced the way in which military operations were carried out. In this case Ostrys and Chelchal appear to have acted on their own initiative to initiate a massacre of the enemy forces inside a valley (the hollow place) in all probability because they had been instructed to do so by Aspar. It is possible that Aspar wanted to weaken the Amali Ostrogoths so that Leo could not use them against the Thracian Ostrogoths led by Theoderic Strabo. The probable reason for this is that the conflict between the Pannonian and Thracian Ostrogoths was now too large and that Aspar must have feared that Leo could use the Pannonian Ostrogoths against the Thracian ones. If he managed to kill large numbers of the Pannonian Ostrogoths treacherously, it was doubly beneficial. It made the Pannonian Ostrogoths suspicious of any overtures made by Leo while it also diminished their numbers.

It is likely that it was now that Ardaburius, son of Aspar, killed Bigiles/Vigiles, king of the Getae (i.e. of the Goths), which is mentioned by Jordanes (*Romana* 336) because this incident took place after Anthemius had been dispatched to the West but before Basiliscus had been sent against the Vandals in 468 (Jord. *Rom. 337*). The reason why Ardaburius was in the Balkans is that he had been sacked by Leo for conspiring against him. It is very likely that Ardaburius accompanied Ostrys and Chelchal and he may even have been the de facto commander of Aspar's corps even if Ostrys was clearly its official commander. It is unfortunate that we do not know how the abovementioned Vigiles was related to the Amali.

There were several reasons for Aspar's quite apparent disloyalty. Firstly, Leo took the first significant steps in asserting his own power over Aspar in about 464/5 by deciding to support the Sciri against the Ostrogoths, but even more important steps were taken in 466/7. In about 466 the Isaurian chieftain Tarasicodissa from Rhusumblada came to Constantinople bearing the news that *MVM per Orientem* Ardaburius had written treasonous letters to the Persians. It is not known with certainty whether this was the case or whether Leo and Tarasicodissa had formed a plot together, but I would not rule out the possibility that Ardaburius could indeed have exchanged rebellious letters with the Persians at this time. It is obvious that the relationship between Leo and Aspar had grown tense because Leo had shown too much independence, of which the best example is his decision to support the Sciri against the Ostrogoths. Therefore it is even likely that father and son had started to plot against Leo. Whatever the truth, Leo sacked Ardaburius and replaced him with Jordanes, son of John the Vandal,[23] but even then Leo was not yet powerful enough to move against Aspar. Leo's immediate reaction was to form a 300-strong new bodyguard unit *Excubitores* to guard the side exits of the Palace, which appears to have consisted of the Isaurians possibly brought to Constantinople by Tarasicodissa. However, it is also possible that the *Excubitores* were formed out of those Isaurian soldiers who fled from Rhodes to Constantinople at about this time. Furthermore, Leo rewarded Tarasicodissa with the position of *Comes Domesticorum* with the implication that he probably commanded both the *Excubitores* and the *Protectores Domestici*. Leo also gave his daughter Ariadne in marriage to Tarasicodissa, who at the same time changed his name to Flavius Zeno, because there had already been one famous Zeno from Isauria. All of these measures suggest that there was indeed a plot to kill Leo at this time and that Leo rewarded the whistleblower amply. Zeno was also appointed as *MVM per Orientem* by 469 which was also the year when he served as consul.[24]

The Persian Front in 468–471

The Armenian and eastern sources refer to a war between Persia and East Rome under Leo I and Peroz of which we known very little. All we know is that there were troubles in Lazica/Colchis, which may have changed its allegiance from East Rome to Persia, that the Persians presented financial demands to the Romans, and that there may have been a short war between the two. Then in about 467–69 it was not the beginning of the trouble but the culmination of a series of troubles caused by the Lazicans and others against the background of already existing grievances felt by the Persians. The Persian interpretation of the previous peace agreement was different and it was because of this that they felt that the Romans had not followed up the clauses of the treaty. As Blockley (1992, 74) notes, the relationship between the two empires had deteriorated to the point of war by 467, and this was the time the East Romans could ill afford a war on their eastern front as their forces were committed to a massive western campaign (detachments given to Anthemius; naval force under Basiliscus; land forces sent from Alexandria to Tripolitania). I will first present an overview of how the relationship between the two soured.

Yazdgerd died in the same year as Marcian, 457, and was succeeded by Hormizd III. However, in 459 his brother Peroz overthrew him with Hepthaelite help, and it was now that the troubles began. Peroz owed money to his helpers, on top of which there was a drought and a seven-year famine. Peroz needed the support of the magi for his rule and therefore accused the Jews and Monophysite Christians for the troubles – the Nestorian Christians appear to have been spared possibly because their loyalty towards Persia was not suspect. It was now that Leo broke the previous agreements with Persia. He granted an asylum to the refugees. The troubles with the Caucasian Albanians and in particular with the Kidarites however distracted Peroz for the moment, but they did not prevent him from dispatching an embassy in 464 to Leo. Peroz was unable to pay the traditional tribute to the Kidarite Huns and was therefore forced to fight. To make matters worse Peroz had then tried to fool their king Kunchas with a marriage pact, but instead of sending his own sister he sent a servant. When Kunchas learned of the trick, he played a ruse of his own and asked Peroz to send him generals to lead his armies against his enemies. Peroz sent 300 with the result that some were killed and the rest were sent back mutilated. In these circumstances, Peroz complained that Leo had not abided by the agreements, having received refugees from Persia and persecuted magians. He also demanded that the Romans pay for the upkeep of the fortress of Iouroeipaach at the Caspian Gates or at least send soldiers to guard it. He also demanded that the Romans help to finance his war against the Kidarites because the Persians were essentially fighting on their behalf. The Roman answer was to deny everything. They denied that they had received refugees, claimed that they had not persecuted magians, and refused to contribute either money or men for the wars the Persians fought. Leo's answer to Peroz was given by Constantius, who was prefect, patrician and consul. At first the Persians did not allow Constantius into their territory, and when they finally did, Constantius had to travel all the way to Gorga where Peroz was fighting against the Kidarites. Peroz dismissed the envoy without answer.[25]

At about the same time in 464 immediately after a fire had destroyed a very significant portion of the city of Constantinople, Leo received the Lazican king Gobazes who arrived with Dionysios. The burning of the eight regions of the city of Constantinople was a grave disaster, the worst fire that had affected the city so far, so the Lazican king had arrived at the very worst moment. The Roman officials accused Gobazes of rebellion, but in the end the entreaties of Gobazes together with the Christian symbols he was carrying convinced Leo and the officials of the court that he should be granted a pardon. It is unfortunate that we do not know the reason for the accusation as it took place at the same time as there were troubles in the Caucasus region. One possible reason could be the one that is mentioned later in which the king of Lazica had asked for military assistance from the Romans against the Persians but had then dismissed them back once they had reached his lands.[26]

It was at about this time that the Romans received the abovementioned embassy from the sons of Attila, but more importantly it was just after this embassy that the Sadaguri, who had previously formed an alliance with the Romans in about 463/4, marched to the Caspian Gates to attack the Persians in about 465/6. When they found this route blocked (had the Romans informed them that this area could be vulnerable because the Persian envoys had implied this or had the Romans informed the Albanian rebels so that they could block the route?), they used another route (presumably the Alan Gates) and invaded Iberia and Armenia. This begs the question, was this invasion a diversionary invasion with a proxy force against the Persians? The sources unfortunately fail to give an answer, but in my opinion this is very likely. Then there is the problem that according to Elishe the Persians also used Huns in their war against the Albanians by opening up the so-called Gate of the Alans. It is actually possible to reconcile the sources if one assumes that when the Romans learnt that the Persians intended to use the Huns against the Albanians, the Romans then used this information to their advantage by inciting the Huns to attack Iberia and Persarmenia at the same time as they devastated Albania. However, it is also possible that we are dealing here with two separate invasions that took place in successive years. Whatever the truth, the Persian reaction to the attack of their territories in Iberia and Persarmenia was not long in coming. Since the war against the Kidarites was still ongoing, they demanded once again that the Romans would either send money or men for the defence of the fortress of Iouroeipaach, and the Roman answer was once again in the negative, and this despite the fact that the Romans were fighting wars of their own in the Balkans.[27]

At about this time in 466/7 there arose trouble between the Persians on the one hand, and Lazi and the Suani on the other. The Suani had captured a number of Persian fortresses with the result that the Persians planned to invade Suenia and Lazica. The king of Lazica (presumably Gubades) sent an embassy to Constantinople with the request that Leo would send reinforcements from Roman Armenia because they were the closest to the theatre of operations. The king also stated that he could not support them if they arrived and were not needed after all because the Persians would decide not to invade. On the previous occasion when there was a threat of Persian invasion the Romans had dispatched reinforcements under Heraclius (in 463/464?), but in that case the king had dispatched them back immediately because he had been unable to support them in his land. This incident is unknown and it is quite possible that it was the reason why Gubades had been called to Constantinople as discussed above. However, now there was once again need for urgent help. The Romans promised this. It was then that an embassy arrived from Persia, which announced that they had now crushed the Kidarites and had conquered their capital

Balaam. The aim, evidently, was to threaten the Romans so that they would not interfere with their planned war against Lazica. The Romans were unimpressed despite the fact that Leo was already more concerned with what happened in Sicily and how the plans against Gaiseric progressed. The Tzani, however, may have allied with the Persians because they were now ravaging the territory around Trapezus with the result that Leo also sent reinforcements there. This means that Leo did not hand money to the Persians in return for peace, but used all the military means available to defeat the Persians and their allies.[28]

Some of the Armenian and eastern sources claim that at about this time there was indeed a war between East Rome and Persia, and as we have seen the situation just before this was clearly ripe for one. On top of this we have the treasonous letters of *MVM per Orientem* Ardaburius, son of Aspar, who had duly been replaced by Jordanes, dated roughly to the year 466.[29] However, most modern historians are still of the opinion that there was no war and that the Romans either paid the Persians or they just allowed Lazica to slip into the Persian sphere of influence. The reason for this is that the Roman documents mentioned by Menander the Guardsman (Blockley fr. 6.1, 578ff.) state that the kings of the Lazi had appointed the kings of the Suani from the time of Theodosius until the reigns of Leo and Perozes. This has been taken to imply that it was under Leo and Peroz that the Lazi became clients of Persia so that the Romans lost control over Suenia and Lazica. However this is actually not conclusive, because it is possible that the Persians obtained control of Suenia but not of Lazica, or that the procedure of appointing the rulers of Suenia was taken away from the King of the Lazi by the Roman Emperor or by the Persian *Shahanshah*. The second of the reasons is that Tzath, the king of Lazica, sought to be christianized in 522 (Procopius), but once again this does not provide any conclusive evidence for the claim and in fact the quite apparent weakness of the Persians in the Caucasus region during the reign of Zeno suggests the opposite.

Michael the Syrian (Bedrosian/Armenian version 83) claims that when Marcian died and Leo became emperor in 457, the Persian *shahanshah* Peroz started a persecution of Christians and then initiated hostilities which can therefore be dated roughly to 459/60. The Syriac version has two different versions. The first places the war to the sixth year of the reign of Marcian which means approximately 455/6 (Chabot, p.122), but at the same time the text then contradicts itself by stating that the war started only after the death of Yazdgerd II during the reign of Peroz (459–84) which dates the war to the reign of Leo. This same piece of text also states that the Persians were defeated and the Romans got 7,000 captives in the region of Arzoun (Arzanene). This is likely to be a duplicate of the war that took place in 421/2 (see Socrates 7.21 with vol.3) and we can therefore safely say that it is probable that the Romans did not take 7,000 captives in Arzanene. According to the second variant, when Leo I was reigning in the East, Peroz began to persecute Christians and started a war against Rome at the beginning of Peroz's reign, which places the war roughly to the year 459/60 (Chabot, p.126). On the basis of the letter of Sidonius (letter to Lambridius 8.9 dated to 476) it is also clear that the Romans had achieved some very significant military successes against the Persians by about 475 because he states that the *Shahanshah* paid tribute to the East Romans in return for peace and not the other way around.

When these pieces of evidence are taken together it appears probable that the new *Shahanshah* of Persia Peroz began some sort of limited war against Rome, which was accompanied by a persecution of Christians in an effort to bolster his own standing among the nobility and magi. The timing, however, is problematic. On the surface it would seem that Peroz started the war immediately in 459 because by 466 the Roman *magister militum per Orientem* Ardaburius had 'grown lazy in the peacetime' (PLRE 2). However, the dating of the war in the *Chronicle* of Agapius is different and makes a lot more sense. According to Agapius, the war started in the 12th year of Leo I's rule in 469 when the Persians besieged and pillaged Amida, but then adds a confusing claim that it was in the 'same' year that Balas/Valash started to reign over the Persians (a 4-year reign) after which Qabad son of Peroz took power for 21 years. Balas/Valash assumed power in 484, which means that there is a discrepancy in the dates.

There are three important pieces of information that lend support for this later dating. Firstly, there were the troubles that took place in Lazica, Suenia and Tzania roughly at this time in about 466/7. Second, the Sadaguri, who were allied with Rome, had invaded Persian territory in about 465/6. Third, the Persians claimed that the Romans had broken the peace treaty. Fourth, the Persians had defeated the Kidarites in about 466/7 and were therefore free to start a war against East Rome. Fifth, the Romans had sent large numbers of soldiers to support Anthemius in 467 and to crush the Vandals, the latter of which had ended disastrously in 468. Sixth, Jordanes, who had been appointed to replace Ardaburius in 466, was nominated as consul for the year 470, which is indicative that he had achieved a significant success against the Persians in 469 (PLRE2 Jordanes). The most important piece of evidence, however, comes from a Western period source. As noted above, according to Sidonius's letter to Lambridius (8.9) in 476, the East Romans had been very successful against their enemies. The Ostrogoths had crushed the Huns on their behalf while the Persian *Shahanshah* paid tribute to the East Romans in return for peace – the latter can only have resulted from a defeat because it had previously been the Persians who had either received payments or had demanded them.

In sum, when one takes into account all the information provided by Michael the Syrian, Agapius and Sidonius, and combines it with the circumstantial evidence, it is practically certain that there was indeed a war between the Romans and Persians in 469, that Jordanes had inflicted a crushing defeat on the invaders possibly somewhere near Amida, and that it is therefore practically certain that Lazica and Suenia remained in the Roman sphere of influence under Leo. This in turn would mean that, if they ever changed their allegiance to the Persian side, it must have happened later.

The Expedition against the Vandals in 468

As already noted, the initial plan of Leo had been to send Anthemius and Marcellinus to the West with the idea that they would conquer North Africa in 467, but this had been prevented by a storm. At the same time as this happened, the Vandals had raided East Roman territories once again and had sacked Rhodes. It was probably because of this that Leo then decided to take charge of operations himself and dispatch his own forces against the Vandals in 468 so that he would not be at the mercy of West Roman action or inaction. He wanted to make certain that the East Roman coasts would not suffer from Vandal attacks. Leo's plan was truly grandiose in scale and involved also Western Forces and Eastern Forces that had been dispatched West with Anthemius and Marcellinus, which means that he must have communicated his plans to Anthemius and Marcellinus well in advance. Leo's intention was to be the man to destroy the Vandals once and for all.

The most detailed of our sources is Procopius (3.5.22ff.) and it is worth summarizing his statements at greater length. According to him, in about 455 Gaiseric gained the support of the Moors and invaded Sicily and Italy every year at the beginning of spring. When he had plundered these areas to the point that there was nothing left worth plundering, he turned his eyes towards the East and plundered Illyricum, most of the Peloponnesus, the rest of Greece and all the islands which were near it. The pillaging of these in 466 resulted from the sending of Marcellinus to Sicily in 465, which Gaiseric interpreted as the breaking of the treaty of 462. According to Procopius, Gaiseric then turned his greedy eyes towards the West and plundered Sicily and Italy again, presumably in 466 and 467 after Marcellinus had withdrawn to Dalmatia to protect it. In spite of this the Vandals still sacked at least Rhodes and plundered the whole land of the Emperor Leo, after which Gaiseric just kept plundering and pillaging one place after another.

After this relentless pillaging there was no other choice left but to attempt to reconquer North Africa with Eastern forces. Leo wanted to punish the Vandals and gathered a massive force for the campaign in 468. According to Procopius, this army consisted of 100,000 men. This figure has been needlessly suspected: some consider it an exaggeration while others think that the figure includes those sent with Marcellinus and Heraclius. Theoretically one could think that Heraclius' force would have been included in this figure while those of Marcellinus were certainly not, but in the light of Procopius' text even this is improbable. And we should not forget that this was only a part of the force gathered against the Vandals because Leo had already dispatched Anthemius with forces to the West and had also convinced Marcellinus to join the effort. According to Procopius, Leo also collected a fleet of ships from the whole of the Eastern Mediterranean, and demonstrated great generosity to both soldiers and sailors because he feared that a penny-pinching policy could cause trouble for the project. According to Procopius, Leo spent altogether 1,300 *centenaria* of gold on the campaign.

The 100,000-strong army was the one dispatched under Basiliscus. The size of the fleet was exactly twice the size of Belisarius' fleet (Procopius, *Wars* 3.11.1ff.; for details, see vol.6) and it is clear that the East Romans were entirely capable of dispatching such a force. If one assumes that the figure of 100,000 men included the sailors/rowers and marines, then one may make the educated guess that the land forces on board consisted roughly of about 40,000–50,000 men. However, it should still be kept in mind that the sailors/rowers and marines could also be used to bolster the fighting strength of the land forces when necessary, just like the land forces could be used in naval combat so that the overall size of the expeditionary force was truly awesome.

However, we also have other figures with which to compare Procopius' 100,000-man army. John Lydus (*De Magistr.* 3.43–4) claims that Leo put 400,000 men on board 10,000 large ships called *liburnae* and spent 65,000 pounds of gold and 700,000 pounds of silver on the ill-fated campaign with the result that the state was basically bankrupted. I would suggest that the 10,000 *liburnae* should be interpreted as 10,000 marines on board the fleet and that the 400,000 men should be interpreted as 40,000 men for a total of 50,000 fighting men or that there were 400,000 men total in ca. 1,100 ships.

Cedrenus (PG pp.665–668) has 1,113 ships each with 100 men for a total of 111,300 men. I would suggest that Cedrenus' total is close to the total number of men carried on board which must also have included others besides the land army, marines, and sailors/rowers. However, I very much doubt that all of the ships would have had 100 men on board. Rather I suspect that Cedrenus has just divided the overall number of men with the number of ships.

Theodore Lector (p.177) claims that the fleet had 7,000 *nautae*, which usually translates as sailors, but this must be a mistake for the number of marines. If one adds to this figure the probably missing supernumerary men, including those manning the artillery pieces, then one may make the guess that the overall figure would have been roughly 10,000.

Theophanes (AM5961) states that Leo gathered 100,000 ships which he filled up with soldiers and weapons and used 130,000 lbs of gold on the expedition. It is clear that Theophanes has here confused the figure of 100,000 men and 1,100 ships with each other.

According to Candidus (Blockley ed. fr.2), Leo's campaign cost 47,000 lbs of gold from the prefects, from the count of the treasuries 17,000 lbs of gold, 700,000 lbs of silver and additional money obtained through confiscations and from Anthemius. This was indeed a very massive and costly campaign. See also Nicephorus Callistus 15.27.

In sum, I would suggest that the size of the fleet was 1,100–1,113 ships carrying on board 111,300 men of whom ca. 40,000 men belonged to the land forces, ca. 10,000 to the marines and the rest to the sailors/rowers and other staff needed. There is still the distinct possibility that we should accept the figure of 100,000 men as accurate for the size of the land army, because we know that the Romans faced an army of 80,000 Vandals of whom perhaps 50,000 were ready for battle. However, I am of the opinion that the former is more likely.

The following quote from Procopius (*Wars* 3.6.2ff., tr. by Dewing p.55ff.) gives us the best description of the resulting joint and combined campaign of the year 468. I have added comments and explanations in parentheses in italics.

He made Basiliscus commander-in-chief ['*autokratora tou polemou*', i.e. *imperator of fighting, which meant a commander with temporary imperial powers for the duration of the campaign. This means that Basiliscus was not necessarily nominated as Praesental MVM or MVM, but rather as a temporary emperor. According to Priscus, Blockley ed. fr.43, Basiliscus was a successful soldier, but still slow-witted and easily deceived. His prior military career proves that he was indeed a competent soldier (see above), but this campaign does indeed prove that he could be deceived by men who were cleverer than he. I see no reason to attempt to rehabilitate his reputation in the manner Ian Hughes does. Basiliscus was certainly a competent general on land, but clearly not a brilliant commander at sea, and he was clearly also full of himself. It was and is a sign of poor generalship to be taken in by deceivers*], the brother of his wife [*Verina*] ..., a man who was ... desirous of the royal power, which he hoped would come to him without a struggle if he won the friendship of Aspar. For Aspar... was unable to enter upon imperial office, but he was easily strong enough to establish another in it, ...since Aspar was then fearful lest, if the Vandals were defeated, Leon should establish his power most securely, he repeatedly urged upon Basiliscus that he should spare the Vandals and Gizerich. [*In my opinion there is actually nothing improbable in this account and it has been quite needlessly suspected by Ian Hughes (2015, 130–31). The opinions and aspirations of Aspar were quite well-known in 468 and it is also entirely plausible that Procopius or his source(s) would have had access to information regarding the discussions undertaken by the two men. Furthermore, such information would not necessarily have been as secret as assumed by Hughes, because if Aspar had advised Basiliscus, for example in a meeting of the Imperial Consistory, such discussions were and are in the habit of leaking out especially if such discussions afterwards seemed to implicate collusion between Basiliscus and Aspar. The utter destruction of the Vandals would have strengthened Leo's position too much in a situation in which Aspar and Leo were already in public disagreement and Aspar foresaw an opportunity to make his son Emperor. There is nothing improbable in the claim that Basiliscus could also think that by doing a favour to Aspar that he might obtain his support for the throne. After all, Aspar's support had already resulted in the nomination of two emperors. Aspar was clearly the man whose support was needed while Basiliscus was a man of very high aspirations with an overblown ego who did not have the necessary intellectual abilities for the job, as is well proven by the outcome and by the disastrous results of his fortunately short subsequent reign.*] ...Leon had already ... sent Anthemius, as Emperor of the West, ... in order that he might assist him in the Vandalic war [*In other words, the war against the Vandal had been planned by Leo and his advisors and Anthemius obeyed the orders dispatched by Leo just as is also implied by other sources, which describe Leo as the superior of the two.*]. ... [*Geiseric*] kept ... entreating that the imperial power be given to Olybrius, ... when he failed in this [*Geiseric*] ...kept plundering the whole land of the Emperor [*this implies that the Vandals plundered the Eastern Empire more widely in 467.*]. ... Marcellinus, ...held power in Dalmatia himself, since no one dared to encounter him. But the Emperor Leon ... won over this Marcellinus ...and bade him to go to the island of Sardinia, ...he drove out the Vandals and gained possession of it with no great difficulty. ... [*Heraclius*] was sent from Byzantium to Tripolis in Libya, and after conquering the the Vandals of that district in battle, he easily captured the cities, leaving his ships there, led his army on foot toward Carthage. [*The usual conclusion has been to unite this amphibious campaign of Heraclius from Byzantium to Tripolis with the information given by Theophanes AM5963/471–2 which states that Heraclius and the Isaurian Marsos with an army from Egypt, the Thebaid and the desert (presumably either Arabs and Berbers, and/or Nubians/Blemmyes) regained Tripolis and many cities of Libya and caused greater damage to Gaiseric than the fleet of Basiliscus had done, with the result that Gaiseric sent envoys to Leo asking for peace. This is a mistake. There is no need to attempt to unite these. Rather it is preferable to accept them as two separate campaigns undertaken at different times by the same commander. The details are clearly different. In the first campaign Heraclius sailed straight from Byzantium to Tripolis and in the second he marched on land from Egypt to Tripolis. One may also assume that Marcellinus retook Sicily from the Vandals before his invasion of Sardinia. Ian Hughes (2015, 125–7) speculates that the idea was to destroy the outlying Vandal forces so that they could not be withdrawn to protect Carthage and to demoralize the Vandals with the news of these defeats. These conclusions are correct, but in my opinion it is still more likely that the main intention was to fool Gaiseric to dispatch reinforcements to these areas so that he would weaken his own main force. The strategy was clearly to distract the Vandals. Gaiseric, however, was not fooled like his successor was when Belisarius started his campaign, but concentrated his efforts against the main strike led by Basiliscus in person. One may assume that Gaiseric was therefore aware of the enemy plans, and it is not impossible that the enemies of Leo and Anthemius, for example Aspar or Ricimer, could have informed him of them.*]

[A fragment of Priscus, Blockley ed. 53/Theophanes AM5961, clarifies what happened before Basiliscus advanced to North Africa. According to Theophanes, Basiliscus, whose forces had been strengthened with western forces, often engaged Gaiseric in sea battles in which he sent many of his ships to the bottom of the sea and could have conquered Carthage. The strengthening with Western forces suggests the possibility that Marcellinus had joined him in Sicily before both advanced to North Africa and that it would therefore presumably have been Marcellinus who was responsible for the naval victories, but it is possible that Basiliscus had merely taken western troops on board to be shipped to Carthage.]

… Basiliscus with his whole fleet put in at a town distant from Carthage, … *[Basiliscus was at anchor in Cap Bon]* … and if he … had undertaken to go straight for Carthage, he would have captured it at the first onset, … so overcome was … *[Gaiseric]* with awe of Leon as an invincible Emperor, when the report was brought to him that Sardinia and Tripolis had been captured, and he saw the fleet of Basiliscus to be such as the Romans were said never to have had before *[This suggests a possibility that Marcellinus was still in Sardinia when Basiliscus' fleet appeared.]* … *[Basiliscus']* hesitation, whether caused by cowardice or treachery, prevented this … *[Gaiseric]*, profiting by the negligence of Basiliscus, did as follows. Arming all his subjects… he filled his ships, but not all, for some he kept in readiness empty, and they were the ships which sailed most swiftly. And sending envoys to Basiliscus, he begged him to defer the war for the space of five days, …They say, too, that he … purchased this armistice. And he did this, thinking, … that a favouring wind would rise for him during this time. … Basiliscus, either as doing a favour to Aspar …, or selling the moment of opportunity for money, or perhaps thinking it the better course, did as he was requested and remained quietly in the camp, …

[This account is entirely plausible. Gaiseric's ploy worked because his words were what Basiliscus wanted to hear. The previous naval victories had convinced him that the Vandals had already been defeated and it would not hurt to wait for a few days for the Vandals to surrender. This enabled him to respect the wishes of Aspar while still forcing the enemy to surrender as required by Leo. It is quite possible that he may even have accepted the bribe, as claimed by some sources. As a landlubber he did not understand the importance of the winds in this situation, but his enemy did. Contrary to what Ian Hughes (2015, 134–5) claims, the decisions taken by individual commanders were and are usually quite decisive in battles and wars. It is very rare for soldiers to be able to rectify a situation when their commander has made a blunder. This battle is a prime example of military incompetence and the ancient sources are quite correct to call it such.]

… The Vandals, as soon as the wind had arisen …, raised their sails and, taking in tow the boats … they sailed against the enemy. …when they came near, they set fire to these boats …, when their sails were bellied by the wind, and let them go against the Roman fleet. …these boats easily spread fire wherever they struck … And as the fire advanced in this way the Roman fleet was filled with tumult,… as the soldiers together with the sailors shouted orders to one another and pushed off with their poles the fire-boats and their own ships as well, which were being destroyed by one another in complete disorder. And already the Vandals were at hand ramming and sinking the ships, and making booty of such of the soldiers as attempted to escape,

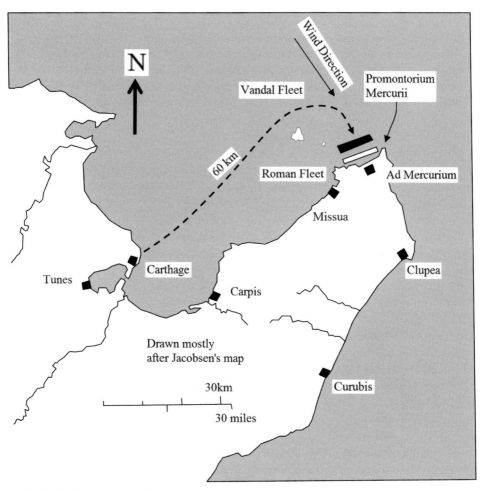

Naval Battle of Cap Bon in 468

and of their arms as well. But there were also some of the Romans who proved themselves brave men in this struggle, and most of all John, who was a general under Basiliscus ... For a great throng surrounded his ship, he stood on the deck, and turning from side to side kept killing very great numbers of the enemy from there, and when he perceived that the ship was being captured, he leaped with his whole equipment of arms from the deck into the sea. And though Genzon, the son of [*Gaiseric*], entreated him earnestly not to do this, offering pledges of safety, he nevertheless threw himself into the sea, uttering one word, that John would never come under the hands of dogs.

... So this war came to an end, and ... [*Heraclius*] departed for home [*i.e. he did not stay in Libya and therefore had to reconquer it two years later*]; for Marcellinus had been destroyed treacherously by one of his fellow-officers. [*According to Fasti Vind. Priores and Paschale Campanum p.305, he was killed in Sicilia. Taken together with Procopius' text this suggests that Marcellinus had already been killed before the landing at Cap Bon, which basically removed the only officer who could have had the authority to challenge Basiliscus when he did not advance immediately against Carthage. None of the sources name who was the culprit, but it is clear that the assassin must have been an officer in the pay of Ricimer who wanted to get rid of his rival. In light of this evidence it is entirely plausible to think that both Ricimer and Aspar were in collusion with Gaiseric to make certain that Leo and Anthemius would not defeat the Vandals.*]

The magnitude of this defeat is pure guesswork, but on the basis of the above and other sources we know that Basiliscus and some other persons escaped from it. Malalas (14.44) appears to be the only source which lists the casualties. He claims that Basiliscus betrayed the ships with the exarchs, *comites* and whole army so that Basiliscus was the first and only one to escape the butchery. He also claims that the Vandals destroyed all the rest, the ships and the army, all of which were sunk at sea. The killed included Damonicus, the *ex-dux*, who was now the *magister militum* of the naval expedition. The PLRE2 suggests that he was *magister militum vacans* in charge of the infantry. According to Malalas, he fought bravely until he was surrounded, captured and then thrown fully armed into the depths. Is he to be identified with the John of Procopius or are these two separate people? The information provided by Malalas suggests a high probability that the Romans lost most of their ships and men, but it is difficult to believe that Basiliscus with his ship would have been the only one to escape. I would suggest, like most modern historians have, that Basiliscus with his ship was not the only one to survive, but that a significant portion of the fleet broke through the Vandal force with him to flee back to Sicily.

In sum, it is probable that the power struggle between Aspar and Leo influenced the outcome of the Vandal war on the grounds that Basiliscus believed that Aspar would win it. It is likely that he wanted to make a service to Aspar when the opportunity for it came in the form of pleas from Gaiseric for an armistice. This was to cost him and the Romans the war. When the disgraced Basiliscus then returned to Constantinople in about 468/9 his sister the Empress Verina saved his life. It is also probable that Leo thought that he could later employ Basiliscus against Aspar, as he was to do. The cost of the war was almost more than Rome could bear, and because of it the East Romans lost ground all round. It forced Leo to resort to all sorts of illegal procedures to obtain money from whatever source possible. From this date onwards they were in serious trouble whenever the Ostrogoths revolted to extort money from them. This was truly one of the greatest military defeats the Romans had ever suffered.[30]

The Balkans in 468–472

There had been other important events both in the Balkans and East that took place before the struggle for supreme power between Aspar and Leo.

Firstly, the war against the Huns had continued after the departure of Anthemius to the West in 467 so that Anagast/Anagastes (definitely as *magister militum per Thraciam* because the *Chronicon Paschale* calls him as such) inflicted a decisive defeat on the Huns and brought the head of Dengizich to Constantinople in 468. It is unfortunate that we do not know if Anagastes had fought a victorious duel against Dengizich or whether he had obtained his head as a result of some other action. This was a major achievement because

it happened against the background of major troop transferrals from the Balkans and the East for the Vandal war, and Anagast expected to be rewarded for his achievement with consulship even if he was epileptic. This was the final nail in the coffin of Attila's short-lived Empire.

The head of Dengizich was brought to Constantinople at a time when chariot races were held, so it was paraded along the Mese and then carried to the Xylocircus where it was fixed on a pole. The head was kept on display for several days so the inhabitants of the city could gaze at it. The accompanying image taken from *Ilias Amrosiana* (drawing by Mai, 1819), which portrays a severed head on a spear, shows how the Romans could also use a similar procedure during a battle for the purpose of demoralizing enemy forces. This quite effective stratagem is something that modern western societies have forgotten when fighting in less developed countries. The displaying of the severed head of the enemy leader was a well-known trick in antiquity.[31]

The absence of the *magister militum Dalmatiae* Marcellinus from Dalmatia to lead the forces of the Western Empire against the Vandals had created a power vacuum in Dalmatia, which had been exploited by the Suevi. They had advanced into Noricum and through it to Dalmatia in about 468/9. The extent of the Suevic occupation of Noricum is not certain. There were still scattered Roman settlements and refuge forts with some small numbers of soldiers who had not received their pay in ages, but there was no longer any regular central administration so it was St. Severinus and some other enterprising individuals who took control of the situation to help the civilians. The Rugii and Alamanni pillaged the area at their will, and it is presumably they that Jordanes meant by the Suavi. Indeed the sources could use Suebi, Suevi, Suavi and Alamanni interchangeably to mean the same or different groups of people. On the basis of the extant evidence, it seems that

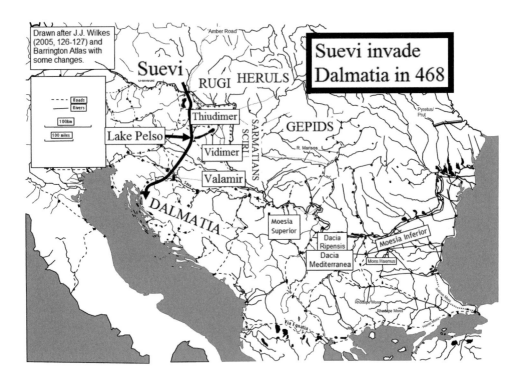

the Suevi had not yet occupied Noricum, but just pillaged it at will and in the absence of effective defence they were able to continue their raids all the way to Dalmatia.[32]

According to Jordanes (Get. 273ff.), Hunimund, chief of the Suevi, crossed over to plunder Dalmatia which was close to both Suevia/Suavia and that part of Pannonia held by Thiudimer. This event can be dated roughly to 468/9. Because of this Thiudimer shadowed Hunimund and when the latter had devastated Dalmatia and was on his way home, Thiudimer made a night attack against the Suevi when they were sleeping near Lake Pelso. The Suevi were completely defeated; some were killed, the rest were taken captive and enslaved; even their king was captured. However, Thiudimer was merciful and eventually granted a pardon to the king; he adopted Hunimund as his son, and then sent him back to his native land together with his surviving followers. This proved to be a mistake, because after a while Hunimund formed a plot with the Sciri, who dwelt above the Danube, to attack the Goths. It is not known when this took place, but one may make the educated guess that it was in about 469/470. The two nations made a surprise attack, but the Goths still managed to gather their forces together. In the ensuing battle, Valamir charged ahead of his troops to encourage them, but the enemy managed to wound his horse with the result that it fell together with its rider. The helpless Valamir was pierced with spears before he could react. The Ostrogoths exacted terrible vengeance against the Sciri in this battle and killed most of them.

The destruction of the Sciri and the growing power of the Amali Ostrogoths frightened their neighbours, with the result that Hunimund and Alaric, the two kings of the Suavi/Suevi, formed an alliance with the Sarmatians led by their kings Beuca and Babai. They were further strengthened by the Gepidae and the remaining Sciri serving under Edica and Hunuulf (Edeco and Onulf), and strong detachments drawn from the Rugi and other tribes of the area. This was clearly a massive army, raised for the sole purpose of crushing the growing power of the Pannonian Ostrogoths. It assembled at the river Bolia in Pannonia where it encamped, presumably to await the arrival of the Ostrogoths. The Ostrogoths were now led by Thiudimer. The two sides fought a battle on a plain, which was presumably close to the encampment. The Ostrogoths filled the plain with the dead bodies which, according to Jordanes, were piled up like hills for more than ten miles. It is unfortunate that he does not specify whether this referred to the width of the plain or to the distance covered up by the pursuing Ostrogoths. If the former is the case then both sides would have had more than 100,000 warriors. If he meant the latter, then it is not possible to make any estimations. However, considering the fact that the Gepidae had previously almost single-handedly defeated the sons of Attila, it is clear that we are here dealing with a major war in which both sides had huge armies, possibly even larger than 100,000 men. It was only with great difficulty that the rest of the motley throng managed to get away. When the Ostrogoths saw the magnitude of their victory, they rejoiced because they had now avenged the death of Valamir. The details suggest that the Ostrogoths were able to defeat their enemies with their typical frontal cavalry charge with lancers. It was simply foolish to engage the Ostrogoths on the plain that favoured their cavalry. It is probable that this war took place in about 471.[33]

Jordanes (*Get.* 280ff.) continues his account with a discussion of a pre-emptive strike conducted by the Ostrogoths during a winter after a certain time had passed. According to Jordanes, the Ostrogoths under Thiudimer exploited the freezing of the Danube, which enabled it to support the footsoldiers, wagons and sledges. I take this to mean that the Ostrogoths went on the warpath during the winter of 471/2. When the river froze, Thiudimer led his army across the Danube and made a surprise attack against the Suavi from behind. According to Jordanes, the Suavi and the Alamanni, who lived together with them, ruled the Alpine heights, and to the east of them lay the lands of the Baiovari (Bavarians), to the west were the Franks, to the south the Burgundians and to the north the Thuringians. Jordanes claims that Thiudimer defeated, plundered and almost conquered all of the Suavi and Alamanni. There are three possible explanations for this war. Firstly, that Thiudimer decided to make a pre-emptive strike against these tribes before they could unite their forces with those of his enemies. Second, that this campaign had been undertaken on behalf of Ricimer (who belonged to a Gothic royal family) against those enemies that posed a potential threat to his Burgundian allies and his remaining supporters in Italy in a situation in which Ricimer and Anthemius were to fight a civil war in 472. Third, it is possible that the Eastern Empire wanted to support Anthemius by destroying the potential allies of Ricimer before they could come to his assistance. The third alternative is probably the most likely if Leo's intention was not to kill Anthemius, but one cannot rule out the others.

When Thiudimer then returned victoriously to Pannonia, he received back his 18-year-old son Theoderic as a gift from Emperor Leo for his great services. This series of wars fought in defence of Roman territory was seen as proof of loyalty in Constantinople. This took place in 472. It was now safe to do this because Leo had by now got rid of Aspar and his sons. What Leo undoubtedly had in mind was the use of the Pannonian Ostrogoths against the Thracian ones, and he wanted to secure the goodwill of the former in a situation in which the latter could pose a threat. However, Leo was still forced to concede the kingship of the Goths to Theoderic Strabo, and it is probable that this was one of the reasons for what happened in 473.[34] Thiudimer gave his son 6,000 retainers (not including the squires, which should be added to the strength because the *foederati* employed these also for combat), which the latter used for a surprise attack against the Sarmatians without the permission of his father. According to Jordanes, the Sarmatian king Babai had just inflicted a defeat on the Roman general Camundus, had captured the city of Singidunum and was puffed up with pride as a result. This suggests that the Romans had continued the war against the Sarmatians when Thiudimer had marched against the Suavi and Alamanni, but with very poor results. It was now that Theoderic, the future Theoderic the Great, demonstrated his great skills as general. He crossed the Danube, killed Babai, captured his treasure and took plenty of slaves, after which he returned to his father. He then attacked Singidunum and captured it from the Sarmatians, but did not return it to the Romans. Considering the locations of his activities, it is likely that he had been given the lands that had formerly belonged to Valamir. It is also clear that his army included other men besides the retainers because the crushing of the Sarmatians and the conquest of Singidunum required more than 6,000 men. It is therefore clear that each of the retainers had at least one to three squires/servants who fought alongside their master.

The Final Showdown between Aspar and Leo in 469–471

The power struggle between Aspar and Leo assumed even more sinister proportions in the Balkans in 469. It was then in the immediate aftermath of the disastrous Vandal campaign that Ardaburius is claimed to have incited Anagastes to a rebellion in 469. The sources give several reasons for the revolt and I would suggest that all of these played a role. Jordanes, his enemy, had been given the consulship for the year 470 presumably as a reward for his successful war against the Persians, and this in a situation in which Anagastes had not been similarly rewarded for his bravery against the Huns. My own educated guess is indeed that Jordanes was rewarded with the consulship because he had achieved some very significant military success against the Persians in about 468/9 and this at a time when the East Romans were facing troubles with the Huns and were still fighting against the Vandals under Heraclius. The hatred between the two was long lasting because it had been Arnegisclus, the father of Anagastes, who had killed Ioannes/Johannes/John the Vandal, the father of Jordanes. Some sources also allege that Anagastes had been denied the same honour because he suffered from epilepsy and could be disgraced by this illness if he ever attended senate meetings, while others claimed that Anagastes simply wanted money.[35]

I would connect the incident in which Anagastes killed Ulith with the beginning of Anagastes's revolt. According to Priscus (Blockley fr.54.1–2), Anagastes killed a fellow Goth named Ulith in Thrace with a ruse. When the two arrived in a defile, Anagast intentionally dropped behind so that Ulith was forced to take the lead. When this happened, Anagastes 'lifted the cap from his head'.[36] There are two alternative interpretations for what happened next. Firstly, it is possible that it was then that Leo gave Zeno as *MVM per Orientem* the task of crushing the revolt and that Ardaburius had incited Anagastes to the revolt precisely so that they could together get rid of Zeno. The other possibility is that Aspar had incited some barbarians[37] to cause troubles in the Balkans (probably the Suevic attack against Dalmatia) with the result that Leo assembled a combined force consisting of the forces of Zeno, Anagastes and Ulith, and that it was in the defile that Anagastes started his revolt and attempted to kill Zeno together with Ulith. Since it was to Serdica (see below) that Zeno fled, it is quite possible that the Romans were on their way to Dalmatia and that Anagastes started his revolt in the Succi Pass. According to Theophanes (AM 5962), *MVM per Orientem* Zeno was ordered to transfer some of his own forces to Thrace for some military purpose (undoubtedly the revolt of Anagast or the Suevic invasion of Dalmatia) with the result that Aspar encouraged them to kill Zeno. Zeno however anticipated the plot and managed to flee to Serdica, from there to the Long Wall, Pylae, and ultimately to Chalcedon. The last-mentioned place suggests that Zeno feared Aspar whose *bucellarii* and loyal federate forces were posted on the European side of the Bosporus. In this situation it is not surprising that Leo appointed Zeno as *MVM per Orientem* in 469. It is possible or even probable that Aspar had already taken control of the praesental forces in the East, the implication of which is that Zeno could not be appointed to this position. The reason for this conclusion is that Theoderic Strabo later demanded the same titles as Aspar had had and was then duly appointed *magister* of both praesental forces (see later). This means that Aspar had probably already managed to force his will on Leo by 469 as a result of the Vandal defeat and the ongoing wars against the Suevi, Sciri, Huns, Vandals and Persians.[38]

Interestingly enough, in 469 there was also a revolt in Isauria led by Indacus whose headquarters was at the hill fort of Papyrius/Papirius. Zeno dispatched men to crush the revolt. The outcome is not known. We also do not know whether the revolt had been caused by rivalry among Isaurian chieftains or whether Aspar had a role in it too. The situation in the Balkans was also pressing because Anagastes had captured several fortresses in Thrace either because he was an able commander or because Aspar had helped him. The revolt of Anagastes, however, was brought to a successful conclusion when the Emperor dispatched envoys to him who managed to persuade him to abandon it. This was clearly a secret operation undertaken without the agreement of Aspar, because it was then that Anagastes revealed the letters of Ardabur which had incited him to revolt. In my opinion we should probably date the end of the revolt to the year 470.[39]

It was probably in late 469 or in 470 that Aspar's position had become once again so strong that he could present additional demands to the Emperor. Zeno had fled to the east, Anagastes was still in revolt in 469–470, and the Vandals had just crushed the Roman invasion attempt. It was now time to demand that the Emperor honour his word and nominate Patricius as Caesar. In other words, I agree with Bury (1.319) that the nomination of Aspar's son Patricius as *Caesar* took place either in 469 or 470 and that the latter year is the more likely. The nomination of an Arian as *Caesar* caused rioting in the Hippodrome. Unsurprisingly, the monks played a leading role in these unrests. Leo pacified the people by promising that Patricius would convert to the Orthodox Faith. The union was further cemented with a bethrothal of Leontia, daughter of Leo, with Patricius – Leo, however, did not intend to honour his word, but was only playing for time.

In a frantic effort to improve his position vis-à-vis Aspar, Leo sought to end the war with the Vandals in 470/1 with a military campaign led by Herakleios (Heraclius) of

Edessa and Marsos (Marsus) the Isaurian. They led an army from Egypt, the Thebaid and the desert, managed to surprise the Vandals so that they once again conquered Tripoli and many other cities in Libya, and harassed Gaiseric so effectively that he dispatched an embassy to seek peace. The timing was good because it was roughly when Leo obtained the surrender of Anagastes together with the proofs implicating Aspar. Leo was more than eager to agree to the peace proposals of Gaiseric, because at this time he needed Heraclius, Marsus and Basiliscus more than ever to get rid of Aspar. It was also during this time that Ardaburius showed his contempt for the Orthodox Church by demanding that St. Marcellus hand over one of his men who had sought a place of refuge; but the threat did not work against the Saint. As if this was not enough, Martinus, an attendant of Ardaburius, informed Zeno that Ardaburius attempted to bribe the Isaurians in Constantinople – in other words, the *Excubitores*. This was the final straw.[40]

In 471 the Emperor invited Aspar, Ardaburius and *Caesar* Patricius to the Palace, where according to Marcellinus Comes the armed eunuchs ambushed them. It seems probable that the use of the eunuchs as *spatharii* (*spatha*-sword-bearers) was not seen to be as threatening as the use of the *Excubitores*, and that it was this that allowed Leo to lull his enemies into a false sense of security and may have been the reason why Aspar and his sons were not accompanied with a heavy security detail – it is possible that they had been left where the *Excubitores* were. In fact, Theophanes states that Zeno was at Chalcedon waiting for news of the murders while Basiliscus with his men was also waiting for the news elsewhere.[41] Aspar and Ardaburius were killed, but Patricius was only wounded and survived. The third son, Ermanaric, was not present and escaped. *Chronicon Paschale* (467) claims that Aspar was killed in the palace while the sons Ardaburius and Patrcius were killed in the house of the Senate. Zeno assisted the escape of Ermanaric to Isauria where he was even allowed to marry a daughter sired by the illegitimate son of Zeno. He returned to the capital after the death of Leo. Zeno's idea was to use this as a way to endear him to some of the followers of Aspar. This treacherous act earned Leo the nickname Butcher (*Makelles*), but as we have seen Leo's treacherous behaviour was quite necessary in the circumstances.[42]

The murders led to unrest in Constantinople because there were large numbers of Goths, *comites* and other followers still loyal to the murdered men.[43] *Comes* Ostrys took the initiative and together with other Goths entered the Palace firing arrows, becoming embroiled in combat with the *Excubitores*. When the *Excubitores* gained the upper hand, killed large numbers of Goths and surrounded Ostrys, the latter fled taking Aspar's concubine with him. Both escaped on horseback to Thrace where they started to pillage estates. This exploit earned Ostrys the fame of being the most loyal friend of Aspar. I would suggest there is a distinct possibility that this incident took place immediately after Aspar and his sons had been ambushed and that Ostrys and his Goths had formed the bodyguard that had failed to protect them, that their attack to the Palace was a last desperate attempt to save the lives of their masters and that the only result of this daring was the saving of Aspar's beautiful Gothic concubine.

It was evidently after their flight to Thrace that Ostrys and whoever had managed to flee with him joined forces with Theoderic Strabo (who was the son of Triarius), Aspar's brother-in-law, and Aspar's *hypaspistês* (bodyguard retainer). According to Malalas, Leo followed the murder of Aspar with a full-scale persecution of Arians, and it would have been this that induced Theoderic Strabo to revolt. However, in my opinion the order of the information in the sources suggests strongly that the revolt of Strabo followed immediately after the murder of Aspar so that the persecution of Arians was not the primary reason for the revolt of the Thracian Federates but rather the murder of their protector and master. It was then that the Goths attempted to storm Constantinople, which is described by Theophanes and implied by Malchus. According to Theophanes, it was only the timely arrival of the forces under Basiliscus and Zeno, who had been waiting for the news of the murders, that prevented the fall of the capital. When the attack failed, Theoderic Strabo was ready to receive the silentiary Telogius (Pelagius?) who had been sent by the Emperor to discuss terms. Theoderic presented three demands to the Emperor: 1) he should receive the inheritance of Aspar; 2) he should be allowed to live in Thrace; 3) he should receive the generalship previously held by Aspar. Leo dismissed the first two demands but agreed to the third if Theoderic Strabo would become his loyal friend. Theoderic decided to add pressure and sent a part of his force against Philippi while he besieged Arcadiopolis. Those sent against Philippi torched the buildings outside but did nothing else. Arcadiopolis was starved into surrender, but the Goths were suffering from the same problem and were forced to send a peace embassy to the Emperor. It was presumably during this time that Armatus/Harmatius, the nephew of Basiliscus, achieved some successes against Strabo so that he was able to capture some Goths whose hands he cut off.[44] This obviously begs the question whether the actions of Armatus were behind the hunger suffered by the Ostrogoths of Strabo. On the basis of the information provided it would seem to be so, which means that Armatus had fought a successful guerrilla campaign against Strabo with inadequate forces. We do not know what position in the military Armatus held when he fought against Strabo, but the usual guess has been that he did this as *MVM per Thracias* (e.g. PLRE2). We do not know this for certain. It is merely an educated guess. The problem with it is that Malchus (frg.8[45]) claims that Strabo later opposed Basiliscus' decision to appoint Armatus *MVM per Thracias* in 475, but this can of course be explained as a mistake because Basiliscus actually appointed him *MVM praesentalis*. Meanwhile, Leo launched a persecution of Arians. Now both sides were ready for peace and Theoderic Strabo was appointed *MVM* of the praesental forces in return for a cash payment of 2,000 lbs of gold for his followers. The Emperor also agreed to consider him to be the only ruler of the Goths and prevent anyone from crossing their territory. In return for this, the Goths promised to fight anyone the Emperor wished.

And who was the other *MVM Praesentalis* whose forces were garrisoned in Bithynia at this time? The PLRE2 names two candidates, namely *patricius* Flavius Marcianus (son of Anthemius who had married Leo's daughter Leontia) in 471/4 and Zenon (*stratêlatês praisentou* who had married Leo's daughter Ariadne) in 473?/474. It is impossible to know which. Whoever it was, Leo kept their forces close to the capital in a situation in which Theoderic Strabo held the other command.

The Final Showdown between Anthemius and Ricimer in 470–472[46]

As already noted the quarrel between the barbarian general and the Emperor was repeated in the west and it would therefore be of great interest to know whether the two barbarian *magistri* coordinated their efforts on behalf of the barbarian blocks. Unfortunately our defective sources fail to state this clearly, but the nagging suspicion remains that there might have been some sort of cooperation between the barbarians in all portions of the Empire. The sources certainly seem to imply this, for example by noting the unwillingness of all the barbarian commanders to engage Gaiseric. It is unlikely to be a coincidence that Ricimer had Marcellinus killed and that successive barbarian commanders from Aspar onwards opposed the policy of attacking the Vandals. It is therefore not surprising that Leo acted the way he did.

The quarrel in the West started in 470 when Anthemius became seriously ill as a result of sorcery, as John of Antioch puts it. This was clearly an attempted assassination with poison and Anthemius acted accordingly. He executed several of those involved in the plot, the most important of whom was *Magister Officiorum* and *Patricius* Romanus who was a close friend of Ricimer. Ricimer fled Rome, gathered 6,000 men and sought a place of refuge in Milan which was close to the forces of the Burgundian Gundobad who was his supporter. However, in early 471 a delegation of Ligurian nobles managed to convince Ricimer to attempt a reconciliation. At their suggestion, Ricimer accepted the Bishop of Ticinum (Pavia), Epiphanius, as envoy. Epiphanius managed convince the two men to agree to a temporary truce, but the hostilities restarted and erupted into war in 472 when Ricimer revolted openly against Anthemius.

According to the sources it was then in 472 that Leo formed a plot to kill Ricimer while publicly claiming to seek reconciliation, because he did not want to lose his nominee in the west. According to Malalas (14.45), Leo dispatched Olybrius to the West with orders to mediate because he was a senator from the west and therefore a person who could be put in charge of such a delicate mission. After Olybrius had managed to convince the two to reconcile their differences, he was to continue his journey to Carthage where he was to convince Gaiseric to become an ally of Leo. Olybrius was similarly an ideal candidate for that mission because he was married to Placidia who was a sister of Huneric's wife Eudocia. However, Leo's real intention was to have both Ricimer and Olybrius assassinated. To make his own plans believable, Leo kept Olybrius' wife and daughter at Constantinople, presumably as hostages. He then dispatched *agens in rebus* (*magistrianos*) with a letter to Anthemius. The letter stated that Anthemius should kill Ricimer like Leo had killed Aspar and that Anthemius should also kill Olybrius. However, Ricimer had posted his loyal Goths at every gate of Rome and also at the harbour with the result that Modestus was searched and the letters were found. Ricimer showed the letters to Olybrius and asked his sister's son Gundobad (Gundobadus) to bring his forces to the city. It would be nice to know whether the original letter of Leo had orders to kill Olybrius or whether this was added by Ricimer. It is also possible to think that Leo had dispatched this letter with the intention of having both Anthemius (his former rival) and Olybrius (his potential rival) killed by Ricimer and his henchmen. Whatever the case, Olybrius was duly appointed Emperor, probably in April 472, with his own full consent, and it did not take long for the rebels to subdue the remaining supporters of Anthemius, so on 11 July 472 Gundobad was able to kill him in the church where he had sought refuge.

The victors, however, had not long to celebrate their victory. Ricimer, vomiting blood, died forty days after Anthemius's murder on 18 August 472, Olybrius was attacked by dropsy and died on 2 November 472. The surviving strongman in the scene Gundobad, the newly appointed *comes et magister militum et patricius*, raised *comes domesticorum* Glycerius as the new Emperor on 3 March 473. It would be nice to know whether Ricimer and Olybrius had been poisoned as their deaths were so convenient from the point of view of Gundobad and Leo. Whatever the case, the appointment of Glycerius was opposed by Leo and he duly prepared to send a fleet under Nepos to oust him in 474. Fortunately for the East Romans, Gundobad was forced to return to Gaul before the arrival of Nepos, possibly because of the threat posed by the Visigoths or because his father had died so that the realm was divided between the brothers Gundobad, Godigisel, Chilperic and Godomar in about 473/4.

The Revolt of the Pannonian Ostrogoths in 473–474

According to Jordanes, the continuous wars had damaged the economy of the Pannonian region so badly that when the booty taken from the defeated enemies was beginning to run out, the Ostrogoths faced the unwelcome prospect of starvation and lack of clothing in 473. The warriors who had earned a living out of fighting considered this a disgrace and demanded that Thiudimer lead them wherever he wanted so that they could obtain a livelihood from fighting. Thiudimer summoned his brother, and they cast lots where to invade. As we shall see later, the Gepids filled up the resulting power vacuum in Pannonia and occupied the territories now abandoned by the Ostrogoths. I would suggest that the second of the reasons for the sudden hostilities against the Romans was the appointment of Strabo as successor to Aspar, which would certainly have increased the eagerness of Thiudimer to attack the Romans in 473. However, when Vidimer entered Italy, he died and was succeeded by his son Vidimer. The Emperor in Italy, Glycerius, chose not to engage the invaders, but bribed Vidimer to continue his march to Gaul where he joined forces with his kinsmen the Visigoths. So, as Jordanes notes, the Goths were once again united as they had been long ago. This time, the united realm of Visigoths and Ostrogoths ruled most of Gaul and Spain.

Thiudimer, the older brother, crossed the river Savus (Sava), and threatened with his great host the Sarmatians who had apparently settled in this area at the same time as they had conquered Singidunum. The Sarmatians chose not to fight because they faced overwhelming odds and allowed the Ostrogoths to march through their territory unmolested. The first object of Thiudimer was Naissus and it was there that he was joined by his son Theoderic and the counts Astat and Invilia. After the city had been taken, Thiudimer dispatched Theoderic together with the two counts to Ulpiana via Castrum Herculis. Ulpiana surrendered without a fight so that Theoderic continued his march to Stobi which likewise surrendered. According to Jordanes, several other places in Illyricum also surrendered. My own educated guess, based on the route of march, is that the town of Scupi was one of them. Theoderic continued his march to Thessaly where he conquered Heraclea and Larissa.

According to Jordanes, when Thiudimer realised that fortune smiled on him and his son, he left only a small guard behind at Naissus and marched against Hilarius the Patrician whose army was located in the city of Thessalonica. This should be interepreted to mean that the Romans were marching along the Via Egnatia to cut off the route of

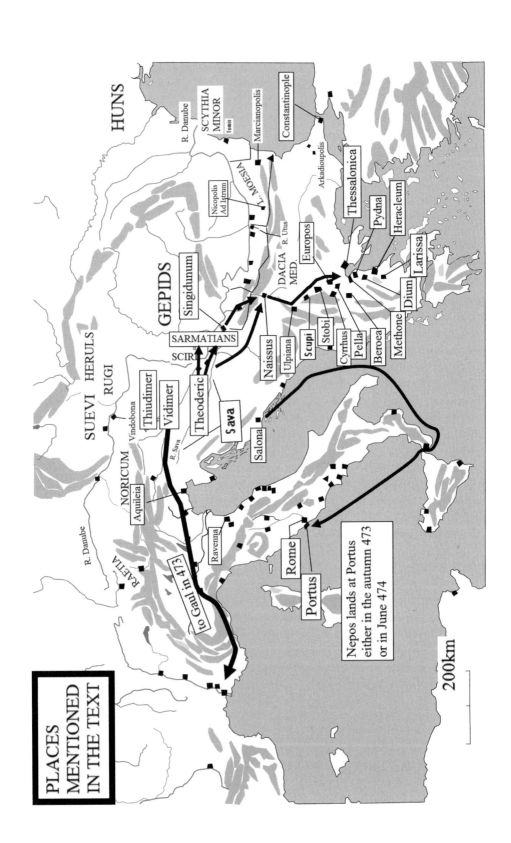

PLACES
MENTIONED
IN THE TEXT

HUNS

SUEVI HERULS
RUGI

NORICUM
Vindobona

RAETIA

R. Danube

Aquileia

R. Sava

Ravenna

to Gaul in 473

Rome

Portus

Nepos lands at Portus
either in the autumn 473
or in June 474

200km

Thiudimer
Vidimer
Theoderic

Sava

Salona

SCIRI
SARMATIANS

Singidunum

GEPIDS

Naissus
Ulpiana
Scupi
Stobi
Cyrhus
Pella
Beroea
Methone
Dium
Larissa
Heracleum
Pydna
Thessalonica

Europos

DACIA
MED.

R. Utus

Nicopolis
Ad Istrum

M. MOESIA

Arkadioupolis

Constantinople

Marcianopolis

SCYTHIA
MINOR
Tomis

R. Danube

retreat from Theoderic who had advanced to Thessaly and that Thiudimer's spies in the enemy camp, which was full of Ostrogoths, informed him of the Roman plans in time so that he was able to intervene. Thiudimer surrounded Thessalonica (map in vol.4) with an entrenchment with the result that Hilarius despaired and sought a negotiated settlement with the enemy. According to Jordanes, without any prior permission to do so Hilarius gave Thiudimer the cities of Cyrrhus, Pella, Europus, Methone, Pydna, Beroea and Dium in Macedonia in return for a truce. If true, this was a risky thing to do by a commander of his own accord. Soon after this Thiudimer fell ill and died in the city of Cyrrhus. It is unfortunate that we do not know if the crafty Romans had had any role in this because they certainly knew how to poison or infect their enemies. If they did, they might have thought that Theoderic, who had been raised in Constantinople, would be preferable as a ruler. Whatever the truth, Theoderic did indeed succeed his father on the throne, but if the Romans thought he would be easier to deal with they miscalculated badly. The death of Thiudimer took place when Zeno had already succeeded Leo so we should probably date the event to winter/spring 474. He was an old man, so he may well have died of natural causes.

The above well demonstrates the weakness of the imperial authorities in the Balkans after Leo had dispatched large forces to support Anthemius in Italy and Gaul in 467 and equally large forces against the Vandals in 468. The situation had been further weakened by the treacherous murder of Aspar, which made all the remaining federate forces serving under Theoderic Strabo disloyal. It is not a coincidence that before this the East Romans had been able to defeat both the Ostrogoths and the Huns with relative ease, but we should still not forget that the murder of Aspar was probably a necessary evil for the Eastern Empire to avoid a similar dependence on barbarian commanders as in the West.

There is also the complication of not knowing when Leo dispatched the naval expedition under Nepos against Glycerius, which landed at Portus near Rome. The problematic part of this is that John of Antioch (Roberto ed. frg. 301.21–27) states that the expedition was sent by Leo while all the other sources claim that Nepos landed at Portus in 474 and was proclaimed emperor at Rome on 19 or 24 June 474 or at Portus on 19 June 474.[47] This account leaves several possible explanations: firstly, it is possible that John of Antioch has made a mistake; secondly, it is possible that Leo did indeed appoint Nepos as commander/Caesar, but that the expedition sailed only after the death of Leo, which is the likeliest alternative; thirdly, it is possible that the plans to dispatch Nepos with East Roman reinforcements affected East Roman plans and made the Emperor prepared to conclude peace with Theoderic in 473; fourthly, it is possible that the expedition sailed in 473 and affected the ability of the East Romans to withstand the invasion of the Pannonian Ostrogoths, and that the official proclamation of Nepos as Emperor took place only later after Zeno had confirmed it during the next sailing season, but this seems far fetched in light of the other evidence. It is probable that Nepos' expedition took place when Vidimer and his Ostrogoths were still in Italy in 474 and that it was partially because of the dual threat that Glycerius decided to surrender without a fight. Whatever the truth, it is certain that East Roman resources were thinly spread after the losses of 468–471.

The Balkans was not the only area that suffered from the disastrous consequences of the losses of the forces sent to the West. The loss of naval forces and the loss of state income were most acutely felt in the Red Sea area, because it was due to these losses that the Alexandrian Fleet was forced to abandon its active operations in the Red Sea theatre and concentrate all of its efforts against the threat posed by the Vandals. Furthermore, the collection of naval resources for the forthcoming expedition against Glycerius must have already started in 473 with the result that the naval strength of the Alexandrian Fleet was not what it used to be. This was exploited by an Arab chieftain called Amorkesos (Imru al-Qais), an ally of the Persians. He exploited the simultaneous weakness of both empires by moving away from the zone controlled by the Persians into that controlled by the Romans. He conquered the Arab tribes below Arabia Petraea and created so powerful a confederacy of tribes that he was able to conquer the Island of Iotabe/Yotabe[48] and throw out the Roman customs officers. However, he was willing to become a Christian and serve under the Romans if the Emperor was prepared to appoint him phylarch of the Arabs in the region occupied by him. Leo was more than happy to accommodate his wishes, because his forces were stretched thin and the alliance with this chief offered him the chance to avoid fighting a war on the Red Sea. Furthermore, if the expedition of Nepos had not yet sailed to Portus, as is likely, the alliance with Amorkesos would have freed resources for a Western adventure. The reception of this fugitive from Persian territory was a breach of the terms of peace between Persia and Rome, but Peroz was powerless to interfere because of the troubles he was facing at the hands of the Hepthalites. Leo invited Amorkesos to Constantinople, which Malchus (Blockley fr.1) criticized strongly because in his opinion the barbarian who was kept at a distance retained an awe of the Empire but when he was given a chance to see the luxury of the Roman cities and how unready these were for war he would start to entertain ideas of invading.

The Inheritance of Leo I the Elder, the Bessian, the Butcher

It was in the middle of the Ostrogothic invasion of the Balkans that Leo died of disease on 18 January 474. Opinions about Leo were just as varied when he ruled as they are today. Most Constantinopolitans saw Leo as a treacherous butcher because he had murdered his benefactor Aspar. The opinion of Malchus (fr.1) was also not that favourable because in his opinion at the time of Leo's death everything everywhere was in a state of confusion. But there were other period sources with a more favourable view of him. The most obvious of these is the Vita of Daniel the Stylite.

One of the unanswerable questions of history is the question what would have happened if Leo had accepted the situation in 470/1 so that Aspar's son Patricius, who had married Leo's younger daughter Leontia, had succeeded him as Emperor. The reason for this question is that, unlike in the West, the Ostrogoths and other barbarians in Thrace had so far been absolutely loyal to the Empire, with the implication that they had become relatively well assimilated into the society. The fact that the populace called Leo butcher suggests that the natives had also accepted the local Gothic officers and soldiers as Romans – after all the Goths had by then been in Thrace for almost 100 years. Furthermore, we should not forget that Theodosius II had been a 'half-breed' which means that even emperors could have barbarian blood running in their veins in the East. The above, however, does not concern the Ostrogoths of Pannonia who were led by the Amals, but those Ostrogoths who had already been given land in Thrace or elsewhere. It was these Goths of Thrace that revolted under Theoderic Strabo after the murder of

Aspar and a large proportion of them subsequently joined their brethren under Theoderic the Amal when he marched to Italy in 488–9, but even then some of them chose to stay. Those Goths who chose to stay in East Rome became completely assimilated into the society. The question therefore is: Would it have been possible to assimilate all of the Ostrogoths of Thrace into Roman society if Leo had accepted Patricius as his successor? We shall never know; but at least Leo was able to get rid of Aspar and his sons. This remains one of the great what-ifs of history.

The reign of Leo can therefore be called as a mixed success. He certainly had had his fair share of troubles and all of his major military endeavours had ended in disaster, although this was not his fault but the fault of the commanders in charge. It had been Basiliscus who had lost the major fleet in 468, but then the commanders Leo put in charge of the operations in Egypt had saved the day. The key problem was actually Ricimer who first murdered Marcellinus and then eventually also Anthemius. Once again it had not been Leo, but Anthemius who had failed to hold his own against the overly ambitious barbarian general. In contrast to him, Leo was able to murder his nemesis, the general Aspar, together with most of his sons, which earned him the nickname Butcher. The key problem with this is of course that this alienated Theoderic Strabo and most of the Gothic *foederati* and that Leo's successor Zeno was therefore given a poisoned legacy. In spite of this, the East Roman Empire was still stable at the time of Leo's death, and before his death he even initiated a new military project to wrest back control of West Rome by dispatching Nepos with a fleet to overthrow Glycerius, and in fact Nepos did precisely that.

In sum, it is fair to say that despite the losses Leo had suffered in the West, he should still be included among the so-called good emperors. For example, it is clear that the contemporary Sidonius Apollinaris had a relatively high opinion of his reign, because according to Sidonius's letter to Lambridius (8.9) in 476, the East Romans had been very successful against their enemies. The Ostrogoths had crushed the Huns on their behalf while the Persian *Shahanshah* paid tribute to the East Romans in return for peace. In short, even if Leo's campaign against the Vandals had been a colossal disaster, he had achieved some very significant successes elsewhere. Furthermore, the ability to dispatch Nepos with a fleet to Rome does suggest that the Empire remained the strongest player in the Mediterranean. The only serious problems left were how to deal with the Ostrogoths who were dissatisfied with the situation, how to deal with the Isaurians who had been brought to the centre of East Roman politics, and how to fill up the empty treasury. The situation was aggravated by the fact that the Ostrogoths were quite rightly suspicious of the motives and plans of Leo's successor Zeno while Zeno himself as an Isaurian was unpopular with the masses.

Leo's reign was also marked by a number of reforms: the forming of *Excubitores*, the increased use of the *silentiarii* as special envoys and operatives and as intelligence officers, the use of the *spatharii* eunuchs and other *spatharii* (presumably *bucellarii*) as the most trusted bodyguards and assassins.

Chapter Nine

Zeno/Zenon in Power (474–475)
Leo II (18 January–7 November 474)

Top: Coin of Leo II and Zeno

Below: Coins of Zeno

(source: Beger 1696)

The Beginning of the Troubled Reign of Zeno in 474–475

The 7-year-old Leo II become sole Emperor when his grandfather Leo I died on 18 January 474, but the real power rested from the beginning with his father Zeno/Zenon who was therefore duly appointed as a co-ruler by his son Leo II on 9 February 474.

As an Isaurian Monophysite, Zeno was extremely unpopular with the army, the Gothic Federates, and the populace of the city of Constantinople. He had tried to cultivate the Federates by saving the son of Aspar and with other gestures, but this was not enough because the Federates knew very well that Zeno was behind their loss of power. The most problematic part of this was that Zeno could not fully trust his native Roman army to act as a counterbalance against the Federates, because the natives hated him as an Isaurian. It is because of this that he could be simultaneously described as an experienced soldier (Anon. Val. 9.39) and as an unwarlike man (Malchus, Blockley ed. fr.5.1–3). He feared to assemble the native soldiers for a campaign. The opinion of the citizens of Constantinople was not as important, but it certainly did not help Zeno that they too were opposed to him.

He was known to be an exceptionally fast runner thanks to his peculiar knee-caps (Anon. Val. 9.40), which must have made him stand out among the light infantry Isaurians at the beginning of his career, but which could be interpreted in a bad way too.

The following quote from Malchus gives us a general assessment of Zeno, but strictly speaking it is accurate only for the period after his return to power in 476, because it refers to Sebastianus who became PPO only in 476 even if we do know that Zeno was from the start of his reign corrupt to the bone.

Zeno, the Roman Emperor, was not by nature as cruel as Leo had been, nor was there inherent in him the inexorable passion such as was constant with Leo. But in many matters he showed ambition for honour, and what he did, he did for the sake of glory …, for show rather than truth. Indeed, neither was he skilled in government nor did he have the brains [*Blockley suggests the education*] by which it is possible for empire to be ruled firmly. He was not given to such love of money and profit as Leo, nor to forge false charges against wealthy men, but, on the other hand, he was not wholly above such business. The Romans would have had a happy reign if Sebastian [*Sebastianus attested to be the PPO in 476–80, 484*], who then held almost equal power, had not controlled him any way he wanted to, buying and selling all government business as if in a market place, and allowing nothing to be done in the Emperor's palace without payment. Moreover, he sold all public offices, taking the payments partly for his private purse and partly for the Emperor's. … Of all the business in the palace there was nothing which he did not buy and sell. If Zeno freely offered an office to someone in his retinue, Sebastian, like a huckster, often took this office from him for a small price and gave it to another for a greater price, keeping the theft hidden from Zeno. Malchus (fr. 9 = Blockley fr.16.2, tr. by Gordon pp.139–40 with one emendation taken from Blockley):

It is no wonder Zeno remained unpopular throughout his reign and that his policies showed no consistency. His policies were entirely opportunistic and based on vainglorious goals – namely on the keeping up of appearances for their own sake.

When he gained power Zeno was acutely aware of his unpopularity and manoeuvred to secure his position, but to no avail. The death of Zeno's son Leo II as a result of illness on 7 November weakened his position beyond recovery so that his enemies were able to form a successful plot against him. It is not known whether Zeno then attempted to make his son Zeno (presumably from his first marriage) his successor, but if he did so in late 474 it must have contributed to his downfall because Zeno the Younger was known for his homosexual extravagances, which were not acceptable among conservative members of society or the Goths. Whatever the case, we know that this Zeno contracted dysentery and died after he had polluted his bed with excrement. Did someone murder him?[1]

To secure his position Zeno rewarded his friends amply and did not make any attempt to find out if any of them was stealing money. As a result of this, the state coffers were emptied and their filling would have required some extraordinary measures. The *PPO* Erythrius (attested as *PPO* for the years 466, 472, 474), who had a reputation for fair dealing, resigned in disgust so that he would not be forced to increase the taxes or force unpaid taxes to be paid (Malchus fr.6, Blockley fr.7). This only increased Zeno's already bad reputation. Erythrius's successor may have been Dioscorus (attested as the *PPO* in about 472 and 474) or possibly already the infamous Sebastian.

The death of Leo I had also dissolved all the treaties that he had concluded. According to Theophanes (AM 5966) and Evagrius (3.2), in the beginning of Zeno's reign (i.e. in 474) the Saracens overran Mesopotamia and the Massagetae Huns Thrace; the other sources add the Vandals and Theoderic Strabo to the list. We know next to nothing about these invasions except that both were eventually defeated. It is possible that Shahid (BAFIC, 114–15) is correct in stating that the Saracen invasion/raid may have been inspired by the Persians as a form of revenge for the acceptance of the refugee Amorkesos as a Roman ally. It is also possible that, even if Evagrius claims that the Massagetae Huns crossed the Danube, this was just his own elaboration added to the invasion of Huns he had read in some source, and that the Huns in question were actually the Goths/Scythians of Theoderic Strabo. In the absence of evidence to the contrary I have here accepted both invasions – the Hunnic and Saracen ones – as accurate. The death of an emperor usually resulted in such invasions.

In addition to the Saracen invasions the eastern provinces were also wrecked by periodic Samaritan and Jewish revolts, which started immediately after Zeno gained the throne. These were the result of their persecution by bigoted Christians. It is clear that the Saracen raids, which were probably instigated by the Persians, and the Jewish and Samaritan revolts, which may also have been incited by the Persians, and the other problems that Zeno faced, influenced directly his policy towards Persia. To avoid an open conflict with Persia in such a situation Zeno appears to have decided to finance Persian military campaigns against the Hepthalite Huns so that his personal representative Eusebius was actually present during Peroz's first Hepthalite campaign in about 474/5–476.[2] This was a clear sign of weakness to outside observers, which they were not slow to exploit.

According to the account provided by Evagrius (3.1–2), it was actually the behaviour of Zeno during these invasions that made these more significant than they actually were. He claims at first (3.1) that Zeno pursued all possible pleasures, both improper and unlawful ones,[3] with complete licence after the death of his son Leo, and that he did not attempt to hide them from the public eye. But later (at 3.2) he modifies this by saying that Zeno led such a life from the beginning and also at the time the Scenite barbarians and Huns ravaged the Roman Empire. The latter is undoubtedly true because the invasions must have already started well before the death of Leo II. This dissolute lifestyle at a time when the Empire was pillaged by the barbarians certainly contributed to the unpopularity of the Emperor.

Gaiseric, King of the Vandals, also exploited the situation and started to raid the Eastern Mediterranean. The sack of Nicopolis in Greece in 474 was a grave blow to the prestige of Zeno. It is also possible that the Vandals sacked Zakynthos the same year. In spite of this, Zeno was forced to placate the Vandals because he faced the revolt of Theoderic Strabo right on the doorstep of his capital, and even if Theoderic had not revolted his previous agreement with Leo included the non-aggression clause concerning the Vandals and in this situation Zeno would also have taken a great risk if he had dispatched native troops against the Vandals that could have been exploited by Strabo. Zeno appointed Senator Severus as *patricius* and dispatched him to negotiate. The purpose was to impress Gaiseric with the high rank of the ambassador. The ploy worked. Gaiseric had continued his piratical raids right up to the arrival of Severus at Carthage, but thanks to the urgency of the situation Severus concluded an endless treaty of non-aggression. Gaiseric even agreed to admit the refugee clergymen back to Carthage because the Catholics posed a lesser threat now that Constantinople was ruled by a Monophysite.[4]

The first to revolt among the Romans was Zeno's Gothic arch-enemy the *MVM Praes.* Theoderic Strabo. We do not known whether he was sacked by Zeno so making this the cause of the revolt or whether he lost his position thanks to his revolt. All that we know is that he lost his title before 475. If Theoderic timed his revolt to occur at the same time as the above Hunnic invasion, then he may have cooperated with them or just exploited the difficulties the new Emperor faced. On the other hand, it is possible that Theoderic had first defeated the invaders and revolted only then because Zeno had failed to reward him. It is unfortunate that we simply do not know any of this. Then there is the problem of what was the position of the Ostrogoths of Theoderic the Amal. We know they sided with Zeno later in 476 and that they were in Novae at the time.[5] My own suggestion is that Zeno concluded a new treaty with Theoderic the Amal but not with Theoderic Strabo when he came to power and that it was because of this that Theoderic the Amal transferred his Ostrogoths to Lower Moesia. Considering the fact that from about 474 onwards Theoderic the Amal was protecting the Lower Moesian frontier it is quite possible that he rather than Theoderic Strabo had defeated the abovementioned Huns on behalf of Zeno or alternatively that his Ostrogoths were just transferred to the Lower Moesian frontier because the Hunnic invasion had revealed a weakness in the defences in that sector. This had the added advantages of separating the two Ostrogothic forces from each other and releasing the army of Thrace for operations against Theoderic Strabo because the defence of the frontier was now conducted by the forces under Theoderic the Amal.

Regardless of the circumstances in which Strabo's revolt took place, it was fortunate for Zeno that he still retained the loyalty of most of the army thanks to his family connection with the previous ruler. The loyal officers included the *MVM per Thracias* Heraclius. According to Malchus, Heraclius, however, was a daring commander, a man of action, who was in the habit of attacking without any forethought. It was because of this that his headlong attack against Theoderic Strabo ended in complete defeat and in his capture. Theoderic Strabo demanded a ransom of 100 lbs of gold for his return, which Heraclius's relatives paid when ordered to do so by Zeno. Heraclius was freed, but when he made a public appearance at Arcadiopolis (this place would also have had Rugi Federates) some Goths who had apparently remained loyal to Zeno killed him in revenge because Heraclius had once punished some Gothic soldiers with stoning in a pit for an offence that did not require such harshness and cruelty, and they did this despite the fact that

Heraclius had a military escort to protect him. The fact that the soldiers bore a grudge against Heraclius proves beyond doubt that the city of Arcadiopolis housed soldiers that had formerly served under him.[6]

However, according to the version given by John of Antioch, Heraclius was killed by Theoderic Strabo near the wall of the Chersonese and that it was this act that declared war against the Romans. He also claims that it was after this that Zeno sent Illus there to help those fighting against Theoderic and that he also achieved some successes against Theoderic. The Isaurian Illus was Zeno's close friend, but we do not know his official position at this time because the first office of his which is known is that of *Magister Officiorum*, which he held from 477 onwards. My own suggestion is that Illus was *Comes Domesticorum* in charge of the *Excubitores* and other Isaurian units that Zeno had presumably brought into (or close to) the capital. It was then that Basiliscus convinced Illus to join him against the Emperor.[7] We do not know what Basiliscus promised but it was enough to convince Illus and his brother Trokoudes/Trocundes. Basiliscus then dispatched Illus with two letters to convince Armatus/Harmatius and Verina to join the plot. Illus met first Armatus, who duly joined the conspirators. This is not surprising because he was a nephew of Basiliscus. It appears therefore very probable that Basiliscus was in charge of operations against Strabo and that Illus had joined his forces. The problem is that we do not know what office Basiliscus held. One possibility is that he held the other praesental position that had been previously held by Zeno up to 9 February 474. Similarly we do not know what position Armatus held in the armed forces. All that we know is that Armatus was clearly in command of some forces in Thrace that were separate from those commanded by Basiliscus and Illus. The fact that Basiliscus appears to have been at Heraclea suggests that Armatus was probably protecting another route of approach to Constantinople. Had Zeno appointed Armatus as a replacement for Heraclius, or was he now *MVM praesentalis* or *magister militum vacans* or something else? My own guess is that he was probably at least temporarily appointed to the office of *MVM praesentalis* because it is likely that Zeno would have appointed a replacement to Theoderic Strabo at least for the period in which he was in revolt in 475 and he may already have held the same position during Strabo's first revolt in 474. Furthermore, what did Basiliscus promise Armatus in return for his support? If he had previously held the office of *MVM per Thracias*, then he definitely promised him the position of *MVM praesentalis*, but if he had not then the former may have sufficed. After this, Illus took the second letter of Basiliscus to Constantinople where he handed it to the *Augusta* Verina, the sister of Basiliscus. The conspirators promised to make her lover Patricius *Augustus*. This was obviously a lie because the plan was to make Basiliscus Emperor and it was this that subsequently soured the relationship between Verina and Basiliscus. Verina then acted with great cunning. When Zeno was watching the chariot races at the hippodrome, she asked him to come to her on the double. When Zeno arrived, she told him he had to flee immediately if he wanted to survive an assassination attempt against him. Zeno believed her. Zeno, Ariadne and Zeno's mother Lallis gathered all the valuables they could from the Palace, then crossed by night to Chalcedon on the ninth day of his consulship (9 January 475), and then fled to Isauria with mules, horses and with those Isaurians who had stayed loyal and who were able to join him in his flight.[8]

According to the second version which is preserved the whole plot had been hatched by Verina because she had quarrelled with Zeno and that Zeno fled immediately because he feared that Verina's assassins in the same Palace could kill him and that his wife Ariadne joined him only later. Theophanes on the other hand states that Basiliscus revolted while staying in Heraclea (Herakleia/Perinthus) with the assistance of his sister Verina and some members of the Senate, and that Zeno and his wife Ariadne fled with plenty of money to Ourba (Olba, mod. Ura north of Seleukeia) and from there to Sbide (mod. Izvit).[9]

In my opinion, the version given by John of Antioch seems likeliest, but I would still suggest it is probable that Basiliscus was indeed at Heraclea when Zeno fled and that Zeno fled together with his wife to Olba and then to Sbide. Then there are the problems of where was Heraclius killed and where was the army serving under Armatus? Malchus claims that Heraclius was killed at Arcadiopolis when he was making a public appearance while John of Antioch claims that he was killed in front of the Wall of the Chersonese. One possible way to reconcile the sources would be to think that Basiliscus and Illus had forced Theoderic to seek shelter behind the Wall of the Chersonese, that Theoderic released him from there, and that it was after this that Heraclius went back to take command of his own Army of Thrace and that its HQ was located at Arcadiopolis. This would also explain why Basiliscus was at Heraclea. The other even more likely alternative is that Theoderic Strabo had been forced to seek shelter in the mountains located between Ainos, the Walls of Chersonese, Heraclea, Arcadiopolis, and Hadrianopolis, and that he just brought Heraclius before the Walls of Chersonese when he released him.

The reason for this educated guess is that this area was where the Goths had sought a place of refuge in the fourth century (see vol.2) and that the Goths would probably have wanted to avoid seeking shelter behind walls. It is also quite probable that the forces garrisoning the Chersonese would have been sufficient to keep the Goths north of the wall. The two known locations of troop concentrations, Arcadiopolis and Heraclea, would have been ideally located to serve as HQs for the Romans if they had isolated the Goths in the mountains north of the Chersonese. One may also speculate that the cities of Ainos and Hadrianopolis had forces in them to isolate the Goths, possibly including the Ostrogoths of Theoderic the Amal if his army had not yet been transferred to Lower Moesia, but my educated guess is that these cities had garrisons of Roman regulars rather than Ostrogothic Federates because the latter would have been considered as a potential threat.

Furthermore, the presence of Theoderic the Amal close to the theatre of operations could have posed a threat to the plotters who sought to ally themselves with Theoderic Strabo. If one takes this line of reasoning a bit further, it is possible that Armatus had been in charge of the army located at Arcadiopolis and that he instigated the Goths to kill Heraclius. However, all of this is mere speculation on my part, and it is quite possible that the Goths just killed a hated leader. Furthermore, it is impossible to know for certain what troops Armatus commanded – all we know is that his support was necessary for the plot to succeed. The above also does not explain when Basiliscus convinced Theoderic to join the plot, and on the basis of Malchus (frg.8)[10] we know that he did join Basiliscus. In light of this, one can also speculate that the murder of Heraclius had been prearranged by the plotters including Theoderic after Theoderic had already released him so that they would be able to get rid of a commander who was not on their side.

Chapter Ten

Basiliscus (January 475–Summer 476)[1]

Basiliscus on a coin
(drawing by Beger, 1696)

Augustus Flavius Basiliscus (475-476)
Source: Hodgkin

When Zeno fled the capital, Constantinople, Verina sought to nominate her lover Patricius as Emperor as had been promised by Illus. However, contrary to her wishes, the military men appointed Basiliscus as *Augustus*. Basiliscus in his turn nominated his wife Zenonis *Augusta* and his son Marcus *Caesar*. When Basiliscus and his forces reached the capital, they began a terrible butchery of the Isaurians who had remained in the city. It is probable that it was then that Illus managed to capture Zeno's brother Longinus, which he was later to use as leverage against Zeno. It was presumably immediately after this that Basiliscus dispatched Illus and Trocundes in pursuit of

Zeno. His idea was presumably to use these two Isaurian chieftains against their fellow tribesman Zeno. Just as Brooks stated more than hundred years ago (p.217), Zeno was in an exceptional position – unlike the previous Roman emperors, he was a tribal chieftain with tribal forces loyal only to him.

I would suggest that Zeno may have been initially unaware of the betrayal of Illus and his brother, so his first object was Tarsus; as we shall see this area formed the core area of Illus' support. He presumably intended to rally these men to his cause with the money that he had brought from Constantinople, or if he was already aware of Illus' betrayal that he tried undermine their loyalty with the money he had brought. His other idea may have been to attempt to bribe the regular forces posted in the East with the same money by sending envoys to Antioch and Seleuceia to test the ground among the Field Army of the East and the Syrian Fleet. However, when it became apparent that he could not get the support of the tribesmen around Tarsus or the support of the regulars posted in the East, he withdrew to the protection provided by his own tribesmen near the town/city of Sbide.

Basiliscus had seven problems facing him after the capital had been purged of the supporters of Zeno: 1) Zeno was still at large; 2) Verina and her lover *Magister Officiorum* Patricius were not happy with the promotion of Basiliscus; 3) he needed to fulfil his promise to Armatus; 4) he needed to fulfil his promises to Illus and Trocundes; 5) he needed to fulfil his promises to Theoderic Strabo; 6) he needed money to bribe his supporters; 7) as a Monophysite he wanted to reconcile the Chalcedonians and Monophysites.

On the basis of a fragment of Candidus, the first problem to materialize was that posed by Verina and Patricius. Candidus states that Basiliscus had Patricius killed because he had angered him, but does not say what it was that had angered him. Presumably the two had a row resulting from the betrayal of promises made. The killing of Patricius was obviously a wise move from the point of view of internal security because he undoubtedly had supporters among the security apparatus as a *Magister Officiorum* and the support of Verina made him a very real threat. Whatever the cause, the killing angered Verina with the result that she started to work in the background to bring Zeno back by supplying money. Basiliscus was apparently informed of this because Candidus states that Verina suffered terribly at the hands of Basiliscus, and had Armatus not taken her out of the church of Hagia Sophia Basiliscus would have killed her.[2]

We do not know what Basiliscus had promised to Illus and Trocundes, but the war and the bribing of the commanders that had supported Basiliscus and the bringing of the Isaurian tribesmen and other armed forces all required money and it was this that Basiliscus started to obtain by whatever means possible. Furthermore, Zeno had emptied the state coffers and had even taken most of the valuables away from the Palace so that Basiliscus had very few legal or pseudo-legal ways left to obtain what was needed. Thanks to the fact that Basiliscus was a Monophysite he exacted taxes from the Chalcedonian bishops, but since this was not sufficient to meet demands, he also exacted taxes from all possible sources including even the artisans. This naturally caused widespread anger, but was still not the most important reason for the hostility felt against him. This was his support of the Monophysite doctrine. The clergy and populace of Constantinople were staunchly Chalcedonian, which meant that he lost the support of the populace of the most important city in the Empire, which included the wealthiest and most powerful men of the Empire among the Senate, and it was the Senate that became active on behalf of Zeno. According to Theophanes AM 5969, it was thanks to the depravity of Basiliscus' ways[3] that the members of the Senate wrote to both Illus and Trocundes to bring Zeno back. However, the key factor in turning both against Basiliscus was actually the fact that Basiliscus had not fulfilled the promises that he had made them. Consequently, both joined forces with Zeno and turned their arms against Basiliscus. The fact that Illus held Zeno's brother Longinus hostage in Isauria made him confident that he could obtain what he wanted from him.

According to the account preserved by Evagrius 3.4ff. and Zachariah 5.1ff., the problems began when Basiliscus received an embassy from Alexandria that had come out to meet Zeno. This embassy asked him to recall Timothy from his exile at Cherson. As a Monophysite Basiliscus agreed to do this. The arrival of this embassy was also seen as a threat by the Bishop of Constantinople Acacius, because one of the monks accompanying the mission was Theopompus who was a brother of Basiliscus' new *Magister Officiorum* Theoctistus, and there existed a danger that Acacius' enemies could attempt to replace him with this man. When Timothy then arrived at Constantinople en route to Alexandria, he and Peter the Fuller, the Bishop of Antioch, met the Emperor and convinced him to send encyclical letters drafted by Paul, one of the members of the embassy, which annulled the decisions made at Chalcedon together with the so-called Tome of Leo (Pope Leo's statement). En route to Alexandria, Timothy then made Paul Bishop of Ephesus. The sending of encyclicals, the appointment of Paul, and the response made to them, worried the Bishop of Constantinople Acacius. Acacius was worried that Timothy, Paul and Peter could attempt to convene a Council against him at Jerusalem and then replace him with Theopompus. So he stirred up the monks of Constantinople together with the populace against the heretical Basiliscus and sent out counter-encyclicals in support of the Council of Chalcedon. He was not a fanatical supporter of the Chalcedon doctrine, but a man whose main concern was his own status and the status of his own see. Basiliscus attempted to gain the support of Daniel the Stylite, but in vain because it was Acacius who managed to convince him to descend from his column and lead the demonstrations against the Emperor. The scale of the public demonstrations frightened Basiliscus, so he went to Hagia Sophia to stage a public reconciliation with Acacius and Daniel. After this, he sent counter-encyclicals in support of the Synod at Chalcedon, but which still left the final decision to the individual. In other words, it was a compromise paper which stressed Basiliscus' own stance of neutrality regarding the doctrinal issue. This was unsatisfactory to all, as all compromises usually are.[4]

It was also in 475 that the East Romans lost their own Emperor in the West. Orestes attacked Nepos with the result that Nepos sailed from Ravenna back to Salona in Dalmatia. Orestes then raised his own son Romulus Augustulus as *Augustus* on 31 October 475. It is quite probable that the Pope, who opposed the religious policies of Basiliscus, contributed to the situation by supporting Orestes in this.

The Suda/Suidas a.3970 has preserved a piece of text that shows what type of person Armatus/Harmatios was and what trouble this caused for Basiliscus:

Given that the Emperor Basiliscus, as Harmatos [*Armatos/Harmatios/Harmatius*] was his relative, unsuspectingly permitted him to meet Zenonis the Empress, [and] since there was frequent converse between them and since their beauty was not easy to overlook, both loved each other extraordinarily. There were castings of glances at each other and continuous turns of their faces and exchanges of smiles; and after these things the problem was one of keeping love hidden from sight. When they had communicated the situation to Daniel the eunuch and Maria the waiting-woman, they managed to cure this with the medicine of intercourse, and Zenonis through flattery convinced Basiliscus that the lover of Zenonis should have the chief positions of the state. But Theoderic seeing Harmatos honoured above all was vexed since he was surpassed in reputation by this young man who thought only of his hair and other bodily training [*note the implication that Armatus trained the military arts with great diligence*]. Harmatos, deranged by the limitless supply of money and honour, supposed no one would surpass him in bravery [*note that this implies that Armatus had probably also fought duels or had at least fought bravely in front of his soldiers*]. And this dementia controlled him to such an extent that he took up the accoutrement of Achilles [*Achilleôs*] and thus rode around on horseback and pranced around his house near the hippodrome [*it is possible that it was not a coincidence that Armatus re-enacted Achilles in and around the Hippodrome, because one of the causeways leading from the Palace to the Hippodrome appears to have been called Achilles according to Ebersolt p.17*]. And being called Pyrrhus by the mob of the people in their acclamations incited him to be fixated on this sort of repute; if they called him this because he had a ruddy complexion they were saying something reasonable, but if it was intended as praise of bravery they were beguiling [him] as [one would] a child; for he did not smite heroes like Pyrrhus, but was a womanizer like Paris.[5] – translated by Jennifer Benedict, vetted by David Whitehead, William Hutton, Catharine Roth at www.stoa.org.

The fact that Armatus and Basiliscus both held joint consulships in 476 cannot have been too popular in the minds of Illus, Trocundes or Theoderic Strabo. The stage was set for a confrontation.

In a very short time Basiliscus had managed to alienate almost all of his supporters and had become so hated that the Senate actually sought to bring back the hated Isaurian Monophysite Zeno. Illus and Trocundes changed sides. After all, Basiliscus had failed to honour his promises while Illus could hope to press his case more forcefully with Zeno thanks to the fact that he held his brother Longinus hostage. It was then that Zeno resorted to the traditional trick used by most of the commanders in one form or another when they needed to instil courage into their superstitious soldiers. Zeno claimed to have seen the proto-martyr Thecla in a dream in which she promised to restore the Empire to him. The use of Thecla was also appropriate because she was an Isaurian saint. This appears to have taken place some time during the summer of 476, because Zeno reached Constantinople by August 476.[6]

Several sources prove also that Zeno or the members of the Senate, who turned Illus and Trocundes against Basiliscus, had been active in the Balkans. According to Anonymous Valesianus, it was Zeno rather than the conspirators among the Senate who sent envoys to the city of Novae in Lower Moesia, and they managed to convince Theoderic the Amal to join Zeno's cause. It was perhaps because of this that we find Theoderic Strabo, the son of Triarius, who was a rival of Theoderic the Amal, staying loyal to Basiliscus even when he was dissatisfied with the rewards he had been given by Basiliscus.[7]

The accounts of Malalas (15.5ff.), Theophanes (AM 5969) and *Chronicon Paschale* (Olympiad 314) allow us to reconstruct what happened next. Zeno divided his forces in two. Trocundes was sent to secure Antioch with a garrison of Isaurians, while Zeno himself together with Illus and a large force of Isaurians marched to Constantinople. The defence of Antioch was actually led by its bishop, Peter, who appears to have been able to hold on to the city until the news of the fall of Basiliscus led to the collapse of resistance, because according to Malalas it was only after his return to power that Zeno removed Peter from his position and exiled him to Euchaita in Pontus.[8] When Basiliscus learnt of the desertion of Illus and Trocundes, he knew that he had to send someone who was loyal and competent as general against them. His choice fell on his nephew Armatus. He obviously trusted that his nephew would remain loyal and would also be able to defeat the approaching enemies because he had already proved himself an able commander against Strabo. The fact that Armatus appears to have been a lover of the Empress Zenonis seems to have worked to his advantage too because the Empress praised her lover to her husband. Regardless, according to Malalas and *Chronicon Paschale*, Basiliscus still made Armatus swear on his holy baptism as a recent convert not to betray him – does this mean that Armatus had been a pagan or Arian?[9]

Basiliscus gave Armatus all available troops, which included those posted in Thrace and Constantinople together with the imperial bodyguard units. These forces cannot have included the Federates under Theoderic Strabo because they were needed to counter the forces of Theoderic the Amal who had joined Zeno. However, the handing of all available imperial forces to the treacherous and amorous Armatus proved to be a grave mistake. When Zeno learned of his approach, he dispatched a message to Armatus in which he promised to make him *MVM praesentalis* for life and *Patricius*, and to proclaim his son Basiliscus *Caesar* and therefore successor of Zeno. The disloyal Armatus duly deserted to the side which promised him more. According to Malalas, Armatus no longer attempted to block Zeno's route of advance but marched towards Isauria by another route. This, however, appears to be false because both Theophanes and *Chronicon Paschale* state that Armatus met Zeno at Nicaea in Bithynia.[10] Theophanes even claims that the army under Armatus frightened Zeno so badly that he was on the point of retreating had not Armatus deserted to his side. Then, at Nicaea, Zeno nominated Basiliscus, son of Armatus, as *Caesar* and confirmed Armatus in his office for life. The united armies then advanced to Pylae/Pylai where the soldiers were embarked on ships. These ships would presumably have been previously used to carry the army of Armatus, so it was really fortunate for Zeno that the latter had changed sides. The use of Pylae to embark the army proved fortunate because the enemy appears to have expected Zeno to cross into Constantinople either from Chalcedon or Chrysopolis, and we should not forget that Basiliscus probably still had most of the Imperial Fleet. It is unfortunate that we do not know what the Imperial Fleet did at this time – perhaps they deserted too – but we know that Zeno was able to land his infantry forces right at the Palace where he and his forces were welcomed by the soldiers posted there, and by the Senate and Verina. When Basiliscus learnt that

Zeno had taken possession of the Palace and that he had been welcomed by all, he took his wife and children and sought a place of refuge in the Great Church of Constantinople. In the meantime, Zeno went up to the Hippodrome where he raised the banner, watched the games and received the welcoming cheers of the people. The public celebration at the Hippodrome is not surprising because, according to Malalas, Zeno had relied on the particular support of the Green Faction when he had entered the capital. In other words, it is probable that the members of the Green Faction had worked tirelessly and effectively in the background to secure the entrance of their favourite ruler. It is clear that we are now entering a period in history in which the importance of the circus factions was rising. Zeno then dispatched Armatus to the church to lure the enemy out, which he managed to do so that Basiliscus and his family were imprisoned.

The captured Basiliscus and his family were exiled to Cappadocia where they were all killed by enclosing them in a tower.[11] As a form of thanks for his success, Zeno dedicated a sanctuary for Thecla in the city of Seleucia (Evagrius 3.8).

What had Basiliscus achieved during his short reign? Not much. He basically left behind an Empire even weaker than it had been twenty months before, in which the position of the restored Emperor was very shaky, in which the Isaurians were even more powerful than they had been before, in which the state finances were in a state of collapse, and in which the religious institutions were also in a state of chaos.

© Dr. Ilkka Syvanne 2014

Armatus re-enacting
Achilles on horseback

Chapter Eleven

Zeno Back in the Saddle (August 476–9 April 491)
The Mighty Struggle for Power in 477–489:
Zeno, Illus, Marcian, Leontius and the Goths

Zeno's First Political and Military Actions in 476–477[1]

Once back in power Zeno's first order of things was to reward all those who had changed sides. This obviously included the rewarding of Armatus, Theoderic the Amal, Illus and Trocundes in particular. It also required money and it is therefore not surprising that Zeno's new PPO Sebastianus put on sale all government businesses, as noted above. According to a fragment of Malchus (Blockley ed. 16.1), he also inflated the prices so that the governorship of Egypt could not be bought with 500 lbs of gold when its previous price had been 50 lbs. This naturally increased the level of corruption and caused difficulties for taxpayers who paid these increases in the form of illegal taxes. Armatus appears to have already been given his rewards: the title of *MVM Praesentalis* for life and *Caesarship* for his son Basiliscus before the overthrow of the Emperor Basiliscus; and it is possible that Theoderic the Amal had also received his titles *MVM per Praesentalis* and *Patricius* already before Basiliscus had been overthrown, but if this did not take place then it certainly took place immediately after Zeno had retaken the capital. The most immediate problem facing Zeno appears to have been that Theoderic Strabo, who had remained loyal to Basiliscus and who had been sacked from his office, was still on the loose in the Balkans. Zeno's solution appears to have been to do nothing and hope that Theoderic Strabo, who was isolated by the forces of Zeno, would be defeated. Strangely enough Illus was not rewarded immediately and had to wait until the next year 477 to receive the office of *Magister Officiorum*. Regardless, it is clear that Illus was the second most important man in the military hierarchy after Armatus even before his official nomination. One may assume that Illus just did not consider the title as important as his de facto position as commander of Isaurian forces. Illus' brother Trocundes kept his position of *magister* (presumably *MVM per Orientem*) that he had received when he had been sent against Antioch. In other words, he had received his reward already before the overthrow of Basiliscus.

In 477 Theoderic Strabo sent envoys to Zeno to ask him to restore Federate status back to the Goths. He pleaded that they had not done as much damage as Theoderic the Amal had to the Romans and that in spite of this it had been Theoderic the Amal who had been rewarded with the titles of *strategos* (*magister*) and friend of the Romans. Zeno convened the Senate to hear their advice on how to proceed. This proves several things: firstly, that Zeno wanted to reward the Senate for the support it had given him; secondly, that the importance of the Senate had grown; thirdly, that Zeno wanted the Senate to have a share in potentially unpopular decisions. The Senate, however, threw the ball back to the

Emperor. The official stance of the Senate was that the state did not have enough money to pay off both Theoderics when it couldn't pay the regulars. So the senators asked Zeno to decide for himself who to pay. Zeno did not want to make the decision alone, so he made a speech to the soldiers of the city and the *Scholae* in which he reiterated all the bad things Theoderic Strabo had done. When the soldiers heard this, they duly shouted in unison that Theoderic son of Triarius and all his accomplices were the enemies of the Romans. It is clear that this whole affair was stage managed and that the officers guided the soldiers in their shouts. Regardless, by doing this it was possible for Zeno to unite all parties behind a decision that he had already made. The demands of Theoderic Strabo were not to be accepted, but Zeno stalled and did not send an answer immediately. First he waited for news of what was happening outside the city.[2]

It was during the hiatus that the security apparatus of Zeno detected three enemy spies inside the city. The medical doctor Anthimos/Anthimus together with Markellinos/Marcellinus and Stephanos/Stephanus had been writing reports to Theoderic Strabo of what had been taking place in the city. They had also dispatched forged letters in the name of high officials with the idea of encouraging Theoderic to continue his revolt. The three men in question were arrested and then interrogated by three senators in the presence of *Magister Officiorum*. They were whipped and condemned to perpetual exile because Zeno was opposed to giving death sentences. This proves nicely that despite being a so-called 'barbarian' from Isauria, Zeno was not barbaric in his treatment of those who opposed him. In the words of Malchus, Zeno did not have the same cruel streak as Leo had.[3]

Western Affairs after 475[4]

As noted, in August 475 there had taken place an important event in Italy that also affected the situation in the East. Nepos, who was a nominee of East Rome on the throne, had been forced to flee by Orestes and had boarded a ship and fled to Dalmatia on 28 August 475. Orestes had then nominated his own son Romulus Augustulus as Emperor on 31 October. Orestes and Romulus had been ousted by Odoacer, the brother of Onulf. Odoacer had been declared King of Italy by his barbarian troops on 23 August 476. This was quite easy to do because the East Romans were in the middle of a civil war of their own. According to Malchus (Blockley ed fr. 14), when the West Romans learnt of the return of Zeno, Augustulus son of Orestes forced the Roman Senate to send envoys to Zeno in which they declared that one Emperor Zeno was sufficient for the Empire and that they had chosen Odoacer as their guardian. They also urged Zeno to give Odoacer the rank of *Patricius* and to confirm him in his military office. As is obvious, it was Odoacer who forced Augustulus and the Senate to dispatch this message on his behalf.

Odoacer's position was by no means strong. An important fragment of Candidus (Blockley ed. fr.1.84ff.) states that the Gauls of the West revolted against Odoacer in 476 and then dispatched an embassy to Zeno to ask his support against Odoacer. This happened against a background in which the Visigoths of Euric had exploited the chaos and had invaded Provence where they had captured Arles and Marseilles again in about 476. The Gauls were naturally quite incensed about the situation in which Odoacer had led the army meant for the defence of Gaul against Orestes. Zeno, who had troubles of his own, appears to have decided to side with Odoacer so as not to upset the balance of power in the Balkans, with the result that the Gauls decided either to seek accommodation with Euric, or full independence, or alternatively they sought protection from some other foreign tribe such as the Burgundians or Franks, and Odoacer in his turn concluded a peace with Euric, which recognized Euric's conquests. This was the end of Roman Gaul. According to Victor of Vita (1.14), the Vandals conceded Sicily to Odoacer in return for tribute in 476, but still kept part of the island for themselves as a naval base. The probable reason for this was the declining health of Gaiseric, but it was still his death on 25 January 477 that brought a real respite for Odoacer and Italy. The end of Vandal raids certainly helped Odoacer, but it did not make his position secure.

Nepos had not been idle either. When he had learnt of the return of Zeno, he had despatched envoys to congratulate him and to ask his support against Odoacer. Verina supported Nepos' demands because his wife was her relative. Zeno was unwilling to commit his forces to combat in the West and therefore opted for a compromise solution. Zeno agreed to nominate Odoacer as *Patricius*, but told him to accept Nepos as Emperor. In consequence of this Odoacer recognized Nepos officially as Emperor and advertised this in his coinage, but as we shall see, in practice he did not obey Nepos. On 9 May 480 Nepos was killed at his villa near Salona by his own followers in a plot organized by Glycerius, and it is of course quite possible or probable that Odoacer played some role in the background. See the discussion later.

On 11 July 477 Odoacer killed *Comes* Brachila at Ravenna to instil fear in the Romans, as Jordanes states. This proves that Odoacer's position among the military was not secure and that he constantly faced the prospect of having to deal with a revolt and/or usurpation in the beginning of the reign. It suggests the likelihood that the Romans and the Senate could have sided with this Brachila, despite his apparent Germanic origins, against Odoacer and that it was necessary for Odoacer to act promptly to put fear into their hearts. This did not work because next year *vir nobilis* Adaric rebelled. Odoacer, however, defeated and executed the rebel with his relatives on 19 November 478. This time the example appears to have worked because the sources do not mention any new revolts for the succeeding years.[5] Odoacer's insecurity during his first years meant that Nepos and the East Romans did not have any reason to fear his intervention in Dalmatia.

There was also a Roman ruler called Syagrius in Gaul. He was the son of Aegidius. Syagrius succeeded Aegidius as lord of the area around Soissons, his capital, after his death in 465. He was known as *rex Romanorum* to the Franks, but was also called *Romanorum Patricius*. Consequently, his domains have been traditionally called a Roman kingdom or the Kingdom of Soissons, but it has also been suggested that he ruled the Roman kingdom together with *Comes* Paulus from 465 until the death of Paulus in 469. It was then as a result of this that Syagrius was left as the only Roman magnate in the north of Gaul while Odoacer formed an alliance with Childeric and advanced against the Alamanni in Italy or Raetia. This brought Odoacer to Italy and from there he went on to serve under the Romans. The sources are silent what Syagrius did during the period 465–486, which suggests that he attempted to stay aloof from troubles. However, in 486 the silence ends. It was then that Clovis, king of the Franks, attacked Syagrius and defeated him decisively. Syagrius sought a place of refuge from the Visigothic king Alaric II at Toulouse, but Alaric handed him over to Clovis who duly executed the last

Roman ruler of Gaul, presumably in about 487. There is no evidence for any contacts between Syagrius and the emperors/rulers in Rome/Ravenna or Constantinople, but it is of course possible that there were some contacts – at least churchmen would have maintained regular contacts with the Pope and it is therefore very likely that legitimate governments were also aware of the existence of Syagrius. Regardless, it is still clear that the legitimate Roman rulers in Italy and Constantinople did not have the military means to influence the destinies of any of these outlying Roman areas, and neither had Syagrius.[6]

Church Matters in 476–477

As soon as he was back in power Zeno removed the bishops of Antioch and Ephesus from their sees because both had opposed him and his supporter the Bishop of Constantinople Acacius. The other bishops asked for forgiveness for having agreed to sign the encyclicals, and were granted it by Acacius. Zeno nominated Stephen as Bishop of Antioch, but the locals were clearly hostile to Zeno and Acacius because 'the sons of the Antiochenes' killed Stephen, with sharpened reed-pens. His successor was one of his followers, John Codonatus, but he was replaced by a pro-Chalcedonian, Stephen, after only three months in early 477. As we shall see, this, however, was not the end of the ecclesiastical troubles in Antioch. Zeno also intended to exile Timothy, the Bishop of Alexandria, but changed his mind when he learnt that Timothy was already old and close to dying. Timothy was allowed to die in peace on 31 July 477. The Alexandrians chose as his successor Peter Mongus. When Zeno learnt of this, he announced a death penalty on Peter and reappointed Timothy Salophaciolus, the successor of Proterius, as bishop and dispatched him back to his see. When Zeno's orders reached Alexandria in early September 477, it caused rioting and bloodshed while Peter fled into hiding.[7]

The Persian Front 475–484[8]

According to Joshua the Stylite (9–11), the Persians fought three wars against the Hepthalite Huns and that it was largely thanks to Roman money that the Persian *shahanshah* Peroz was initially successful against the Huns, presumably in about 474/5, but was then taken prisoner by them. He also states that when Zeno heard of this, he sent money to ransom the king and reconciled the two parties. He then claims that Peroz renewed the war but with the result that his army was completely destroyed and he was taken captive once again. This time Peroz promised thirty mules loaded with silver coins in return for his freedom. But the state coffers were empty because of the wars he had fought and he was able to collect only about twenty loads. Peroz then gave his son Kavadh as hostage for the remaining ten loads and was released. When Peroz returned to his own country, he imposed a poll tax, got together the required ten loads of silver and got his son back. In other words, the Romans did not contribute money this time. Joshua's statement that Peroz was captured twice is usually dismissed (e.g. by Blockley, 1992, 215 n.29), but this is definitely not so because three wars against the Hepthalites explain far better than two wars (474/5 and then again 484) why the Persians remained inactive in the west after 475.

    Furthermore, one can use military analysis of the texts of al-Tabari (i.874–7), Balami (428ff.), Theophanes (AM 5967–8) and Procopius (*Wars* 1.3.1–4.35) to support the case for two captures before the third campaign. All of these sources describe the final defeat, in which the Persians were destroyed with the use of hidden pits and feigned flights in 484, but in addition to this they provide descriptions of two other wars with different details. In other words, the two other wars that were different from each other describe the two other wars mentioned by Joshua the Stylite.

The second Hepthalite war was fought in about 479. The period of recovery from the destruction of the army at the second campaign naturally took longer. The two most obvious reasons are as follows. Firstly, it was difficult to rebuild the army when the Persians still had to pay the ransom for the son held hostage without Roman support. Second, the revolts of Albania, Iberia and Persarmenia[9] in about 481–4 described by the Armenian Lazar Parpeci delayed such operations even further. Lazar's description makes it clear that the Persian armies were not fighting against the Hepthalites at the beginning of these revolts, that the preparations for the campaign began in winter 483, and that Peroz probably launched his campaign later in 483 [esp. Bedrosian tr. pp.273–4, g138; p.288, g145].

In sum, it is clear that the Persians were preoccupied with other problems from 474 until 484 and were in no position to cause serious troubles, despite the best efforts of Illus as we shall see.[10]

Zeno vs. Armatus in 477

As noted above, initially the treacherous Isaurian Zeno honoured his word to the equally untrustworthy Armatus so that Armatus's son *Caesar* Basiliscus sat beside Zeno when he presided over the chariot races and both presented awards to the charioteers. However Zeno was well aware that Armatus had not honoured any of his promises in the past and that there was a danger that when Basiliscus reached manhood Armatus would get rid of him. Illus urged Zeno to kill Armatus because Armatus was also his enemy. It is actually possible that Zeno was initially unwilling to do this because it was possible to use Armatus and his supporters against those who supported Illus, but the fact that Illus held Zeno's brother as a hostage, together with the future danger posed by the adulthood of Basiliscus, was clearly enough to convince Zeno to accept Illus' advice. Consequently, Zeno convinced Armatus' protégé and bodyguard Onulf to murder the man who had done most to promote his career. This suggests a likelihood in which Zeno used Onulf as his assassin precisely because Armatus thought that he had nothing to fear from him. The murder took place near Dekimon when Armatus was on his way to preside over the races. His son Basiliscus was ordained as priest at Blachernae.[11]

The murder of Armatus was popular with the people because he had made himself hated through his behaviour as a wealthy treacherous dandy and seducer.[12] The author who recorded the murder and the reaction of the populace described the event as follows:

> This man had very great influence on Zenonis the empress and on Basiliscus himself. He was killed by the emperor Zeno and the citizens were overjoyed at the slaughter of this man. For in the time of emperor Leo, he cut off the hands of whatever Thracians he caught and sent them to the rebels [*this refers to the revolt of Theoderic Strabo and proves that Armatus had achieved some significant successes against the*

Goths, presumably by guerrilla warfare]. But Onooulphos [*Onulf*] killed him, a poor man who when he had come recently from the barbarians Harmatius had welcomed and first made a count, then the general of the Illyrians, and he readied a great deal of money to hold a banquet [*presumably to celebrate the promotion*]. But he repaid this man's barbaric disloyalty with a murderous hand. Translation of Suda alpha 3968 (Suda online www.stoa.org) by Jennifer Benedict with vetting by Catharine Roth and David Whitehead.

The End of the Vandal war in 477[13]

The death of Gaiseric in 477 had dissolved the previous treaties with the Vandals, and Zeno sought to renew the peace treaty with Huneric their new ruler. He sent Alexander, the guardian of Olybrius' wife, as an ambassador to Carthage. When Alexander and other envoys returned in 477/8, they informed Zeno that Huneric was prepared to renounce all claims that Gaiseric had regarding the confiscated property of Huneric's wife and Carthagian merchants. He was also prepared to forget all the other grievances as well. From other sources, like Victor of Vita (2.2), we know that Alexander was also seeking to obtain concessions for the Orthodox in the Vandal kingdom. Huneric agreed to these too. According to Malchus the real reason for Huneric's readiness to agree to all terms of peace was that the Vandals feared war more than anything else because they had not maintained their military readiness and had grown weak. It is probable that Zeno knew all this, but he had problems of his own and was therefore quite prepared to conclude peace with the Vandals.

Assassination Attempts and Revolts in 477–479[14]

It is probable that the murder of Armatus contributed to what happened next. Zeno wisely attempted to get rid off Illus. Armatus was by no means the only person who posed a threat to the Emperor. According to John of Antioch there were three attempts on the life of Illus. The first attempt was already made before a year had elapsed from the return of Zeno to power. He states that Paulus, who was a member of the Emperor's household and therefore a slave, was detected with a drawn sword to kill Illus. Zeno defused the problem by handing over Paulus to Illus for punishment. He also appears to have attempted to sooth Illus with honours which included the consulship for the year 478. The idea was to lull Illus into a false sense of security.

In the course of the year 477 the position of Theoderic Strabo improved, contrary to the wishful expectations of Zeno. He had managed to increase the size of his own force by adding to its strength some of the followers of Theoderic the Amal and other tribes and forces. These other tribes must have included other Ostrogothic tribes together with the tribes of Alans and Huns who had previously joined the Goths or had been settled in Thrace. In addition to this, it is probable that he managed to add to his army the Rugi who had been stationed at Arcadiopolis and Bizye under Marcian. The weakening of Theoderic the Amal and the strengthening of the position of Theoderic Strabo led Zeno to send envoys to Strabo who suggested peace on terms that he would give his son as a hostage, and would keep his loot and would live in peace as a private citizen as Theoderic

Strabo had once suggested himself. This, however, was no longer acceptable to Theoderic who stated that now that he had assembled the tribes he had to feed them. Consequently, Zeno ordered all the *tagmata* (military units) to be assembled from their garrisons close to the Black Sea and from all Asian and eastern districts. As a result of this, a large army was assembled for the forthcoming war together with the baggage wagons, and cattle and grain and other necessary things were purchased. The soldiers were eager to fight because Illus was in charge of the operations. This proved to be an illusion because Illus was soon to be replaced by Martinianus soon.[15]

The second attempt on the life Illus took place in the midst of the war preparations in 478. According to the official version the plotter was Verina presumably because she detested the influence of Illus, but one cannot entirely rule out the possibility that Zeno was involved as well. This time it was an Alan who attacked Illus in the *schola* of the *magister*. It seems probable that the *schola* of the *magister* means one of the *scholae* in the Palace belonging to the units also called *scholae*, who served under the *Comes Domesticorum* and whose superior was *Magister Officiorum* Illus. I would therefore suggest that Verina had through her own henchmen managed to convince one of the *scholarii* who served under Illus to assassinate him. The would-be assassin however was detected and arrested. The Alan was then tortured and he named the Phrygian Praetorian Prefect Epinicus as the man behind the attempt. According to John of Antioch, Illus then released the man because he did not harbour any anger against him – after all he had only been a gullible fool in the service of others. It is practically certain that Illus knew full well who was behind the attempt even though he could not find any concrete evidence for it. He was prepared to bide his time. The news of another failed attempt on the life of Illus frightened Zeno. He sacked Epinicus immediately and confiscated his property in an effort to appease Illus. However, Zeno did not stop at this. According to John of Antioch, Zeno also bought a peace with Theoderic Strabo, presumably because he urgently needed someone to act as a counterbalance against Illus. Illus in his turn dispatched Epinicus to Isauria under guard.[16] It is probable that the reference to the peace between Zeno and Theoderic Strabo telescopes the events and that it actually took place later in 479 after the return of Illus to the capital (see below) unless of course there were more changes in the allegiances of each party than are known.

According to the version preserved by John of Antioch, Illus wanted to interrogate Epinicus in person and he was only seeking an excuse to do so. It was the death of his brother Aspalius that gave him this excuse. He left the capital to attend the funeral in 478. Epinicus revealed that Verina was behind this plot. It was because of this that Illus stayed in Isauria until Zeno recalled him to Constantinople to protect it against Theoderic Strabo after the earthquake had damaged the walls of the capital in September 479. The earthquake had apparently damaged the walls significantly so that additional manpower was sorely needed for the protection of the capital. When Illus reached Chalcedon, he brought his friend and supporter Pamprepius to him. Pamprepius was a black man who had been born in Panopolis, Thebaid, Egypt, and who was openly a Hellene (pagan) Neoplatonic philosopher. Illus had promoted his career before his leaving for Isauria, but once he had left the capital his enemies had convinced Zeno and Verina to exile him to Pergamum in Mysia. From this date onwards, Pamprepius would serve as Illus' permanent advisor and companion much akin to the relationship of Marcellinus with

Sallustius or King Arthur with the wizard Merlin. Military men needed wise philosophers as their advisors. Zeno met all the dignitaries at a distance of 50 stades (6 miles) in front of Chalcedon and it was there that Illus' representatives presented the evidence against Verina. Illus demanded that Zeno hand Verina over to his wife's brother Matronianus who would then escort Verina to be consecrated in the church at Tarsus. Zeno agreed, but Verina was then transferred to Dalisandus and then to Cherris. In addition to this, Epinicus was released as a reward for his confession and Pamprepius was rewarded with the office of *Quaestor*.

Malalas (15.12) and Theophanes (AM5972) have preserved for us an entirely different account. According to them, Zeno and Illus conspired together to exile Verina so that Zeno sent Illus to Isauria to release his brother Longinus who was being held hostage by Illus. Then, as agreed with Zeno, Illus dispatched a message through Verina in which he claimed to be afraid of Zeno and therefore stayed in Isauria. Zeno then persuaded Verina to go to Illus and convince him that it would be safe to return to Constantinople with Longinus. Verina was duly imprisoned in Isauria and Longinus brought back to Constantinople in the company of Illus. Longinus was then made *MVM praesentalis* and consul. These appointments, however, can be dated to have taken place only after 485. Consequently, in this case the account of John of Antioch is to be preferred because it fits the other evidence better, like the *fasti* of consuls.

The War against the Ostrogoths 478–479

Thanks to the failed assassination attempt and the subsequent self-imposed exile of Illus in Isauria, Zeno was forced to appoint Martinianus as *strategos* (general) of the campaign against Theoderic Strabo. We do not know what the official title of Martinianus was, but it is possible that he was *MVM praesentalis* as the PLRE2 suggests because it is clear that the commander of a large army would have needed some official standing to command his subordinates. On the other hand, Malchus claims that his appointment disordered the army immediately to such an extent that the soldiers bribed their superiors so that they would not have to fight. This implies that the soldiers did not have any trust in his abilities and possibly also that Martinianus was not given any high military rank now or before this.[17]

The second part of Zeno's plan was to use Theoderic the Amal against his namesake. Zeno sent envoys in which he stated that Theoderic the Amal should prove himself worthy of his title as Roman *strategos* (general) and engage the Ostrogoths of Theoderic Strabo. Theoderic the Amal's answer was that he would fight if Zeno and the whole Senate swore that they would never make a treaty with Theoderic Strabo. The Senate swore that they would not make any treaty unless Zeno wanted it, and Zeno swore that he would abide by the current agreement unless Theoderic the Amal broke it first.[18]

The two sides then agreed to a plan according to which Theoderic, whose army was then at Marcianople/Marcianopolis, would move his forces to the gates of the Haemus range where he would be met by the *MVM per Thracias* with 2,000 horsemen and 10,000 footmen. The Romans also promised that Claudius, the paymaster of Gothic Federates, would meet them with the money. Once the Amal Ostrogoths had crossed the Haemus range, they would meet at the river Hebrus near Adrianople another army consisting of 6,000 horsemen and 20,000 footmen, and if this was not enough the Romans had more men available for combat at Heraclea and other towns and forts near Byzantium (Constantinople).[19]

It is clear that the force under the *MVM per Thracias* belonged to his field army and those garrisoning the towns and forts near Byzantium belonged to the praesental forces and other forces that had now been assembled near the capital. This leaves the problem of which forces were stationed near Adrianople and under whom they served. The size of the contingent is consistent with the size of one praesental army and it is possible that it was the western praesental army and that the eastern praesental army together with reinforcements had been assembled near the capital, but it is equally possible that the two forces mentioned were both under the *MVM per Thracias* so that these forces included the Thracian field army, the *limitanei* and those Federates that had stayed loyal. If the East Romans had maintained their forces close to the official establishment figures but with the inclusion of loyal Federates, the *MVM per Thracias* would certainly have had access to 8,000 cavalry and 30,000 infantry, but we simply do not know this with any certainty because Malchus fails to state who was leading the forces near Adrianople, even if the fact that he did not name any commander can be taken as evidence that they belonged to the Field Army of Thrace. However, as shall be made clear, it is practically certain the entire force was under the Master of the Soldiers of Thrace.

There are basically two versions of what happened next. According to the Ostrogothic version, when Theoderic the Amal then marched his forces to the gates of Haemus as had been agreed there were neither the Master of the Soldiers of Thrace nor the soldiers stationed at the Hebrus near Adrianople there to meet him. This can also be taken to mean that the forces stationed near Adrianople served under the *MVM per Thracias*. This version claims that the Romans had purposely kept away from the place of meeting so that the two Ostrogothic forces would fight against each other and thereby weaken themselves. According to the Roman version, which is presented as a list of complaints made by Zeno to Theoderic the Amal by Malchus, the traitor was none other than Theoderic the Amal himself. Theoderic the Amal had first promised to fight on his own, but had then demanded help from the Romans and when the Romans had then promised to send the soldiers, he had still secretly communicated with Theoderic Strabo. When the *MVM per Thracias* then learnt of the secret negotiations between the Ostrogothic leaders he had not dared to meet him or combine his forces with him because he feared a trap. The reference to the combining of forces once again suggests that the *MVM per Thracias* commanded all 8,000 horsemen and 30,000 footmen. This version receives further support from Malalas (15.9) who states that Theoderic the Amal became afraid of Zeno after he had seen what had happened to Armatus. The problem with this is that Malalas associated this piece of information with the details of the later revolt. Regardless, the distrust of Theoderic in the immediate aftermath of the murder of Armatus would certainly explain why he might have started to make feelers towards his tribal opponent.[20]

According to the Ostrogothic version, when the Amal was then marching through the central wilderness he came to the area around the Mountain Sondis which barred the way if the enemy force occupied it, and now it was occupied by the army of Theoderic Strabo. The two sides attacked each other and took as booty cattle, horses and other valuable things. This seems to suggest a successful ambush by the forces of Theoderic

Strabo. Theoderic, the son of Triarius, resorted to the use of psychological warfare and rode close to the Amal camp, insulted the leader as a child and betrayer of their race and claimed that the Romans had lured Theoderic the Amal there at the gates with false promises so that the two Ostrogothic armies would fight against each other while no Roman blood would be spilled. This proves that Theoderic Strabo was well aware of the Roman plans and what the Romans had promised to Theoderic the Amal, and if the Roman version is correct then the source of this information would have been Theoderic the Amal himself. The disgruntled followers of the Amal voiced their complaints. On the following day, Theoderic Strabo went to a hill overlooking the Amal camp and continued in the same vein. This time he also accused Theoderic the Amal as a destroyer of their race and stated that he was leading them to destruction. Strabo claimed that the followers of Theoderic the Amal had begun their campaign with two to three horses each but were now horseless and forced to go on foot. This actually suggests that Theoderic Strabo had somehow managed to ambush the forces of Theoderic the Amal with the result that he had managed to capture most of the horses in the encounter mentioned. The end result of all this was that the followers of Theoderic the Amal demanded that he join forces with his namesake. So the two leaders met on opposite banks of a river and made an agreement not to fight against each other, after which they both sent envoys to 'Byzantium'.[21]

It is impossible to know which of the versions is correct, but on balance it would seem likely that, despite all the treacherous behaviour of the Romans and Zeno in particular and Malchus' claim of Roman duplicity, the two Theoderics had agreed on a common plan and that the idea had been to force the Amal Ostrogoths to join forces with their brethren so that they would stand united against the Romans. The main reason for this conclusion is that even the Ostrogothic version makes it clear that Theoderic Strabo was fully aware of all of the movements and plans of the Amal forces and that the Romans did indeed accuse Theoderic the Amal of having made secret promises of friendship to Theoderic Strabo. Furthermore, Theoderic the Amal did nothing to prevent his namesake from attempting to turn his men against the Romans. This has all the earmarks of being a barbarian conspiracy as claimed by Zeno.

Now that the Ostrogoths stood united, both leaders dispatched envoys to Zeno. Theoderic the Amal accused Zeno of the betrayal of the promises and demanded land with sufficient grain to support his forces until the next harvest season and the sending of distributors of revenues called *domestici* to him immediately. Otherwise his men would have to pillage to obtain what they needed. To lend weight to his words, Theoderic advanced his army into Thrace. Theoderic Strabo, son of Triarius, demanded that Zeno implement the agreements made by Leo, and that those relatives of his who were alive were to be returned to him. If they had died, Strabo demanded that Illus and other Isaurians whom he trusted were to swear this on oath.[22]

Zeno's response was to accuse Theoderic the Amal of being a traitor, but still he promised him 1,000 lbs of gold, 40,000 lbs of silver and a yearly income of 10,000 *nomismata*[23] if he attacked and defeated Theoderic Strabo. In addition to this, Zeno promised the daughter of Olybrius or some other noblewoman as his wife. This would have made Theodric the Amal a member of the imperial family. The plot failed. Theoderic the Amal stayed loyal to the Ostrogothic cause with the result that Zeno ordered his soldiers to assemble and prepare for war and be in good spirits because he would lead the campaign in person.

This took place clearly at a time when Illus had already departed to the east. The soldiers were elated because bravery in front of the Emperor was a sure path to glory. Now they were so eager to fight that whereas they had previously paid their officers bribes to avoid having to fight, they now paid a bribe to join the campaign. The enthusiasm showed. The soldiers captured the scouts Theoderic the Amal had sent, and the guards of the Long Wall (presumably of Chersonese) defended it successfully against the bodyguard *moira* of Theoderic. But then the soldiers were betrayed in their high hopes of glory. According to Malchus, it was immediately after this that the true cowardly character of Zeno demonstrated itself again. He abandoned the campaign and returned to the capital with the result that the soldiers became mutinous. The soldiers demanded to be led against the barbarian enemies who were sacking their cities. More favourable explanations for the abandonment of the campaign would of course be that Zeno withdrew to the capital because of the earthquake that had damaged the walls of Constantinople in September 479 and the capital now needed extra defenders, and/or that the return of Illus to Chalcedon at the head of his army required Zeno's attention. In my opinion, we should date these two events to have been simultaneous with the abandonment of the campaign so that it was then in about October 479 that Zeno and Illus were reconciled in the manner described above. When the acting commander Martinianus learnt of the mutinous state of the army, he recommended its immediate disbanding before the soldiers would unite and revolt. Zeno agreed and ordered the soldiers back to their winter quarters.[24]

Zeno's next move was to seek peace with Theoderic Strabo, whose forces were near the Rhodope Mountains, on whatever terms possible. The arrival of Illus with his Isaurians would have strengthened Zeno's hand. The other alternatives are that Zeno sought peace with Theoderic before he had reached accord with Illus so that his hand in those negotiations would be stronger, or that he just sought peace with both in order to solve the situation. Theoderic's terms of peace were: food and pay for 13,000 men chosen by Theoderic; command of two units of *scholae*; the return of property; the position of *magister mililitum in praesenti*; the return of relatives. Zeno conceded all, removed Theoderic the Amal from office, and distributed money immediately to the Goths.[25]

Theoderic the Amal had been checkmated and was forced to evacuate Thrace in about October 479. According to Malchus, he had also lost many men to the military action of Roman *stratêgoi* (generals) and was facing a dire situation. He led his army west and pillaged everything en route including the city of Stobi in Macedonia. When the citizens of Thessalonica learnt of his presence, they suspected that Zeno wanted to hand the city over to him. This resulted in a riot in which the statues of Zeno were overthrown and the prefect John (Ioannes/Johannes) would have been killed had not the officials and priests calmed the men while he was taken to safety. The people, however, did not trust the prefect. They took away the keys of the gates and gave them to the archbishop, and then organized guards and citizen patrols while still keeping the local *stratêgos* in office because they considered him loyal to the Romans.[26] The situation was clearly not healthy when both the soldiers and civilians suspected the Emperor of colluding with the barbarians, and were prepared to overthrow him. We do not have to wait long for this discontent to materialize in the capital.

When Zeno learnt that nobody was willing to fight on his behalf, he asked Theoderic to send envoys to him to discuss terms of peace. Theoderic agreed to do this while he advanced to Heraclea in Macedonia. The bishop of the city sent him and his men gifts so that Theoderic did not ravage their countryside. Zeno dispatched Adamantius to offer land in Pautalia with the idea that if Theoderic Strabo caused trouble he could use Theoderic the Amal against him, and if Theoderic the Amal caused trouble he could use the forces of Illyricum and Thrace against him. He also gave Adamantius 200 lbs of gold to transport adequate supplies for the Ostrogoths in Pautalia because it was now past the harvest season. While the envoys were still at the capital, Constantinople, Zeno received the news that some of the soldiers had ambushed John the prefect of Thessalonica. Zeno ordered Adamantius to settle the quarrel, which he promptly did.[27]

In the meantime, Theoderic the Amal had asked Sidimund, who received regular pay from the Emperor as a federate in his estate located close to Epidamnus (Dyrrachium) in Epirus, to find a way to capture the city of Epidamnus. This Sidimund was of the same tribe as Theoderic and also a cousin of Aedoingus, who in his turn was a close associate of Verina and a commander of the *Domestici*. This suggests a likelihood that both Theoderic and Sidimund were aware of the imprisonment of Verina and of the potential problems this could cause for her protégés. Sidimund was more loyal to his tribe with the result that he convinced the inhabitants of Epidamnus/Dyrrachium to abandon their city and seek a place of refuge on the islands or in some other city because the Emperor had sent Adamantius there for the purpose of handing over the city to Theoderic. He told the same story to the 2,000-strong garrison and convinced them to leave the city too. This force would have been sufficient to hold the city against any Ostrogothic attack, which shows well how the Ostrogoths were able to play the distrust felt by the people and soldiers against Zeno to their own advantage. Both were quite prepared to believe the worst. When the news of this was brought to Theoderic, he demanded that the inhabitants of Heraclea, who had abandoned their city and fled to a fortress, provide him with supplies of grain and wine. The inhabitants refused with the result that Theoderic burned most of the city and then marched his army through the difficult and narrow road. Theoderic ordered his cavalry to advance at the double and surprise the defenders on the heights occupying the wall blocking the route, which they did. The Roman garrison panicked when they saw the Ostrogothic cavalry and fled without closing the gates, so the Ostrogoths were able to walk in. Theoderic then took the leadership of the van while Soas commanded the centre and Theodimund the rear. When they reached level terrain, Theoderic was convinced that no-one was following them and allowed the wagon train and baggage animals to march at their leisure while he advanced at the double with the cavalry to capture the city of Lychnidus by surprise. The attempt failed due to its advantageous location. On top of this, it had a plentiful supply of water thanks to the springs located inside the fortress and the plentiful supplies that had been stored there. So Theoderic bypassed it and advanced to Scampia, which he managed to capture because the inhabitants had fled. After this he marched at the double to Epidamnus which he was able to capture without any trouble because the city was undefended thanks to the stratagem of Sidimund.[28] In other words, Theoderic the Amal was just as duplicitous as the Romans accused him of being. Theoderic acted as if he would agree to conclude the peace, but in truth used this lull in hostilities to his own advantage.

When Adamantius learnt of the duplicity of his foe, he was still prepared to negotiate because the situation was now very grave. Theoderic had occupied a port city in the

Adriatic, and the Romans were in a state of panic. They did not need another Gaiseric roaming the seas. Adamantius dispatched one of the imperial mounted couriers, who were called *magistriani* (*agentes in rebus*), to Theoderic with the message to stop where he was and not to capture any ships before he arrived to negotiate. Adamantius also asked Theoderic to send a hostage as a pledge for his own safety during the negotiations. After this Adamantius left Thessalonica and met Sabinianus at Edessa. Adamantius informed Sabinianus that he had been appointed as the acting *stratêgos* of all forces in the region, i.e. he had been made *MVM per Illyricum*, while Philoxenus informed Onulf that he had been removed from office. It was probably because of this that we find Onulf later serving under his brother Odoacer in Italy. After this, Adamantius and Sabinianus discussed what to do next. The problem was that Sabinianus had with him only some of his own mercenaries (*misthoforôn oikeôn*, i.e. the *bucellarii*), which were insuffient for a full scale war. The regular *stratiotai* (soldiers, presumably the footmen in this case) and *tagmata* (units, presumably the cavalry) were scattered throughout the cities and a part of the army was with the *stratêgos* (*magister militum per Illyricum*) Onulf. Therefore the men decided to inform everyone of the appointment of Sabinianus first and then to assemble the army. They also decided to continue the negotiations, undoubtedly because this was the wisest course for them when the army was dispersed.[29]

The above information regarding the locations of Roman military forces (see the accompanying map) is interesting also for its strategic implications. On the basis of it we know that Onulf was not in Dyrrachium though he was still somewhere in Illyricum. This brings up the interesting possibility that Onulf, as brother of Odoacer, had placed himself and his forces somewhere close to Nepos, possibly at Epidaurum so as to threaten Salona if Nepos made any move against Odoacer. In other words, there is a possibility that Onulf was using the regular forces of East Rome to threaten Nepos. However, the fact that Zeno was able to remove Onulf from office proves that the forces he commanded were still primarily loyal to East Rome and therefore likely to consist mostly of regulars – after all Onulf owed his position entirely to Armatus and was therefore unlikely to possess any sizable force of his own. The problem with the above is that there is of course no definite evidence for it; it is possible that Onulf was actually in Macedonia and that his forces were among those that Sabinianus assembled at Lychnidus (see below).

It was then that the previously sent *agens in rebus* arrived together with a Gothic presbyter. Adamantius and Sabinianus took the men with them and marched to Lychnidus after which Adamantius sent Theoderic the message to come to a place close to Lychnidus to negotiate, or if he wanted Adamantius to come to him to send Soas and Dagistheus as hostages. Theoderic sent the men, but told them to remain at Scampia until Sabinianus gave his oath that the men would be returned safely. Sabinianus refused to swear the oath because he never swore anything for anyone. Adamantius attempted to make him change his mind, but to no avail.[30]

If this is true then it proves that Sabinianus was at least superficially an honest man because he did intend to attack the Ostrogoths, but at the same time perhaps it would prove that he was not a great commander fully abreast of the situation. A more ruthless commander might have given his oath to fool his enemies to capture their generals, but on the basis of the above, this was not for Sabinianus. Famous Roman commanders such as Trajan, Caracalla, Gallienus and Belisarius, or the Persian Suren/Surenas (vs Crassus)

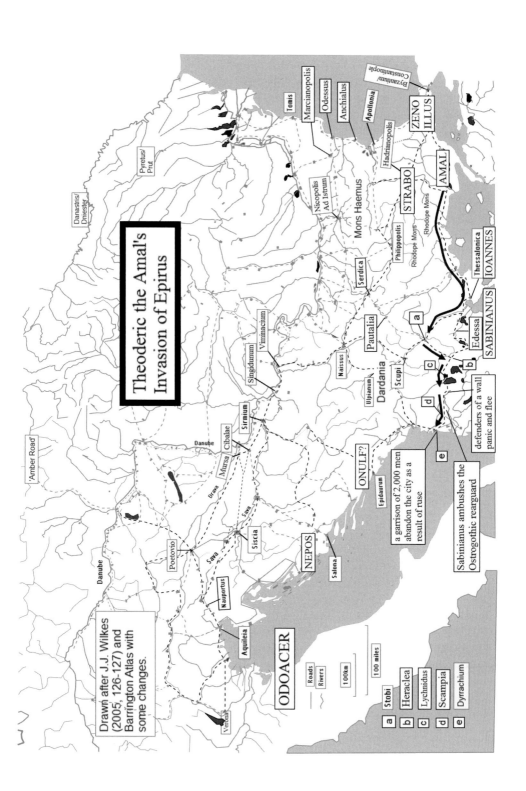

Theoderic the Amal's Invasion of Epirus

Drawn after J.J. Wilkes (2005, 126-127) and Barrington Atlas with some changes.

a garrison of 2,000 men abandon the city as a result of ruse

Sabinianus ambushes the Ostrogothic rearguard

defenders of a wall panic and flee

a	Stobi
b	Heraclea
c	Lychnidus
d	Scampia
e	Dyrrachium

Roads
Rivers

100km
100 miles

ODOACER

NEPOS

ONULF?

ZENO
ILLUS

STRABO

AMAL

IOANNES

SABINIANUS

Byzantium/
Constantinople

Tomis
Marcianopolis
Odessus
Anchialus
Apollonia
Nicopolis
Ad Istrum
Hadrianopolis
Mons Haemus
Rhodope Mons
Rhodope Mons
Philippopolis
Serdica
Thessalonica
Edessa
Pautalia
Scupi
Naissus
Ulpianum
Dardania
Vimnacium
Singidunum
Epidaurum
Salona
Sirmium
Cibalae
Mursa
Danube
Drava
Sava
Sava
Sisicia
Nauportus
Poetovio
Aquileia
Verona
Danube
'Amber Road'
Pyretus/
Prut
Danastris/
Dniester

and Shapur I (vs. Valerian) certainly felt no compunction about lying under oath. Nevertheless, on the basis of subsequent events it is clear that Sabinianus was a very good commander, on a par with Theoderic the Amal who definitely deserved his title the Great – but it should be noted that in contrast to Sabinianus, Theoderic the Great did not have any problems in giving his oath to the Romans and then betraying it at the first opportunity, and neither should have Sabinianus. This brings up the other and even likelier possibility which is that Sabinianus wanted to sabotage the peace negotiations so that he could fight the war that he had been dreaming about. On the basis of the above reaction of the native Roman soldiers to the news that the Emperor would lead them against the barbarians and then their reaction to the abandonment of the campaign, the natives had had enough of the appeasement of the barbarians and were yearning to fight. It is very likely that Sabinianus was one of these men. He wanted to fight and he wanted to prove his worth as a military commander. He wanted to see barbarian blood shed for the crimes they had committed against the Romans.

Sabinianus' attitude had made the situation unbearable for Adamantius. At nightfall, he took 200 mounted soldiers and marched through the hills to a guard tower near Epidamnus/Dyrrachium. He asked Theoderic to meet him there. The two men then held a discussion across a river. Theoderic accused the Romans of duplicity which had forced him to join forces with Strabo while Adamantius reminded him of the honours bestowed on him and accused him of duplicity. Our source, Malchus, is of the opinion that Theoderic was right in this case, but as I have noted above, in my opinion it is actually more likely that it was Theoderic who had been duplicitious in this case. Adamantius' suggestion was that Theoderic would evacuate Epirus and move to Dardania which was fertile and depopulated and which therefore offered the Goths land to farm and support themselves. The idea was of course to move the Ostrogoths away from the Adriatic. Theoderic claimed that he would be glad to accept this, but that his men would not. They wanted to rest after their long march and stay where they were through the winter. He promised to go to Dardania once the spring started if the Romans would send a guide for this purpose. In addition to this, Theoderic promised to place his baggage and all the non-combatants in any city the Emperor chose, presumably as hostages, in addition to which he promised his mother and sister as hostages and promised to take 6,000 of his best soldiers to Thrace. Theoderic promised to use these men and the Illyrian army and whatever forces Zeno gave him for the purpose of destroying Theoderic Strabo on condition that the Emperor would make him praesental *magister* instead of Theoderic Strabo and would receive him in Constantinople as a Roman citizen. This may imply that Theoderic Strabo had revolted again in support of Marcian (see later), but is not conclusive because he was still the office holder in this discussion. The Amal was also ready to go to Dalmatia and restore Nepos to power in Italy if the Emperor preferred this. Adamantius answered that he would need to consult the Emperor first. It is impossible to know if Theoderic made these promises in good faith because subsequent events made all these plans futile, but on the surface these promises imply that Theoderic was quite prepared to ally himself with the Romans.

In the meantime, while Adamantius was on his mission, Sabinianus, who had assembled the Roman army at Lychnidus, learnt that the Ostrogoths under Theoderic's brother Theodimund were taking their baggage together with most of their wagons and

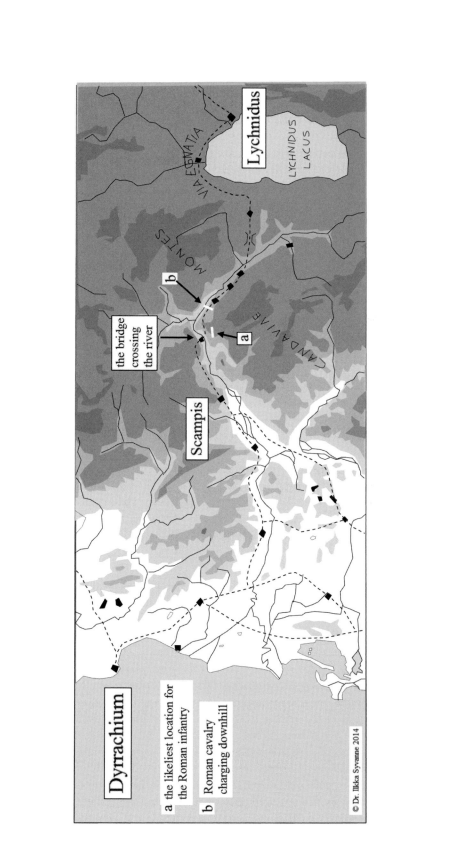

Dyrrachium

a the likeliest location for the Roman infantry

b Roman cavalry charging downhill

the bridge crossing the river

Scampis

Lychnidus

LYCHNIDUS LACUS

VIA EGNATIA

MONTES

CANDAVIAE

© Dr. Ilkka Syvänne 2014

rearguard overconfidently from the Candavia Mountains down to the plains. Sabinianus realized that it would therefore be possible to surprise them, and he also realized that it would be possible to sabotage the peace negotiations by attacking the barbarians while Adamantius was negotiating. He took command of the cavalry in person and sent the infantry through the mountains to attack them from the flank, with precise orders when and where to attack. After this he ate dinner, collected his forces and marched out during the night. At daybreak Sabinianus led his cavalry against the Goths when they had already started their march. Theodimund and his mother did not attempt to organize any resistance, but fled immediately down to the plain, crossed a river and then broke the bridge so that it was impossible to follow them. This move also cut off the route of retreat for their own men with the result that despite their small numbers the remaining men regrouped and faced the attacking Roman cavalry. But when the Roman infantry appeared on the heights, they gave up any hope of resistance and scattered in flight. Sabinianus captured 2,000 wagons, more than 5,000 prisoners and plenty of booty most of which had been previously looted from the Romans. After this, Sabinianus returned in triumph to Lychnidus. It was there that he met Adamantius, who had just returned. According to Malchus, each was unaware of the other's exploits during the previous two nights, which actually appears to be true. It is unlikely that they would have cooperated and coordinated their actions, because if they had Sabinianus would have sworn the oath. Furthermore, subsequent events prove that the two men competed with each other for imperial favours. Without this knowledge it would be possible to suggest that the two men had formed a plot to lull Theoderic into a false sense of security which they would then have exploited by attacking the rearguard. This was clearly not the case. Sabinianus clearly wanted to sabotage any peace negotiations and preferred the military option as this made him the man of the hour with the potential to gain imperial favours. Before the capture of the Gothic wagons Sabinianus had also ordered the local cities to hand over wagons for his army, but now that he had captured the Gothic wagons there was no need for this, and Sabinianus was now able to advertise his success among the populace by informing them that he no longer needed the wagons.[31]

By comparing the number of captured Gothic wagons with the number of wagons in the Roman army under Aristus in 498/9, it is possible to make an educated guess regarding the overall size of the tribal army (retinue and levy) under Theoderic the Amal at this time. Aristus had 15,000 men and 520 wagons (Marc. 498), and if Theoderic's forces possessed a similar number of wagons, then Theoderic would have had ca. 57,692 tribal warriors altogether. This is of course only speculation, but it would help to explain why it was so difficult for the Romans to defeat the Amal Goths and why the areas that were given to the Amal Goths were insufficient to support them and their families.

The two men on the scene, Adamantius and Sabinianus, then launched PR campaigns by sending envoys to Zeno. Adamantius informed the Emperor of the negotiations he had conducted while Sabinianus (*strategos*, general) and Ioannes/Johannes (presumably now *hypostrategos*, second-in-command) wrote what they had achieved, magnified the importance of their victory and stated that there was no need to conclude any peace with the barbarian because they could either force him out of the country or wear him down with guerrilla war. News of the victory convinced Zeno and he recalled Adamantius. The likeliest reason for Zeno's readiness to fight now is that he was aware of the mood of the native population and what had taken place at Thessalonica. He undountedly thought that had he decided to appease Theoderic the Amal after the victory, he would have faced a revolt, and in fact this is what happened regardless. Therefore, Zeno ordered Sabinianus and Gento to resume combat. Gento was a Federate commander who had married a Roman woman in the area of Epirus and therefore was presumably eager to fight in defence of his and her estates. When Adamantius learnt of the decision, he assembled the soldiers, informed them of the Emperor's decision, praised their valour and ordered them to fight nobly.[32]

The Revolt of Marcian in late 479 and Theoderic Strabo[33]

Some time in late 479 a very serious incident took place in Constantinople, namely the usurpation attempt of Marcian (Marcianus) against Zeno. John of Antioch's dating for this is the end of Zeno's consulship. It is unfortunate that we cannot pinpoint the timing more precisely, but we know that it took place after two signal events: 1) Zeno and Illus had been reconciled with each other; 2) Zeno had concluded peace with Theoderic Strabo who was still far away from the capital. My own educated guess is that the coup took place in November or December.

Marcian (Fl. Marcianus) was the son of the Emperor Anthemius, and Aelia Marcia Euphemia daughter of the Emperor Marcian. He had also married Leontia, the younger daughter of the Emperor Leo. He had held consulships both in the West in 469 and in the East in 472. Leo had also made him *MVM Praesentalis* and *Patricius* (ca. 471–4). In short, he was better qualified to be emperor than Zeno. Marcian's claim for the throne however was based on the fact that his wife Leontia was born in the purple, while Zeno's wife Ariadne had been born when Leo was not yet Emperor. He had supported Basiliscus against Zeno but had apparently then changed sides because Zeno had not exiled him.

Marcian detested the treatment of Verina and decided to act against Zeno. The time was ripe for this because the native soldiers detested their 'cowardly' Isaurian Emperor. He formed a plot with his brothers Procopius Anthemius and Romulus, and Theoderic Strabo. According to John of Antioch, Marcian assembled a force of barbarians and local native Romans at the house of Caesarius. He had taken control of all the ferry boats between Chalcedon and Constantinople so that Zeno and Illus would be unable to bring help from across the straits. The commanders in charge were Marcian and Procopius so that one of them led his men against Zeno in the Palace and the other against Illus in the district of Varanus. The attack was timed to take place at midday (the 'siesta') when the Palace and the streets were all quiet. The attack on the Palace proceeded through the Stoa of the Delphax where the Delphic pillars varied their colours. John of Antioch says that on the side of Marcian fought Busalbus ('*hegoumenos stratiôtikou tagmatos*', commander of a *tagma* of soldiers, meaning presumably a unit of the bodyguards), Niketas (office unknown), and Theoderic son of Triarius. This implies that the attackers included Theoderic, but the account of Malchus (Blockley ed. fr. 22) implies that Theoderic only sided with Marcian and was not actually present in Constantinople. The attackers defeated the guards in a fierce and bloody battle and almost captured Zeno as well. The citizens of Constantinople fought on the rebel side and threw all kinds of objects on the soldiers supporting Zeno. In other words, they rather sided with the mostly Germanic forces fighting on behalf of Marcian against the Isaurians and other loyal forces which presumably included the *scholarii*. This proves how hated Zeno had become among the populace who yearned for a real native warrior to take charge of the realm. The rebels also took control of the house of Illus.

Then, at the moment of his triumph, Marcian made a fatal error. He halted his attack for the night and did not immediately proclaim himself Emperor. Even without the interference of Pamprepius, Marcian would still have won. According to Malchus (Blockley ed. fr. 23.24ff.), Illus was in a state of despair as a result of Marcian's revolt and it was only the encouragement of the philosopher Pamprepius that caused Illus to continue to fight on behalf of Zeno. During the night, Illus managed to obtain ships from Pylai, which he then used to ship his Isaurian soldiers from Chalcedon to Constantinople. He also managed to bribe some of the supporters of Marcian to desert to his side during the night. The rebels were in a state of jubilation and did not realise the need to take precautions. They apparently did not understand that the enemy could obtain ships from other sources and they did not understand the power that money had on some men. Consequently, Illus managed to surprise and capture Procopius and Romulus when they were bathing at the Bath of Zeuxippos.[34] It was then Illus' turn to be careless, because both of them managed to escape to Theoderic Strabo and then to Rome. Zeno demanded that Theoderic hand them over, but Theoderic refused. This means that if Theoderic had been present in person, he had managed to fight his way out of the capital where the brothers then joined him. However, as stated above, on the basis of Malchus it is likelier that Theoderic was not present in person. He had only formed an alliance with the rebels. In other words, in the course of the night, Illus neutralized at least half of the enemy force with a surprise attack. So when morning arrived, the loyalists had the upper hand. Marcian and his supporters were forced to abandon the Palace, which was then duly occupied by Zeno. Marcian and his men retreated to the Precinct of the Apostles and en route torched the house of Illus. Zeno stayed in the Palace and dispatched forces, presumably under Illus against the usurper. Marcian was defeated, sought safety from the Church of the Apostles, surrendered, was made a priest, and then was sent to Caesarea in Cappadocia. His wife Leontia was 'exiled' among the Sleepless Monks of Constantinople, and the property of those who had fled to Theoderic Strabo was confiscated.

According to Malchus (Blockley ed. fr. 22), when Theoderic Strabo learnt of the usurpation of Marcian, he assembled his forces and advanced towards Constantinople with the pretence that he was coming to the aid of Zeno. As noted above, it is probable that this is only partially true. Theoderic appears to have been party to the plot and had just arrived too late to participate in it. When Zeno learnt of this, he dispatched an envoy to announce that Theoderic's services were no longer needed and that the revolt had been put down. Theoderic claimed that he would not yet turn around because he needed to rest his men. His real idea was to exploit the situation because he saw that there were no defenders on the walls and he thought that the populace would side with him out of hatred of the Isaurians. This was precisely what Zeno feared. So Zeno sent Pelagius with a large sum of money to convince Theoderic to abandon his plans. This Pelagius did by handing money both to Theoderic and to other Goths and by using a combination of promises and threats. The greediness of the Goths prevented the wholesale destruction of the city because the Isaurians were not prepared to abandon it without a fight and had prepared long poles (*kontoi*) with linen and sulphur with the idea of setting the city on fire if attacked.

After Theoderic had left, Zeno dispatched a succession of envoys to Theoderic Strabo with the demand that he should hand over to him Procopius, Busalbus and their followers. Theoderic's reply was that it was not right for him to hand over those who had sought a place of refuge among his tribe, so these men lived with the Goths farming a small plot of land until some of them made their way to Rome.

Marcian, Ostrogoths and other troubles in 479/480–483

The withdrawal of Theoderic Strabo did not end Zeno's troubles. He faced troubles all around. Isauria, his home territory, was in revolt and the Isaurian rebels captured Corycus and Sebaste at about this time in 479/80. Unfortunately we do not know who was in charge of the operations against them, but one possible candidate would be Trocundes, brother of Illus. Furthermore, Marcian fled from Caesarea and gathered a great mass of peasants with which he attempted to capture Ancyra in Galatia. Trocundes, who was presumably *MVM per Orientem*, reached the scene first and defeated Marcian and his followers. He captured Marcian and his family and imprisoned them in Isauria. The PLRE2 dates this event to 479, but it may have taken place in 480. As a reward, Zeno appointed Trocundes as *MVM praesentalis* instead of Theoderic Strabo in 480 (see below), and placed Aetius (probably as *Comes Isauriae*) in charge of the war against the Isaurians. At about the same time, probably during the summer/fall of 480, Epinicus, *PPO* Dionysius and Thraustila formed a conspiracy, but were caught before they could launch their revolt. Epinicus was the former *PPO* who had attempted to murder Illus on behalf of Verina and who had been exiled to Isauria. It is therefore not surprising that he was involved in a plot to kill Zeno. It is possible, if unprovable, that Illus had urged him and the other conspirators to do this and that the subsequent assassination attempt against Illus himself was the result of this failed attempt on the life of Zeno, but the sources are silent on this. In fact, John of Antioch follows up this piece of text by describing the murder attempt against Illus, which must therefore have followed after the previously mentioned attempt against Zeno. The principal argument against this is that at the time Illus appears not to have had a candidate for the throne if Zeno had died. Therefore, it is still possible that he was not involved.[35]

According to a fragment of John of Antioch (fr. 212 Roberto ed. fr. 304), during the reign of Zeno a man called Theosebius usurped power in the east by claiming to be Procopius Anthemius, son of the usurper Marcian. The usurper bore resemblance to the real Procopius with the result that his usurpation met with some success before it was crushed. The fragment does not give us any details regarding the precise date or how the revolt was crushed. My own educated guess is that it must have taken place very soon after the failed second revolt of the real Marcian for it to have been feasible. It is also likely that it took place before the death of Sabinianus on 9 May 481 because the fragment is found before the 'Sabinianus fragment' in the sequence of fragments. It is unfortunate that we do not know the name of the person responsible for the crushing of the revolt. It is possible that it was once again Trocundes, or Aetius, Illus or some other general. My best educated guess however is that it was Trocundes again, that the revolt took place in about 480/81, and that Trocundes was possibly rewarded with a consulship in 482 for the effective and fast suppression of the two revolts.

Unsurprisingly, the quite apparent role of Theoderic Strabo in the Marcian conspiracy and his refusal to hand over the conspirators soured the relationship between Zeno and Theoderic with the result that Zeno removed Theoderic from office in 480 and appointed Trocundes as his successor. Theoderic Strabo's response was to renew his alliance with Theoderic the Amal. The Amal, however, was unable to bring any assistance to Strabo thanks to the fact that the forces of Sabinianus isolated Theoderic's Goths in Epirus. In spite of this, the alliance was still beneficial for Strabo because the Romans had to take into account in their plans the threat that the forces of the two Theoderics could unite. Sabinianus was therefore forced to concentrate most of his efforts on isolating the forces of Theoderic the Amal. This in turn meant that Theoderic Strabo was able to pillage cities throughout Thrace with relative impunity.[36]

Illus and his forces were still located in the capital, but Zeno was afraid to lead these or any other native and/or Isaurian force out against the foe. Zeno, however, rose to the occasion and formed an alliance with the Bulgarians/Huns. This is the first time the Bulgarians are mentioned in the sources, but we shall hear a lot more about them in the future. It is possible that it was thanks to Zeno's diplomatic activities that they turned their attention towards East Roman Thrace. In fact Zeno invited them to invade Thrace against Theoderic Strabo. Theoderic son of Triarius was not a novice in military matters. He advanced against the enemy and defeated them in battle. It is possible that the Roman plan had been to unite these Bulgarians with the forces posted in the capital, but if this had been the plan, the fast response of Theoderic had made it futile. Theoderic exploited his victory by advancing against the capital itself with the idea of taking it with a surprise attack, but Illus was too fast for him. Illus posted his forces at the gates before Theoderic's forces reached them. According to Evagrius and Theophanes, the reason for the failure was that Theoderic's army included high ranking relatives who were plotting to kill him. Theoderic moved his forces to Sycae (modern Galata) and tried to ship them across the Golden Horn, but this attack was once again defeated. The location makes it clear that there was a naval battle between Theoderic and the Imperial Fleet. Theoderic changed his strategy once again and moved his forces to *Pros Hestias* (presumably an area close to *Leosthenion*) and *Leosthenion* (see the Map of Hellespont and Bosporus) and tried to ship them to Bithynia. This attempt also failed, because the Imperial Fleet again defeated Theoderic in battle. Constantinople remained impregnable as long as there were enough men to man the walls and gates and the Imperial Fleet protected the sea walls. It is clear that Theoderic Strabo had recognized the same thing as the Crusaders of the Fourth Crusade later in 1204: it was easier to attack the city from the sea.[37]

Theoderic son of Triarius had no alternative but to try his luck on land. According to John of Antioch, Theoderic, together with his son Recitach, two brothers and wife, led his about 30,000 strong force of Scythians towards Greece (other sources claim Illyricum) but then disaster struck when he reached a place called *Stabula Diomedis* (the stable of Diomede).[38] According to the official version, Theoderic Strabo was mounting his horse one morning when it bolted and threw him onto an upright spear held in place by a thong/loop at the side of his tent or beside his carriage. John of Antioch mentions that it was rumoured that Theoderic was killed by his son Recitach because Theoderic had beaten him. Even if one cannot entirely rule this out, if the father was very forgiving towards his son, this still appears to be untrue, because, according to Evagrius, Theoderic died of the wound only a few days later. Whatever the truth, Recitach and his uncles succeeded Theoderic as rulers either in late 480 or in 481. Recitach murdered his uncles shortly after this and ravaged Thrace with even greater ferocity than his father had. The reference to 30,000 Scythians by John of Antioch should not be interpreted to mean the total force available for Theoderic and then to Recitach. Rather it should be seen as the personal retinue of Theoderic Strabo. To it one should add the squires accompanying them and the levy of all those tribes following Strabo. This figure would then be much higher, perhaps 80,000–100,000 fighting men.[39]

The Emperor Nepos was murdered by his *comites* Viator and Ovida at his villa near Salona on 9 May 480. Malchus (Blockley ed. fr.1.18ff.) claims that the assassination was organized by Nepos' personal enemy, his predecessor Glycerius, but I would suggest that possibly there was more to this than meets the eye. It is of course possible that this version is the whole truth and nothing but the truth, but there are three other possible explanations for the sudden success of this murder.[40]

Firstly, one should consider the possibility that it had been organized by Odoacer. The extant coins prove that Odoacer had recognized Nepos as his figurehead Emperor as required by the Eastern Empire – Zeno had no other alternative because Nepos was married to a relative of Verina. The sacking of Onulf as Master of the Soldiers in Illyricum could have been interpreted as a sign that the Eastern Government was no longer satisfied with the situation and was planning to oust Odoacer and install Nepos as de facto ruler of Italy. If Odoacer then learnt of the intention of Theoderic to install Nepos on the throne, this could have been all that was needed for him to initiate a pre-emptive strike to kill Nepos. However, this is unlikely on the grounds that we find Ovida defending Dalmatia against Odoacer after this, unless of course one or the other double-crossed the other.

Second, we should consider the possibility that the murder was organized by none other than Zeno. This theory obtains support from the situation facing Zeno precisely in 480. The Isaurian Zeno was highly unpopular and it could have been possible for either Theoderic the Amal or Sabinianus to use Nepos as a figurehead ruler to oust him. The suggestion of Theoderic the Amal to escort Nepos to Italy would have stressed the existence of this danger. Furthermore, the fact that we find Ovida protecting Dalmatia against Odoacer could be interpreted as evidence of Zeno's involvement and that Zeno had placed Ovida in control of Dalmatia. However, this alternative is unlikely on the grounds that Zeno recognized the Western consuls until 486 while Odoacer recognized Zeno as Emperor in his coins.

Third, it is possible that Theoderic the Amal had a role in the murder because Ovida was a Goth and one can think that Theoderic's plan could have been to expand his domains northward when he was isolated from the south and east by the Roman forces. Once again there is no evidence for this alternative either.

Whatever the truth, it is clear that the death of Nepos at this precise junction in history was very fortuitous for both Zeno and Odoacer. If Zeno was behind the murder, there are four possible explanations for what happened next: 1) that Zeno used Odoacer against Ovida because Ovida had seized Dalmatia against Zeno's wishes; 2) that Zeno's wife and her relatives demanded vengeance against the murderers of Nepos, and Zeno had to comply and betray his own henchmen; 3) that Zeno had planned to double-cross Glycerius and Ovida from the start and used Odoacer for this purpose; 4) that the seizing of Dalmatia by the Gothic Ovida against the wishes of Zeno could have given Theoderic the Amal the chance to form an alliance with him so that it was necessary to use Odoacer against Ovida.

In the absence of any concrete evidence for the above alternatives, it is probably safest to accept the version preserved in the sources, which is that Nepos was indeed murdered by his *comites* at the behest of Glycerius and that Ovida just exploited the situation by seizing Dalmatia for himself.

Immediately after the assassination of Nepos in 481 we find Odoacer invading Dalmatia and Ovida in charge of the defence of Dalmatia against him. Odoacer won the contest over Dalmatia and Ovida was executed in 481 or 482, on 9 October, 27 November or 9 December. The fact that Zeno recognized the Western consuls until 486 suggests that Odoacer's invasion of Dalmatia was approved by Zeno. After the seizing of Dalmatia by Odoacer the strategic situation was such that Sabinianus was blocking Theoderic the Amal in Epirus from the east and Odoacer from the north.

Theoderic the Amal was still in possession of Epirus in 480/1, but in Zeno's eyes the main source of trouble was not actually Theoderic but Sabinianus who was conducting the war against the Ostrogoths with success. According to Marcellinus Comes, 'Sabinianus Magnus' kept Theoderic the Amal at bay with shrewdness rather than with manliness. Marcellinus even went so far as to say that Sabinianus was so good an administrator and old-school disciplinarian in military affairs that he could be compared with the past Roman commanders. Here the Romans had a soldier who could be compared with the great commanders of the past. Therefore perhaps it is not a surprise that, according to John of Antioch, Zeno had Sabinianus assassinated in 481. His replacements were the *stratêgoi* John the Scythian (*Iôannês ho Skuthês/Johannes Scytha*) and Moschianus (Moscianus1 in the PLRE2), but they proved unable to contain Theoderic. This implies that the command was now divided between two men to lessen the danger of usurpation. Despite the conspicuous lack of success, this appointment proved important for the future, if the suggestion of the PLRE2 is correct that we should identify this Moschianus1 with the Moschianus2. This identification would make Moschianus a relative of the future Emperor Anastasius so that it is possible that this elevation of Moschianus to a higher rank made him so important a military figure that he could have had a role in the appointment of Anastasius as Emperor. Unfortunately this is impossible to know with certainty.[41]

As noted, the change of Roman leadership was not fortuituous for the Roman war effort against Theoderic the Amal. Theoderic managed to break through the Roman cordon, pillage Macedonia and Thessaly, and sack the city of Larissa. The sources fail to state why the Romans were so singularly unsuccessful now. This question is particularly important because later events prove John the Scythian to have been among the best commanders of the period. My own educated guess is that the principal reason for the troubles was the division of command between two commanders. The second of the reasons must have been, even if not stated by the sources, the alliance previously concluded by Theoderic Strabo and Theoderic the Amal. This gave the Ostrogoths the critical mass to overcome all Roman forces in Thessaly, Macedonia and Thrace.[42]

The imprisonment of Verina to please Illus brought with it serious domestic and dynastic troubles for the Emperor Zeno. His wife Ariadne demanded that Illus release her mother, but to no avail. It was then that Ariadne made an ultimatum to her husband Zeno. He had to choose between Illus or her. Zeno had no alternative but to obey because his position depended on his marriage. Zeno or Ariadne ordered *praepositus sacri cubiculi* Urbicius to find someone to assassinate Illus. The choice to use a *cubicularius* for this delicate task was a natural one because the Isaurian *excubitores* could not be trusted in this case. Urbicius hired a *scholarius* named Spanikios/Spanicius or Sporakios/Sporacius. When Illus was ascending the *kochlias* (spiral strairaise) of the Hippodrome and/or going through the *Poulpita* to *Dekimon*, Sporacius attempted to kill him with a sword-cut to the head, but Illus' *spatharios/spatharius* (sword-bearer/bodyguard) protected his employer by taking the cut on his right arm. In spite of this, the tip of the sword cut off Illus' right ear. The *scholarius* was killed on the spot, or according to the alternative version Zeno had the *scholarius* beheaded to hide the truth. Illus was rescued by his retinue and carried home, and from there was taken to Bithynia for safety. Zeno claimed innocence, but Illus naturally suspected him and soon after asked Zeno to send him to the east because he was still weak from the wound. Zeno complied and appointed Illus *Magister Militum per Orientem* in late 481.[43]

This was not the only murder attempt or assassination that took place at this time. The years 480–1 saw a rash of assassinations or assassination attempts, and it is difficult not to suspect that most were done on behalf of Zeno, as was suspected at the time.

Of note are the roles of the *scholarius* and *spatharius*. The *scholarii* were still the principal military force guarding the Emperor even if they were now in the process of becoming a parade ground corps thanks to the widespread corruption which resulted in ambitious and rich but unwarlike people to buy their way into the financially lucrative service. The fact that the emperors no longer served in the field made the corps attractive to those who did not actually want to fight. The *spatharius* who protected Illus would not have been a member of the Palace *cubicularii* because it is very unlikely that Zeno would have given Illus access to them.[44] Here we are dealing with a *spatharius*/sword-bearer who belonged to Illus' private retinue, who would have held the rank of officer (*doruforos*) in this private corps of *hypaspistai/bucellarii*. This is a good example of the loyalty of these private retinues to their employers, which they demonstrated again and again.[45]

It was only a matter of time before Zeno and Illus would have to fight it out and both men knew this. It was because of this that Zeno and Illus both failed to provide any support for the Persarmenian rebels against the Persians despite their initial promise of help in 481. Illus set about to accomplish his goal by endearing himself with the Easterners and with the Chalcedonians. The highly unpopular Zeno sought to do the same, but in addition to this he had to deal with the fact that Theoderic the Amal was roaming free in Macedonia and Thessaly and that Moschinus and John the Scythian could not contain him. The approaching showdown with Illus forced his hand. He was forced to buy peace from Theoderic the Amal with concessions in 483. These included his appointment as *magister militum in praesenti* (or as *magister militum per Thracias* according to Theophanes) and as consul for the year 484, the handing of gifts, the erecting of an equestrian statue, and the settling of his people in Dacia Ripensis and Moesia Inferior. The sources fail to state what the Ostrogoths under Recitach did during this time, but the fact that we find

Recitach in a suburb of Constantinople in 484 suggests that he had also concluded peace either before, at the same time, or after Theoderic the Amal. My own educated guess is that both concluded the peace at the same time, but in such a manner that Theoderic's treaty was advantageous in comparison with that of Recitach, which made the latter envious. According to John of Antioch, when Zeno realized that Recitach was jealous of Theoderic, he demanded that before Theoderic set out to fight Illus he should kill his cousin and personal enemy Recitach. This Theoderic did quite willingly. Recitach was duly killed in the suburb of Constantinople called Bonophatianae. Gordon and other modern historians have suggested that it might not have been Zeno but Theoderic who demanded the killing of his competitor Recitach, before he could embark on a war against Illus. This is a distinct possibility, but it is perhaps still best to accept the version of John of Antioch. The stage was now set.[46]

The showdown with Illus in 484, and the East until 489[47]

The third assassination attempt against Illus soured the relationship between Zeno and Illus permanently so that both parties started to undermine each other while attempting to gather support for themselves. Despite his popularity Illus was not a native Roman so he needed to court the opinions of important sections of society in the East. One of the important arenas of competition for the two men was naturally the church, and in particular the See of Alexandria because control of this city would have meant control of supplies both to Constantinople and the eastern field armies. It is clear that Illus also sought support from the pagans through his friend Pamprepius. The Hellenes hoped that Illus would restore full freedom of worship for the pagans. Publicly, however, Illus was a staunch supporter of the Chalcedonian doctrine, because he could not appear to be a pagan.[48]

The Alexandrian supporters of Peter Mongus appear to have sent a deputation to Constantinople in 481 to urge Zeno to reappoint Peter to his see once Timothy Salophaciolus was dead. Timothy in his turn sent another deputation to counter this, probably in late 481, to demand that his successor belong to the same faction as himself. The head of this mission was John Talaia, a monk from Canopus and steward, *oikonomos*, of the Alexandrian Church. Zeno suspected that this John was seeking the bishopric for himself and that he was also a supporter of the *strategos* Illus who was preparing an insurrection. Consequently, Zeno demanded on oath that John would not seek the See himself, while still granting the local community the right to choose their bishop. Illus instructed John to obey. After this, Illus gave John a letter to take to Theognostus, the prefect (*praefectus Augustalis*), who was one of his co-conspirators. John and presumably therefore also Illus promised Theognostus the royal vessels that Arcadius had given to the church in return for the bishopric, and when Timothy died soon after in February 482, John gave Theognostus the promised bribe and got the bishopric as a representative of the Chalcedonian party. John gave a report of this to his patron Illus who was at Antioch, but, more importantly, he did not inform Zeno of his nomination. This was effectively a declaration of loyalty to Illus. Zeno could be ignored.[49]

When this was reported to Zeno, he replaced Theognostus with Pergamius, and then on the advice of Acacius, Zeno rewrote the recent pronouncement of Martyrius

Augsburg II helmet reconstruction by Vicus Ultimus.

Augsburg II reconstruction by Vicus Ultimus.

Augst reconstruction by Vicus Ultimus.

Berkasovo II reconstruction by Vicus Ultimus.

Reconstruction of a helmet after Ch. Miks by Vicus Ultimus.

Burgh Castle reconstruction by Vicus Ultimus.

Christies reconstruction by Vicus Ultimus.

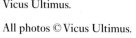

Deurne reconstruction by Vicus Ultimus.

Deurne from behind, reconstruction by Vicus Ultimus.

Budapest knife. Reconstruction by Vicus Ultimus.

Bonn-*spatha*. Reconstruction by Vicus Ultimus.

Burgh Castle francisca.

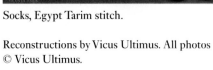

Socks, Egypt Tarim stitch.

Draco standard.

Reconstructions by Vicus Ultimus. All photos
© Vicus Ultimus.

A Gothic village – Masłomęcz, Poland. Reconstruction by Vicus Ultimus. (© *Vicus Ultimus*)
The Gothic *foederati* in Roman service could be housed in similar villages on Roman territory.

Image in San Maria Maggiore, Ravenna ca. 500 (public domain). Note the use of large shields and two spears with the implication that the soldier was expected to throw at least one before making contact with the enemy.

Hejmstead, Romo – North Sea coast. Reconstruction by Vicus Ultimus. (© *Vicus Ultimus*)

A Gothic village – Masłomęcz, Poland. Reconstruction by Vicus Ultimus. (© *Vicus Ultimus*)
The Gothic *foederati* in Roman service could be housed in similar villages on Roman territory.

Hejmstead, Romo – North Sea coast. Reconstruction by Vicus Ultimus. (© *Vicus Ultimus*)

Male and female re-enactors outside the Gothic village – Masłomęcz, Poland. Reconstruction by Vicus Ultimus. (© *Vicus Ultimus*)

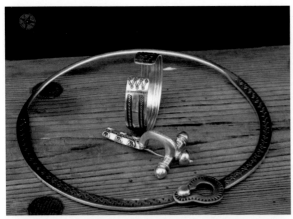

Above left: Fancy gear worn by men as reconstructed by Vicus Ultimus.

Above right: A reconstruction of a hunting knife after British Museum example 4–5th Century AD.

Centre left: A reconstruction of a bracelet.

Below: Musée Parc archéologique des Temps Barbares.

All photos © Vicus Ultimus.

Image in San Maria Maggiore, Ravenna ca. 500 (public domain). Note the use of different types of helmets by the cavalry. The horseman on the right may use a ridge helmet (unless the lighter colour is meant to present a reflection of the sun), but the two others appear to wear single bowl helmets.

Top: Members of the Vicus Ultimus at Hejmstead, Romo – North Sea coast.

Centre right: Detail from muscle armour.

Bottom left: A reconstruction of a *spatha*-sword Ejsbol-Sarry subtype 2, variant 2.

Bottom right: Manica arm-guard.

Reconstructions by Vicus Ultimus.
(© *Vicus Ultimus*)

An image in San Maria Maggiore, Ravenna ca. 500 (public domain). Note the use of the spiked shields described by the sixth century *Peri Strategias/Strategikes*.

An image in San Maria Maggiore, Ravenna ca. 500 (public domain). Note the size of the shields on the left which resemble closely the huge shields described by the sixth century *Peri Strategias/Strategikes*.

Two images in San Maria Maggiore, Ravenna ca. 500 (public domain). Note the large shields described by the sixth century *Peri Strategias/Strategikes*, and also the use of two spears with the implication that the soldier was expected to throw at least one before engaging the enemy in mêlée.

A coin of Leo I.

A coin of Zeno (nummus), British Museum. (*Photos by author*)

A bust of Emperor Leo the Butcher (457–74). (*Wikimedia Commons, released by the photographer into the public domain*)

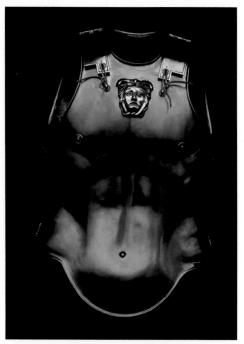

Musculata – armour. Reconstruction by Vicus Ultimus. (© *Vicus Ultimus*) The Romans continued to use this very ancient style of armour and this is a good modern reconstruction of one of the variants.

Bottom left: Kunzing shin guard.
Bottom centre: Manica arm guard.
Bottom right: A *semispatha* was a short-sword used usually when fighting against infantry.

Reconstructions by Vicus Ultimus. (© *Vicus Ultimus*)

Author's drawing of Armatus on a chariot representing how he could have appeared when he re-enacted Achilles on the circus. The other way he could have re-enacted Achilles on horseback is included in the text proper.

A coin of Nepos.
British Museum. (*Photos by author*)

A coin of Romulus Augustulus.

Left: A modern reconstruction of Carnuntum with tents and other military equipment.

Above: *veruta* (light javelins), *lancea* (lance/spear), *spiculum* (heavy javelin). Reconstruction of period equipment by Vicus Ultimus. (© *Vicus Ultimus*)

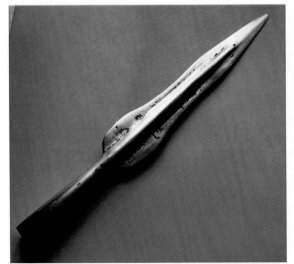

Top left: A spearhead (24 cm) at the Museum Peronne. Photo by Vicus Ultimus. (© *Vicus Ultimus*)

Top right: Squamata robh (scale armour).

Centre left: Nydam quiver.

Bottom left: Hjemstead Romo. A period warrior.

Bottom right: Nydam bow.

Reconstructions by Vicus Ultimus. (© *Vicus Ultimus*)

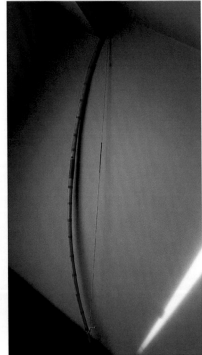

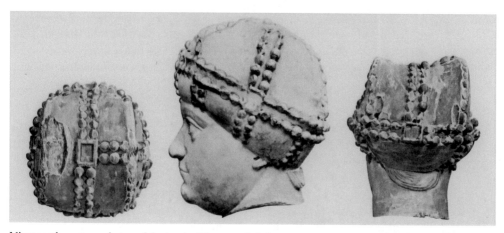

Nineteenth century photos of the head of Empress Ariadne.

Bottom left: Medallion of Theoderic the Amal/the Great (a nineteenth century photo).

Bottom right: Spatha – Snipstat – Illerup. Reconstruction by Vicus Ultimus. (© *Vicus Ultimus*)

Left: A diptych variously attributed to Anastasius, Justin I or Justinian I. (*Wikimedia Commons – released by the photographer into the public domain*)

Below left: Noze-style knives. Reconstruction by Vicus Ultimus. (© *Vicus Ultimus*)

Below right: A coin of Anastasius I. One of the best emperors East Rome ever had, British Museum. (*Photo by author*) of Jerusalem and called it *Henoticon*, which was then published on 28 July 482. Zeno's aim was to reconcile the two hostile parties in Alexandria, Egypt, Libya and Pentapolis – the Monophysites and Chalcedonians – with each other. When Pergamius then reached Alexandria he found out that Peter had fled into hiding eventually managing to find his way to Rome. It was there that John claimed that he had been sacked because he had been a firm supporter of the doctrines of Pope Leo and Chalcedon. Zachariah and Evagrius fail to state what happened to Theognostus, but considering that Peter had fled it is possible that Theognostus had done the same. The new prefect, Pergamius, persuaded Peter Mongus to support the *Henoticon* and the return of Bishop Proterius's Chalcedonian party if they accepted the *Henoticon* of Zeno and Acacius. When Peter agreed to do this, he was duly reappointed as Bishop of Alexandria. In the presence of the prefect, the duke, the chief men, the clergy, the monks, the sisters and the believers, Peter then read the *Henoticon* to the populace and explained it so that it abrogated Chalcedon. He did this to retain the support of his Monophysite followers while presenting a conciliatory stance towards the Chalcedonians.[50]

Pope Simplicius reacted to the news by dispatching a letter to Zeno in which he accused Peter of being a Eutychian and protested his restoration to the See of Alexandria. Zeno, however, excused himself by saying that John had broken his oath. Simplicius died on 10 March 483 before he had learnt that the *Henoticon* of Zeno 'abrogated' Chalcedon. When the clergy and people assembled in the church of St. Peter to choose a new Pope, Odoacer made it clear to all through his representative Praetorian Prefect Basilius that they had to choose a successor acceptable to Odoacer. In other words, Odoacer assumed imperial powers in this case. This suggests strongly that the Arian Odoacer knew how to use the Catholic Church to his own advantage and that it was his policy decision to appoint a Pope who would support Illus against Zeno. It was then that the Bishop of Antioch, Calandion, wrote to Zeno about Peter and called him an adulterer. Since Antioch belonged firmly to the sphere of influence of Illus, who already in 482/3 was openly preparing to revolt, it is possible or even probable that this was a public insult to Zeno for his support of the overthrow of the bishop who belonged to the opposing party led by Illus. Whatever the case, Zeno believed that he was a supporter of Illus and exiled him to the Oasis once he had gained possession of the city. Zeno's replacement as Bishop of Antioch was Peter the Fuller. He was a supporter of the *Henoticon*, as was the Bishop of Jerusalem Martyrius. The other Eastern bishops supported Calandion and asked the new Pope, Felix, for help. They suffered a similar fate, exile, when the day of reckoning came.[51]

Meanwhile, Peter Mongus was in trouble. The *Henoticon* had been cautiously worded so that the different sides could be united under it, but it still failed to achieve its purpose because the Monophysites wanted a clear revocation of Chalcedon, while the Chalcedonians would not tolerate the abrogation of the Council of Chalcedon in any form. When Peter's Monophysite supporters separated themselves from communion with Peter despite his claims that the *Henoticon* abrogated Chalcedon, Peter repeated this publicly by anathematizing the Council of Chalcedon once again. When this was brought to the ears of Acacius he sent a deputation to investigate Peter's actions with the result that Peter claimed never to have done such a thing and also wrote a memorandum in which he presented witnesses to the contrary. This public denial endangered Peter's standing among the Monophysites.[52]

John Talaia, meanwhile, had managed to convince Pope Felix to depose Peter with a letter that was sent via the Sleepless Monks of Constantinople (supporters of Chalcedon) to Acacius. Acacius refused to accept it. John then accused Acacius of unlawful contacts with Peter Mongus, as a result of which Felix convened a Council against Acacius at Rome on 28 July 484. Cyril, the leader of the Sleepless, had sent a letter to Felix in which he reproached him for his slowness in reacting to the situation. The Council decided to expel Peter as a heretic and demanded that Acacius be sent to Felix to be examined. When the envoys of Felix arrived, Zeno and Acacius had them arrested at Abydos. It was then in 484 that the news of the persecution of the Orthodox by Huneric king of the Vandals reached both Felix and Zeno. This was certainly a source of distraction to Felix.[53] In fact, it is possible that Huneric supported Zeno in this because Zeno was at the time fighting against the Chalcedonians who were allied with Illus. Zeno's response was that John had needlessly bothered him and had broken his oath, and that Peter had been ordained with all due scrutiny. At the same time the letters of Cyril and other archimandrates of Constantinople, together with the bishops and clergy of Egypt, condemned Peter as a heretic. Cyril even dispatched some of the Sleepless monks to Felix to stress the situation. All of these claimed that John was a good Orthodox while Acacius and Peter were accomplices in crime. The conflict between Acacius and Felix ended up as the so-called Acacian schism, when the Council held at Rome anathematized Acacius on 28 July 484. This schism was to last until Justin I came to power in 518 and ended it in 519.[54]

This appears to have been the situation in about 484. The above account suggests that Illus sought support from the Chalcedonians quite actively and in fact managed to secure the support of most of the bishops of the East with the exception of Peter Mongus. Therefore the See of Alexandria was the only place where Zeno's actions had met with success before the start of the revolt of Illus. However, this success was crucially important, because it was this that secured Zeno the grain supplies of Egypt for Constantinople. Had Illus managed to keep his men in position at Alexandria, the situation could have been quite bad for Zeno. In contrast to Zeno, Illus even managed to secure the support of the Sleepless monks and some of the archimandrates of Constantinople. Illus then exploited this by attempting to gain the support of the Pope by using the Sleepless monks, archimandrates, Eastern bishops and John against Acacius and Zeno. The support of the Pope in turn strengthened the stance of Illus among the Orthodox Chalcedonians. It is also probable that Illus tried to use this as leverage to obtain the support of Odoacer against Zeno. After all, it was the Roman Pope who supported Illus against the heretical leaders of the East! The fact that Odoacer had in practice elected Pope Felix implies that he was actively involved in the undermining of Zeno's position and that Illus had every reason to expect help from him.

In 483 after the conclusion of peace with the Ostrogoths, Zeno felt strong enough to start presenting actual demands to Illus.[55] Zeno ordered Illus to release his brother Longinus and when Illus refused he dimissed Illus from office and appointed John the Scythian as his successor. At the same time he expelled Illus' relatives and supporters from Constantinople and gave their property to the cities of Isauria with the intention of undermining Illus' support there. Illus' response was to rebel openly either late in 483 or in January 484. His allies naturally included the Isaurian Trocundes, his brother, and Marsus, who had previously been in charge of a campaign against the Vandals. He sent envoys to Odoacer and the rulers of Persia and Armenia with proposals of alliance. Odoacer refused to send any help, but the request still made Odoacer suspect in Zeno's eyes which was to have consequences later. The rulers of Armenia and Persia promised help if Illus would send envoys. After this, Illus released Marcian and appointed him as ruler, but then, unfortunately for him, fate intervened. The Hephthalites killed Peroz and annihilated his entire army in January 484. Armenia, under its rebel leader Vahan Mamikonean, was unable to provide help as he was in the midst of his revolt against Persia. It is of course possible that John of Antioch meant only the satraps of Roman Armenia; indeed, the Armenian satrapies, which were part of the Roman Empire, sided with the rebel Illus against the Emperor Zeno in 484 (Procopius, *Buildings/De aed.* 3.1.17–29).

I divide the campaign of Zeno against Illus into three stages, because I accept the consensus view that Leontius was actually sent by Zeno against Illus with a military force, as stated by Joshua the Stylite (14) and was not Illus' accomplice from the start. According to Joshua the Stylite (14), Zeno's initial reaction had been to send some important men to meet Illus at Antioch with the message that Zeno would be willing to pardon him if he would apologize. Illus, however, refused because he despised Zeno. This would mean that Zeno's immediate reaction was to try to negotiate.

It was presumably then that Zeno dispatched a military force under the *strategoi* (generals), Conon the Isaurian Bishop of Apamea, and Linges/Lingis//Lilingis[56] the bastard half-brother of Illus, which is mentioned by John of Antioch (fr. 214.4, Roberto ed. 303.10ff.). The implication is that this force would have consisted mostly of Isaurians and its purpose was to undermine Illus' standing among the Isaurians and those who supported the religious view presented by Conon. Lilingis was known in the later Isaurian war as an exellent horseman, which means he was probably in charge of the cavalry during both wars (Marcellinus 491/492). John of Antioch (fr. 214.5, Roberto ed. 303.13ff.) follows this with the release of Verina by Illus to crown Leontius, but it is clear that John has here omitted the events preceding this. According to Joshua the Stylite, Zeno appointed the *stratelates* (likely to mean *MVM per Thracias*) Leontius as commander of the forces sent against Illus. He bribed him with the title of *Patricius* and may also have appointed him as an honorary consul for the year 484. The forces serving under Leontius are likely to have consisted mostly of the Thracian Field Army. We do not know how well Conon and Lilingis performed their mission or what the new *MVM per Orientem* John the Scythian did during this time. My educated guess is that Conon and Lilingis managed to secure most of Isauria while John the Scythian was fighting against the Armenian satraps who supported Illus. The reason for my conclusion is that Leontius was apparently able to advance up to the Gates of Cilicia without having to fight against Illus or his allies and satellites in Isauria and satrapies – or at least the sources are silent about this – which means that the other commanders had already secured the route of march, for example by shielding the main army of Leontius.[57]

Illus' response to the threat posed by Leontius was ingenious. He bribed him with a vast quantity of gold and promised him the emperorship. This was a believable proposition because as an Isaurian Illus was not acceptable to the Romans. The greedy Leontius swallowed the bait. Illus released Verina and brought her to Tarsus to proclaim Leontius as Emperor. Marcian was dismissed from office. In the official document which was spread throughout the East Verina declared that it had been her who had crowned Zeno and that she was now transferring it to pious Leontius because Zeno had proved himself unworthy of the office. Theophanes (AM 5976) claims that Leontius entered Antioch on 27 June 484, but according to the contemporary astrologer Palchus, the crowning took place on 19 July 484. The two likeliest ways to reconcile the sources are: 1) it is possible that, despite being contemporary, Palchus has confused the date of entry to Antioch with the crowning so that the crowning took place on 27 June; 2) it is possible that Theophanes has confused the months so that Leontius was crowned on 19 July and entered Antioch on 27 July. Of note is the fact that Palchus' comments refer to the horoscope of Leontius which was undoubtedly at least partially drawn by Pamprepius. Unsurprisingly, it promised success for Leontius.[58]

Leontius
Source: Beger 1696

Now Zeno had no alternative but to send Theoderic the Amal with his Goths against the enemy. Theoderic's forces were united with those of John the Scythian. Notably, despite the fact that Theoderic was nominally John's superior as praesental *magister*, John was actually the overall commander of the army as *magister militum per Orientem*. The obvious reason was that John was regarded as loyal while Theoderic was not. John of Antioch (fr. 214.4, Roberto ed. 303.25ff.) claims that Zeno recalled Theoderic when he reached Nicomedia, but still used his Gothic forces against Illus. All the other sources place the recall later and I agree with this consensus view. It is inherently more likely that Theoderic accompanied the army as long as there was a chance that they would have to fight a pitched battle. However, there is one possible way to reconcile the sources, which is to assume that Theoderic was actually sent twice against Illus. First under Leontius (or under John the Scythian if he fought a separate campaign against the Armenian satraps) when he would have been recalled to get rid of Recitach, and a second time under John the Scythian when he would have been recalled after Illus had been put under siege. However, in the absence of any definite evidence for this, it is safest to assume that the consensus view is correct in this case.

The extant fragment of John of Antioch (fr. 214.4, Roberto ed. 303.25ff.) states that Zeno dispatched Rugians under Herminericus, the son of Aspar, against Illus after the recall of Theoderic. These Rugians would presumably be those who had been settled in Thrace under Marcian. This does not date the sending of the Rugians precisely, but on the basis of military probability it seems likely that Zeno replaced the Gothic cavalry of Theoderic with the Rugians only after Illus had been put under siege. The implication is that the Rugians were better suited to siege warfare and must therefore have consisted predominantly of infantry. The same fragment states that at the same time Zeno also dispatched a separate fleet under *nauarchoi/navarchoi* (admirals) John (Ioannes) and *sacellarius* Paul (Paulus).[59] This command structure combined the military man John with the financial expert Paul, which ensured better control of the men if there was a need to bribe them.[60]

The problem with this fragment is the dating of the naval expedition, because it allows two different interpretations. Was it simultaneous with the land campaign led by John the Scythian or was it dispatched only after Theoderic had been recalled? From the point of view of the military situation both are possible. If the naval force was dispatched simultaneously, the idea was obviously to neutralize the Syrian Fleet based at Seleucia, to isolate the enemy and cause Illus to divide its forces so it would be easier to defeat on land. On the other hand, if the naval force was dispatched only after the loyalists had besieged Illus, then the initial plan had been to keep the Imperial Fleet together in Constantinople for its protection and to dispatch a detachment of the Fleet to occupy the coastline of Asia Minor and Syria only after it had become quite clear that the enemy would not be able to mount an amphibious operation against the capital. The aim would have been to blockade the besieged. It is also likely that Illus' forces included Isaurian pirates so that one of the purposes would also have been to eliminate them.

According to Joshua the Stylite, when Illus and Leontius learned that Zeno had dispatched a large force under John the Scythian, they became frightened and so did the population of Antioch. The Antiochenes feared the city would not be able to withstand a siege and urged the two men to leave the city and fight a battle outside it. This piece of evidence actually suggests that Zeno had dispatched the Imperial Fleet at the same time as he dispatched the land army, because the Fleet was certainly required for the siege of Antioch. Joshua also claims that Illus' men planned to abandon the city and flee to the east bank of the Euphrates with the result that Illus sent Matronianus with 500 horsemen to establish a capital for them at Edessa but the Edessans closed their gates and guarded the wall. It was thanks to this that Illus' men were forced to fight a pitched battle against great odds. The usual assumption is that this means that a battle was fought near Antioch or close to Isaurian Seleucia.[61] In my opinion, this is very unlikely because the subsequent place of refuge for Illus was Cherris-Papyrios. In light of this it is inherently more likely that Illus and Leontius left Antioch and advanced along the road which led to Iconomium so that the two armies met each other somewhere south of Iconomium.

We know the names of some of the commanders of Zeno's army. The overall commander, the *strategos*, was clearly John the Scythian, and his second-in-command, the *hypostrategos*, was Theoderic the Amal. It is probable that his army also included Conon, the warrior bishop, and Lilingis, the general. It is also likely that Kottomenes/ Cottomenes and Longinus of Kardala, both probably Isaurians, accompanied the army. It is clear that this army was composed of infantry and cavalry and it is likely that the cavalry forces were deployed either on the flanks or in front of the infantry. Typically the cavalry would have been placed on the flanks, but the presence of very large numbers of Ostrogothic cavalry may have resulted in the use of cavalry in advance of footmen. John of Antioch implies that the battle was fought between the vanguard of Illus, which consisted of Artemidoros, who was a *hypaspistes* (*bucellarius*) of Trocundes, and Papimus, the cavalry commander (*hipparchos*) of Illus, that it was this force that was defeated and fled to Cherris-Papyrius[62] and that Illus, Verina and Leontius joined them there only later. In my opinion this seems very unlikely because Joshua the Stylite clearly implies that Illus and Leontius accompanied the army because they were among the fugitives. Illus was therefore undoubtedly the overall commander on the other side even if Leontius was the nominal commander. It is also clear that the army included Trocundes, who is likely to have been the de facto *hypostrategos* of the army, and Marsus. We also know that the pagan philosopher Pamprepius accompanied the army, but we do not know what his role was, probably because he did not have a military role. It is likely that he encouraged the army with encouraging prophecies and predictions just like Christian priests in the army did.

Illus' army was also a mixed force of infantry and cavalry and once again it is likely that his cavalry was placed either on the flanks or in front of the infantry. It is unfortunate that we do not know any details of this very decisive battle which must have involved massive numbers of soldiers on both sides. All that we know is that the forces of John the Scythian prevailed, destroying most of the enemy and scattering the rest. It is likely that the Ostrogoths of Theoderic played an important if not decisive role in this battle. They were arguably the best and most effective cavalry force of their day and it is not difficult to see how a very large force of these brave elite warriors would have been able to surround and crush the enemy.[63]

Illus, Leontius, Marsus, Verina and Pamprepius fled to the impregnable mountain fort called Cherris/Papyrius (the fort had two names). Illus had prepared the fort as a place of refuge well in advance by placing in it sufficient supplies under the management of his wife. The fort had only one very narrow path leading to it and was therefore ideal as a place of refuge. However, there was not enough room for the entire army, so all those not admitted were forced to seek a place of refuge from a number of small fortresses and caves which surrounded the area. Verina died nine days later and Marsus thirty days later. After this Illus appointed Indacus Kottounes as commander of the fort and spent his days reading books. Leontius became utterly depressed and spent his days in fasting and lamentation.

When Zeno learnt of the flight of Illus and Leontius, he appointed Kottomanes/ Cottomanes as *magister utriusque militiae* and made Longinus of Kardala/Cardala *Magister Officiorum* in 484. He also recalled the army of Theoderic and replaced them with the Rugians commanded by Herminericus. On the basis of Jordanes (*Getica* 289), it is possible that Theoderic was now given a triumph in Constantinople because it is difficult to see any other possible time for such an event in the career of Theoderic in Zeno's service. This would mean that Theoderic and his Goths had played an important role in the defeat of the enemy, or at least that Zeno wanted to flatter the vanity of their commander.

The morale of the defenders of Papyrius suffered a bad setback when John captured and beheaded Trocundes when he attempted to sneak out of the fortress to assemble a force of barbarians (i.e. Isaurians). This convinced Illus and Leontius that Pamprepius had been a false prophet, and they had him executed. Both men were apparently quite silly individuals for having believed that. It was then that John put his siege engines to work and captured the counter-fort, the outworks, with the result that the fort became isolated. This dampened the morale of the defenders, but in spite of this and the best efforts of John, who used all the siege engineering skills he could muster and all his ingenuity for the invention of stratagems, the siege lasted for four years. The renewed revolt of the Ostrogoths in 486 may have played a role in this, but it is still likelier that it was the impregnability of the place that frustrated his efforts. When all had failed, John tried to convince Zeno to grant a pardon, but to no avail.[64]

Some time during the mopping up operations in 485, John's forces managed to release Zeno's brother Longinus from some Isaurian fortress. Zeno duly made Longinus *magister militum praesentalis* and appointed him consul for the year 486. We know on the basis of Procopius' *Buildings* (*De Aed.* 3.6.23) that during his tenure as *magister* Longinus fought a war against the Tzani and that he built a marching camp called *Longini Fossatum* (*the Trench of Longinus*) and that at a later date the Emperor Justinian built a fort there which was called Bourgousnoes. It is unfortunate that Procopius does not give us any details of this war, in the absence of which it is impossible to know what its significance was or how it ended. My educated guess, however, is that it was fought in about 485/6 and that it ended just like all the rest of the minor revolts against the East Roman Empire in the defeat of the rebels.[65] It is also unfortunate that the sources fail to specify who lost the office of *magister militum praesentalis* when Longinus was appointed to this post. On the basis of this it would be possible to speculate that Zeno had replaced Theoderic the Amal with his brother, which in its turn caused the latter to revolt in 486 (see below), but it is of course possible that the office had not been filled after Trocundes lost it as a result of the revolt of his brother Illus. In fact, in light of the evidence the latter is likely.

According to *Chronicon Paschale* (484), John Malalas (15.8) and Procopius (*De Aed.* 5.7.5–9), the Samaritans revolted under a bandit chief called Iustatas/Justatas during the reign of Zeno, which the *Chronicon* dates to 484. He is claimed to have taken control of Caesarea, where he then presided over chariot races and killed many Christians. Justatas also burned the Church of St. Procopius (St. Probus in the *Chronicon*) at Caesarea when Timothy was its bishop. Procopius adds that the Samaritans butchered the Christians in Neapolis and killed the bishop Terebinthus. The governor of First Palestine was Porphyrius, but he was apparently powerless to do anything. Asclepiades, the *dux Palestinae*, with his forces, and Rheges, the *lestodioktes* (dignitary) of Caesarea and the commander of the *Arcadiani* (as *tribunus?*), led their forces against the rebel, defeated him in battle and then beheaded Justatas. The Samaritans were also expelled from their Synagogue which was located on Mt. Garizin/Garizim (Gargarides in the *Chronicon*) and it was handed over to the Christians who dedicated it to Mary Mother of God. Asclepiades also garrisoned the city below the Mountain with soldiers and placed ten soldiers to guard the Church. The Church of St. Procopius was duly rebuilt. In addition to this, Zeno issued an Edict which forbade the Samaritans from entering public service and confiscated the property of the rich Samaritans. This secured the area, but the seeds of the second even more violent revolt were planted because the Samaritans were not completely wiped out. The PLRE2 does not accept the dating given by the *Chronicon*

Paschale on the grounds that the Samaritan revolt would have taken place simultaneously with the revolt of Illus, but in my opinion the dating should stand as it is, even if the source for it is unreliable. It is easy to see how the Samaritans could have exploited the troubles the Romans and Persians were facing in 484.

Irfan Shahid has shown on the basis of one of the letters of Barsauma, the Metropolitan of Nisibis, to his superior Acacius, the Nestorian catholicus of Nisibis, that the Persian Arabs raided Roman territory in 485 and that the Roman Arabs responded in kind. On the basis of the Persian reaction, the raids had not been approved by the Persian high command, which is not surprising in light of the difficulties the Persians were facing after the disastrous reign of Peroz. The local Persian satrap Qardag Nakoragan mediated and suggested that both parties return their loot. The new *shahanshah* Balash (in truth Sukhra Karin) ordered the satrap of Beth-Aramaye to Nisibis to meet his Roman counterpart. Barsauma persuaded the Roman commander to attend. The meeting between the commanders was friendly, but the Persian Arabs/Saracens raided Roman territory with impunity because the Roman troops had been assembled before Nisibis. The Romans naturally suspected treachery, but apparently still decided to conclude a truce/peace – or at least the sources fail to mention the continuance of hostilities. It was not in the interest of either empire to initiate full scale hostilities while both had quite enough other troubles.[66]

In the end, the fortress of Papyrius was betrayed from the inside in 488. According to Theophanes, the fort was taken as a result of the betrayal of Trocundes' brother-in-law who had been sent to the fortress for this purpose by Zeno, but John of Antioch has preserved us a more detailed and more likely version. According to him, Indacus Kottounes was the man who betrayed the fort. The other men in the plot were the 'rustic Conon', Longinus, another Longinus (possibly son of the former), and Artemidoros. Indacus convinced Illus and Leontius to post their men outside the fort so that the enemy would not be able to disturb their sleep. When this then took place, Indacus lowered a rope from the fort during the night and let the besiegers in. They killed the guards at the gates and then shouted '*Vinci Zenone Augusto!*' They killed Indacus on the spot, but Illus and Leontius managed to flee to the shrine of Conon where Illus prevented Leontius from killing himself. The attackers naturally did not respect the sanctuary and captured the men. Illus begged Paulus and Illus, who had been his slaves, to bury his deceased sister at Tarsus, and to protect his wife Asteria and daughter Thekla. This they did, but the rest of the defenders including Illus and Leontius were taken outside the fortress and beheaded. Their executioner could not stomach his duty and went mad. The presence of Paulus among the besiegers means that he had joined them after his duty as admiral had ended. Zeno posted the heads on poles outside Constantinople to serve as a warning. Verina was given a proper burial. Most of the fortresses in Isauria were destroyed so that they could not serve as places of refuge in the future, but as we shall see, Isauria would be in flames again soon.

The Troubled See of Alexandria and the Acacian Schism in 485–489

At the height of the schism Peter Mongus was forced to repeat his abrogation of the Tome of Leo and Council of Chalcedon to a commission set up by the separatist Monophysites.

This convinced the members of the commission, but failed to convince all the separatists. Peter's reaction was to expel his enemies from their monasteries by force of arms. When news of the troubles was brought to Zeno by Nephalius in 487, Zeno dispatched one of his bodyguards, called Cosmas, to investigate the situation and force Peter to unite with the other separatist monks. Thirty thousand separatist monks then assembled at the gates of Alexandria to present their case against Peter. Cosmas allowed only 200 of them to enter the city for security reasons. Peter once again anathematized Chalcedon and the Tome of Leo, but most of the monks refused to accept this as evidence because Peter was in communication with bishops who, while accepting the *Henoticon*, still refused to abrogate the Council of Chalcedon. Of particular note is the fact that the populace of Alexandria sided with Peter, which was naturally a good thing for internal security and the only thing that really mattered. When Cosmas brought back his report, Zeno dispatched Arsenius, with extraordinary powers as controller of Egypt and its military units, to force the separatist monks into union. If this failed, he was to dispatch some of the separatist monks to the capital to hold discussions with Zeno. And so it transpired, and Zeno was forced to hold long discussions with these monks to try to convince them to return to the union. But the discussions proved fruitless as Zeno refused to anathematize Chalcedon.[67]

On 26 November 489 Acacius died and was succeeded by Fravitta. Fravitta died after a short rule of four months in March 490 without having achieved anything of great importance. His successor was Euphemius who, when he received the synodical letters that Peter Mongus had dispatched to his predecessor Fravitta, was horrified to find that they abrogated the Council of Chalcedon. Because of this Euphemius cut off communion with Peter. Fravitta had tried to establish good relations with both Felix and Peter, but Euphemius had a different stance. He tried to reconcile with Pope Felix, but not with Peter. However, his attempt proved a failure when Felix demanded that Euphemius remove the names of Acacius and Fravitta from the diptychs, which Euphemius naturally refused to do. In my opinion it is very likely that the conflict between Odoacer and Zeno had a role in the background in this. Peter's situation was resolved by his death on 29 October 489, but his successor Athanasius (who occupied the see until his death on 17 October 496) and his successors followed up the position adopted by Peter so that this conflict between Euphemius and Alexandria remained unresolved until the reign of Anastasius who eventually expelled Euphemius.[68]

The Ostrogothic menace and Odoacer in 486–488[69]

Theoderic the Amal revolted again in 486. The probable reason for this was once again the chronic shortages of food in the areas inhabited by the Ostrogoths which the central government failed to address adequately or his removal from office if Longinus replaced him in 485. The expectation of the government was apparently that the Gothic settlers would be able to obtain their supplies locally from the land given to them, because it is quite clear that had the Emperor wanted he could have easily supplied the Goths in their places of abode by shipping the necessary foodstuffs via the Danube. The best proof of this is that the Romans were easily able to supply their own massive cities from the foodstuffs available to them in their less disturbed areas. The Ostrogothic nation was certainly very populous but the Roman cities were more so.

Consequently, Theoderic revolted against Zeno in 486 and ravaged Thrace. On the basis of Malalas it is possible that Theoderic first went from Constantinople to Selymbria where there were stationed *numeri*. At the time Leo rose to power these included the *Mattiarii* legion. It is therefore possible that the *numeri* garrisoning Selymbria included native units that joined Theodoric. These would have been the forces serving under Theoderic if he was still the praesental magister as Malalas' text suggests. The problem with Malalas is that he has confused the earlier events (for example the murder of Armatus) with the later ones. Theoderic marched first to Sycae/Sykai (mod. Galata) with the probable intention of capturing boats and ships, and when this failed he cut the city's aqueduct (presumably the Aqueduct of Valens). Theoderic's apparent aim was to extort concessions from the Romans as had been done so many times in the past, but this failed for the moment. *The Panegyric of Theoderic* by Ennodius (19) proves that Zeno resorted once again to the use of Bulgars as his proxies. Zeno simply could not spare any troops in a situation in which he was still engaged in war with Illus and his Isaurian satellites. The Bulgars invaded but were defeated, this time by Theoderic the Amal. Theoderic renewed his offensive in 487 and advanced against Constantinople. This time he marched as far as the city of Melantias about eighteen miles from Regium. Zeno decided to buy peace with bribes. He sent his own sister as a wife, giving her a plentiful sum of money to serve as a dowry. This was enough to convince Theoderic to return to Novae.

In the meantime, according to John of Antioch, Zeno had concluded an alliance with the Rugians of North Noricum against Odoacer because Odoacer was preparing an alliance with Illus. The reference to Illus at this place is odd because Illus was enclosed inside the fort of Papyrius, but still possible. The sentence would actually make a lot more sense if one replaced Illus with Theoderic, but this is of course mere speculation. Another possible reason would of course be that Zeno suspected that Odoacer could support Illus. Whatever the truth, Odoacer struck first in late 487. He marched to Noricum, defeated the Rugians on the other side of the Danube, and captured their king Feletheus/Feba. Feletheus and many other prisoners were taken to Ravenna and executed. His son Fredericus (Frederic) however managed to flee to regroup the remnants of the tribe while Odoacer pillaged Noricum. Odoacer sent a part of the spoils to Zeno as a gesture of his loyalty, and Zeno pretended to accept this and publicly rejoiced the victory of Odoacer over the barbarians.[70] In early 488 Fredericus and the surviving Rugians returned to Noricum, but Odoacer despatched his brother Onulf with a great army against them. Fredericus and his men were forced to flee, and they subsequently joined Theoderic at Novae in Moesia. Meanwhile Onulf evacuated what Romans there were left in Noricum Ripenses and transferred them to Italy. This was the sad end of Roman Noricum.[71]

It was in 488 that Zeno decided to use Theoderic and his Goths against Odoacer in Italy. Some sources claim that the idea for this came originally from Zeno while others claim that Theoderic was the one who suggested it. It appears likely that it was Theoderic who suggested it originally in 478 and that the situation was now ripe for the implementation of this plan in the eyes of both. The flight of Fredericus to Theoderic gave him an excuse to wage war against Odoacer. He was avenging the murder of Feletheus. However, the real reason was of course, as suggested by Ian Hughes and many others like Wolfram, the quite accurate calculation that Theoderic's forces would eventually prove too weak to resist the East Romans if he stayed in the Balkans.[72] The end of the revolt of Illus in 488 would have released adequate forces from the East to make certain that this would be the case. When Theoderic was given the official go-ahead, he started to assemble his fellow tribesmen all over the East Roman Empire and any other forces willing to join his trek against Odoacer. He even dispatched envoys to the Crimean Goths with the suggestion that they join him – they declined.

The sources fail to give any accurate head count for this assembled force, but it must have been very considerable even if many Gothic nobles and their forces chose to remain. After all, the assembled army of Theodoric included most of those who had served under Theoderic Strabo, his own tribesmen, the Rugians of Fredericus and many native Romans too, and the sources point out how difficult it was for Theoderic to obtain enough supplies. The usual suggestion is that it consisted of roughly 20,000–30,000 warriors and their families, but even as small a figure as 10,000 has been suggested. In my opinion, of the major historians of the modern era, Hodgkin in his classic *Italy and Her Invaders* (vol.3) is closest to the probable sizes when he suggests a fighting strength of 40,000 and the size of the Gothic nation 200,000 souls, and notes that this is likely to be an underestimation because fifty years later the Goths had 150,000 men in their field army besieging Rome. Hodgkin notes that even greater figures had been suggested in the past: Pallmann had suggested 300,000 for the Gothic nation and 40,000–50,000 for the Rugian.[73]

In my opinion, Hodgkin had a point. Most modern estimates for the Ostrogoths are definitely too small. But in my opinion it is likely that Hodgkin's estimation is too small as well. We should remember that Theoderic had to defeat the combined forces of the Torcilingi, Sciri, Heruls and other barbarians making up the 'praesental army' of Italy and its well-fortified sizable cities. The experience of Galerius before the gates of Rome in 307 (see vol.1) should be proof enough to put these underestimations finally at rest. Galerius and his field army, which certainly had more than 20,000 men, were too few to besiege Rome.[74] This is in contrast to the Gothic forces of Theoderic the Amal or Theoderic Strabo. They besieged Constantinople several times, even if they lacked the logistical means, the navy and siege skills needed to take the city. They certainly had enough men for this. Merely by adding together the retainers of both Theoderics one has 36,000 warriors plus their squires for a likely total of ca. 48,000 men,[75] but as discussed above this was not the entire armed strength of the Ostrogothic nation. In addition to these we should count the tribal levy which accompanied Theoderic the Amal and also the forces of Fredericus and the Romans joining them. In fact, Ennodius (*Pan.* 29) describes the Ostrogothic nation as 'innumerable as sand and stars'! My own educated guess is that Theoderic had a minimum of 150,000 warriors in his army when one includes the tribal levy of all men able to bear arms. This is based on Procopius' (*Wars*, 5.16.11; 5.24.3) figure of 150,000 men for the Ostrogothic field army besieging Rome in the sixth century, which was also the reason for Hodgkin's suspicions that the Ostrogoths had more men than he included in his conservative estimate.[76] Of note also is the fact that the 150,000 Goths represent only the size of the field army in a situation in which the entire Gothic army consisted of 200,000 men (Procopius, *Wars* 7.4.12). However, since this represents the size after years of relative peace, it is safest to assume that it was closer to 150,000 men when Theoderic began his trek. I would divide this figure so that Theoderic's cavalry forces consisted of at least 80,000 (mostly lancers and cataphracts) and the rest of infantry (mostly heavy infantry). On the basis of what we know of Ostrogothic combat practices the only portion of the army that was considered ready for combat was the cavalry. The infantry would have been used only for the protection of the wagon laager and for the protection of cavalry if it was forced to retreat.

The Ostrogothic invasion of Italy 489–493[77]

The opposition Theoderic faced in Italy was no longer the West Rome of early fifth century but a rump of it. The Visigothic king Euric had exploited the chaos in which West Rome was in 476 by invading Provence and by capturing Arles and Marseille. The fragment of Candidus (fr.1) also proves that the Gauls had revolted against Odoacer and presumably therefore submitted to Euric or to other local rulers. The Gauls had decided to abandon the Roman Empire. Spain, Britain and North Africa had been lost well before this, and Sardinia, Corsica and the Balearic Islands were held by the Vandals. Odoacer held most of Sicily in return for paying tribute, but the Vandals still maintained a naval base on the island. Basically all that was left for Odoacer were Italy, Dalmatia and parts of Raetia and the deserted Noricum. His army consisted of the Turcilingi, Sciri, Heruls, Rugians and other tribal units. It is probable that he possessed some remnants of native units as well, but their numbers were neglible in comparison to the tribal *foederati*. On the basis of the very few references to the fighting tactics of these units, most of these forces appear to have consisted of footmen, with the implication that Odoacer's forces were more evenly balanced than the army of Theoderic which relied mainly on its cavalry to win its battles.[78] It is quite probable that Odoacer also had access to well over 100,000 men in Italy, and it is quite possible that he had even more men than Theoderic because infantry was cheaper to maintain than cavalry. Italy was certainly able to maintain even greater numbers of tribal soldiers[79] so this should be seen as a very conservative estimate for his forces.

The Battle of the River Ulca in about February 489

Theoderic began his trek along the Danube after the harvest in late 488. After Sirmium, Theoderic's advance was blocked by the Gepids who had in the meantime occupied the lands previously held by the Ostrogoths. The sources do not tell us why the Gepids sought to prevent the enemy's advance. It is therefore possible that Odoacer and the Gepids had formed an alliance. But it is also possible that the longstanding bloodfeud between these two tribes was enough to cause the hostility between them. Whatever the reason, the Gepid cavalry *turmae* occupied the opposite bank of the River Ulca where a battle was fought in February 489. The River Ulca is likely to be located at *Hiulca Palus* as suggested by Hodgkin and the *Barrington Atlas*. The location fits the description of the battle given by Ennodius in his *Panegyric of Theoderic*. It was a morass/fen-country, and the intention was to slow down and stop the Gothic cavalry charge in this difficult terrain. Theoderic had no alternative but to attack, because his followers were already suffering from the effects of hunger.

One may speculate whether the positioning of the men behind the river in a defensive posture could have lowered the Gepids' morale, because they could clearly see that

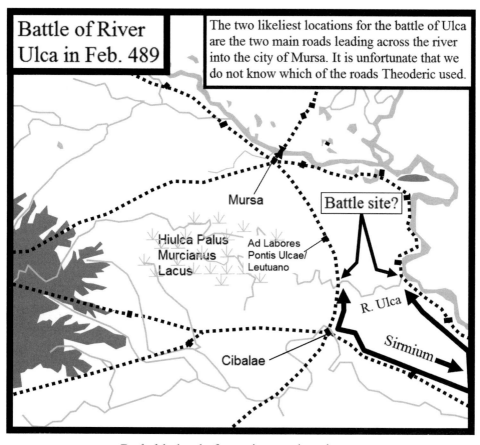

Battle of River Ulca in Feb. 489

The two likeliest locations for the battle of Ulca are the two main roads leading across the river into the city of Mursa. It is unfortunate that we do not know which of the roads Theoderic used.

Mursa

Battle site?

Hiulca Palus
Murcianus
Lacus

Ad Labores
Pontis Ulcae/
Leutuano

R. Ulca

Sirmium

Cibalae

Probable battle formations and tactics

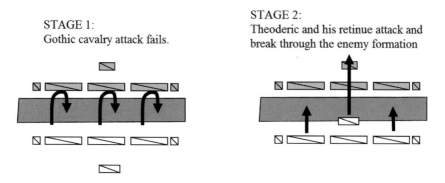

STAGE 1:
Gothic cavalry attack fails.

STAGE 2:
Theoderic and his retinue attack and break through the enemy formation

their king, Trapsila, did not trust them to hold their line at the sight of the fearsome Gothic cavalry charge. This may suggest a clear numerical advantage for Theoderic's side. However, there is a more likely possibility: that Trapstila/Thraustila was copying the previously successful Gepid tactic. After all, the Gepids had defeated the Huns and Ostrogoths at a river called Nedao, not far from the River Ulca. The location was very familiar to the Ostrogoths, because they had migrated from this area just sixteen years before.

It is fortunate that Ennodius has preserved for us a description of this battle. According to him, Theoderic was forced to attack because his followers were suffering from hunger. As has already been noted by Hodgkin (3.187), Theoderic deployed his cavalry in at least two lines so that he sent first his front line (in Hodgkin, 'the van') to the attack across the river. Those Goths who managed to reach the other bank of the river, despite the rough terrain and swift current, faced tighly packed *turmae* of Gepid cavalry and were forced to retreat because the Gepids engaged them with missiles and *lanceae*-javelins which wreaked havoc among their forces. It was then that Theoderic rallied his men by shouting encouraging words and then by taking a cup for the sake of good auspices, after which he led the attack. According to Ennodius, Theoderic ordered the standards (*signa*) to be raised to show that he was attacking in person. This means that the attack was now spearheaded by Theoderic and his retainers who had been in reserve before this. Theoderic loosed his reins and attacked at a gallop. He rode through all of the enemy formations and nobody among the enemy was able to withstand his charge. According to Ennodius, Theoderic's attack brought destruction like a lion to a herd or drought to a crop. It is probable, as already noted by Hodgkin (3.188), that Theoderic had noted some causeway that he was able to use to break through the enemy formation. The Gepids scattered in flight, but still suffered horrendous losses. Only nightfall put a stop to the butchery. The Gepid king Thrapstila lay dead on the ground. The most important part of the victory was that the Goths gained possession of the Gepid wagons filled with supplies drawn from the Roman cities of the area. It was thanks to this that Theoderic was able to alleviate the hunger from which his followers were suffering.

From the point of view of military history it is important to note that Theoderic the Great did not employ his cavalry as a single line without reserves but was using at least two cavalry lines of which the latter consisted, among others, of his personal retainers under his own leadership. The size of the force makes it clear that it was deployed in at least two lines. On the basis of this it is possible to speculate that as a Roman *magister militum*, he may have used the Roman cavalry array. Unfortunately this is inconclusive because at a later date we find the Ostrogoths employing a typical Germanic cavalry array with a personal reserve under the king/general behind the front line if he did not lead the charge from the start, rather than the Roman cavalry array. On the other hand, the Ostrogoths had fewer men in these battles than they did during their trek to Italy.[80] Regardless, it is clear that Theoderic fully understood the importance of the use of the reserve in cavalry combat and also the importance of personal example if the situation required it. Furthermore, he was also clearly a first class fighter.

The Battle of Pons Sontii on 28 August 489

Some time after the battle of Ulca but before the Ostrogoths reached Italy, Theoderic encountered and defeated the Sarmatian army. We do not know for certain whether the Sarmatians lived to the north-west of the Gepids or were on a raid when they encountered the Goths. They clearly did not possess adequate numbers to challenge Theoderic's force. Theoderic rested his army until the summer and then continued the march along the traditional invasion route via Emona to the River Sontium/Sontius. Meanwhile the Saxon king Odoacer appointed Tufa as *magister militum* on 1 April 489. Later we find Tufa in Milan; it seems likely that Odoacer posted him there with a part of his army to protect Liguria and other areas in north-west Italy against possible attacks from Visigoths or Burgundians.

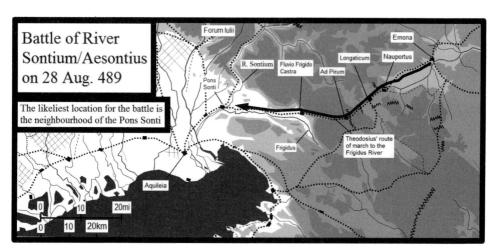

Meanwhile, Odoacer took charge of the defence of Italy against Theoderic and assembled his forces at *Pons Sontii*. He built a very strong fortified marching camp and used it and the river as his defensive bulwark against the invader. According to Ennodius (*Pan.* 36), Odoacer's army consisted of a multitude of nations led by their own kings. He also claimed that the size of this host was so large that it was difficult to supply, but noted that the numbers were no substitute for a unified leadership. Odoacer's plan for the battle was to prevent the crossing of the river at the bridge and to hold the river line. This proves that Odoacer feared in particular the impact that the Gothic lancer charge could have on his men. He clearly adopted the same defeatist formation that the Gepids had used at Ulca. In my opinion, the positioning of the men thus was bound to lower morale, and so it proved. Odoacer's men could see that he did not trust them to hold their positions when the Gothic cavalry charged them. Even if Odoacer's army included warriors who had taken part in the famous battle of Nedao in 453, his men would still have known the result of the battle of Ulca. On the basis of the military treatise of Urbicius (*Epitedeuma* e.g. 2, 7) which dates from the reign of Anastasius (491–518), it is clear that the Gothic/ Scythian cavalry charge had a reputation for being unstoppable and required exceptional measures from infantry forces to counter it.[81]

It is unfortunate that Ennodius fails (*Pan.* 37ff.) to give us any details of this important battle besides some generalities. All he says is that Odoacer's men were only good for constructing the ramparts but not for defending them and in fact fled immediately when the Gothic host made its appearance with the result that the gates of the camp were open to enter. In short, the river and ramparts could not hold back the Goths. The defenders' morale was clearly very low as the next battle also proves.

The Battle of Verona on 30 September 489

Odoacer withdrew and pitched a fortified camp (*fossatum*) on a plain not far from Verona on 27 September. The location suggests that Odoacer may have received some tribal reinforcements from the north via the Brenner Pass, but if he did the sources are silent about it. Odoacer's plan for the combat proves how low the morale of his army was. It is no wonder that it did not put up any resistance at Pons Sontii. It was not, as Ennodius stated, an army at all, but a conglomeration of many disparate tribes without cohesion or discipline. Odoacer's plan was to force his men to fight by making flight almost impossible. This approach was later criticised by the *Strategikon*, but that does not mean that it would not have been or would not continue to be one of the standard stratagems used by desperate commanders to force their men to fight to the death.

Theoderic followed Odoacer, pitched a camp opposite the enemy *fossatum*, presumably on 29 September, and a battle ensued on the 30th. The first to attack was Odoacer. This time he wanted to take the initiative and not be surprised in his camp. Ennodius describes the battle as follows (*Panegyric* 40–47, tr. by Haase, 27–29 with my comments in parentheses):

Odoacer's men [*this would of course be Odoacer himself*] carefully chose a position in a region which was useful not so much for fighting as for catering to fear, so that not even the first flight of runaways was the result of chance ... already the war tumpets were sounding hoarsely, already the army forgetting itself was calling for you. As you encased your chest in a protection of steel, armed yourself with greaves and fitted your sword, the avenger of freedom [*note the symbolic importance of this sword, which must have been of exceptional quality*], to your side, you offered your respected mother and venerable sister ... courage with such words: 'You know, mother, ... This is the day when the plain will announce the manhood of your son! ... There stands before my eyes my father, of whom fortune never made sport in battle, who himself made her auspicious for him, his strength creating his successes. One must fight under such a leader who feared not uncertain omens, but who himself was aware of omens favourable to him. You, however, fetch the embroidered cloaks and the woven cloths! More conspicuous than on festive days may the battlefield see me. Who shall not know me by my charge, let him recognize me by my splendour! Let the preciousness of my garments invite the eyes of jealous men! Let my splendid image indicate who must be struck at! ... After you had spoken such words, your steed received you on its back, restless with longings for the war trumpets [*Theoderic was to lead the cavalry attack again*]. But while you were devoting yourself to your address your legions were hard pressed by the enemy's onset. [*In other words, Odoacer attacked first while Theoderic was still equipping himself inside the marching camp. The reference to the legions may imply the use of Gothic infantry in front of their camp, but this is not conclusive because period authors could use cavalry and infantry terms interchangeably, or to mean any units of soldiers in general. However, I am in this case inclined to believe that the legions would indeed mean infantry because the fighting took place just in front of the Gothic wagon laager and the infantry legions were probably protected by cavalry wings.*]

You gave confidence to the cowardly [*Odoacer and his men*] while you delayed ... At once a host of slaughtered displayed to the enemy your arrival [*One of the standard Roman tactics, most famously used by Julius Caesar, was to let the enemy attack one's own camp and then send cavalry through the gates to attack the disordered enemy force. I would suggest that Theoderic used this tactic when he delayed his cavalry attack*]. ... without delay they took wings which Panic provided, and chose their destruction in headlong flight ... waves of the river Atesis [*Athesis, mod. Adige*] were billowing with corpses [*The river blocked the route of retreat, which suggests that Theoderic had outflanked the enemy's left wing and forced the enemy against the river.*] ... See that plain, which had been covered with armed men, shone ennobled by the whiteness of human bones [*Odoacer's army was effectively wiped out, which means that the army under Tufa that subsequently surrendered to Theoderic must have been a separate army*].

The above account suggests that Theoderic had purposely allowed the enemy to attack his infantry phalanx which probably had cavalry wings that he had posted in front of his marching camp so that the enemy would become disordered in the process. The idea was to attack the enemy the moment their flanks became exposed due to the round shape of the Gothic wagon laager.[82] A variant version of this same tactic had been used by the Goths in the battle of Adrianople and one may assume that the Goths retained a tribal memory of this same event, even if one cannot exclude the possibility that Theoderic could have also learnt of this tactic from Roman sources when he served as a hostage in Constantinople. The problem with this conclusion is that Anonymous Valesianus (2.50) claims that great numbers of men fell on both sides at this battle. This could imply that the battle was hard fought and that it was evenly matched, but in my opinion this is not the case. There is actually no real discrepancy between these two accounts when one takes into account the circumstances. It is quite easy to see that when Odoacer's men were forced against the River Athesis they would have fought desperately and that the cost of victory would have been great, as was noted by Hodgkin (3.194) well over a century ago. Germanic honour dictated that warriors should fight to the death with their leader rather than surrender, but as we have seen this was not always the case.

It is clear that this did not concern Odoacer, who fled before his army was completely entrapped. According to Anonymous Valesianus (2.50), he fled to Ravenna on 30 September 489. Paul the Deacon (15.16, p.214), however, claims that Odoacer fled first to Rome, but when he found the gates closed he fled to Ravenna. This has been doubted by historians, but in my opinion it is quite possible that this is what happened.

Theoderic did not follow Odoacer, but chose to march to Milan instead. It is clear that Verona and many other cities surrendered to him before this. When Theoderic reached Milan (Mediolanum), Odoacer's *magister militum* Tufa and most of his remaining army surrendered to him. Theoderic was experienced enough to know that chasing Odoacer was not the right thing to do. He clearly knew that the key to victory was the elimination of the enemy's army, and this he did by advancing against Tufa, but it was then that he made the greatest blunder of his career.

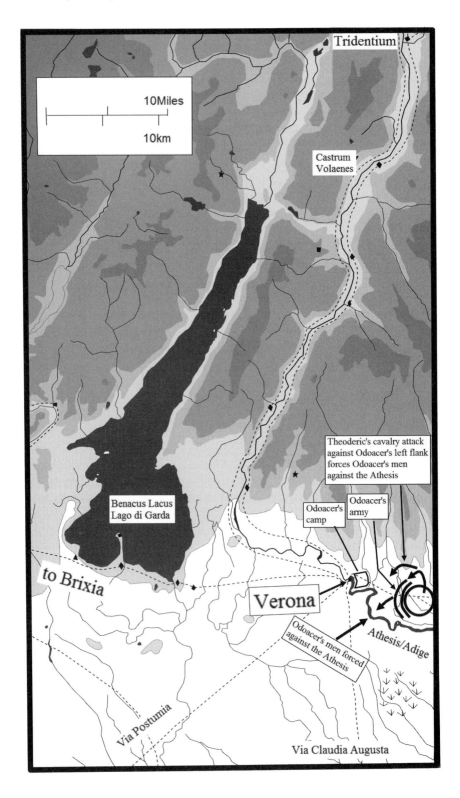

Tridentium

Castrum
Volaenes

10Miles

10km

Theoderic's cavalry attack
against Odoacer's left flank
forces Odoacer's men
against the Athesis

Odoacer's
army

Benacus Lacus
Lago di Garda

Odoacer's
camp

to Brixia

Verona

Odoacer's men forced
against the Athesis

Athesis/Adige

Via Postumia

Via Claudia Augusta

The Winter Season in 489–490

It is clear that Theoderic trusted Tufa because he gave him an army and dispatched him together with his *comites* against Odoacer later in the same year. The *comites Theoderici* presumably means Theoderic's trusted generals/friends/nobles in this case. When Tufa reached Faventia and besieged it, Odoacer left Ravenna and marched there, and Tufa betrayed his new Gothic employer and handed over to Odoacer the *comites* of Theoderic who put them in irons and took them to Ravenna. After this, Odoacer and Tufa apparently marched to Cremona where they rested their army through the winter season. The idea was presumably to isolate Theoderic and his forces behind the River Addua/Adda. Theoderic in his turn wintered his army at the city of Ticinum (Pavia) where its bishop, Epiphanius, managed to negotiate the release of prisoners from both belligerents, including native Romans.

The War in Italy in 490

The Burgundians under their king Gundobad invaded Liguria with a large army in the spring of 490 and took large numbers of captives back to Gaul. This is the first time the sources mention him after he had left Italy in about 473/4. We do not know whether he had come there as an ally of Odoacer or whether he just invaded Liguria (Milan was its capital) on his own account to plunder it. Whatever the truth, it is still clear that Theoderic somehow managed to force Gundobad to sign a treaty with Theoderic that Gundobad felt compelled to respect. We do not know whether Theoderic achieved this with force or by some other means, but what is certain is that Gundobad did not join forces with Odoacer, which in its turn enabled Theoderic to concentrate his efforts against Odoacer. It is also possible that the reference to the treaty means actually the treaty of the year 494 when Theoderic ransomed the captives taken in Italy in 490 and the two men concluded a marriage alliance in which Gundobad's son Sigismund married Theoderic's daughter Ariagne.[83]

Odoacer appears to have declared his son Thela as *Caesar* in 490. The likeliest date for this would have been before Odoacer began his campaign, and the purpose would have been to foment loyalty among the troops. The nomination of his son as *Caesar* would also have been an occasion in which the troops were bribed with a donative of gold. Odoacer began his advance towards Milan presumably in the spring of 490. If Gundobad had acted on his own initiative, it is possible to think that it was actually the advance of Odoacer that forced the Burgundians to evacuate Liguria and to sign the treaty with Theoderic, which the panegyrist then explained in the most favourable light possible, but as said, it is also possible that Theoderic had achieved this by force or by other means before the advance of Odoacer.[84] Odoacer took Milan without opposition, after which he vented his anger against those who had welcomed Theoderic to Milan in the previous year. Odoacer now had the initiative thanks to the clear numerical superiority achieved through the treacherous behaviour of Tufa, and it was because of this that he was able to force Theoderic to remain inside Ticinum (Pavia) where he was then besieged by Odoacer.

The Battle of Addua on 11 August 490

Theoderic, however, had not been idle during the winter. He had concluded an alliance with the Visigothic king Alaric II. Alaric's army included Theoderic's own blood relatives thanks to the fact that his uncle Vidimer had led his Ostrogoths to Gaul in 473 and then after his death his son Vidimer (cousin of Theoderic) had led them to Gaul where they had joined the Visigoths in 473. Therefore, even if according to the sources Theoderic received assistance from the Visigoths, it is actually possible to think that Alaric sent only the Ostrogoths to Italy and no Visigoths at all.

Ennodius (*Panegyric* 51–52) also appears to refer to an Italy-wide conspiracy on behalf of Theoderic. This has naturally caused speculation. Ennodius' sentences clearly state that Theoderic made some loyal friends all over Italy who were privy to his secret designs through which deserters would be punished in a sort of sacrificial slaughter, and that the Italian clergy was also privy to these designs. It is therefore not surprising that it has been suggested, quite rightly in my opinion, that this conspiracy was a sort of Sicilian Vespers for the supporters of Odoacer in Italy and that those who had deserted to his side or were his supporters were killed all over Italy on the same day by the members of this secret conspiracy. This massacre of supporters of Odoacer appears to have taken place in the summer of 490.[85]

The existence of such a plot explains why Odoacer failed to obtain any support from the Italians and in my opinion it would also explain the abovementioned incident before the gates of Rome. Odoacer had made himself hated throughout Italy thanks to his avarice and corrupt practices. The existence of this plot also suggests the existence of some sort of cabal for the overthrow of Odoacer before the arrival of Theoderic and that he had also been in contact with the members of this cabal and that these men were now implementing Theoderic's secret designs with great efficiency. The ability to maintain secrecy bespeaks of high coordination and discipline among the plotters. The participation of the priests may suggest that it had been organized by the members of the clergy, but it is also possible that it had been organized by the East Roman secret services (possibly by the *agentes in rebus*, or by the officers of the bodyguard units like the *scholarii, domestici, excubitores* etc.) among those Italians who were known to be loyal towards the Roman Republic. Still another possibility is that the plot was organized by persons of Gothic origins throughout Italy, but the former alternatives would seem more likely. In my opinion the most likely of these is that the plot was organized by the East Roman secret services.

The arrival of the 'Visigoths' in August changed the balance of power in the area and Odoacer raised the siege and started a retreat towards Cremona. The Goths caught up with Odoacer when he had reached the river Addua/Adda on 11 August 490. It was impossible for the infantry-based army to flee from the Gothic cavalry and the enemy was once again pushed against a river. Odoacer had no alternative but to accept battle and if he did this by choice he repeated the same mistake he had made at Verona.

No details of this battle are known except that it was hard fought, that many men fell on both sides, that it ended in the complete defeat of Odoacer, and that his *Comes Domesticorum* Pierius fell in the battle. True to his style, Odoacer, however, managed to escape from the trap formed by the river and flee to Ravenna. We also know that Tufa and

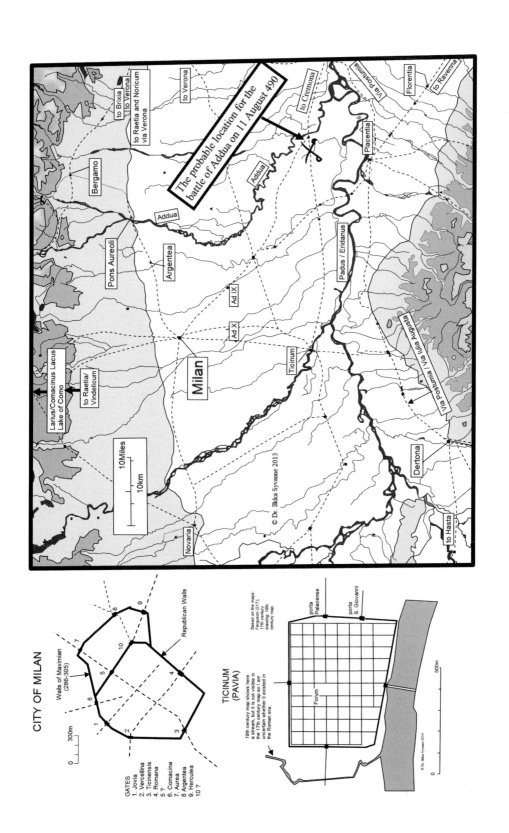

CITY OF MILAN

Walls of Maximian
(286-305)

Republican Walls

GATES
1. Jovia
2. Vercellina
3. Ticinensis
4. Romana
5 ?
6. Comacina
7. Aurea
8. Argentea
9. Herculea
10 ?

0   300m

TICINUM
(PAVIA)

19th century map shows here
a stream, but it is not visible in
the 17th century map so I am
uncertain whether it existed in
the Roman era.

Based on the maps:
Ferguson (217);
17th century
drawing; 19th
century map

porta
Palacense

porta
S. Giovanni

Forum

0   500m

© Ilkka Syvänne 2014

Larius/Comacinus Lacus
Lake of Como

to Raetia/
Vindelicum

10Miles

10km

© Dr. Ilkka Syvänne 2013

Novaria

Bergamo

to Brixia
to Verona

to Raetia and Noricum
via Verona

to Verona

Pons Aureoli

Addua

Argentea

Addua

The probable location for the
battle of Addua on 11 August 490

to Cremona

Ad IX

Ad X

Milan

Ticinum

Padus / Eridanus

Placentia

Via Postumia

Florentia

to Ravenna

Via Postumia / Via Iulia Augusta

Dertona

to Hasta

a significant portion of the army survived, but we do not know whether he was present in this battle. It is also possible that this was not really a regular battle at all and that the Goths caught up with their enemy when it was in the process of crossing the river so that they destroyed only that section of the enemy force which was still west of the Addua. In this case, Tufa and Odoacer would have probably already crossed the river while Pierius was still on the other side. It is therefore unfortunate that we do not possess any details of this very significant battle which decided the fate of Italy for decades to come.

Tufa retreated to the valley of the river Athesis which lay between Verona and Tridentium (Trent). This terrain enabled him to negate the advantages that the Gothic cavalry had while also enabling him to obtain allies from the north, or alternatively the chance to retreat from Italy altogether.

The Siege of Ravenna 490–493

This time Theoderic followed his prey to Ravenna where he established a camp (*fossatum*) at Pineta (Pine Grove) three miles south of the city with the idea of blockading it as effectively as he could without a fleet. The lack of naval assets and the inability to capture Classe, the main harbour, meant that the blockade was incomplete. But it was still effective enough to cause the price of food to rise to famine level. At this time Odoacer still maintained control of Ariminum (Rimini) with its fleet of *dromones*, and probably also Dalmatia because its conquest by Zeno or Theoderic is not mentioned by any source.

Despite the ongoing siege Theoderic was now effectively lord of Italy. He therefore dispatched Flavius Rufius Postumius Festus, the chief of the Senate, to inform Zeno and obtain his recognition together with the imperial robes as promised. Festus, however, was unable to accomplish his mission because Zeno died in April 491 and his successor Anastasius refused to recognize Theoderic. This left Theoderic in a constitutional limbo, so he sent another envoy, Anicius Probus Faustus iunior Niger (consul 490, west), to Anastasius the following year, 492. Faustus was also unable to obtain recognition and was back in Italy by 494.

In the meantime much had happened. The arrival of Herulian reinforcements from the Danube, which had apparently been shipped to Ravenna thanks to the fact that Odoacer's supporters apparently still held Dalmatia, enabled Odoacer to resume his offensive. Odoacer, his *magister militum* Libila/Livila/Levila, and the newly arrived Heruls sortied out of the city against the Goths either on 10 or 15 July 491. The battle was very hard fought, but in the end the sortie ended in a terrible failure in front of the Gothic *fossatum*, and Libila was killed in the river Bedentis/Bedetis/Bedesis during the retreat. Odoacer, however, once again managed to flee to the relative safety provided by the walls of Ravenna.

The Vandals had also exploited the chaos in Italy by raiding Sicily, but they were so badly mauled in 491 that they concluded a treaty in which they gave up the tribute that Odoacer had been paying to them in return for peace. This proves that the Romans, who now recognized Theoderic as their lord, possessed adequate military means in Sicily to oppose the Vandals. These must have been positioned there by Odoacer well before this conflict. Another possibility would of course be that the East Romans had dispatched a fleet to Sicily, but none of the sources mention so.

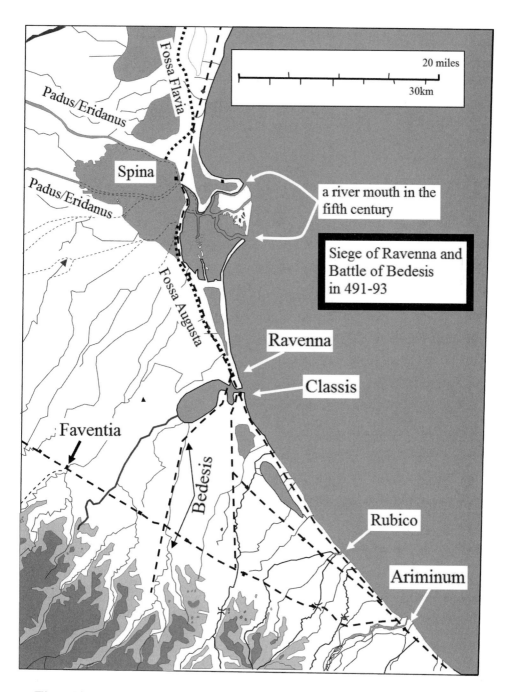

Then Theoderic received another piece of bad news. The Rugians under their king Fredericus/Frideric, who had been left behind at Ticinum, were causing serious problems with their unruly behaviour towards the native Romans. This was intolerable in a situation in which Theoderic wanted to appear as the saviour of Italy. Theoderic travelled there in person and disciplined Fredericus, either on 18 or 22 August 491,

Modern Reconstruction of the Fifth and Sixth Century Ravenna

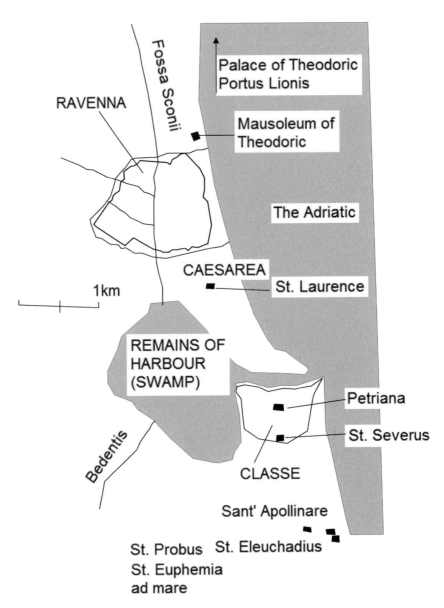

Fossa Sconii

Palace of Theodoric
Portus Lionis

RAVENNA

Mausoleum of
Theodoric

The Adriatic

CAESAREA

St. Laurence

1km

REMAINS OF
HARBOUR
(SWAMP)

Petriana

St. Severus

Bedentis

CLASSE

Sant' Apollinare

St. Probus   St. Eleuchadius
St. Euphemia
ad mare

but this did not produce the desired result. Instead, the humiliated Fredericus and his Rugians deserted and joined Tufa somewhere north of Verona where Theoderic then isolated them by posting additional forces in the area. The reason for this conclusion is that the newly allied Tufa and Fredericus were unable to advance into Italy. The alliance, however, proved short-lived and the two men quarrelled and fought a battle in the area between Verona and Tridentium presumably in the river valley. The end result was the defeat and death of Tufa. This took place either in 492 or 493. After this, Theoderic defeated Fridericus, but we do not know any details of how this was achieved. The two most likely alternatives are that Fridericus was defeated by the forces sent to isolate him and Tufa, or that he managed to invade Italy and was then defeated either by Theoderic in person or by his general in 492 or 493. The situation was fast becoming hopeless for Odoacer.

Ravenna suffered an earthquake on 26 May 492, but unfortunately for Theoderic this did not give him an opportunity to enter it, so he was forced to continue his blockade of the city. It was then in 492 that Theoderic finally decided to tighten the blockade by obtaining ships, which he actually should have done at the very beginning of the siege. Theoderic led his forces against the city of Ariminum, which he captured together with its *dromones*. This proved decisive because now he led these *dromones* to Lion's Harbour, six miles north of Ravenna, where he built his Palace called *Fossatum Palatioli*.

Theoderic was now able to squeeze the defenders inside the blockade to such an extent that the famine became intolerable and Odoacer was forced to begin negotiations for peace. The two agreed to rule Italy jointly. On 25 February 493 Odoacer handed over his son Thela as a hostage to prove his honesty, and the next day Theoderic entered Classis/Classes and made it his headquarters. On 27 February they concluded the peace agreement while the Archbishop of Ravenna, John, acted as a mediator. On 5 March 493 the Ostrogoths finally rode through the gates of Ravenna and took control of the city. On 15 March Theoderic invited Odoacer to attend a banquet. Odoacer came with his *comitatus*, but this was not enough to protect him from what followed. Theoderic had hidden his men on both sides of the banquet hall. Two of them pretended to be supplicants and grasped Odoacer's hands, and at that moment the others rushed in with swords in their hands, but those whose duty it was to kill Odoacer hesitated out of fear, according to John of Antioch. So Theoderic rushed forward and struck Odoacer on the collarbone with his sword. Odoacer is claimed to have shouted, 'Where is God?' and Theoderic shouted, 'This is what thou didst to my friends,' and then made a sword cut that went all the way through Odoacer's body as far as his hip. Theoderic was amazed and said, 'I think that the wretch had never a bone in his body.'[86] His brother Onulf was shot by arrows attempting to flee, while his son Thela was exiled to the Visigothic nation. However, when Thela later escaped and entered Italy, he was also killed. Odoacer's wife Sunigilda was imprisoned and starved to death. The official reason for the massacre was that Odoacer had been planning to do the same, but even if this is plausible it was probably merely an excuse for Theoderic to get rid of his enemy.

The elated Ostrogoths recognized Theoderic as their king, which should be interpreted that they now recognized Theoderic as King of the Goths and Romans and not only King of the Gothic nation. This means that Theoderic had decided that he had waited long enough for the official recognition which had not been forthcoming from Anastasius and that it was now his right to start calling himself King of the Romans or Italy just as Odoacer had and not wait for the Emperor's permission to do so.

Theoderic the Great was to rule for thirty-three years until his death on 30 August 526. He would have already deserved his title for his achievements, but he was to do even more than this. He was to become the most powerful ruler of his times.

The Final Years of Zeno 489–491: Peace at Last

In about 489 there was a serious factional riot at Antioch. Factional riots became ever more common in the course of the next decades. In this case it was the Green Faction which murdered the Jews in Antioch without mercy. Malalas states that the removal of *Comes Orientis* Theodorus from office pacified the rioters. According to him Zeno was angry with the Greens of Antioch and upbraided them for having torched only the dead Jews while not torching the living ones, which then supposedly ended the whole affair. It is unfortunate that Malalas (15.15) fails to give us the exact circumstances for the riots and why the removal of the magistrate and the Emperor's racist but possibly ironic statement worked.[87]

The last two years of Zeno's life were marked by worsening health, superstitious fears and by misrule by the Isaurians who had been raised to dominant positions by Zeno. Zeno trusted in particular the advice of *Comes* Maurianos because he was supposed to be able to foresee the future. Zeno's readiness to resort to the use of such means of prediction shows nicely how the approach of death was weakening the mind of this aging ruler. Maurianos predicted that an ex-silentiary would succeed Zeno as Emperor and marry his wife. As a result, Zeno became suspicious of Pelagius who was not only a learned man but also an *ex-silentiarius* and patrician. Zeno duly arrested him, confiscated his property and had him strangled. The Praetorian Prefect Arcadius did not approve, and when the Emperor learnt of this he ordered him to be killed as he entered the Palace. But Arcadius was warned, presumably by those who did not approve Zeno's order, and fled to the Great Church of Constantinople where he escaped death because the Emperor for some reason decided to respect the sanctity of the church. Zeno merely confiscated his property.

After 488 Zeno made no pretence in his favouritism of Isaurians like Cottomenes or Longinus of Cardala or his relatives such as his brothers Longinus and Conon. The latter two misused their position and helped anyone in return for payment. Longinus for example, who expected to succeed his brother Zeno on the throne, became particularly notorious for his lifestyle, perhaps because he had been in prison for so long. His lust was insatiable: he was not satisfied with only whores but also forced married women to have sex with him – even the wives of public officials – and nuns. This made him intensely hated, in particular among those whose opinions counted. Zeno also became intensely unpopular in the capital – even more so than before if that were possible – finally dying of epilepsy or dysentery on 9 April 491. This must have been a great relief for all those who the Isaurians had been mistreating.

However, there is an alternative version of the circumstances of Zeno's death. According to two late sources, Cedrenus (622) and Zonaras (14.31–35), Zeno was buried alive when unconscious, and when he woke up and started to shout from within the sarchophagus his wife Ariadne did not allow anyone to open it. When one connects this event with the story of Zachariah of Mytilene (7.1) that the future Emperor Anastasius, while still a soldier, had been favoured by the Empress Ariadne, as Haarer does (p.4), then the circumstances of Zeno's death become suspicious. Had he been murdered by Ariadne on behalf of her lover Anastasius? Unfortunately it is impossible to know which of the versions is true, but in my opinion the latter more sensational one is actually the more likely and explains why it was that this unknown person *decurio silentiariorum* Anastasius became the ruler. If the story is true, Anastasius and Ariadne must have loved each other dearly.

Zeno the Isaurian as Emperor

As we have seen, the reign of the very unpopular Isaurian *Henoticon* Zeno (474–491) was dominated by attempted coups and by his need to play one military faction against the other. There was the constant threat that if he campaigned in person, the native soldiers would simply kill him. Consequently, with one exception, he did not lead armies in person, and usually sought to maintain peace on all frontiers so that he would not have to fight simultaneously against domestic and foreign enemies. Persia and Rome were both facing serious external and internal troubles, which meant that neither wanted to fight against each other. This was important because it was during Zeno's reign that the Jews and Samaritans started to seek Persian help against the Romans. On top of that the Romans lost the support of the Christians of Persia when Kavadh (Kawad/Kavad/Qubad/Qubadh, son of Peroz) gave his support to the Nestorian Church in about 486.

In the field of religion Zeno's goals were enlightened because he at least tried to reconcile the different churches with the so-called *Henoticon* of Zeno. In a sense this was a success, because under his rule most of the Eastern bishops came to accept this compromise. However, the reception was not as good in the West where the popes launched a steady attack against the *Henoticon*. The end result of this was the so-called Acacian Schism which lasted until the reign of Justin I. This was obviously bad for the cooperation between the Eastern and Western Churches, but at the same time it can be said to have been meaningless because the West was fast becoming relatively unimportant for the East. At this stage the West was practically impotent in the field of military matters and was entirely dependent on the support of the East for its survival, and in fact Zeno did launch a campaign against the leader of the West, Odoacer, which ended in the destruction of the latter.

Zeno's reign was marked by constant upheaval, and he was not a good military commander, but he still managed to hold on to his life and position. This was actually a great achievement and he deserves credit for it. Zeno was indeed a first rate schemer and plotter, in fact so much so that nobody but his closest relatives trusted him.

Zeno also deserves credit for having finally solved the Gothic problem in the Balkans by dispatching them under Theoderic to Italy. This can actually be called his only real policy success.

Augustus Flavius Zeno (474-491). Source: Hodgkin

The way in which he achieved all of this, which was the favouritism of that faction of Isaurians (his tribal followers) which favoured him, was the poisonous legacy that he left for his successor to solve. He also left the state treasury and the civil service in miserable condition thanks to his spendrift habits and corrupt practices. But after Zeno's reign East Rome stood proud and strong, unlike West Rome. This was not a bad accomplishment in the circumstances, but I would still hesitate to include him among the so-called good emperors.

Chapter Twelve

Anastasius (11 April 491–9 July 518)[1]

Augustus Anastasius I (1 April 491 - 9 July 518)
Drawings of coins by Beger 1696

M alalas (16.1, tr. by E. Jeffreys, M. Jeffreys and R. Scott, p.220) describes the appearance of Anastasius as follows: 'He was very tall, with short hair, a good figure, a round face, both hair and beard greying; he had a grey pupil in his right eye and a black one in his left though his eyesight was perfect; and he shaved his beard frequently.' This is clearly in evidence in his coins. He had a nickname Dicorus (twin-eyes).

The Coronation on 11 April 491[2]

Zeno died on 9 April 491 and on the following day the Senate, the Patriarch Euphemius, Empress Ariadne and other powerbrokers met at the Palace to discuss the question of succession while the soldiers and citizens waited in the hippodrome. This was high theatre in which the main roles were played by the *Praepositus Sacri Cubiculi* Urbicius, who is not to be confused with the *MVM per Orientem* Urbicius, the writer of military treatises, and Empress Ariadne. The expectation of Longinus, brother of Zeno, and the Isaurians in the capital was that Longinus would succeed his brother. This was not to be. At the meeting of the powerbrokers in front of the Delphax in the Palace, the *PVC* Urbicius took the lead and suggested that the choice of who would succeed Zeno should be left in the hands of Ariadne. Ariadne in her turn chose the 60-year-old silentiary Anastasius, a native of Dyrrachium in Nova Epirus. It is clear that this was merely theatre and that the decision to nominate Anastasius had been made well before this by Ariadne, Urbicius and their backers among the military who cannot have included any Isaurians. The worsening health of Zeno had been known for months and the key players must have started to make plans well before his death. The Isaurians were now so hated that they had to choose a native as Zeno's successor. As noted above, it is possible or even probable that Anastasius was Ariadne's lover, so the choice was a natural one. As a long serving silentiary, the 60-year Anastasius had in all probability once been a subordinate of Urbicius at some point so that these two men knew each other – Zeno had placed the *silentiarii* under the *Magister Officiorum* (Delmaire, 39), but the fact that both men had been in office for decades makes it clear that they knew each other. It is therefore clear that the principal players behind Anastasius's nomination were precisely Ariadne and Urbicius, but it is still quite clear that these two must have obtained the backing of the key military men for their choice in advance. In my opinion, these must have included the unknown *Comes Domesticorum*[3] and other commanders of the *Scholae* and *Domestici*, because in this case the *Excubitores* included too many Isaurians to be trusted, and it is clear that the conspirators kept all of this hidden from the overall commander of the bodyguards, the *Magister Officiorum* Longinus of Kardala. One may also speculate that Ariadne and Urbicius exploited the above-mentioned prediction that an ex-silentiary would succeed Zeno to press their case among the superstitious.

The only thorn in the situation was the Patriarch Euphemius who vehemently opposed the nomination of Anastasius. Euphemius knew that Anastasius held a favourable attitude towards the heretic views of Eutyches. Anastasius had also given private sermons in the Great Church in 488/491, which had resulted in riots. This had led to the interference of the Patriarch and Zeno with the result that Euphemius was able to silence Anastasius. John of Nikiu even claims that Zeno exiled Anastasius to Egypt, but this is not accepted by most historians even if it is still clear that Anastasius had at least visited Egypt at some point. It is clear that Anastasius was a charismatic speaker and a religious person; he had even posted himself as a candidate for the Patriarchate of Antioch in 488. It is therefore not surprising that Euphemius agreed to carry out the coronation on 11 April 491, but only after Anastasius had signed a written declaration in which he accepted the Council of Chalcedon. To secure the legality of succession Ariadne married Anastasius on 20 May 491 so that the two lovebirds were finally united officially. This was certainly a marriage of love and not only a marriage of convenience for political reasons.

The Isaurians were presented with a *fait accompli*, and not unnaturally they were not satisfied with the situation. It is therefore not surprising that a purge of Isaurians from all positions of power followed soon after this. Very soon after Anastasius took the reins of power, Ariadne informed the populace that Julianus had been appointed as the new *Praefectus Urbis Constantinopoleos* (Urban Prefect of Constantinople). He was a native of Alexandria and a scholar whose actions provoked a riot, especially when he imposed restrictions on theatrical shows.[4] The latter resulted in a riot in the Hippodorome, and after that a more widespread riot engulfing the city in fire. So Anastasius replaced Julianus with his brother-in-law Secundinus to satisfy the populace while still suppressing the revolt with a harsh hand. He accused the Isaurians of having instigated this revolt, and it is possible that they did, but it is also possible that he just exploited this for his own purposes. It appears probable that the Isaurians in Isauria revolted immediately after they had heard of Anastasius' nomination, so that one can certainly consider it probable that those in the capital had the same tendencies. The simultaneous revolt in Isauria made all Isaurians even more suspect than they already were. The revolt in Isauria appears to have started under the leadership of Conon the ex-bishop of Apameia and Lilingis, the *Comes et Praeses Isauriae*.[5]

According to Malalas (16.2), Anastasius was also a supporter of the Red Faction at Constantinople so he took active measures against the Greens and Blues, who in their turn caused disturbances throughout the realm. One may also wonder whether the Green Faction in particular, which had been favoured by Zeno (Malalas 15.5), was behind this rioting. My suggestion is that the Greens sided now with their Isaurian backers and that the rioting had indeed been instigated by the Isaurians against the newly appointed *PVC* Julianus who failed to crush the revolt and was therefore replaced with one who could.[6]

Zeno's brother Longinus was exiled to the Thebaid where he died of hunger eight years later. His mother, wife and daughter were exiled to Bithynia where they had to subsist on charity. The *Magister Officiorum* Longinus of Kardala, senator Athenodorus, and other Isaurians were expelled from the capital and their property confiscated to reward Anastasius' supporters and to finance the war against the Isaurians. The expulsion of the unruly and badly behaving barbarian Isaurians from the capital was a crowd-pleaser and sure to make the Emperor's position in the capital more secure. Anastasius cancelled the yearly donation of money to the Isaurians introduced by Illus in 484 and continued by Zeno. This was another wise move that saved money and punished the barbarians. He ordered the fortress at Papyrios to be demolished, probably to prevent it from becoming the place of refuge it had been during the previous revolt. His forces were apparently able to do this because the rebels had not yet managed to widen their revolt, which seems to have taken place only after the arrival of those who had been expelled from the capital.[7] It might actually have been wiser to massacre the Isaurians than expel them, but it is probable that the situation was such that the expulsion was actually the better alternative because it removed the threat from Constantinople with less trouble.

It was also now that Anastasius purged the *Excubitores* from the Isaurians and replaced them with native Romans or Germans so that from this date onwards they were loyal to him. I would also suggest that it is likely that the future Emperor Justin I was now promoted as its commander with the title *Comes Excubitorum*, a title which he definitely held in 515–18, because he was probably a member of this corps. He was born into a poor peasant family and was uneducated, possibly even illiterate, Orthodox, and of Thracian or Illyrian descent, all of which made him an ideal candidate as a commander of the bodyguard.[8] With this background it was difficult to think that he would rise to become Emperor, but as we shall see this is precisely what happened, and to the benefit of the Empire. He was to be one of the 'good emperors', as was Anastasius.

Anastasius started military reforms immediately after gaining power because the first piece of legislation was addressed to *magister militum* Longinus in 491. The aim of this law was to prevent the tribunes and other officers from stealing the pay of the troops. At the same time he sought to prevent the commissaries (*actuarii*, *optiones*, and *chartularii*) from stealing army provisions and from exploiting their position to make the soldiers pay for these provisions. He also ordered that the officers called *ergatores* were to pay the *solatio* directly to the soldiers, and that the actuaries could not demand exorbitant interest on any debts. Anastasius made it easier for the soldiers to obtain leave so that the tribunes could authorise leave for up to thirty men. The idea was presumably to make it less easy for the officers to extort payment in return for leaves. Next year in 492, Anastasius gave the *duces* judicial powers over all troops serving under them and prevented the soldiers from facing prosecution simultaneously in civilian and military courts. The fragments of imperial edicts preserved in inscriptions prove that Anastasius issued other edicts too that sought to prevent corruption in the military. In short, Anastasius sought to make service in the military more lucrative and to prevent the military corruption which spilled out into the civilian sphere in the form of the support that corrupt officers could give to local rich men.[9] The rooting out of corruption in the military was also very good for the exchequer because money and supplies went to the troops rather into the pockets of the officers so that there were now actually more men in the service than before. It was also beneficial for the gathering of taxes because civilian rich men could no longer use the soldiers so easily for their nefarious purposes. In combination with subsequent reforms of coins, taxation and administration this was all to have a very positive result for the economy and tax base.

The Isaurian War 491–498[10]

Longinus of Cardala and Athenodorus then joined their brethren in a revolt led by Conon and Lilingis. As the highest ranking person, Longinus took charge and armed and supplied the rebels from the stores prepared by Zeno. According to Theophanes the army comprised 150,000 Isaurians, barbarians and bandits, while according to John of Antioch (Roberto ed. fr.308.33ff., esp. 40–44) the army of Lilinges and Athenodorus, Conon, *magister* Longinus and another Athenodorus comprised 100,000 Isaurians and Romans. Both figures are plausible for a major army collected from those who had stayed loyal to Longinus, but I would suggest that 150,000 should be thought of as the overall number with non-combatants included, while the figure of 100,000 would have represented the actual fighting strength of the rebels. Considering the fact that most of these consisted of Isaurians it is very likely that the vast majority of the army consisted of light foot equipped (see Proc. *Pan.* 9) with javelins, swords and shields. However, it is probable that the rebels also possessed cavalry because one of the commanders, Lilingis, achieved renown for his skills as a horseman and was probably in charge of rebel cavalry (Marcellinus 491/2). According to Procopius of Gaza (*Pan.* 9), Theophanes (AM5985) and Zonaras (14.3.22), the rebels pillaged a number of cities in the vicinity of Isauria and advanced to Kotyaeion/ Cotyaeum in Phrygia probably with the idea of marching to the capital.

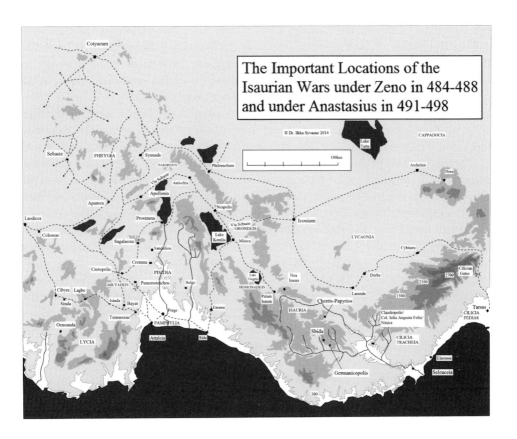

Anastasius had not been idle. According to Procopius (*Anecdota* 5.38.4ff.), he had assembled a large army under John the Hunchback (*Ioannes to epiklên Kurtos; Ioannes qui et Gibbus*) against the Isaurians. According to John of Antioch (Roberto ed. fr. 308.45ff.) and Theophanes (AM 5985), the army was under two commanders, John the Scythian and John the Hunchback. This army was drawn from Thrace so both could have been *magistri militum per Thracias*. On the basis of this it is generally assumed that this army was under the joint command of these two Johns. However, on the basis of Procopius' statement and the success of the operation, it is in my opinion more likely that John the Hunchback was the overall commander, the *strategos*, while John the Scythian was his second-in-command, the *hypostrategos*, even if it is clear that Anastasius was in the habit of dividing the command which is well-proven by the Persian War of 502–6. It is therefore quite probable that the PLRE2 is correct in suggesting that John the Hunchback would have held the position of *magister utriusque militiae praesentalis* as stated by Malalas (16.3) rather than the position of *magister militum per Thracias*, while in my opinion John the Scythian would have held the rank of *magister utriusque militiae per Thracias* (or less likely *MVM per Orientem* or *per Illyricum*[11]), but it is of course impossible to know for certain. It is also quite possible that both were praesental *magistri* because Longinus of Cardala had lost his title and no praesental *magister* is known after Theoderic the Amal marched to Italy, and I would suggest that this was indeed the case. According to John of Antioch, the *hypostrategoi* of the Imperial Army were Justin from Bedriana near Naissus (the future

Emperor), the Gothic Apskal/Apsical, Hun Sigizan, Hun Zolbo/Zolbon, and the *Comes Scholarum* Diogenianus/Diogenes, a relative of the Empress. John of Antioch claims that the size of this Imperial Army at Cotyaeum was about 2,000 men, which is clearly an underestimation and also contradicted by Procopius. I would suggest that it refers to the number of *Scholarii* present on the battlefield under Diogenianus.[12]

On the basis of the sources, it is probable that most of the regular army of the East sided with the Isaurians while the Imperial Army consisted mostly of the soldiers posted in Thrace, which in turn included the Praesental Army under John the Hunchback posted in Thrace, the Field Army of Thrace under John the Scythian, the Gothic Federates under Apskal, the Huns under Sigizan and Zolbo, the *Scholarii* under Diogenes, and the *Excubitores* plus some other soldiers under Justin. The reason why I give Justin more men than the *Excubitores* is as follows: even if he would have been able take the entire 300-men contingent with him – and this was not possible – this would not have made him a field commander. There is evidence from later periods for the use of the *Comes Excubitorum* or his subordinates in command of entire armies or units of soldiers, and I would suggest that this is the case now.[13] Malalas (16.3) adds to the list the Bessoi. Should the Bessoi be identified with Bessas? The composition of the army, as detailed by John of Antioch and Theophanes, makes it clear that the Imperial Field Army consisted solely of forces posted in Thrace. My estimate based on the paper strengths is that one Praesental Army had 6,500 cavalry and 30,000 infantry; the Thracian Army 3,500 cavalry and 40,000 infantry; 10,000 Goths and Bessoi; 10,000 Huns; 2,000 *Scholarii*; and 2,000 other horsemen under Justin.[14] My estimate for the overall size of this force is therefore 70,000 footmen and 34,000 cavalry. The armies would therefore have been evenly matched as far as numbers are concerned, but there was one significant difference: most of the Isaurians would have consisted of light infantry better suited to the mountainous terrain of their native land (Proc. *Pan.* 9) than facing the massed cavalry and the massed heavy infantry phalanx they were now facing. It is very unlikely that the Isaurians even with their Roman reinforcements would have had as many horsemen as the Imperial Army they were now facing. The two Johns then led this Imperial Army to Cotyaeum where they engaged the Isaurian army under its leaders.

It is unfortunate that we do not even know the date of this very important and decisive battle. On the basis of the sources, it is possible that it took place during the winter, either very late in 491 or at the beginning of the year 492, or at the end of 492. On the basis of Marcellinus Comes the most likely of these dates is the winter 491/2, but one cannot know for certain.[15] The only details that we know of the battle of Cotyaeum are that Lilingis, who was slow on foot but a superb horseman, was the first to be killed by the Imperial Army, and when this happened the Isaurians panicked and fled.[16]

According to Theophanes (AM5985), the Imperial Army destroyed most of the enemy army and would have ended the war then and there had they not stopped to loot. It was thanks to this that the remnants of the Isaurian force managed to flee to the mountains and its secure strongholds. This means that the Isaurians were not disciplined enough to form a hollow infantry square/oblong or double-fronted formations in which they could have retreated, but rather that they panicked immediately when the enemy killed their cavalry commander and outflanked them. Consequently the Imperialists were once again forced to fight a prolonged campaign which consisted of sieges and guerrilla warfare in the mountains.

On the basis of the above and the composition of the forces, one may make the educated guess that both sides deployed their cavalries on the wings and that the battle was decided immediately when the cavalry wings engaged each other, which resulted in the death of the rebel cavalry commander Lilingis. This would mean that the battle was decided by the superior numbers and quality of the Imperial cavalry, and in particular by those who killed Lilingis at the very beginning of the battle. Perhaps it was because of this that John of Antioch (Roberto ed. 308.46–7) claimed that the Imperial Army consisted of only about 2,000 men. It would have been these 2,000 men who engaged and killed Lilingis and those around them, and if my speculation is correct then this 2,000-man unit would have consisted of the *Scholarii* under Diogenius/Diogenianus, and it is quite possible that it was because of this that he received the title of *Patricius* mentioned by Malalas.[17] Readers, however, should keep in mind that this reconstruction of the main features of the battle is merely conjecture based on the details given and period combat doctrine.

The Isaurians scattered around the mountains and the Imperial Army did likewise in order to deal with the enemy guerrillas in different places and to besiege all of their different mountain strongholds. Thanks to the previous Isaurian War, the Imperial Army and its leaders, especially John the Scythian, were thoroughly familiar with the way this war was to be conducted and how the Isaurians were to be defeated. One of the places which the Imperials besieged was Claudiopolis on the Calycadnus, which fell to the forces led by Diogenianus in 493. It is clear that in this case the force that captured the city cannot have consisted solely of the Imperial Bodyguards but also of large numbers of regulars. As noted above, it is probable that Diogenianus had been promoted as a result of the battle of Cotyaeum to the rank of *patricius* which usually carried with it the title of *magister militum* possibly *per Orientem*. The Isaurians under Bishop Conon reacted with a counter-attack, marched against Diogenianus and put him under a siege in the very same place he had besieged previously. It did not take long for the Imperials to start suffering from lack of victuals, but fortunately for them John the Hunchback had assembled a relief force. John's forces marched through the passes of Taurus, captured the guards (i.e. surprised them) and then made a surprise attack against the besieging force while those inside sortied from the city. The Isaurian besiegers were destroyed and Bishop Conon was fatally wounded with a spear. Theophanes calls this the second very great victory for the Romans over the Isaurians, and this is defininitely true. After this, the Isaurians did not dare to face the Romans in open battle again.[18]

Enemies naturally exploited the civil war between the Romans and Isaurians. Marcellinus Comes' statement that the *magister militum* Julianus was struck and killed by Scythian iron (a sword) when fighting a night battle against the Scythians proves that the transferral of the Roman forces from Thrace to fight against the Isaurians had left a power vacuum in the area which their enemies were not slow to exploit. It is usually suggested that these Scythians were Bulgars, and I concur. The Bulgars are the most likely culprits. The statement of Marcellinus, however, leaves open who won the encounter. On the basis of his Latin it appears that it had been Julianus who attacked the Bulgars during the night, but this is not absolutely certain because the text can be understood either way. However, if it indeed had been Julianus who attacked the Bulgars, then the battle could have gone either way because the death of the commander could have resulted in the failure of the attack, but since Marcellinus does not say anything about Bulgars exploiting the death of

Julianus, and Anastasius himself claimed to have defeated all invaders in 491 (see below), it is safest to assume that the Bulgars lost and then fled back to their side of the border. The PLRE2 assumes on the basis of the location of the battle that Julianus was *MVM per Thracias*, which is indeed possible but it is possible that he just had the title *magister militum*. If John the Scythian had held this position, then Julianus was his successor after John had presumably been made praesental *magister* or *MVM per Orientem*, but as noted above in my opinion it is probable that John the Scythian was praesental *magister* already in 491.

The Persian *shahanshah* Kavadh had also been active. He demanded that the Romans pay the upkeep of the Persian garrisons in the Caucasus as agreed before. Anastasius answered that he would pay if the Persians returned Nisibis. Kavadh's response was to send his Arab allies to raid Phoenicia Libanensis, which they did as far as Emesa in 491/2. This was useless. Anastasius still refused. Furthermore, the harsh stance of Anastasius against the Persians encouraged the Persarmenians to revolt against the Zoroastrian persecutors in about 491/2. It is possible that Anastasius had encouraged them to do so. This distracted the Persians, at least for a while. On top of this, according to Joshua of Stylite (20), Anastasius bragged to Kavadh that he had faced and defeated the Germans (Gepids?), the Blemmyes and others (which includes at least the above-mentioned Bulgars). This suggests that at the beginning of his reign Anastasius had faced a series of raids resulting from the fact that the death of Zeno had made treaties void and had not only faced but also defeated all of the raiders.[19] It is clear that it was thanks to this that Anastasius was unable to commit all of his forces against the Isaurians.

After the Isaurians realized they were no match for the Imperialists in battle, they resorted to their specialty: guerrilla warfare. Longinus of Cardala, 'the *magister*', and Athenodorus remained on difficult terrain where they harassed the Imperials, while Longinus of Selinus, who lived in Isaurian Antioch, shipped food from abroad and then transported it to the rebels in the mountains. This meant that the war became even more prolonged.[20]

This prolonging of the conflict led Anastasius to try other means to put a stop to the fighting, and he started negotiations with the Isaurians. He confided that he had done so to the Patriarch Euphemius and asked him to convene the bishops of Constantinople to pray that the negotiations would bring about a peace with the Isaurians. Patriarch Euphemius then revealed this secret to the patrician John who was father-in-law of the Isaurian rebel Athenodorus. When Anastasius learned that Euphemius had revealed the contents of their confidential discussion he had the necessary excuse to get rid of the pro-Chalcedonian Patriarch, and he had been looking for the right excuse for a long time. Euphemius had intervened in Church matters all over the East on behalf of the Chalcedonian faith and this was too much for Anastasius to bear. An assassin attacked the Patriarch with a sword, but Paul the Deacon took the blow on his head and then killed the assassin. Then there was an ambush at a liturgical gathering, but Euphemius managed to flee in disguise. After this Anastasius sent soldiers against the Patriarch who found the Emperor's written oath to follow the Chalcedonian faith and then took it away from Euphemius by force. After this, Anastasius convened a Synod which found the Patriarch guilty of Nestorianism and exiled him in November 496. Anastasius appointed Macedonius as his successor, but the people rioted in support of Euphemius. This did not alter Anastasius' policy. Macedonius was duly made to sign the *Henoticon* to prove his loyalty.[21]

The experienced John the Scythian and John the Hunchback knew how to deal with the difficult situation. By combining the accounts of Theophanes (AM 5987–8), Evagrius (3.35) and Marcellinus Comes (a.498), it becomes clear that the leaders divided their responsibilities. John the Scythian advanced against Longinus of Cardala and the Athenodori and Theodore,[22] while John the Hunchback advanced against Longinus of Selinus and Indes and the other rebels. John the Hunchback divided responsibilites further by placing *Comes* Priscus in charge of the operations against Longinus of Selinus at Antioch while he himself hunted down the rest of the rebels.

According to Priscus of Caesarea (*Pan.* 103ff.), the rebel fleet was destroyed in a storm that threw the ships against the Lycian shore, but we should not take this to mean that the Roman fleet would not have had any role in it because we know from later East Roman naval treatises that the Romans could time their naval attack to coincide with a storm and the exploitation of stormy weather by Constantine the Great's fleet against the Licinians is a proof that this was not a later idea but one of the combat methods used by the Roman navy probably throughout its history.[23] In light of this it is more than likely that the Roman fleet had attacked the Isaurians at the very moment the storm hit them to ensure that the enemy fleet would end up on the shore. It was thanks to this dual operation that the enemy was completely isolated.

John the Scythian was the first to achieve his objectives. He besieged and captured Longinus of Cardala, both Athenodori and Theodore. The prisoners were beheaded so that the head of one of the Athenodori was sent to Tarsus where it was fixed on a spear in front of the gates to rot away as a warning of what would happen to rebels. The heads of Longinus, the other Athenodorus and Theodore were cut off and sent to the Emperor Anastasius. He fixed them on poles at a place called Sycae opposite Constantinople. John the Scythian was rewarded with a consulship for 498.

In 498 John the Hunchback achieved his objectives. Priscus captured Antioch with Longinus of Selinus while John himself captured Indes. Longinus, Indes and others were paraded in chains through Constantinople and the Hippodrome in a triumph for the victorious Emperor Anastasius after which they too were beheaded. John the Hunchback was rewarded with a consulship for the year 499. The Isaurian problem was then permanently solved by transporting masses of Isaurians away from Isauria to Thrace where they were used as soldiers against any invading barbarian force. The forts and strongholds of Isauria were demolished so that they could not be used as safe havens for bandits. This strategy worked. The Isaurians never again posed any serious problem for the East Romans.[24]

The sending of Theoderic the Amal with the Ostrogoths to retake Italy from Odoacer had created another problem for Anastasius, and this at a time when he was forced to fight against the Isaurians. Theoderic dispatched an embassy to Zeno in late 490, but it arrived in Constantinople at about the time or soon after the death of Zeno in April 491. Theoderic asked the Emperor to recognize his position as ruler of Italy, but the situation was complicated by the fact that Theoderic had not yet defeated Odoacer who still held Ravenna, Rimini with a fleet, and apparently Dalmatia. It was presumably thanks to this uncertainty that Anastasius withheld his recognition. Theoderic's second embassy to

Anastasius in about 492/3 was equally fruitless, but apparently included the concession according to which Theoderic got the right to nominate one of the consuls but not the right to appoint him to the office which still rested with the Emperor. It is probable that Anastasius wanted more effort from Theoderic to convince the Pope to heal the so-called Acacian Schism by accepting the *Henoticon* than Theoderic was willing to supply in a situation in which he wanted to secure his own rule over the Italians. Basically, Theoderic sought the support of the Italian Church and its nobility by respecting their rights as long as they recognized his superior position.[25]

After the death of Odoacer, Theoderic felt no longer constrained to wait for the official recognition of the Emperor; he allowed himself to be called King of the Romans and Goths in 493 which was an open insult to the Emperor. The relationship between the two obviously soured, but did not lead to open conflict thanks to the fact that the Isaurian War preoccupied Anastasius while Theoderic also needed to secure his newly won position. His international standing was secured with marriage alliances between his family and with the barbarian rulers of the west. In addition to this, Theoderic may have sought to undermine the position of Anastasius in the Balkans through the Pope. It is therefore not surprising to find Pope Gelasius declaring that his spiritual authority included temporal power and that Anastasius should be submissive to his will. In other words, where Anastasius as a temporal leader with his observance of the Henoticon Edict claimed authority over religious doctrine, church and Pope, the Pope as a religious leader claimed to possess temporal powers over the Emperor. This quarrel was undoubtedly in the interest of Theoderic in a situation in which he and Anastasius were not on friendly terms even if they maintained superficially friendly relations.[26]

When the Isaurian war was drawing to its end the situation changed. Theoderic faced the prospect of having to face the wrath of Anastasius. It was probably because of this that Theoderic wanted to find some sort of agreement with Anastasius and it was probably because of this that he ensured the nomination of the pro-Eastern Anastasius II as Pope in 496 and dispatched Festus to the Emperor Anastasius in 496. This resulted in the official recognition of Theodoric as ruler of Italy and in the sending of the ornaments of the Palace in January 497. This recognized Theoderic as king even if it did not recognize him as Emperor. Theoderic kept up this pretence by not assuming imperial prerogatives, but it did not mean that he did not behave as if he were an Emperor. Furthermore, even Italian senators called him *Augustus*, which is shown for example by the inscription set up by the Decii, which calls him '*semper Aug(ustus)*'. In return for the above and for the recognition of Rome's superiority over the See of Alexandria and the removal of Acacius' name from the diptychs, Festus had promised that Pope Anastasius II would accept the *Henoticon* with the implication that he recognized the Emperor Anastasius as his superior and the Patriarchate of Constantinople as equal to that of Rome. This, however, was not to be because when Festus then returned, he found that Anastasius II had died. This resulted in a schism within the Western Church because now Festus through bribery and intrigue obtained the nomination of *pro-Henoticon* Laurentius as Pope in the Church of Santa Maria while his political enemy senator Faustus (envoy in 491/2) and most of the bishops nominated *anti-Henoticon* Symmachus as Pope in the Latern Basilica. Both were nominated as popes on the same day, 22 November 498. The Senate and clergy were divided, but the vast majority supported Symmachus. Both popes sought recognition from Theoderic at Ravenna. Contrary to the expectations of Festus and Laurentius, Theoderic decided in favour of Symmachus despite what Festus had achieved. They had failed to understand that Theoderic had already obtained what he wanted, namely official recognition. It was not in his interest anymore to allow Anastasius to get what he wanted. So Laurentius was dispatched as Bishop of Nuceria in Campania. In 501 Symmachus was accused of not celebrating Easter properly, immoral intercourse with women and illegal alienation of Church property, but he was found not guilty in the so-called *synodus Palmaris* undoubtedly because he had the backing of Theoderic. It is therefore unsurprising that relations with the East plummeted under Symmachus, but, as we shall see, this was a reflection of what was taking place simultaneously in the temporal field.[27]

And why would Anastasius have been willing to conclude peace with Theoderic in 497 at a time when the Isaurian War was coming to its end? There were several reasons. Firstly, it is clear that by now Theoderic had secured his position in Italy through his alliances with the ruling Italian elite and the Catholic Church. Secondly, he had secured himself with marriage alliances and other alliances that he had concluded with neighbours. Thirdly, it is probable that Anastasius thought it possible to end the Acacian Schism with the help of Theoderic, if he recognized him. In my opinion, however, the decisive and most important reason for Anastasius' readiness to conclude the peace at this time was that the Isaurian War had been very costly both in manpower and money. The Romans must have lost a minimum of 100,000 soldiers in this war, perhaps 150,000, and it took a while to build up military strength after such a culling. Anastasius was in no position to start a war in the West. Subsequent events on the Eastern frontier prove that his forces were ill-prepared to fight against the Persians as well. Not only had Anastasius lost most of the field armies posted in the East, as these had sided with the Isaurians because at the time most of them were Isaurians, but the walls of the cities, towns and forts in the East had also been allowed to decay thanks to lack of upkeep during the very long peace with Persia.

In fact, the continuation of the Isaurian War and the beginning of operations to retake control of the trade route to India in 498 (see later) meant problems for the Balkans even after Anastasius had concluded peace with Theoderic. According to Marcellinus Comes (1 September 498 – 31 August 499), the *magister militum per Illyricum* Aristus, with 15,000 men and 520 wagons, marched against the Bulgars who had invaded Thrace. The use of the Illyrian army proves nicely that the regular forces of Thrace were still in the East. The two armies met in combat beside the River Tzurta and the Romans were defeated. The Romans lost 4,000 men killed either in flight or when the riverbank collapsed (the Bulgars apparently forced the Romans against the riverbank, which collapsed). The Romans lost four *comites* (counts) Nicostratus, Innocentius, Tancus and Aquilinus in this battle, which proves how costly it was to the Romans. It is also clear that the defeat lowered the morale of the army because the next year Anastasius sent a donative with *tribunus notariorum* Paulus to the Illyrian soldiers. The aim was clearly to restore the morale of the soldiers after their defeat. By this time however, the situation in the Balkans would have already been stabilized because the ending of the Isaurian War would have enabled Anastasius to transfer forces from the East back to their stations in the West which were now also strengththened by the Isaurians who were transferred to Thrace.

The Reforms of Anastasius

Anastasius appears to have launched a series of economic and administrative reforms after the Isaurian War during the period 498–502. In 498, probably at the instigation of *comes sacrarum largitionum* John the Paphlagonian, he reformed the coinage by introducing extra large bronze coins marked with a value on the reverse: M meant 40 *nummi* and was also known as *follis*; K meant 20 *nummi*; and I meant 10 *nummi*. The introduction of these coins cleared up the confusion surrounding the small bronze coins and quelled inflation thanks to the fact that now the state controlled the weight and the numbers of bronze coins, which meant that the exchange rate between the gold coins and bronze coins became steady. This first portion of the reform was already a success, but it was modified, presumably as an answer to problems noted, in 512 by doubling their weight and by introducing another smaller coin with the letter E meaning 5 *nummi*. The reform had actually been copied from the Vandals, who had introduced a similar system under Gunthamund in 487–8. The system was such a success that Theoderic the Amal copied it too. In short, the Vandals were actually the forerunners in the financial reforms at this time. It was partially thanks to this reform that Anastasius was able to fill the treasury, because the new bronze coins brought money into it.[28]

In 498 Anastasius also abolished the hated *chrysargyron* (*auri lustralis collatio*) which had been introduced by Constantine the Great together with the *collatio glebalis* on the senators. Marcian had already abolished the senatorial tax, but now Anastasius also eased the taxes of the common folk, the traders, fishermen, merchants, market-gardeners, artisans and prostitutes. The abolition of this tax was significant because, although yielding only about one twentieth of what agriculture produced in taxes, it was still responsible for tens of thousands of pounds of gold per year. (Note how small the sums paid to the barbarians or Persians were in comparison.) The cancelling of these taxes allowed trade and industry to flourish, which was good for the morale and well-being of the people and defence of the cities. How did Anastasius fill the gap in the budget? He took the money from his private income controlled by the *res privata* created originally by Septimius Severus. It seems probable that Anastasius received a great windfall of property as a result of the confiscations of Isaurian and their supporters' property so that he was able to place these and some other Imperial properties under the *comes sacri patrimonii*, who was created or recreated by Anastasius for this purpose, and who then transferred the money to the *sacrae largitiones* to replace the money lost thanks to the cancelling of the *chrysargyron*. Anastasius was satisfied with the funds that remained in the *res privata*.[29]

Soon after the reforms of 498, followed the reform of how taxes were collected. This reform is usually connected with Marinus the Syrian so that it took place probably at the beginning of the sixth century, either when Marinus had become *tractator* so that the reform took place between 498 and 502 or when Marinus became the *PPO* so that it took place in 506/7. The reform was the introduction of the so-called *vindices* (sing. *vindex*), who were appointed by the Praetorian Prefect and who were sent to supervise the collection of taxes by the *curiales* (the city councils). The idea was to root out the corrupt practices of the rich and powerful landowners who could avoid the paying of taxes and who were also in the habit of stealing a part of the taxes meant for the state and city. This

A coin (Follis) of Anastasius I
D(ominus) N(oster) ANASTASIUS
P(er) P(etuus) AUG(ustus)

reform proved a great success so that the tax burden of the poor lessened at the same time as the state coffers were filled with money. Anastasius may also have strengthened the position of *pagarch*, who enforced the payment of taxes. In addition, Anastasius strengthened the position of the bishops in the city administration by including them among those who nominated *defensores* (sing. *defensor*) for the communities. The *defensor* was an imperial officer in charge of protecting the lower classes against the rich landowners and governors. Anastasius also strengthened the position of these *defensores* so that the net effect was very beneficial for taxpayers despite the grumbling of the traditionalists like John Lydus.

Anastasius also introduced legislation in 500 which eased the tax burden on the communities when some of their lands were uncultivated, and rationalized the *coemptio* (produce sold at fixed prices for the army) with two sets of legislation in 491 and 498 so that he finally abolished it altogether in about 512 from all other areas except Thrace. That Thrace was not included had serious consequences (see later). Anastasius also eased or cancelled taxes for a number or years in many places that had suffered either as a result of natural calamity like an earthquake or as a result of manmade disasters like wars. And if this was not enough, Anastasius was also able to launch major fortification projects throughout the Empire while still revitalizing the cities with new communal buildings like baths, shops, porticoes, basilicas, churches etc.[30] Anastasius' handling of state finances was far superior to his more famous successor Justinian, who was also famous for his building projects but who overspent.

Anastasius' nominations to high civilian offices were not based on the corrupt practice of selling them or on birth, but on the ability, experience and learning of the person in question. It was because of this that we find several capable administrators among them. Haarer lists the following as examples: Polycarp rose from the position of financial clerck to become Praetorian Prefect. Leontius had been professor of law at Beirut before he rose to the same position. The praetorian prefects Zoticus, Sergius and Marinus were all promoted to this position thanks to their learning and literary talent. Anastasius could also require his generals to be learned, of which the best example is Celer. One can consider the civilian administrators to have been great successes in their fields, because the economy flourished under Anastasius.[31] However, in my opinion Anastasius' track record in military appointments is mixed, as the following account will make clear.

The Eastern Front 491–502

At the beginning of his reign Anastasius was in no position to take offensive actions against any neighbouring nations thanks to the Isaurian War and the various invasions of Roman territory, but this does not mean that he did not formulate a policy to be implemented after the Isaurian War had ended. According to Haarer (29–47), this consisted of the reorganization of the alliance structures with the various Arabic tribes and confederations and of religious and cultural policies meant to cement these alliances.

As has already been noticed, Kavadh had demanded that the Romans honour their old treaty and provide money for the upkeep of the Persian garrison in the Caucasus. Anastasius's answer was that the Persians should first return Nisibis to the Romans. It was because of this that Kavadh then dispatched his Arab allies to raid Roman territories in 491/2. They penetrated Phoenicia Libanensis as far as Emesa thanks to the fact that the Romans were distracted by their civil war, but this did not bring the desired outcome. Anastasius still refused to pay. On the basis of Joshua the Stylite's statement, the Romans defeated all invaders.[32]

Kavadh was in no position to initiate full-scale hostilities because his position was still weak, and made worse by his own foolish religious policies that had resulted in a revolt of Armenia under Vahan Mamikonean in 491/2. According to [Pseudo-] Joshua the Stylite (20–24), Kavadh restarted the persecution of Christians with the result that when the Persarmenians learned of the refusal of Anastasius I to pay tribute to the Persians, they revolted again under their charismatic leader Vahan in about 491/2.[33] Furthermore, the initial defeat of the Isaurians at Cotyaeum in 491/2 had released most of the Roman troops for possible use against the Persians.

The next time we hear of events on the eastern front is in 497/8. Kavadh had used the Mazdakite Sect, which has been characterized as an early form of communism, to try and undermine the position of the nobility and Zoroastrian clergy. This backfired. These groups had deposed him and had then placed on the throne the more malleable Zamasp either in 496 or 497. Kavadh had sought a place of refuge among the Hepthalites. He returned to power with their help in 499. However, before that several important developments had taken place for which our sole pieces of evidence are references in Theophanes AM 5990 (497/8) and Evagrius 3.36 and al-Tabari i.945–6.

According to Evagrius, the Scenite Arabs (tent-dwelling Arabs) raided Roman territory in Mesopotamia, and in both Phoenicias and the Palestines not on their own behalf but on behalf of the Persians. After they had been defeated by the Roman commanders they retreated back into their own territory. According to Theophanes, in 498 the Tent-Dwelling Arabs raided Euphratesia but were defeated by the local commander Eugenios at Bithrapsa.[34] The invaders were allies of Persia from the tribe of the phylarch Naaman. The location of Bithrapsa is not known, but it is usually suggested that it must be Rufasa/

Rufesa/Sergiopolis. At the same time, Romanus, who was the commander of the army fighting in Palestine, defeated and captured in battle, thanks to his good planning and superior generalship, Ogaros, son of Arethas, son of Thalabene, taking many prisoners. Before that the same Romanus had defeated another Tent-Dwelling Arab called Gabalas (Gabala/Jabala) who had been raiding Palestine before Romanus had arrived on the scene. At that time, Romanus had also captured, after fierce battles, the island of Iotabe/Yotabe from the Tent-Dwelling Arabs (see the reign of Leo).

The sequence of events given by Theophanes seems to advance from the later events towards earlier ones so that the first action of the year 497 had been the operation to recapture the island of Iotabe from the Arab allies, or alternatively the operation was a response to the pillage of Palestine by the Ghassanid Gabalas/Jabala if he had succeeded the Ghassanid/Jafnid Amorkesos/Imru al-Qays as suggested for example by Irfan Shahid (BAFIC 61ff., 125–6). The identification is uncertain, but still the most likely. It is, however, clear that the entire area was under one chieftain called Gabala (Jabala) and that the most likely alternative is that he was a Ghassanid/Jafnid.[35]

This means that Anastasius either responded to the raids of Gabalas in *Palestine Tertia / Salutaris*, the territory which Gabalas was supposed to protect as its Phylarch, or initiated a project to regain the possession of the trade route to India and Africa at the first opportunity he got after the defeat of half of the Isaurians by John the Scythian in 497. The obvious question is why would Gabalas have suddenly started to raid? If he started these raids on his own initiative roughly at the same time as the Persian Arabs raided, then the root cause could have been a drought, but in my opinion one should see both operations in the light of imperial politics. My own educated guess therefore is that Anastasius initiated the operation to regain possession of Iotabe and the India/Africa trade to obtain the lucrative customs duties. It is unlikely to be a coincidence that Anastasius had received an elephant as a gift from India just before the reconquest of Jotabe in about 495–6 (Marcellinus, 1 September 495 – 31 August 496). I would suggest that some unknown Indian ruler and Anastasius had formed an alliance for the purpose of bypassing the Persians, and it is not too far-fetched to think that this Indian ruler was an enemy of Kavadh.

The next stages of this operation are detailed in the following pages. The first part was the sending of Romanus to retake the island of Iotabe which he managed to achieve after an amphibious operation and fierce battles. It is likely that this formed only a part of a major naval operation along the Red Sea.[36] Gabala responded by starting to pillage Palestine before Romanus' arrival, which on the basis of Evagrius can mean Palestine III with Palestine I or even Palestine II. This presumably means that Gabala had not been in the area of operations at the time Iotabe was captured or if he was he had then retreated into the desert from where he launched an attack against the Palestines while Romanus was taking Iotabe. The latter is more likely. When Romanus then arrived on the scene, he defeated Gabala immediately and forced him back into the desert. After this Romanus marched against Ogaros son of Arethas who had invaded one of the Palestines (Palestine I?) and defeated and captured him. The identification of this Ogaros and Arethas and Thalabene has caused quite a bit of disagreement among historians. Some have thought Ogaros (Hujr?) to be a ruler of the Mudar tribe or the Kinda tribe or Ghassanids/Jafnids,[37] but in my opinion the likeliest alternative remains that Ogaros was a chieftain of the Ghassanids/Jafnids and it was because of this that he was invading Palestine at the same time as Gabala.

The raid of the Arabs of the phylarch Naaman (al-Numan?) into Euphratesia on behalf of the Persians probably in early 498 would presumably have been a Persian attempt to exploit the continuing Roman wars against the Isaurians now under John the Hunchback while Romanus was still fighting against the Ghassanids in Palestine. Even if Theophanes fails to state this, the obvious aim would have been to attempt to extort money from Anastasius for the new government of Zamasp with the excuse of using it to cover the cost of maintaining garrisons in the Caucasus against the Huns. As noted, this attack ended in a miserable failure just like the previous ones.

The years 497 and 498 were good ones for the Emperor Anastasius. His commanders defeated the Isaurians, Ghassanids and Arab allies of Persia. This, however, was not the end of the Arab attacks. According to Theophanes AM 5994, the Saracens raided Phoenicia, Syria and Palestine after the death of Ogaros under his brother Badicharimos in 500/501. The raid was over as fast as it started because Romanus was unable to catch the invaders despite giving hot pursuit. The implication is that the Romans had probably held the captured Ogaros hostage until about 500 after which he had been killed, but according to Arabic tradition both brothers actually outlived their father Arethas who died in 528. If correct, this would mean that we should consider the raid of Badicharimos as a means to put pressure on the Romans to reach an agreement with his father Arethas, which would also include the release of the hostage. The result appears to have been the famous treaty between Anastasius and Arethas mentioned by Theophanes AM 5995 (tr. by Mango and Scott, 223: 'In this year [*502*] Anastasios made a treaty with Arethas [*known as the son of Thalabene*], the father of Badicharimos and Ogaros after which all Palestine, Arabia, and Phoenice enjoyed much peace and calm.' This Arethas has usually been identified with the ruler of the Kinda, but it has also been suggested that he was ruler of the Mudar or Ghassanids/Jafnids. My own view is that this Arethas must have been a Ghassanid/Jafnid because Yaqubi and Ibn Khaldun refer to the treaty made between the Ghassanids and Anastasius.[38] Whatever the truth, it is still clear that this treaty pacified the southern section of the Eastern front for the duration of Anastasius' reign and that this was a very timely decision because it was in the same year that the Persians invaded.

The conquest of Iotabe in 498 enabled Anastasius to begin his project of reform for the vitalization of the India/Africa trade while improving the defensive organization in the area. The evidence for this has been preserved in an imperial edict which created a new office of *commercianus* for Clysma who served under the Praetorian Prefect. This change took away from the *comitiva sacrarum largitionum*, the administration of customs of this important trade. In addition to this, Anastasius regulated the recruitment and promotion of officials, which improved the efficiency of the organization and diminished the possibility for corruption. Furthermore, he regulated the distribution of supplies and improved the serving conditions of the soldiers for the same reasons.[39]

Anastasius also initiated religious and cultural projects to connect the Arabs, Himyarites and Aksumites more closely to the Roman Empire. The main idea was to spread Christianity among them because, as events of the past proved, and events of the future were to prove, Christian rulers were friendlier towards the Romans than the pagans or Jews who usually favoured the Persians. At some unknown point in time Anastasius dispatched the Monophysite bishop Silvanus to Himyar to organize the ecclesiastical hierarchy in the area. We do not know when this took place, but the usual guess is that it must have been when Himyar was ruled by the Christian king Marthad'ilan Yanuf who according to Rubin was placed on the throne by Aksum in 500.[40] However, al-Tabari (i.945–6) claims that the dominion of Aksum over Yemen lasted for 72 years, which would date the operation to install Yanuf on the throne to the year 498. This would connect the operation in Yemen with the operation to take Iotabe, and in my opinion is to be preferred over the dating of 500 proposed by Rubin because it is in agreement with the other sources.

In my opinion, this means it is likely that Anastasius had either already begun to negotiate with Aksum before the conquest of Iotabe or immediately after it for the purpose of launching a joint-combined military operation to install a Christian ruler on the Himyarite throne, and when this succeeded he dispatched Silvanus to organize the Church in the area. The former is more likely so that the initial stage of the operation would have been the conquest of Iotabe with an amphibious landing under Romanus who would then have been dispatched back to Palestine to protect it against the Ghassanids. In my opinion, it is very likely that the Romans were also actively involved in the operation to install the Christian ruler on the Himyarite throne by dispatching a naval detachment with transport ships in support just as they had been in the habit of doing ever since the Principate.[41] The naval involvement is more than likely on the basis that the Romans were already operating a fleet on the Red Sea theatre for the purpose of occupying the island of Iotabe with an amphibious landing. It means that by about 500/502 Anastasius had managed to secure the trade route from Clysma to the mouth of the Red Sea with Roman naval bases and alliances concluded with the Christian rulers of Aksum and Himyar. It is therefore not surprising that we see a further development in the system of alliances precisely in 502.

The Persian War 502–506[42]

Persian Invasion in 502–503

Kavadh owed his return to power in 498/9 entirely to the Hephthalites. Their help, however, had not come cheap. Kavadh owed them a considerable sum of money in 502 which he did not have. After he had regained his throne he had immediately dispatched envoys to Anastasius with the demand for money which Anastasius supposedly owed him on the basis of the old agreements and when a succession of these embassies had come back empty-handed Kavadh assembled his forces. On the basis of the extant evidence most modern historians are of the opinion that in the end Anastasius promised to give the money in order to avoid the conflict, but only as a loan, which Kavadh considered an insult. However, according to Procopius (*Wars* 1.7.1–2), it was Kavadh who actually asked Anastasius to loan the money on the last occasion, which Anastasius then refused to lend because he agreed with the advice given to him by his friends, which was that it was not in the Roman interest to promote good relations between Kavadh and the Hephthalites. In this case I am inclined to follow Procopius' version because it fits the circumstances better than the other version. Kavadh could easily have taken the loan and then refused to pay it back.

By refusing to give the money, Anastasius' aim was not to cause a war – after all, previous refusals had not resulted in wars. As has been noted, for example by Geoffrey

Greatrex, had Anastasius really wanted to initiate hostilities, or expected them from the Persian side, he would surely have helped the Persarmenian rebels and would surely have assembled his armies for war. He did none of these things, because he expected that the Persarmenian revolt, and the rebellions of the Tamuraye (possibly an Iranian mountain tribe) and Kadishaye, the latter of which were besieging Nisibis, would keep Kavadh preoccupied.[43] Contrary to expectations, this did not work, because the only source left for Kavadh for the money was to loot it from Roman territory. Furthermore, the Tamuraye and Kadishaye concluded peace with Kavadh when the latter promised to take them along to the Roman side of the border where the pickings were richer. The Romans were clearly aware that the Persians had assembled their army, but they appear to have made the miscalculation that it had been assembled merely to crush the Persarmenian revolt. Consequently the Romans made no defensive preparations against any possible Persian invasion. This time, and contrary to expectations, the Persarmenians were immediately defeated by the combined force of Persians, Hephthalites, Tamuraye, Kadishaye and Saracens, on top of which they were ready to sign a peace with Kavadh and provide forces for him in return for religious freedom and autonomy. The fact that the Romans had not provided any help made this decision all the easier. When the bad news was brought to Anastasius, he dispatched Rufinus as his envoy with orders to hand over the gold to Kavadh if the latter had not yet crossed the border, but when Rufinus arrived at Caesarea he learnt that Kavadh had already invaded and was advancing towards Amida.

Kavadh initiated hostilities by crossing the border on 22 August 502 and advancing towards Theodosiopolis (Erzurum). The walls of the city were in bad condition due to lack of maintenance and its commander Constantine betrayed the city to the Persians after the siege had lasted only a few days and obtained in return a military command in the Persian army. Constantine was a civilian governor with the title *Comes Armeniae* that had been created by Zeno, but oddly enough he was also a military commander at the time, expected to lead the feudal forces of the Armenian satrapies in combat. Therefore, at the time of the invasion the forces at his disposal were very limited. He simply had not had enough time to assemble the forces of the different satrapies. I am inclined to agree with the PLRE2 that we should consider him a military commander with some forces under his command. The betrayal of the city enabled Kavadh to pillage it to the satisfaction of the Hephthalites and other forces accompanying him. Joshua the Stylite claims that the city was destroyed, but, as has already been noted by several historians, this is untrue because Kavadh placed a garrison to defend it. This was a strategically sound decision because Theodosiopolis could be used as a bulwark for the protection of Persarmenia just as it had served for Roman Armenia, or vice versa it could serve as a forward base for invasions into Persarmenia or Roman Armenia.

After this, Kavadh turned south to pillage the poorly defended Armenian satrapies, which was preferable to advancing deeper into Roman territory where he could have faced far more serious opposition while his own line of retreat and supply route could have been threatened by the Romans. Now Kavadh was able to march through Chorzane to Asthiane passing through the *cleisura* (passes) of Saphcae and Illyris en route to Sophene where the local satrap Theodore promised Kavadh two years' taxes in return for not pillaging Martyropolis. Kavadh accepted the bribe, annexed Sophene and nominated

Theodore as its satrap. Anastasius later forgave Theodore this treachery because the walls of Martyropolis were considered indefensible. After this Kavadh continued his march to Amida, a day's march south of Martyropolis, which he decided to besiege because of its riches despite the fact that it was already 5 October 502.[44]

Siege of Amida on 5 October 502–12 January 503

This time the defenders did not surrender. The inhabitants of Amida had strengthened the walls in preparation for the siege. They were mostly civilians, presumably drawn from the citizen militia who served under their own leaders so that the top echelon of the

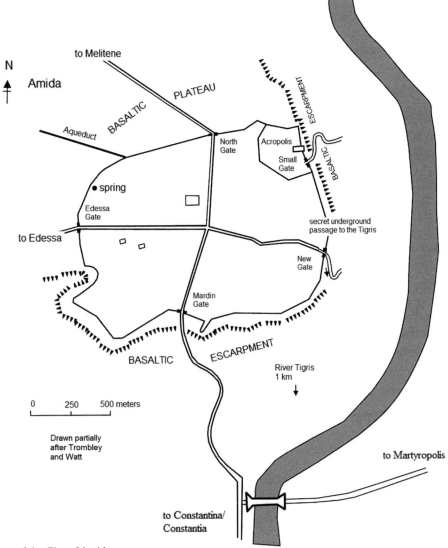

Siege of the City of Amida

command structure consisted of the civilian *praeses* (governor) of Mesopotamia Cyrus and the city council of whom the most important were Leontius the chief councillor, and Paul Bar Zainab the steward. In short, the governor and the civilian city administrators were in charge of the militiamen and defence and as we shall see their combat performance was exemplary – even better than had been the performance of the professional soldiers during the siege of 359 (see vol.1). In fact, Procopius (*Wars* 1.7.4) states that there were no soldiers present at all, but, as has been noted by Geoffrey Greatrex (1998, 84), this must be an exaggeration. The governor undoubtedly had some soldiers in his staff, and there may also have been other soldiers in the city, for example on leave, but the role of these professional soldiers was clearly limited because none of the sources mention any role for them.

Rufinus reached Kavadh just when he had arrived before Amida. Rufinus still offered Kavadh the gold, if he abandoned his campaign. Kavadh's response was to imprison Rufinus for the length of the siege and then send him back to the Emperor with the news. Despite hasty reparation of the walls, the defences of the city must have still been weak enough after years of neglect to tempt Kavadh to make an attempt on it even in the middle of winter.

Kavadh first built battering rams which were directed against every part of the wall, but the citizens broke their heads by dropping timbers on them, or prevented them from damaging the walls by hanging protective bundles of padding from them. When Kavadh saw he was getting nowhere he built a mound on top of which he placed a battering ram. The city-dwellers countered this by two means: they built the walls higher, and they dug a mine/tunnel beneath the mound which they propped up with timbers. Geoffrey

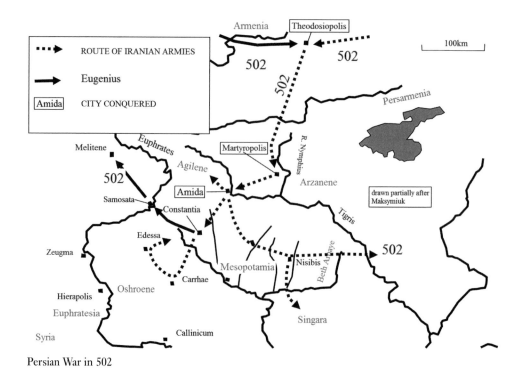

Persian War in 502

Greatrex is surely correct in suggesting that the mound was directed against the northern section of the wall because the Persians used the monastery of Mar John for building materials for the mound. When the mound was finally finished, the Persians brought a battering ram to the top of it and started to batter away. The battering brought down the newly added section of the wall because it had not yet settled, but as this happened the timbers in the tunnel/mine, which had been set on fire when the Persian attack started, collapsed and masses of Persians fell to their deaths.

While the mound was being built, Kavadh had dispatched his forces to forage. The Hephthalites, presumably as they were not good at sieges, foraged and pillaged the area north-west from Amida to a distance of one day's march (Endiclon/Ingilene/Agilene). During one such raid, the Hephthalites came across a 'holy man' called Jacobus. For some reason they found themselves unable to shoot him and because of this Kavadh granted Jacobus the right to protect fugitives who had come to his place of abode.

The second force, consisting of Persians, Hephthalites and Arabs, advanced southwards towards Constantia/Tella, but when on 19 October they spread out to pillage the villages around the city, the *dux* of Tella (i.e. the *dux* of Mesopotamia) Olympius and the *dux* of Melitene (*dux utriusque Armeniae*) Eugenius attacked the scattered Persians in the villages.[45]

After this, the *duces* turned back to the city but were informed that there were 500 Persians in a certain ravine not far from them (Joshua 51, tr. Wright, 40 with my additions in parentheses): 'They were ready to go against them, but the Greek [*Roman*] troops that were with them had dispersed themselves to strip the slain; and because it was night, Olympius gave orders to light a fire on the top of an eminence [*Trombley/Watt: hill-top*] and to blow trumpets, that those who were scattered might rejoin them. But the Persian generals [*Trombley/Watt: marzbans*], who were encamped at the village of Tell Beshmai, when they saw the light of the fire and heard the sound of trumpets, armed all their force and came against them [*this means that the duces had destroyed only some of the Persian forces scattered in the villages but had missed the main force under the marzbans and the 500 men in the ravine*]. When the Greek [*Roman*] cavalry saw that the Persians were too many for them, they turned [*their backs*]; but the infantry were unable to escape and were constrained by the fight. So they came together and drew up in battle array, forming what is called the chelône or tortoise, and fought for a long time. But as the army of the Persians was too many for them, and there were added to these the Huns and Arabs, their ranks were broken, and they were thrown into disorder, and mixed up among the cavalry, and trampled and crushed under the hooves of the horses of the Arabs [*Trombley/Watt: Tayyaye*]. So many of the Greeks [*Romans*] were killed, and the rest were made prisoners.'

Eugenius realized that he had too few men to fight a pitched battle against the combined enemy forces and therefore decided to withdraw into Armenia, but when he did this he marched against the Persian garrison at Theodosiopolis. Eugenius proved himself once again to be a first-rate commander. He destroyed the entire enemy force and recaptured the city for the Romans.

The third force consisting of the Arabs commanded by the Lakhmid sheik al-Nu'man advanced south-westward to pillage the region of Carrhae and Edessa. It is probable that this force had accompanied the division that advanced against Constantia. They reached the region of Carrhae on 26 October, plundered at their will and took captive people, cattle and property, after which they advanced to Edessa. They took 18,500 prisoners altogether. This attack was particularly effective thanks to the fact that it coincided with the vintage so that people were outside their walled cities where they were completely taken by surprise. The Edessans reacted by strengthening the walls, digging up ditches, and blocking the gates and sluices of the river.

Kavadh's next idea was to build a mound so high and close to the city walls that it would be possible to make a gangway from it to the wall. The city-dwellers once again undermined it from below. When the mound was finished the archers started to provide covering fire for the 500 armoured Persians who mounted the mound. The Persians then laid their beams on the wall, but the townspeople were once again prepared. They responded by throwing on the gangway strings of just-flayed ox-skins soaked in vetch and myrrh-oil, which made the gangway slippery. At the same time they set fire to the timbers in the tunnel. The battle lasted for six hours during which the Persians failed to make any headway. Then the mound collapsed in a fiery blaze, some of the Persians were burned while others were bruised and/or killed by stones thrown from the wall.

This setback did not put a stop to the siege because Kavadh was determined to take the city. He ordered a new mound to be built on top of the previous one and to place a battering ram on it. His men wore multilayered wet cotton coverings to withstand fire-attacks and arrows. The Amidenes, however, were prepared even against this eventuality. They built a 'scorpion' which used torsion springs of sinew to launch rocks of 300 lbs against the coverings. The men and battering ram were destroyed in a continuous barrage of stones. The Persians were by now utterly demoralized and ready to return home. Joshua the Stylite claims that they had lost 50,000 men in the siege. This figure is comparable with the figure of 30,000 lost at the siege of Amida in 359 (Amm. 19.9.9 with *MHLR* vol.1) and therefore may well be roughly accurate; in 359 the Romans actually made a headcount of the killed after the siege.

Persian rulers always considered their peasant infantry as expendable cannon fodder in offensive sieges. Kavadh could have brought with him an army of well over 100,000 men, a figure which modern historians usually do not accept, but which is consistently stated by ancient sources whenever the Persians under their ruler advanced into Roman territory prepared to undertake prolonged sieges.

Now Kavadh had had enough, but he still sent a message to the Amidenes in which he demanded that they should pay him a small sum of silver in return for abandoning the siege. The Amidenes, however, had grown overconfident so that when the governor Cyrus assembled the city council it was decided to present demands to the Persians instead. The Amidenes demanded financial compensation for the lost harvest, and according to Procopius (*Wars* 1.7.18–19) the courtesans exposed their private parts from the walls as an insult. This insolence was the last straw for Kavadh who now decided to continue the siege. The magi claimed that the exposure of the private parts was a good omen. Luckily for him, a *marzban* called Kanarang the Lame (Zachariah 7.4) – who was encamped on the western side of the city opposite the so-called *Tripyrgion* tower (location not known) which was guarded by monks under their Persian archimandrite[46] – noted that a thieving fellow called Kutrigo was in the habit of making daring nightly raids in which he captured cattle and goods from the Persians precisely from this location and that this man used an underground stream/aqueduct/sewer[47] through a wall next to the *Tripyrgion* as his route outside and inside. When this Kutrigo made his next raid, Kanarang pursued him up to the *Tripyrgion*. Unluckily for the Amidenes, someone had given wine and food to the monks who were all asleep. Consequently, when Kanarang noted that the defenders failed to react, he gave orders for his men to set up ladders against the wall while others entered the city through the aqueduct/stream. The tower and the battlements next to it were all captured and the king was informed.[48]

The townsmen from the next tower noticed and rushed to bring help to the monks who were being killed, but were not able to do so because the Persians killed them with arrows. Cyrus rushed to the scene in person with torches lighting the way and it was thanks to this that the Persians hiding in the darkness were able to wound him with an arrow so that he was forced to retreat. Kavadh reached the scene when it was already morning and ordered the scaling-ladders to be put against the wall. The attack, however, did not progress well. Very many of the attackers were killed by arrows, stones or spear thrusts, or because their ladders were thrown back. This caused panic among the Persians who started to flee down the ladders. Kavadh advanced just behind them and ordered all those who fled to be killed as cowards. This threat worked and the Persians were able to reach the wall thanks to their vastly superior numbers and to take one tower after another while the defenders were still trying to dislodge them from the first tower by collapsing it.[49]

One of the defenders, called Peter of Amkhoro, distinguished himself in this action. He was a huge man equipped with a coat of iron (mail?)[50] and was able to hold one of the battlements alone against those attacking from inside and out without any assistance. He stood his ground and prevented the Persians from making any progress, killing them with his spear until the Persians had captured five or six towers from the Amidenes, after which he retreated unharmed. Peter was clearly a true warrior hero, as stated by Zachariah – a superb martial artist whose exploits on this occasion have deservedly gained eternal glory. The Persians had by now gained possession only of the western wall, and the defenders had not yet given up. The Persians were forced to spend the entire night and the following day (12 January 503) fighting their way through the defenders to able to descend from the wall to the level ground and open the gates so that the rest of the Persian army could enter the city. It was only then that the defenders were forced to give up their fight. Kavadh ordered the soldiers to kill all the men and women inside the city for three days, and the men were happy to comply after their hardships.[51]

The butchery went on until the ruler entered the city on an elephant on the third day and was met by a priest who begged mercy for the remaining captives. Kavadh granted this but ordered the rest of the population to be made slaves. The king left a garrison of 3,000 men (their servants/squires should be added to this figure because they could fight too), with some remaining Amidenes as slaves under the Persian commander Glones,[52] and marched with the prisoners to the mountain of Singara where he left 20,000 men to winter while the rest of the army scattered to their various other winter quarters. Those left behind in Amida collected the corpses and heaped them up in two piles outside the North Gate. According to the sources, the number of killed was more than 80,000, but this figure did not include those left inside buildings, or those that the Persians killed on the mound or threw into the Tigris. Paul Bar Zainab the steward was killed, Leontius and Cyrus were publicly humiliated and taken together with the other prisoners to the city to be built for the prisoners called *Veh-az-Amid-Kavadh* (the Better Amida of Kavadh) south-east of Khuzistan, and others were sent to the Caucasus.[53]

The Roman counter-attack in 503

Kavadh released Rufinus to convey the news of the defeat to Anastasius. The news of the fall of Amida caused panic among the cities east of the Euphrates and the population started to flee westwards. Jacob, the *periodeutes*,[54] wrote letters in an effort to calm the situation; the role of the priests as upholders of morale was of the utmost importance during these wars. When news of the troubles was brought to Anastasius, he sent a large force to winter in these cities so that the enemy would not be able to threaten them and the citizens would choose to stay. The cities would have been defenceless if the populations had not chosen to stay and fight. From February 503 onwards each possessed a garrison to protect them. Kavadh, however, was not bent on attacking them because he was on his way back home and trusted that he had already done enough to press his case. He dispatched envoys with the same message as before: pay me gold or face war. This was extortion on a grand scale.[55]

In May 503 Anastasius sent additional men to the eastern front with the mission to retake Amida and prevent another enemy invasion. According to Joshua (54), this force was placed under Areobindus, Patricius, Hypatius and many others, while according to Procopius (Wars 1.8.1ff.), the supreme command of the campaign was divided between four *strategoi* and it was largely thanks to this that the commanders failed in their task (but as we shall see this is not exactly true). The commanders Procopius mentions are: Areobindus, the *magister militum per Orientem*, son-in-law of the Emperor Olybrius; Celer, the *Magister Officiorum*; Patricius the Phrygian; and Hypatius, the nephew of the Emperor. With them served: Justinus (Justin) the future Emperor; Patriciolus with his son Vitalianus (Vitalian); Pharesmanes, a native of Colchis (Lazica) who was a man with exceptional abilities as a warrior; the Goths Godidisklus and Bessas; and many others. Apion the Egyptian was placed in charge of financial matters and supply. He was given an authority equal to that of the Emperor so that the army would not lack anything. He was therefore a special Praetorian Prefect specifically in charge of supplying the armies posted in the East. Theophanes (AM 5997) adds Zemarchos to the list of sub-commanders.

The details provided by Joshua the Stylite (54ff.) make it certain that Procopius has condensed his account here and later, and that he has forgotten to mention the garrisoning of the cities in the winter of 503 and the successes achieved by the commanders. Most importantly Celer arrived only later in the autumn of 503 to reinforce those already sent to the scene of operations, and it is also probable that Patriciolus with his son Vitalianus arrived later but before Celer to reinforce the forces already sent. It is also probable that Justinus arrived with Celer. Pharesmanes arrived with Patricius and Hypatius. It is not known when the Goths Godidisklus and Bessas arrived, but I would suggest they arrived with Areobindus because Theophanes claims that the Goths, Bessi (probably Bessas and not the tribe), and other Thracian races were dispatched by Anastasius under Areobindus, who was *magister militum per Orientem* and exarch. The use of the exarch in this case has created an insoluble problem.[56] One possibility is that it refers to the title *Comes Foederatum*, a title which had been held by his famous grandfather Areobindus in 422 (see vol.3). Areobindus was certainly in charge of the Goths and other Thracians during this war. The problem with this is that the usual assumption on the basis of Theophanes AM 6005 is that Patriciolus, who was probably of Gothic descent, was the *Comes Foederatum* at this time.[57] My suggestion is that both Areobindus and Patriciolus probably had Goths in their forces (Bessas with Areobindus and Godidisklus with Patriciolus?). It is possible or even probable that the position of the *Comes Foederatum* was also divided between two commanders both of whom had Gothic blood in their veins[58] just as the position of *Comes Domesticorum* was at times, but it is also possible that Patriciolus replaced Areobindus as *Comes Foederatum* when he arrived. However, the division of this command appears more likely. See also my analysis of this position during the revolt of Vitalianus.

The details provided by Joshua make it clear that it was not because of the divided command that the Romans failed, even if it is clear that the commanders were envious of each other and quarrelled. In my opinion it is very unlikely that the command was divided, because Patricius, as commander of the first ('great') praesental army, was clearly the *strategos* while Hypatius was his *hypostrategos* as commander of the second praesental army;[59] Zachariah (7.4) even states Patricius was the commander-in-chief. Even if the command was divided as claimed by Procopius, despite what Zachariah states and the circumstantial evidence, it is still clear that Patricius and Hypatius coordinated their actions with each other and also with Areobindus. According to Zachariah, Patricius was an old man, just and loyal, but deficient in mental power. This is probably too harsh a judgment on the man, because despite his initial defeat (see later) he was still able to maintain his command throughout the war and even inflict a very serious defeat on the Persians. Regardless, it is still clear that he was not among the greatest military commanders or thinkers of his time.

The Roman counter-attack that began in May consisted of three elements. Areobindus with 12,000 men (on the basis of the details of combat, all cavalry) advanced to the border between Dara (not yet fortified to serve as a base) and Ammudin where he pitched a camp to act as a shielding force to the 40,000 men (a massive mixed force of infantry and cavalry as stated by Malalas 16.9) under Patricius and Hypatius who besieged the Persians at Amida, while Apion/Appion stayed at Edessa to make certain that both armies and the soldiers garrisoning Edessa and other cities would receive their supplies and salaries.[60]

Modern historians[61] have noted that Procopius (*Wars* 1.8.1–4, esp.3) calls the resulting army such that had never been assembled by the Romans against the Persians either before or after that time; but they make the mistake of thinking that this would have meant only the 52,000 men mentioned above by Joshua the Stylite. In truth, when one reads the text carefully Procopius includes in the army the later reinforcements under Patriciolus and Celer, and may also have included the reinforcements already sent to the scene in the winter of 503. In short, we do not know what the size of this army was, but we know it was massive, and that it was not assembled together as one united force. Altogether it must have been well in excess of 100,000 men, on top of which one should include the men already on the scene, namely the Field Army of the East, *limitanei* and Arab allies. It is no wonder the Persians failed to make any real progress, even though the Romans were poorly led.

When Kavadh learnt from his scouts that Areobindus had only a few men at his disposal, he ordered the 20,000 that he left at Singara to proceed at once against

Areobindus. However, contrary to Kavadh's expectations, things went badly for the Persians despite their numerical advantage. Areobindus routed the Persians repeatedly and forced them to flee to the gate of Nisibis where the panicked fugitives suffocated each other as they struggled to get inside. According to Theophanes, Areobindus' forces had been strengthened by Romanus[62] who had advanced from Euphratesia to join him, which implies that Areobindus had more than 12,000 horsemen. His forces also included Arabs under their phylarch Asouades and many other commanders. Theophanes claims that Areobindus led this force against Kavadh who was located at Nisibis, defeated the Persians in many battles and drove Kavadh out of Nisibis. According to Theophanes, a Scythian soldier killed the greatest of the Persian generals in one of these battles and then brought his sword and bracelet as proof of his achievement to Areobindus who then sent them to the Emperor as tokens of his victory.[63]

Joshua the Stylite, Theophanes and others do not give us any more details, but on the basis of military probability, which is based on the known combat doctrines of both, there are two possible ways to interpret the above. It is possible that there were several cavalry battles which Areobindus won, or it is possible that there was just one cavalry battle consisting of several stages. In the latter case, it is probable that Areobindus had deployed his cavalry in two lines (with two divisions in reserve) or in three lines (with four divisions in reserve plus the rear guards) so that his forces had adopted a shallower formation with fewer ranks than the enemy so he was able to match the width of the enemy array after which he charged with his line of cavalry lancers at the double against the Persians, as instructed later by the *Strategikon*, so that Areobindus defeated the first Persian line (the first defeat/rout), after which the Persian second line had moved forward to protect their comrades only to be defeated by the Romans (possibly by the pursuing first line alone or with the help of the second line) so that the Persians suffered their second defeat/rout and fled in complete panic to Nisibis.

In July 503 the Persians received reinforcements from the Huns and Tayyaye (the Lakhmids of Hira). According to Theophanes, this force had been assembled by Kavadh who had just been obliged to retreat from Nisibis. This force was placed under Constantine, who had just betrayed the city of Theodosiopolis to the Persians. When Areobindus learnt of their arrival from his scouts, he sent Calliopius the Aleppine to Patricius and Hypatius with a plea for urgent help because the enemy was about to attack him with vastly superior numbers. They paid no attention to this plea because they had just finished the building of three siege towers covered with iron plating. Everything was therefore ready for the final *coup de main*, as Trombley and Watt (p.67, n.318) say in their commentary of Joshua the Stylite, and it is possible that this was the main reason for their refusal to help. However, this was not to be because the Persians under their Roman commander defeated Areobindus's forces with the result that the Romans were forced to abandon their camp with all their baggage and flee to Constantia/Tella and Edessa. According to Theophanes (AM 5997), the praesental commanders refused to help because they envied Areobindus. This has usually been dismissed as a groundless accusation, but I would not preclude the possibility that it could have influenced the decisions. Personal relationships between commanders are known to have played a very important role in war throughout the ages, and in this case it is clear that the relationship between the officers was hostile, because Theophanes (AM 5998) specifically notes the personal hostility of Hypatius towards Areobindus.

When this news was brought to Patricius and Hypatius, they torched their towers, left behind Pharesmanes/Pharazman/Farzman and Theodore with cavalry forces (according to Zachariah Pharesmanes had 500 horsemen) to harass the Persian garrison at distance, and advanced against the Persians but were unable to catch them. This proves that Patricius, Hypatius and Areobindus all acted according to a pre-agreed plan, but that Patricius and Hypatius failed to support Areobindus in time because they thought that they could take the city of Amida when their towers were ready. This is not proof of a divided command, but proof of a grave miscalculation by the praesental commanders. Areobindus, however, felt that his superiors had failed to support him and threatened to return to Constantinople. It was thanks to the intervention of Apion, who was also at Edessa, that he stayed.

Meanwhile Pharazman/Farzman/Pharesmanes and Theodore had ambushed the Persians in a pass near Amida. They had placed a flock of sheep there as bait, and when the Persians saw them they sent 400 horsemen to capture the sheep and the Romans killed or captured all of them. The captured *marzban* promised to deliver the city of Amida to the Romans and when this news was brought to Patricius and Hypatius they returned at the double. The *marzban* however was unable to convince those inside the city to open the gates, and the *stratelai* (generals) ordered him to be strung up. According to Zachariah, Pharesmanes performed many similar feats of bravery against the Persians, the least of which was not the ambush of Glon with his men. (In my opinion this event belongs to the year 504 when Pharesmanes had been appointed second-in-command of Patricius.[64])

It is probable that the events described by Zachariah of Mitylene at the beginning of his Chapter 7.5 took place immediately after this. He states that Patricius invaded Arzanene with the implication that he retook Sophene and Martyropolis because both lay on the route. This means that the Romans had retaken both major cities previously lost to the Persians in Armenia. The invasion of Arzanene was obviously a cavalry raid and not a real invasion. In the meantime, Areobindus and Hypatius advanced against Nisibis but failed to capture it despite the fact that its citizens were fighting half-heartedly in its defence due to their favourable attitude towards the Romans. It is possible that the hostility of Hypatius against Areobindus (mentioned by Theophanes AM 5998) played a role in the Roman failure to take the city. According to Zachariah, it was then that Kavadh had assembled his army and advanced against the Romans.

This would also explain what Areobindus was doing for the month after his defeat by Constantinus. There was surely plenty of time for him to regroup his forces and on the basis of Zachariah's account he did precisely that. He united his demoralized force with that of Hypatius and then, together with him, advanced in front of Nisibis to restore morale with a demonstration of power, after which the Roman commanders deployed their army once again in depth so that Areobindus served as an advance force with the purpose of harassing the advancing Persian army until it met the main Roman army under Patricius and Hypatius who were presumably preparing to resume the siege of Amida.[65]

The Persian Tayyaye (Lakhmids) had also invaded Roman territory, on their own. Timostratus, *dux* of Callinicum (i.e. of Oshroene), intercepted and defeated them. It

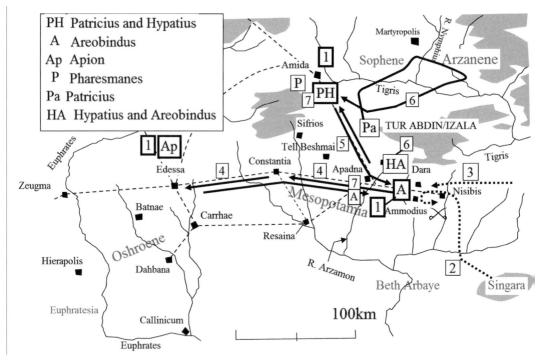

War in 503: Phase 1, the Roman counter-attack:
1) Patricius and Hypatius besiege Amida with Areobindus's forces posted between Ammodius and Dara to act as a shielding force. Apion at Edessa is in charge of the supplies.
2) Kavadh sends 20,000 horsemen from Singara to attack Areobindus. Areobindus defeats them and forces them to flee to Nisibis.
3) Persians receive reinforcements. Areobindus asks his colleagues to assist, but they refuse probably because they were now ready to make the final attack against Amida and because they envied the successes of Areobindus.
4) Areobindus flees to Constantia and Edessa. Apion convinces him to stay.
5) Patricius and Hypatius leave Pharesmanes behind to isolate Amida while they advance against the Persians, but the Persians have fled before their arrival.
6) Hypatius and Areobindus attack Nisibis, but fail to take it. Patricius ravages Arzanene and presumably returns Sophene to the Roman Empire even if the sources fail to mention this.
7) Patricius and Hypatius both return to Amida when the captured Persian commander promises to deliver the city. When this fails, the Persian *marzban* is executed. Then both resume the siege of Amida. When Hypatius marched north, Areobindus' army became the shielding force, but with the difference that Areobindus was now at Apadna closer to his superiors than before.

is uncertain whether this contingent was advancing directly from al-Hira or whether it was part of the force that had previously defeated Areobindus after which it had avoided contact with the praesental *magistri*. Whatever the case, it is clear that the Persian Arabs had left their capital al-Hira defenceless because we find the Roman Tayyaye called the Thalabites (the Ghassanids) advancing against it. The Ghassanids attacked and destroyed a caravan en route there, but did not attack the city itself because its population had abandoned it and fled into the inner desert.

The Battle of Opadna/Apadna/Apadana in August 503

The assembly of the Persian army took until August to accomplish because it consisted of many nationalities (Persians, Hephthalite Huns, Qadishaye and Armenians). According to Joshua the Stylite (57), Kavadh led this massive force as far as Opadna/Apadna (mod. Tell Harzem), which was 40 km west of the Dara-Ammudin line previously held by Areobindus.[66] The accounts of the resulting battle of Opadna/Apadna by Procopius (*Wars* 1.8.13ff.), Joshua the Stylite (57) and Zachariah (7.5) are almost irreconcilable, but an attempt at it will follow.[67] My above analysis of Zachariah, which builds upon the analysis of Greatrex, explains what happened before the battle.

According to Procopius, the forces of Patricius and Hypatius engaged a Persian vanguard of 800 Hephthalites and killed almost all. Since both men were unaware of the presence of the Persian main army, under Kavadh, they allowed their men to relax and take lunch next to a small stream. The men washed pieces of meat in the stream and bathed in it, and the water became muddy. The Roman commanders were clearly guilty of gross neglect of duty when they failed to post scouts around their army when they stopped. Kavadh had learnt what had happened to his vanguard and was advancing against the Romans. When Kavadh saw the mud downstream, he realised the enemy was unprepared for an attack. The Persian cavalry charged at full speed and caught the Romans by surprise, eating and disarmed. The Romans panicked and scattered in flight. Procopius claims that not a man got away except Patricius and Hypatius who fled immediately at the beginning of the attack.

Joshua, on the other hand, claims that when Patricius' men heard of the invasion of Kavadh, they marched towards the enemy but were surprised by the Persians before they had drawn up their battle array. According to him, the Persians first defeated the Roman vanguard which fled to the main army, which was still in the process of forming up its battle array, and the Roman army panicked. The first to flee was Patricius himself, and his army followed his example and turned tail. It retreated across the Euphrates and sought safety behind the walls of Samosata. The comments of Trombley and Watt regarding this flight are to the point. They note that the flight of the army past many fortified cities all the way behind the Euphrates proves that it had ceased to exist as a fighting force and that its commander Patricius thought it safest just to attempt to prevent the crossing of the Euphrates and nothing more. Joshua also notes that the Lakhmid commander al-Numan was wounded in this battle, and that a Roman officer called Peter fled with his men to the fortress of Ashparin.[68] The pursuing Persians surrounded him there with the result that the frightened inhabitants handed him and his men to the Persians. The Persians took him captive but killed his men. The officer was valuable for his knowledge and as a bargaining chip, but his men were not.

Zachariah's version 7.5 concerning the events preceding the battle (tr. by Hamilton and Brooks, 161) is as follows: 'But at last Patrick [*Patricius*] went down to Arzanene of the Persians, and carried off captives, and subdued fortresses there. And Areobindus and Hypatius went down to Nisibis and did not subdue it, although the citizens were favourably inclined towards the Romans, and showed themselves lazy in the fight. However, the king of the Persians hearing of it, came with an army against the Romans; and they fled before him, and they left their tents and the heavy baggage which they had with them. Areobindus fled from Arzamena and Aphphadana [*Arzamon and Apadna, both the same place*], and Hypatius and Patrick and others from Thelkatsro. And they lost many horses and their riders, who fell from the cliffs of the mountains, and were bruised, and perished, and were mangled.' This account would imply that there was no real fighting at all because the Romans just fled when Kavadh approached, and in fact this seems to have been the case. Note also the implication that both Roman forces consisted solely of cavalry and that no infantry was present.

It is unfortunate we do not know the size of the cavalry contingent under Patricius and Hypatius because it cannot have been as small as the approximate paper strength of the praesental cavalry forces in the early fifth century *Notitia Dignitatum* which was 12,500 horsemen. This would have made their force equal in size to the cavalry force under Areobindus. One wonders whether the 15,000 men that Marcellinus Comes (a.503) claims to have been the size of the army Anastasius sent against the Persians refers to the size of the praesental cavalry forces. In light of Areobindus' reaction to the size of the enemy force, even this figure would make their readiness to engage the Persians quite strange. There are four possibilities. Firstly, that the East Romans had increased the proportion of cavalry in the praesental forces after the *Notitia Dignitatum* had been written and that because of this they were now able to take a far larger proportion of cavalry with them to the East while they still left half of their infantry contingents behind to protect Constantinople. Secondly, it is possible that the number of horsemen had been increased by adding *foederati* or other Thracian forces for the campaign army. Thirdly, it is possible that the size of their cavalry contingent had been bolstered with the *limitanei*, *foederati* and Arabs already posted in the East just as they had bolstered the size of Areobindus's force before the fighting. Fourthly, it is possible that the commanders expected Areobindus to withdraw towards their army so that the size of their cavalry contingent was adequate for the task. My suggestion is that the praesental commanders had 15,000 cavalry to begin with (Marcellinus' figure for their army), which had been bolstered with *foederati*, *limitanei* and Arabs, and that they expected Areobindus to reinforce them before the battle, and that it was because of this that they were ready to fight. What is certain, however, is that the praesental commanders must have thought that they had a minimum of about 20,000 horsemen plus the retreating 12,000 horsemen of Areobindus for them to engage the Persians.

I would suggest all the versions are mutually supportive. The Romans had deployed Areobindus as a shielding force at Apadna as they had done previously while Patricius and Hypatius were about to begin the siege of Amida again. When the Romans then learned of the approach of the enemy, Patricius and Hypatius presumably left their infantry somewhere behind but not at Siphrios because there were no infantry forces there when the pursuing Persians reached it. It is quite probable they did not take their infantry with them, but left it behind to follow them at a leisurely pace when they advanced forward at the double with their cavalry just like Belisarius was to do later during the Vandal war (see *MHLR* Vol.6 518–565, with Syvänne, 2004). Patricius and Hypatius wanted to avoid repeating the mistake they had made previously, so they took their cavalry with them and advanced to help Areobindus. However, they were hopelessly late if their intention was to reach Apadna in time to help Areobindus. They were encamped at Siphrius when the Persians were already attacking Apadna.

When the commanders learnt that the enemy was already at Apadna, they marched south at the double with their cavalry. The speed of the Persian attack, however, took the Romans by surprise so that when the Persians approached the demoralized forces of Areobindus, his men fled immediately westwards without attempting to unite with the main army. But there is another possibility: that Procopius has confused the Persian attacks against Areobindus and Patricius with each other so that it would have actually been Areobindus who engaged the 800 Hephthalites and then allowed his men to relax so that Kavadh was able to surprise him. This would explain why the details of the battle are so different in Procopius and Joshua, and why Areobindus did not retreat towards his colleagues, while also explaining the severe criticism of Areobindus' behaviour in most sources. For example, John the Lydus (*de Magistr.* 3.53.6ff. esp.10–11) accused Areobindus of too much fondness for song, flute and dance, and that he lost because of his softness.

When Patricius and Hypatius learnt that the Persians had already reached Apadna, they advanced there at the double, but were once again surprised by the speed of the Persian advance. Because of the complete defeat of his forces, Areobindus had been unable to withdraw to his superiors and warn them of the imminent arrival of the enemy. The praesental commanders had posted a vanguard to shield their army when it was being arrayed for combat, but the Persians attacked before the Romans could deploy. When Patricius then saw his vanguard in flight, he was the first to flee because he knew that the Persian cavalry would be upon his force immediately. The Persian attack was again fast and furious. The other alternative is that the praesental commanders surprised the Persian vanguard, as stated by Procopius, and then allowed their men to relax and were thereby surprised by the Persians who had already routed Areobindus. However, it is more likely that Procopius has actually confused the actions of Areobindus and Patricius for the reasons given above.

According to Roman combat doctrine (*Strategikon* 4.3.87ff.; 7.2.8) the cavalry vanguard of one to two *banda*/flags (ca. 200/400–400/800 men) were to be deployed at a distance of ca. 1.5–3 km in front of the cavalry array, and it is obvious that if the commander and his men saw this force in flight before the actual battle array was ready for combat it was best to flee immediately, which they did. In short, the Romans lost the battle thanks to poor intelligence gathering. Combat doctrine called for the use of scouts well in advance of the vanguard and on this occasion it is clear that they had not done their job properly, if they had been posted at all. The fact that the commanders probably expected Areobindus to do this on their

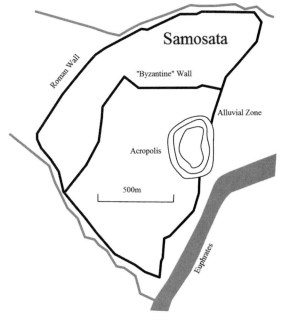

behalf is not really a valid excuse for their negligence. The Roman army scattered in flight and suffered very serious losses during the flight, but it was not entirely annihilated as claimed by Procopius, because the remnants of this army were regrouped at Samosata, as were the forces of Areobindus at Edessa. Still, it is clear that Patricius' army had ceased to be a viable fighting force, usable only for the defence of walls, bridges or a river line.

None of the sources give us details of what happened to the infantry accompanying the praesental commanders. All we have are the references to the destroyed army or destroyed cavalry forces. Because of this I would suggest that the commanders had left their infantry behind when they advanced against the Persians, so we do not have any descriptions of the Persians attempting to crush retreating infantry formations as we have near Constantia in 502 (above). The Roman infantry simply withdrew when they learnt of the defeat of their commanders. The other possibility is of course that the Persians simply annihilated the infantry and that the sources fail to mention any details of this, but this conclusion has the problem that the praesental commanders once again had infantry at their disposal when they resumed the siege of Amida later. If the cavalry contingent accompanying the praesental commanders was 15,000 horsemen plus the additions to it, then the infantry force would have consisted of 25,000 footmen plus the local additions to it.

According to John the Lydus (de Magistr. 3.53.6ff. esp.11), the reason for the defeat of Patricius and Hypatius was that they were inexperienced and cowardly. The official inquiry, however, appears to have found Hypatius to have been the main culprit for the defeat because he was recalled to Constantinople in 504 while Patricius was left in his office. But it is also possible that the sole reason for this dismissal from office was his hostility towards Areobindus, as stated by Theophanes AM 5998. It is easy to see why these two men would have been hostile towards each other. Both were connected to imperial families and could see each other as enemies. It is also easy to see that Hypatius would have considered Areobindus' failure to retreat towards him, and in particular his failure to inform him of the approach of the Persian army, as the principal reason for the defeat. He would certainly have accused Areobindus of this. It is actually probable that both played a role in the hostility felt, and it is also very probable that the men just did not like each other.

In May 504 Apion was replaced by Calliopus while he went to Alexandria to organize further supplies from there. The reason for the replacement at the same time is not known. Perhaps he had failed to deliver adequate supplies for the forces near Dara as the absence of a fortified city there was later stated to be one of the causes of Roman troubles. However, the reason for his subsequent dismissal from office is clear. After Celer had arrived on the scene, Apion and Hypatius were both accused of sabotaging the war effort through their hostility towards Areobindus and both were recalled to Constantinople.[69]

The conclusion that Hypatius was the principal culprit for the defeat appears to have been sound, because Hypatius as hypostrategos would have been in charge of the first cavalry battle line and it is also clear that he was in charge of the vanguard and the scouts. In this position, it would have been Hypatius' duty to make certain the army received timely information of enemy activities and that its battle array would have been ready to engage the enemy when it was at hand.

Kavadh exploits his victory: Constantia, Carrhae, Batnae, Edessa, Callinicum, Palestine, Arabia

Kavadh planned to exploit his victory by advancing against Areobindus at Edessa. Al-Numan encouraged him in this, but, according to Joshua the Stylite (58), a Christian Arab from al-Hira had said that Kavadh should not march against Edessa because Christ said the city would never fall. This angered the pagan al-Numan and he promised to make Edessa suffer. But as soon as he said this his head began to swell because of an injury he had suffered in the battle. He was taken to his tent where he died two days later. Kavadh was thus forced to appoint a new ruler for the Lakhmids, who was actually not a Lakhmid at all. His name was Abu Ja'fur b. Alqama and he ruled until he was succeeded by al-Mundhir either in 503 or 505 who was a member of the family.[70]

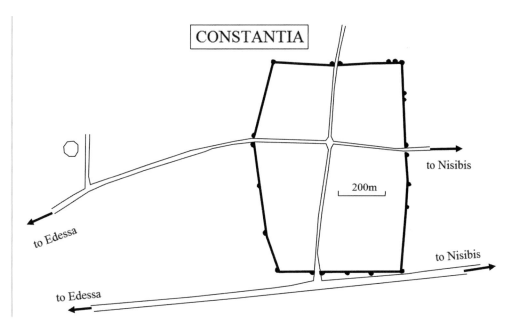

The first city en route to Edessa was Constantina/Constantia/Tella, which Kavadh proceeded to besiege. What happened next is described by Joshua (58, tr. by Wright 47–8 with my comments in italics in parentheses):

... and the Jews who were there plotted to surrender the city to him. They dug a hole in the tower of their synagogue, which had been committed to them to guard, and sent word to the Persians regarding it that they might dig into it [*from the outside*] and enter by it. This was found out by the count [*komês, comes*] Peter, who was in captivity [*captured at Ashparin/Siphrios*], and he persuaded those who were guarding him to let him come near the wall, saying that there were clothes and articles of his ... which he had left in the city. ... The guards granted his request and let him go near. He said to the soldiers who were standing on the wall [*note that all cities east of the Euphrates had garrisons after the winter of 503*] to call the count Leontius, who at the time had charge of the city, and they called him and the officers. Peter spoke with them in the language of the Romans [*I have here changed the text to follow the more accurate Trombley & Watt translation; note how the Persian guards were unable to understand what Peter said while he was able to communicate with the Persians; clearly this Peter was fluent in at least two languages*] and disclosed the treachery of the Jews. In order that the matter might not become known to the Persians, he asked them to give him a pair of trousers [*Trombley & Watt has a change of clothes*]. They at first made a pretence of being angry with him; but afterwards they threw down to him from the wall a pair of trousers, ... Then they went down from the wall, and as if they had learned nothing about the treachery of the Jews ... they went round and examined the foundations of the whole wall, ... This they did for the sake of Peter, ... At last they came to the place which the Jews were guarding, and found out that it was mined ... When the Greeks saw what was there, they sallied out against them with great fury, and went round the whole city, and killed all the Jews whom they could find, men and women, old men and children. This they did for [*several*] days, and they would scarcely cease from killing them at the order of the count Leontius[71] and the entreaty of the blessed Bar-hadad the bishop. They guarded the city carefully by night and by day, and the holy Bar-hadad himself used to go round and visit them and pray for them and bless them, commending their care and encouraging them, and sprinkling holy water on them and on the wall of the city. [*Note the importance of the bishops and priests in the upkeep of morale during the sieges, which was a typical phenomenon after the fourth century.*] He also carried with him on his rounds the eucharist ... He also went out boldly to the king of the Persians and spoke with him and appeased him. [*It is noteworthy that the Persians allowed him to move so freely. Perhaps it was because they wanted to use him as a go-between.*] When Kawâd saw the dignified bearing of the man, and perceived too the vigilance of the Greeks, it seemed to him of no use to remain idle before Tellâ with all that host which he had with him; firstly because sustenance could not be found for it in a district that had already been ravaged [*pillaged in November 502, see above*]; and secondly, because he was afraid lest the Greek generals might join one another and come against him in a body. [*The generals Areobindus, Patricius and Hypatius clearly still had enough men left to challenge Kavadh's army if they joined forces. This is actually not that surprising because even in defeat most of the defeated cavalry survived to fight another day.*] For these reasons he moved off quickly towards Edessa and encamped by the River Gallab, which is also called [*the river*] of the Medes for about twenty days. [*Greatrex, 1998, 103 notes that in this position Kavadh threatened both Edessa and Carrhae.*] Some of the more daring men in his army traversed the district and laid it waste [*the men probably foraged*].

The noteworthy points in the above are the treacherous behaviour of the Jews who had been entrusted the defence of that portion of the wall against which their synagogue was placed despite the general persecution of Jews by Christians at this time, and the preparedness of the city to defend itself when there was a garrison in place. The persecution of the Jews that had started under Constantine the Great and was then intensified under Theodosius II had finally resulted in the almost complete alienation of the Jewish population to such an extent that they could consider the Persian invaders their saviours. Trombley and Watt (Joshua, p.72) note that as far as we know Anastasius had not legislated against the Jews and had also intervened on their behalf when they had been subjected to persecution, but it is still clear that at this time the Jews felt quite unwelcome in the Christian Empire. In light of the persecution they received it is not surprising that they acted as they did. What is surprising is that it was expected that they would defend their city loyally.

The Edessenes prepared for siege on 6 September by tearing down all the monasteries and inns situated close to the wall and torched the village of Kephar Selem/Neghbath. Additionally, they cut down all the hedges and trees, and brought in the bones of the martyrs. The former were necessary because the defenders needed a clear shooting range around the city. It also ensured that the enemy would not be able to use the trees and stones to build mounds. The bones of the martyrs were important as talismans to protect those who possessed them. The citizens made coverings of haircloth on top of the walls and brought weaponry onto them. These coverings were an important feature in the defence, because they protected the defenders from enemy archery.

On 9 September Kavadh sent a message to Areobindus in which he asked him to allow his *marzban* to enter the city or come out to negotiate himself. Kavadh's real purpose was either to use *marzban* and his men as his commando strikeforce, or to ambush Areobindus if he came out. Areobindus was suspicious of Kavadh's motives and agreed to meet the envoy only in the church of Mar Sergius just outside the Great Gate on the east side of the city. According to Joshua, the Persian envoy Bawi was an '*astabid/astabadh*', the highest ranking military officer in Iran, the equivalent of *magister militum*. He demanded 10,000 lbs of gold immediately and the customary gold thereafter each year in return for peace. Areobindus said he would be able to give only 7,000 lbs of gold. The men argued with each other for several hours but could not reach an agreement. When the Persians were unable to find a way to attack Areobindus, because he was guarded by Roman soldiers, the meeting ended.[72]

Since the attempt to take Edessa with a stratagem had failed, Kavadh turned his attention to the surrounding areas. The Arabs were detached to raid Batnae/Serug. They bypassed the city and plundered and pillaged everything up to the Euphrates without facing any opposition. In the meantime, Kavadh marched with his Persians and Hephthalites and presumably with the other foreign contingents against Carrhae/Harran. It was then, according to Joshua (59), that Rifaya sortied secretly from Carrhae and attacked the Persians, killed sixty of them and captured the chief of the Hephthalites. I would suggest that this Rifaya surprised the Hephthalites who were probably acting as a vanguard. The name Rifaya is otherwise unknown. It has been suggested that it referred to Rufinus, or that it meant *ripensis* (= *ripensis militia*), or an Arab leader named Rifaya. It is clear that this was a well-conducted surprise attack against the Persian forces. The leader of the Huns was a person held in very high honour by Kavadh, and Kavadh wanted to get him back alive and well. So Kavadh promised he would not attack Carrhae if its defenders returned the Hun to him. According to Joshua, the defenders were frightened and chose to return the Hun together with a gift of 1,500 rams and other items. This worked. The Persians needed food. Kavadh kept his word and marched to the Euphrates where he joined forces with the Arabs, after which he marched to besiege Edessa – perhaps the

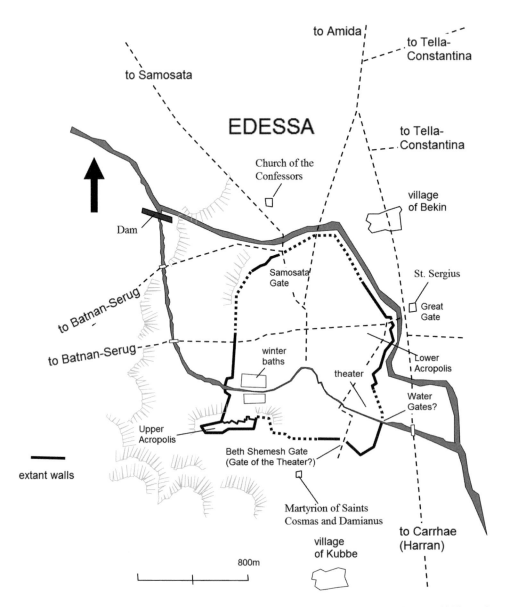

to Amida

to Tella-Constantina

to Samosata

EDESSA

to Tella-Constantina

Church of the
Confessors

village
of Bekin

Dam

Samosata
Gate

St. Sergius

to Batnan-Serug

Great
Gate

to Batnan-Serug

winter
baths

theater

Lower
Acropolis

Water
Gates?

Upper
Acropolis

Beth Shemesh Gate
(Gate of the Theater?)

extant walls

Martyrion of Saints
Cosmas and Damianus

to Carrhae
(Harran)

village
of Kubbe

800m

1,500 rams and other booty provided enough supplies to contemplate the possibility of besieging Edessa. When Kavadh reached Edessa on 17 September 503 he dispatched another force northwards to act as a shielding army against the Roman forces posted at Samosata.[73]

In the meantime, the Roman reinforcements under Patriciolus and his son Vitalianus had arrived at Samosata. According to Joshua (60), Patriciolus was still full of fearless confidence because he had not been among those who had been defeated and it was then because of this that he crossed the Euphrates and attacked one of the Persian officers on the other side, defeated and annihilated him. This force would have been the shielding force posted for the protection of Kavadh's besieging army. After this, Patriciolus aimed

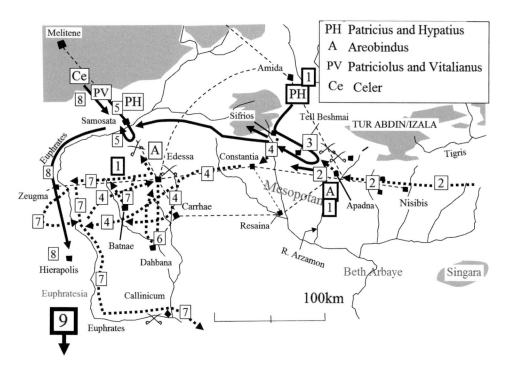

War in 503: Phase 2, the Persian counter-attack:

1) Patricius and Hypatius besiege Amida with Areobindus's forces at Apadna to act as a shielding force. Apion at Edessa is in charge of supplies.

2) Kavadh surprises Areobindus by the River Arzamon close to Apadna before Patricius and Hypatius, who are encamped at Siphrios, are able to reach him. Areobindus flees to Edessa.

3) Kavadh surprises Patricius and Hypatius, who flee all the way to Samosata.

4) Kavadh advances first to Constantia, but fails to capture it when the Jewish plot to hand it over to him is exposed. Kavadh continues his march against Edessa, which he tries to take through a ruse. When this fails, Kavadh sends his Arab allies towards Batnae while he advances to Carrhae. The defenders of Carrhae capture the Hephthalite leader and Kavadh leaves the city unmolested in return for his release. He joins forces with the Arabs along the Euphrates and proceeds to besiege Edessa on 17 September. He posts forces opposite Samosata to shield his main army.

5) Patriciolus and his son Vitalianus reach Samosata. They cross the Euphrates, defeat the shielding force, but are too late to advance to Edessa and so retreat to Samosata.

6) The battle in front of Edessa on 17 September in conjunction with the defeat of his shielding force convince Kavadh to accept Areobindus' suggestion to accept 2,000 lbs of gold twelve days later in return for abandoning the siege. When Kavadh reaches Dahbana/Dabana he demands part of the sum immediately. The Romans refuse and Kavadh attacks Edessa again, but is defeated severely by defenders on the wall and by villager slingers in front of the walls. Kavadh abandons the siege.

7) Kavadh marches to the Euphrates in a bold gesture meant to restore the morale of his battered army and to mislead the enemy when his real intention is to retreat. The Persians capture Batnae because its walls have crumbled. The Arabs raid across the Euphrates. The Persians learn of the approach of Celer and retreat at the double along the river. Close to Callinicum their vanguard is defeated by *dux Oshroenae* Timostratus and its commander captured. Kavadh leaves the city unmolested in return for the captive.

8) Celer, who has arrived from Constantinople, gives a pursuit of Kavadh, but then abandons it when he learns at Hierapolis that Kavadh has escaped.

9) Far to the south of the map, al-Munhir, son of al-Numan, raided Roman Arabia and Palestine with impunity either in late 503 or in early 504 because there provinces were left without adequate forces when the *dux* Romanus had joined the field armies.

to march to Edessa, but he abandoned his plan when he learnt from the refugees that Kavadh had already surrounded the city. Patriciolus returned to Samosata. His plan had clearly been to reach Edessa before the Persians could besiege it. He was a brave man quite ready to place his neck in the noose for the sake of the Roman Empire.

As noted above, the siege began on 17 September and it is well described by Joshua (60, tr. by Wright) as follows:

His [*Kavadh's*] camp extended from the church of SS. Cosmas and Damianus [*Martyrion of Mar Cosmas and Mar Damian in Trombley & Watt*], past all the gardens and the church of S. Sergius and the village of Běkin, as far as the church of the Confessors; and its breadth was as far as the steep descent of Serrîn. This whole host without number surrounded Edessa in one day, besides the pickets which it had left on the hills and rising grounds (to the west of the city). In fact the whole plain (to the E. and S.) [*and to the north*] was full of them. The gates of the city were all standing open, but the Persians were unable to enter it because of the blessing of Christ. [*The intention was to demonstrate to the enemy that the defenders did not fear them and thereby to lower the morale of the attackers. The other point of having the gates open was of course to make it easier to sally out of the city against the attackers, as happened.*] On the contrary, fear fell upon them [*i.e. the ploy worked*], and they remained at their posts, no one fighting with them, from morning till towards the ninth hour. Then some went forth from the city and fought with them [*Trombley & Watt's translation specifies that a few people went out, with the implication that they were civilians*]; and they slew many Persians, but of them there fell but one man. Women too were bearing water, and carrying it outside the wall, that those who were fighting might drink; and little boys were throwing stones with slings. So then a few people who had gone out of the city drove them away and repulsed them far from the wall, for they were not further off from it than about a bowshot; [*the implication being that regular soldiers were manning the walls and protecting the villagers with their bows even if Joshua fails to give the regulars any role in the defence*] and they went and encamped beside the village of Kubbê.

The following day, 18 September 503, Areobindus went out of the Great Gate to negotiate with the Persians. Kavadh agreed to withdraw if Areobindus handed over hostages as a guarantee that he would not attack Kavadh when he withdrew. The destruction of his shielding force together with the battle in front of the city on 17 September had clearly convinced Kavadh to accept the terms. In return for Kavadh's withdrawal Areobindus therefore handed over *comes* Basil together with the captured Persians and promised to pay Kavadh 2,000 lbs of gold at the end of twelve days. After this Kavadh left Edessa and marched to Dahbânâ/Dabana, but then contrary to the agreement sent Hormizd back to Edessa with the demand to send 300 lbs of gold immediately. Areobindus assembled the city council, which steadfastly refused to hand over the gold because Kavadh had not kept his promise. This emboldened Areobindus to send an insulting message to Kavadh in which he stated that he was not king at all because he had not kept his promise and demanded that Kavadh send back Basil.[74]

Then follows one of the most dramatic episodes of the war, which is described by Joshua (62–3, tr. by Wright):

The Kawâd became furious, and armed the elephants which were with him, and set out, he and all his host, and came again to fight with Edessa, on the 24th of the month of September, a Wednesday. He surrounded the city on all sides, more than on the former occasion, all its gates being open [*see above*]. Areobindus ordered the Greek soldiers [*the Roman soldiers in Trombley & Watt*] not to fight with him, that no falsehood might appear on his part; but some few of the villagers who were in the city went out against him with slings, and smote many of his mail-clad warriors, whilst of themselves not one fell.[75] [*The villagers of the surrounding area were undoubtedly very eager to exact revenge on the Persians for the pillaging and murdering they had done in this area in 502 and were therefore highly motivated to kill.*] … His legions were daring enough to try to enter the city; but when they came near its gates, like an upraised mound of earth [*Trombley & Watt translate this that the Persian legions were drawn up in formation like a tortoise, which is indeed the likeliest meaning for the mound in this case when the legions approached the gates. Note how Joshua compares the Sassanian infantry to the legions and how the Persian infantry was also using the tortoise array when it approached the enemy. Were these legionaries the murmillones of Ammianus who are likely to have been the descendants of the former Roman soldiers of Niger? For the former, see vol.1 and for the latter, see Herodian 3.4.7ff.*] they were humbled and repressed and turned back [*presumably under the hail of arrows, javelins, slingshots, and stones either thrown from the towers beside the gates or shot by stonethrowers*]. Because, however, of the swiftness of the charge of their cavalry, the slingers became mixed up among them; and though the Persians were shooting arrows, and the Huns were brandishing maces [*Trombley & Watt translate the problematic word as maces or as thongs and note that the meaning could also be clubs, axes, or lassoes; they also note that the Sassanid clibanarii carried with them lassoes and slings with stones; considering that here we are talking about Hephthalites, all of these are possible, but lassoes would probably fit the circumstances best*], and the Arabs were levelling spears at them [*the Arabs were famous as superb light cavalry lancers*], they were unable to harm a single one of them. After they saw that they were able neither to enter the city nor to harm the unarmed men who were mixed up with them, they set fire to the church of S. Sergius and the church of the Confessors and to all the convents that had been left [*standing*], and to the church of [*the village*] Negbath, which the people of the city had spared.

When the *stratêlatês* Areobindus saw the zeal of the villagers, and that they were not put to shame, but that [*divine*] help went with them, he summoned all the villagers that were in Edessa next day [*25 September 503*] to the [*Great*] Chruch, and gave them three hundred dinars [*denarii*] as a present. Kawâd departed from Edessa, and went and pitched on the river Euphrates [*probably to Zeugma, because the Arabs crossed the river unopposed and the Persians captured Batnae*]; and thence he sent ambassadors to the emperor to inform him of his coming. [*This was a ruse to mislead the enemy when the actual intention was to withdraw, as is noted by Greatrex, 1998, 107.*] The Arabs that were with him crossed the river westwards, and plundered and laid waste and took captive and burned everything in their way. Some few of the Persian cavalry went to Batnae, and because its wall was broken down, they could not resist them, but admitted them without fighting and surrendered the town to them.

The above account proves the fighting spirit of the Edessenes and villagers when their defences were bolstered by the presence of professional soldiers under Areobindus. In fact the fighting spirit and combat performance of the civilians put the professionals to shame. It is of course possible that Joshua has purposely magnified the exploits of the civilians to demonstrate the help provided by Christ for the city of Edessa, but I would still suggest that his account is accurate. In contrast to the professionals who had just been defeated and were therefore not in high spirits, the local civilians were protecting their homes, property and families, and they had every reason to be eager to exact vengeance against the Persians and their allies for the ravages of the previous year. The combat performance of the village slingers against the elite Persian cavalry, the Hephthalites and the Arabic lancers was superb. It was a true David and Goliath battle that ended in the victory of the former. It is remarkable how good the villagers were, both at long and short distance, against the much better equipped foes. The ancients evidently considered slingers to be particularly effective against cataphracts, but none of the military manuals recommended their use at a short distance. This instance proves that brave lightly-armed civilians could humiliate a professional enemy elite even at close quarters. One wonders whether the villagers had received some sort of martial arts training that made this possible or whether it was just their sheer enthusiasm.

The spirited defence of Edessa by the villagers had broken the fighting spirit of the Persian army, and the subsequent pillaging of those areas that were undefended was just meant to save face and restore some fighting spirit into the army, after which Kavadh started his retreat along the Euphrates past Callinicum. The threatening message to Anastasius and the raiding of the territory west of the Euphrates were just meant to mislead the enemy of Kavadh's intention to retreat. The frightened Anastasius had also dispatched *Magister Officiorum* Celer with a large army in late August. Note the use of the term 'large army' by Joshua (64), which implies that he arrived with a very significant number of reinforcements. According to Marcellinus Comes (a.503), Celer brought with him only 2,000 men as reinforcements, but this is clearly a mistake. The size of the *Scholae* accompanying their commander to the battlefield is also contradicted by Joshua. It is likely that the future Emperor Justin arrived with Celer and held the position of *Comes Excubitorum*. The news of the arrival of Celer appears to have frightened Kavadh because he retreated on the eastern side of the Euphrates faster than Celer advanced on the western side. The reason for this conclusion is that when Celer had reached Hierapolis, one of the traditional assembly points for the Roman army, he learnt that Kavadh had already managed to slip away too far to catch him. He had already passed Callinicum. So Celer summoned the Roman commanders, rebuked them because they had not cooperated, and then assigned cities for each to stay for the winter until the next campaigning season.[76]

During the winter break Celer reorganized the command structure of the army. He made Areobindus his second-in-command and then removed from office Hypatius because he could not cooperate with Areobindus. This must have taken place when the commanders were assigned to their winter quarters because we do not hear of Hypatius when Patricius started his operations in early winter 504. Celer also removed Apion from office for the same reason, but this took place in May 504, and Apion was not yet dismissed completely because he was dispatched to Alexandria to organize the sending of *bucellatum* (hard tack) from there to Seleucia and the eastern front. Apion was particularly suitable for this mission because he was a native of Egypt. Once he had organized this, the Emperor recalled him.[77]

There was another pressing reason for the retreat of Kavadh from Roman territory, which is mentioned by Procopius. Procopius (*Wars* 1.8.19) falsely places the retreat of Kavadh to have taken place immediately after he had defeated Patricius and Hypatius because the Huns had invaded his land. It is clear that the invasion of the Huns must be placed to have coincided with the arrival of Celer in the east. The Huns in question cannot be the Hephthalites because they were accompanying Kavadh, unless they now suddenly deserted him. This, in fact, is quite possible because after this there are no longer any references to the Hephthalites fighting in the Persian army. However, there are two other possibilities: either that these Huns were located north of the Caucasus (the Sabirs?) as usually suggested; or that they were actually the Kidarite Huns who at this time dwelled in north-west India. Whoever they were, their action helped the Romans at precisely the right time. It is likely that Roman diplomacy had contributed to this. After all, as *Magister Officiorum* Celer was also in charge of Roman foreign policy and it would not be too far fetched to suggest that he had bribed the Sabirs, Hephthalites or other Huns to invade Persian territory at this time. As we shall see, he was a crafty fellow. There is a reference to such a Roman diplomatic manoeuvre for 504 in Zachrariah the Rhetor (7.3). The extant version of Zachariah claims that in the thirteenth year of Emperor Anastasius, the Romans promised to give the Huns who lived on the north-western territory twice the sum of tribute that the Persians paid. This would of course identify the Huns either as Sabirs (the Huns located in the north-west) or as Hephthalites (the Persians paid tribute to them). The principal problem with this is that the extant version of Zachariah has confused the reigns of Kavadh and Peroz with each other so that it claims that the above event took place during the reign of Peroz and that the Huns killed the treacherous Persian monarch.

In the Caucasus the Romans could have contacted the Huns quite fast and it would not have taken them too long to do the same via the sea route to India, if they had dispatched envoys in 502. It would also have been possible to convey the message to the Hepthalites by using a captured Hephthalite as a messenger. Regardless, it is also clear that Procopius has once again condensed the events because he has left out the details of how Kavadh exploited his initial victory over the Romans and failed to achieve anything of any importance – in fact he was outgeneralled by the Romans, and even the Roman peasants humiliated him and his elite forces. As has often been noted Procopius' intention was to magnify the successes of Justinian and Belisarius by diminishing the successes achieved by Anastasius and his commanders.

The fact that Kavadh marched to Beth Aramaye, the Sassanian province of Asuristan-Babylonia, to winter his army proves that the immediate reason for the withdrawal was not the invasion of the Huns but the arrival of Celer in the aftermath of the humiliating incident at Edessa. Clearly Kavadh spent the winter in his capital Ctesiphon because it was located in that province, and he spent the winter well because his army was ready for action in the spring 504. But then came the news of the Hunnic invasion, whoever they were. I will discuss this matter in greater detail in the context of the events of the year 504.[78]

The Persian withdrawal along the Euphrates back to Persia took them in front of the city of Callinicum, HQ of the *dux Oshroenae* Timostratus. Kavadh dispatched a *marzban* against the city, but Timostratus marched outside, annihilated the entire Persian force and took its commander captive. The Persians appear not to have learnt their lesson. This is the second time a Roman commander defeated and captured the commander of the Persian vanguard in a very short time. This time however, the careless vanguard consisted of native Persians and not of Hephthalites, and apparently involved a real pitched battle probably with an ambush, rather than an ambush without a battle. Instead of just killing sixty soldiers as they had at Carrhae, the Romans now annihilated the entire vanguard. When Kavadh then reached the city with the main army, he threatened to destroy the city with all its inhabitants if they did not hand over the captive *marzban*. According to Joshua, the size of the enemy host frightened the *dux* so much that he handed over the captive, and so the retreat of the Persians continued.

In the past it was often suggested that in the later Roman period the frontier forces, the *limitanei*, had become next to useless soldier farmers that could not be used for military duties. This view has now been dated for well over a decade, but the above should finally put at rest this false idea. During the reign of Anastasius, the *limitanei*, or even the civilian militia, performed extremely well against the Persians and Arabs, while the combat performance of the mobile field armies left much to be desired. The *limitanei* were regular soldiers who often outperformed the *comitatenses* in combat thanks to their greater experience of operations in the field. The stellar performances of the civilian militia during the sieges of Amida and Edessa show that civilians could outperform regular professionals, the *comitatenses* included, when well motivated.

According to Geoffrey Greatrex, some time either in late 503 or early in 504, al-Numan's son al-Mundhir exploited the absence of Roman troops from Arabia and Palestine by invading those areas. He is claimed to have caused great damage and to have taken plenty of captives. It is probable, if Greatrex's dating is correct, that he had by then succeeded his father as *sheikh* so that Kavadh's appointee Abu Ya'fur had made room for him. However, it is also possible that this raid took place later in c. 509.[79]

There had also been trouble in Constantinople. According to Theophanes (AM 5997) two factions fought against each other during the chariot races with the result that many died, among them the illegitimate son of Anastasius. This angered the Emperor and he punished the culprits either with death or exile. It seems likely that this incident had nothing to do with the bad news coming out of the East, but it certainly cannot have helped the already distressed Emperor.

On 25 December 503, the Emperor gave a most welcome Christmas gift to the inhabitants of Mesopotamia. He released them from the *synteleia*, meaning he gave the inhabitants tax remission, which he repeated yearly for the next seven years so that the area had a chance to recover from the ravages of war.[80] This is a good example of the sound judgment of Anastasius as a ruler and how well he handled the finances. It is no wonder his reign came to be remembered with such fondness by those who were not bigoted Chalcedonians.

The Roman Counter Attack in 504

On the basis of the order of events in Joshua (66), Patricius started his operations before 19 March 504, a very unusual time for this. The abovementioned Hunnic invasion kept Kavadh away from the Roman frontier for the rest of the war so the Romans were free to take the initiative. We know very few details of this war, but on the basis of Zachariah (7.3) it is possible to make some educated guesses.

The version preserved in the extant version of Zachariah of Mitylene (7.3) is as follows. The 'Huns' invaded through the gates guarded by the Persians and through the mountains so that they invaded Persia proper in the 13th year of the reign of Anastasius (491–518, i.e. in 504) while Peroz was the ruler of Persia. Peroz then assembled an army and went to meet them and enquired why they had attacked. The Huns responded that they lived by their weapons, the bow and sword, and the Romans had promised through their ambassador (Eustace the merchant from Apamea, i.e. a spy in disguise) to pay twice the money the Persians paid as tribute, if they would wage war against the Persians. Peroz noted that his army outnumbered the enemy, but still decided to use a ruse to weaken them even further. He promised to pay them the same. Peroz met Eustace and the 400 leading Huns and promised to hand over the tribute to these 400 Huns if they would stay there on the mountain while the rest of the Huns retreated back to their country. On the tenth day, when Peroz knew that the Huns would be far away, he then broke his oath and prepared for war. When Eustace and the Huns noted this, Eustace advised the Huns to fight despite being outnumbered. They proceeded to kill Peroz together with a large part of his army, after which they pillaged at their will and returned to their country. The corpse of Peroz was never found and he received the nickname 'liar'.

It is obvious that the extant version of Zachariah has confused reigns and events with each other. However, if we assume that this version of Zachariah has preserved a garbled account of what really happened, then it is indeed possible to think that the above events took place in about 504, because with the exception of the death of the Persian ruler at the end of the account, the rest of this version does fit the dating and the circumstances prevailing under Kavadh. He had started his war against the Romans because he owed the Hephthalites tribute money. There were also Hephthalites in his army, at least in the initial stages, but even with the capture of Amida and other booty, it is by no means certain that Kavadh would have been able to pay the money he owed to the Hephthalites. It is easy to see how the Romans could have bribed the Hephthalites in these circumstances. Furthermore, Procopius (*Wars* 1.7.1–2) specifically refers to Roman efforts to disturb the relationship between these two. In my opinion it is therefore very likely that the Romans did indeed manage to break up the alliance between Kavadh and the Hephthalites with money or with a promise of money.[81]

If we then replace Peroz with Kavadh and change the confused ending it is possible to think that events progressed as described by Zachariah, Procopius and Joshua. The Romans would have bribed the Hephthalites with promises in 503 with the result that they invaded through the walls of Gurgan and then through the mountains into Persia in 504. Kavadh, who had spent the winter at Ctesiphon, advanced against the invaders, after which he betrayed the Hephthalites with promises. However, it is clear that the Hephthalites would not have retreated as claimed by Zachariah, but would have stayed somewhere close by so that the Persians faced the entire enemy army in the ensuing conflict in which Kavadh was defeated (but not killed as claimed in the confused account of Zachariah). It was then thanks to the failure of this ruse that the war became prolonged so that Kavadh was prepared to negotiate with the Romans.

According to Joshua (66), when the Roman army had departed to its winter quarters in late 503, it had abandoned its tight watch of the city of Amida as well. Consequently, the Persians opened up the city gates and organized a market in front of the city where the merchants traded their food and wares. When Patricius learnt of this, he left his winter quarters at Melitene and marched to Amida where he killed all the merchants he found on the site and then resumed the siege of the place. After this he apparently left the infantry and part of the cavalry behind to continue the siege while he with the rest of the cavalry crossed the river Nymphius and advanced into Persian Arzanene. There his forces attacked and killed the Persians who had been commissioned to bring arms, grain, and animals to Amida. When Kavadh learnt of this, he sent a *marzban* against Patricius. Trombley and Watt suggest that this *marzban* was either the military governor of Armin (Persarmenia) or Adurbadagan (Azerbaijan). Then, when Patricius was leading his men against this force, they told him that they were not yet ready to fight the Persians after the previous defeat. Patricius knew that it was not advisable to fight with an army that feared the enemy so he ordered a hasty retreat, and they ended up against the river Nymphius. As it was winter the river was flooding and impossible to cross. Some of the men tried anyway with the result that they and their horses drowned. It was then that Patricius spoke to his men and encouraged them to fight with all their strength, because it was preferable to die honourably by the sword rather than drown as a coward. The Romans had no choice but to fight, and they certainly did. The Roman cavalry turned around and charged furiously against the enemy. The Persian host was utterly destroyed and its commanders were captured alive. When Patricius had defeated the relief force, he returned to Amida to continue its siege.[82] The stain of last year's defeat was now gloriously washed away with enemy blood.

One wonders whether Patricius, who had just been leading his forces against the Persians to fight a battle but who had been forced to abandon his plans, had lead his army purposely to a place where it would have to fight. I would suggest that he did, in which case the risk paid off.

Celer started his operations in March and with this in mind he or Areobindus had ordered from the people of the church of Zeugma a miracle which encouraged his men to fight with greater zeal. Joshua obviously represents the miracle as genuine, but any rational person recognizes the classical methods used throughout the ages by all cynical military leaders in situations of war. In this case a goose supposedly laid an egg on 19 March 504 which had a cross (possibly a *labarum*) on it with a text written in Greek saying, 'The Romans will conquer!' The people of the church sent this information together with the egg to Areobindus who was duly impressed, as apparently were his men.[83]

Celer concentrated his forces at Resaina-Theodosiopolis. His subordinate commanders included at least *hypostrategos* Areobindus, *Comes* Justin, and the *duces* Bonosus, Timostratus and Romanus. In the meantime Kavadh had sent about 10,000 men to attack Patricius at Amida. On the basis of the size of this force it is clear that the purpose was to harass the besiegers into discontinuing the siege, as it is improbable that this force would have been large enough for a pitched battle against the remnants of the praesental

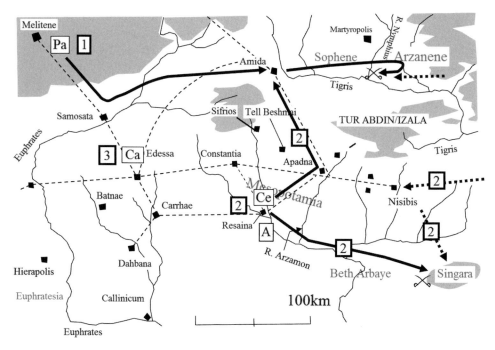

War in 504: The Roman counter-attack in the winter and spring:
1) When Patricius learnt that the Persians were holding markets at Amida, he marched out of his winter quarters at Melitene (some time in January-March 504), attacked Amida and then marched to Persian Arzanene where he captured an enemy convoy heading towards Amida. Kavadh dispatched a general against him. When Patricius learnt from his men that they were too frightened to fight, he attempted to retreat, but was forced to fight because the river Nymphius was flooding. It is also possible that this was just Patricius' stratagem to force his men to fight. The Persians were defeated and Patricius returned to Amida to resume the siege.
2) Kavadh dispatched an army against Patricius who was besieging at Amida, but it was forced to abandon its planned attack because Celer had concentrated his army at Resaina. The Persians moved their horses to pasture on Mount Singara. When Celer learnt of this, he ordered the *dux* of Callinicum Timostratus with 6,000 men to attack those who were looking after the horses in Singara. Timostratus defeated the Persians and captured their horses, thereby immobilizing the Persians at Nisibis. Celer was now free to join Patricius at Amida.
3) Calliopus arrives at Edessa to take charge of the supplying in May 504.

armies even after the defeat of the previous year. None of the sources mention casualties for the praesental infantry and it is also clear that most of the praesental cavalry survived the battle of Apadna because they had started their flight immediately after they had seen the Persians. When the Persians reached Nisibis they stopped for a rest and sent their animals to pasture on the Mount of Singara.[84] Geoffrey Greatrex has rightly pointed out that the probable reason for the inactivity of this force is that when it found out that Celer was located at Resaina it became impossible to even consider the prospect of advancing against Patricius because had they done so they would have been placed between two numerically superior enemy forces.[85]

When Celer learnt of the pasturing of the horses at Mount Singara, he ordered the *dux* of Callinicum Timostratus with 6,000 men to attack those who were looking after the horses. Timostratus had clearly now joined the main field army and did as ordered. He routed the guards, captured the horses and flocks, took much booty, and returned to Resaina. It is clear that most of the *limitanei* cavalry were assembled with the field armies at this time and their combat performance was outstanding while the *limitanei* infantry forces were left behind to man the fortresses and cities. After this Celer joined his army with Patricius to besiege Amida more effectively.[86]

Meanwhile Patricius had undermined the wall with a tunnel, but they had succeeded in collapsing only the outer section of the wall and the inner portion remained standing. Patricius decided to make a longer tunnel. When this was accomplished, the Romans entered it, but were unfortunately noted by one Amidene woman who shouted in great joy that the Romans were coming. This was heard by the Persians who rushed there and speared the first Roman to enter. The Gothic tribune Ald[87] was just behind him; he charged out and speared/stabbed three Persians immediately, but his example was not followed by those behind him and he decided to retreat. However, he was like the US Marines[88] of our own era who do not leave behind any fallen comrades-in-arms. He grabbed his dead comrade and pulled his body inside the tunnel. As he did so, the Persians wounded him, but apparently he still managed to retreat, because the next thing the Persians did was to fill the tunnel with water which would have taken some time to accomplish. After this, the Persians dug a moat inside the wall which they filled with water to prevent tunnelling.[89]

Joshua (72) notes that after this there was a serious incident that resulted in a change of strategy. There was a young man who had the duty of looking after the camels and asses. One day one of the asses went to graze just under the wall, where the boy was naturally afraid to go. One of the Persians noted this and lowered himself on a rope to capture the ass because the Persians had eaten all their meat. He was seen by a Galilean soldier, who drew his sword and charged with a shield in his left hand. The Persians on the wall

Scouting ladder

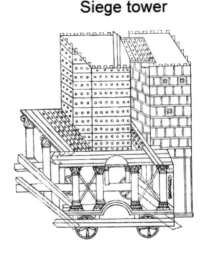

Siege tower

threw a large stone, which hit the man, so the Persian started to climb the rope. When he was halfway, one Roman officer behind the cover of two shield-bearers shot an arrow at him, and he fell beside the Galilean. After this both sides were roused to combat, and the Romans crowded against the wall and got the worst of it. The Romans lost 40 killed and 150 wounded while the Persians lost only 9 dead. This resulted from the fact that the Persians had built extra protection for themselves on top of the walls in the form of small huts so that they were not visible to the Romans. Does this suggest that the Romans used siege towers or scouting ladders/cranes to observe the enemy? It is impossible to say, but one may assume they would have used at least the latter to direct their archery fire, for which see the accompanying illustration. They had used siege towers in 502, but if they had used them on this occasion one would expect they would have been brought close to the wall for assault, but we hear nothing of this at this time.

So Celer and the commanders came to the conclusion that it was not in their interest to fight against the garrison, but rather either to force it to surrender by defeating Kavadh or to force it into submission through hunger. But Celer did not invade enemy territory immediately because Joshua clearly keeps him and the other commanders at Amida at least until July. The probable reason for this is that Celer needed to organize the supplying of expeditionary forces with Calliopus before he could undertake them.[90]

In June Constantine, the commander who had surrendered Theodosiopolis and who had defeated Areobindus, deserted back to the Roman side when it became apparent the Persians were losing. He had in the meantime married two women and it was with them that he travelled through the wilderness for fourteen days to reach the Roman Arabs who then took him to a *kastron* called Sura and from where he was sent to Edessa. Anastasius forced him to become a priest and to stay away from all public business. At about the same time further defections followed in the form of a Persian Arab called Adid (either Aziz or Yazid) who did so with his entire army. One wonders whether this Adid had helped Constantine and his wives across the desert. In July the Persians of Amida managed to kill the *dux* of Arabia, Gainas, with ballistae bolts (arrows in Joshua) because he had loosened his armour because of the heat.[91]

According to Joshua (75ff.) it was then, in July, that Celer led his army into Persian territory while he left Patricius in charge of the siege. At the same time he also dispatched Areobindus into Persarmenia. It is unfortunate that Joshua fails to give any details regarding these targets of invasions and the routes taken, but fortunately we know from Marcellinus Comes that Celer's invasion was directed south. Furthermore, it is probable that he has telescoped some of the events and left out the invasion of Arzanene (Joshua 79) by the Roman officers besieging Amida (i.e. probably Patricius), which is likely to have taken place at the same time as the two other invasions so that Patricius would have invaded the central portion of enemy territory when the others invaded areas north and south. On the basis of Zachariah's description of the exploits of Pharesmanes it is also likely that he was left in charge of the siege of Amida when these Roman officers invaded Arzanene. However, if we assume that Joshua has retained the correct order of events, then it is possible that the invasion of the central portion of the enemy front at Arzanene followed after the invasions of Celer and Areobindus. I will here give both alternatives. In addition to this, Joshua (79) states that the Roman Arabs crossed the Tigris and plundered and destroyed Persian territory. Unfortunately once again he fails to specify which section of the frontier the Arabs invaded, but perhaps the likeliest is the part where Celer led his forces.

The invasion of Persarmenia by Areobindus was a great success. He destroyed 10,000 Armenians and Persians presumably in combat, and captured 30,000 women and children together with 120,000 sheep, oxen and horses. After this he marched south along the Tigris, crossed it and bypassed Nisibis. Here he laid an ambush for the local *marzban*, placing his booty under a light guard so that when the *marzban* saw it he led his forces out of the city. Areobindus' men then feigned flight and the *marzban* followed them and fell into the ambush. Seven thousand Persians were killed, which undoubtedly heightened Areobindus' reputation as a commander still further. Joshua follows this with the information that Mushleg the Armenian, who has been identified as Mushleg the Mamikonean, deserted with his soldiers to the Roman side.[92] He fails to specify when and in what circumstances this defection took place, which means that it could have taken place during the invasion of Persarmenia or as a result of it. My own suggestion is that he defected at the same time when the invasion took place because the Mamikonean domains lay along the western frontiers both at Tayk and Taron, and it is very probable that his defection had been organized in advance of the invasion.[93]

Trombley and Watt suggest a route across the Tigris south of Martyropolis into Persian Arzanene round Tur Abdin and then along the Tigris to Nisibis. They also suggest that the figures for booty suggest the pillaging of thirty villages.[94] However, on the basis of the above, I would suggest Areobindus' invasion actually took place further north into the heartland of Persarmenia as stated by Joshua so that he advanced first to Theodosiopolis and then either to Tayk or Taron[95] and from there southwards, because it would seem strange if all the invasions were directed across the Tigris in the neighbourhood of Arzanene. After all, the city of Theodosipolis had been built to serve as an advance base for military operations deep into Persarmenian territory.[96]

The evidence we have clearly suggests that Celer and his generals and Arabs invaded the entire length of the Persian front in the absence of Kavadh in order to convince him to give up Amida and to sign a peace/truce. The fact that Kavadh was unable to intervene in any effective way suggests that he was actually somewhere in the east rather than in the north fighting against the Sabirs as usually suggested. It would seem strange if Kavadh had been unable to make personal appearance in Arzanene or south of it if he was in the Caucasus fighting the Sabirs when one remembers the long distances covered by Roman commanders at the time. However, it is still probable that the Sabirs also invaded the Persian territory at this time because they were in possession of the Caspian Gates as allies of Rome at some point in time during the period 506–518 (see later), but it is equally clear that Kavadh cannot have been there facing them with his main army because he could have otherwise marched south against the Romans relatively fast.

Joshua (75) fails to give us any details concerning the invasion route taken by Celer, but according to Marcellinus Comes (tr. by Croke 33–4):

Meanwhile Celer, the Master of the Offices, while leading his armed soldiery through Callinicum, a city in Mesopotamia, diverted to ravage Persian farms. He killed cattle, very many farmers engaged in their rural labours, led off shepherds of diverse flocks with their numerous herds, invaded a fort constructed of brick and

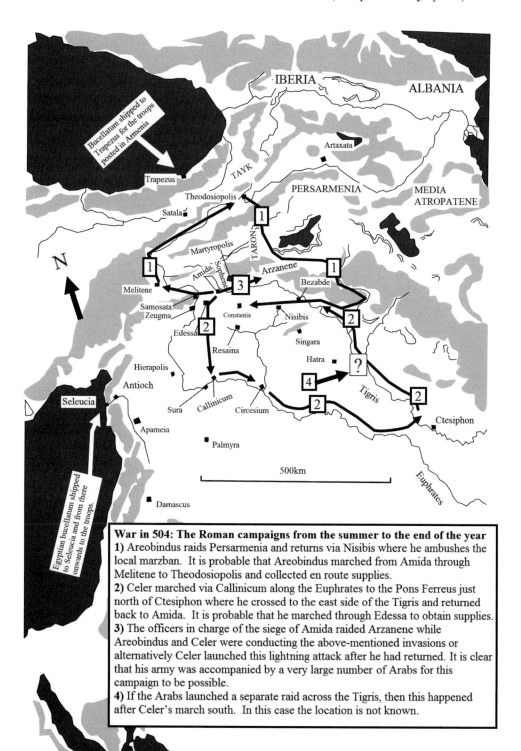

War in 504: The Roman campaigns from the summer to the end of the year
1) Areobindus raids Persarmenia and returns via Nisibis where he ambushes the local marzban. It is probable that Areobindus marched from Amida through Melitene to Theodosiopolis and collected en route supplies.
2) Celer marched via Callinicum along the Euphrates to the Pons Ferreus just north of Ctesiphon where he crossed to the east side of the Tigris and returned back to Amida. It is probable that he marched through Edessa to obtain supplies.
3) The officers in charge of the siege of Amida raided Arzanene while Areobindus and Celer were conducting the above-mentioned invasions or alternatively Celer launched this lightning attack after he had returned. It is clear that his army was accompanied by a very large number of Arabs for this campaign to be possible.
4) If the Arabs launched a separate raid across the Tigris, then this happened after Celer's march south. In this case the location is not known.

214 Military History of Late Rome AD 457–518

mud and advanced as far as the so-called Ironbridge [*Pons Ferreus*] by laying waste everywhere. After taking possession of all the booty and enriching the soldiery, he returned to the common camp [*presumably in front of Amida, which makes it possible that he did lead the invasion of Arzanene in person as claimed by Procopius, even if Joshua fails to say so*]. Some time after, he resolved to conclude a treaty with the Persians when Armonius …had been sent to him to draft the treaty.

The *Pons Ferreus* has been identified with the bridge which leads over the Tigris in the heights above Ctesiphon. This means that Celer marched first along the Euphrates (on its eastern side) all the way up to the bridge close to Ctesiphon after which he marched on the eastern side of the Tigris north until recrossing it again to march back to Amida. According to Theophanes (AM 5998) the Romans overran many forts in Persian territory at this time. He also claims that the Romans almost took Nisibis, which I take to imply that after the death of its *marzban*, the Romans, probably under Areobindus, attacked the city.[97] It is even possible or probable that Celer recrossed the Tigris close to Nisibis, because Areobindus' invasion would have neutralized its garrison, so that the two invasion forces would have pillaged the entire length of enemy territory. I would also suggest that we should connect the crossing of the Tigris by the Roman Arabs with this operation so that Celer's army was accompanied by very large numbers of Arabs which were particularly useful in operations in the areas under discussion. The inability of the Persians to do anything would obviously have resulted from their troubles with the Huns. On top of this, Theophanes (AM 5998) and Zachariah (7.6) claim that the Kadishaye/Kadisioi, Tamaraye and other races had revolted against the Persians. The Persians were in deep trouble.

It is clear that Celer's campaign was a huge success the like of which the Romans would not be able repeat for a long time, and it is also clear we should include Celer among the greatest commanders of his age, even if he was not strictly speaking a military man. It is not without reason that Malalas (16.9) called him a learned man while Theophanes (AM 5998) judged him a man with good sense and learning of all kinds while also brave. If the campaign against Arzanene (see below) took place after this, then Celer continued his unbelievable string of military successes with another lightning campaign very late in the same year or in early 505, but I would suggest that this campaign was probably conducted on his behalf by Patricius and other officers in August-September 504.[98]

Joshua the Stylite (79) describes the invasion of Arzanene by the Roman officers who were besieging Amida *after* he has described the campaigns of Areobindus and Celer, but in my opinion it is more likely that they were simultaneous, even if one cannot entirely rule out the other option. It was then that these officers conducted raids into Persian territory, destroying everything while taking captives and booty. The Persians withdrew in front of them with the Romans in pursuit. The Persians assembled an army of 10,000 men for a counter-attack behind the Tigris, but this did not deter the Romans who crossed the Tigris and routed the enemy force.

The area targeted must be Arzanene once again, and it is possible that we should connect this with the invasion of Arzanene by Celer mentioned by Procopius (Wars 1.8.21–22) as has been done by most modern historians. However, it is possible that Procopius has made a mistake here, just as he did when he claimed that nobody was made commander-in-chief, and when he implied that all of the commanders arrived at the same time. I would suggest it is more than likely that Joshua is correct in stating that the invasion was conducted by the Roman officers in charge of the siege rather than by Celer, and that Procopius has just put their action to have taken place under his name. In fact, contrary to what all modern commentators state, it becomes clear that if one pays close attention to what Joshua actually states, that he nowhere claims that Celer was accompanying the army. To quote the latest translation by Trombley and Watt (Joshua 79), which describes the situation immediately after the defeat of the 10,000 Persians:

> They looted the property of all those who had fled, burned many villages, killed all the men in them twelve years or above, and took captive the women and children. In fact, the *magistros* had thus ordered all officers, that if any of the Roman soldiers were found sparing a male of twelve years or above, he should be executed instead of him, and whatever village they would enter, they should not leave a single house standing in it. On this account he had detached some strong men from the soldiers, and also numerous villagers who joined them as they went down [*into Persian territory*], and after the roofs had been burnt and the fire gone out, these people pulled down the walls. They also cut down and destroyed the vineyards, olives and all other trees.

The *magistros* Celer is clearly not the commander of the operations. He is the *magistros* who has given the orders to the officers and men on how to conduct their operations and who has dispatched the men and villagers for this task. The commanders of this operation are called throughout the text 'they' or 'officers', although it is still possible that the *magistros* Celer accompanied the army.

Joshua describes the above invasion of Arzanene after his description of placing the civilians of Amida inside the amphitheatre (see below), but in my opinion he has here telescoped the events because the same incident is also described by Zachariah (7.5) from an eyewitness account. In his account this event followed after the ambush of Glon by Pharesmanes and in my opinion his version should be preferred. In short, if the invasion of Arzanene took place at the same time as Celer and Areobindus invaded Persian territory, then Patricius would have left Pharesmanes as acting commander in charge of the siege of Amida so that Pharesmanes conducted the siege from a distance rather than at close range so he could avoid taking casualties in the manner described above. Celer's strategy was to starve the Persian defenders slowly while conducting punitive raids into Persian territory. It was then because of this strategy that Pharesmanes' ruse against the Persians worked. If the invasion of Arzanene took place only after Areobindus and Celer had returned, then it must have taken place under Patricius and Areobindus, because it is strange that Joshua refers to officers in charge of the siege of Amida. But of course one cannot entirely rule out the possibility that Procopius was right after all.

According to Zachariah, a crafty fellow called Gadono of Akhore,[99] who was a hunter and fisher and who brought food for the Persians, suggested to Pharesmanes that he would lure out the Persian commander Glon to an ambush. Pharesmanes agreed to the plan. He placed about 100 Romans with 500 horses at a distance of seven miles from the city in a place called Afotho Ro'en. Gadono told Glon about them and Glon dispatched his scouts to check the information. When Gadono's story was confirmed, Glon together with 400 horsemen and Gadono on a mule advanced to the place and were duly ambushed. Glon's head was cut off and placed on display at Constantia.

This angered the son of Glon and the two *marzbans* to such an extent that they enclosed 10,000 civilians and the two or three remaining rich men inside the amphitheatre, thereby preventing them from gaining access to the food markets. However, the Persians made an exception in the case of women. They gave them food in return for sex until there was so little food left that they stopped doing even this. By this stage the Persians were no longer leaving their posts in the wall for fear of the enemy. They brought handmills and small ovens onto the walls so that they could grind, bake and eat the barley without leaving their posts. They also brought up large kneading-troughs in which they planted vegetables, which they ate.[100]

Eventually the situation became unbearable for the civilians. According to Joshua (77, tr. by Wright),

many women then met and conspired together, and used to go forth by stealth into the streets of the city in the evening or morning; and whomsoever they met, woman or child or man, [*this means that the Persians no longer cared to guard the civilians inside the amphitheatre*] for whom they were a match, they used to carry him by force into a house and kill and eat him, either boiled or roasted. [*The women who had sold sex in return for food would have been in better physical condition, so it would have been relatively easy for them to overpower the people they met, adult males included. Possibly they had reason to hate men in particular. According to Zachariah 7.5, the women ate more than 500 men.*] When this was betrayed by the smell of the roasting, and the thing became known to the *marzban* who was there [*in command*], he made an example of many of them and put them to death, and told the rest with threats that they should not do this again nor kill anyone. He gave them leave however to eat those that were dead, and this they did openly, eating the flesh of dead men; and the rest of them were picking up shoes and old soles and other nasty things from the streets and courtyards, and eating them. To the Greek troops [*Romans*] however nought was lacking, but everything was supplied to them in its season, and came down with great care by the order of the emperor. Indeed the things that were sold in their camps were more abundant than in the cities whether meat or drink or shoes or clothing. All the cities were baking soldiers' bread (*boukellaton*) … by the order of Calliopus the hyparch [*This was exemplary performance by both the Emperor and by Calliopus. Such great care for the wellbeing of soldiers was a rare phenomenon during the late Roman period*].

The Peace Negotiations 504–505[101]

The ravaging of Persian territory in combination with the ongoing war against the Huns, and the desperate situation of the defenders of Amida, finally convinced Kavadh to seek peace. He dispatched an *Astabid* (*spahbad/spahbod*, presumably meaning *Eran-Spahbad/ Eiran-Spahbod*) with 20,000 soldiers to negotiate with Celer at the end of 504. The intention was clearly to impress Celer with the rank of his counterpart (the highest-ranking military commander in Persia) and to demonstrate that the Persians still had troops to oppose the Romans. The *Astabid* brought with him generals Peter, Basil and other hostages and gave them as gifts to demonstrate goodwill towards the Romans. He also returned *dux* Olympius, but since he had died (of natural causes) he was handed over in a coffin. He had been dispatched as an envoy to the Persians at some point but had not been allowed to return. Celer dispatched the others to Edessa, but intended to execute governor Cyrus and *comes* Peter because of their negligence. Celer therefore accused Cyrus of having allowed the walls to decay and allowing the enemy to enter the city because the Tripyrgia was not guarded adequately. Peter was presumably accused of having allowed the civilians to negotiate with the enemy which resulted in his and his men's surrender to the enemy. Both men however appear to have survived, despite the anger felt by Celer and the Emperor.[102]

The *Astabid* pleaded Celer to release the defenders of Amida in return for the hostages returned by the Persians, but Celer refused to allow this. Then the Astabid pleaded that he might at least be allowed to send food to the men. Celer promised to allow this and Astabid asked Celer and his officers to swear this on oath. Celer, however, sent one of his *duces* called Nonnosus away so that he would not be party to the deal. The idea was to allow Nonnosus to attack the convoy and then claim innocence. The Persians were justifiably suspicious of Romans intentions but were unable to prevent the convoy from being attacked. On the other hand, the Persians had not been exactly honest either: the destroyed convoy included arrows besides the food supplies. Consequently, when the *Astabid* complained about the attack he did not press his case but began to negotiate terms of peace.[103]

The negotiations went on for several days until the weather became very cold and there was snow and ice on the ground. Then the Roman soldiers started to desert their posts, taking with them the booty they had captured, some heading back to their homes, others to Constantia, Resaina and Edessa. When the *Astabid* noted this, he sent a more threatening message to Celer: Either send the defenders of Amida back home or face war! Celer dispatched Justin after the deserters to reassemble the army, but when it became apparent this was impossible, Celer concluded the peace with the *Astabid* on condition that it was accepted by both the *Augustus* and the *Shahanshah*. He therefore allowed the Persians to go home and gave a one-time gift of 1,100 lbs of gold in return for the city of Amida. According to Zachariah, Pharesmanes was the person responsible for making the treaty, but this is clearly untrue even if it is probable that Pharesmanes acted as Celer's representative to the Persians and Amidenes when the Persians were allowed to leave the city.[104]

It is possible or even probable that events in the Balkans played a role in the readiness of Anastasius and Celer to conclude peace, now in the winter of 504/5 and then later in 506. In 504 Theoderic the Amal exploited the Persian war by sending *Comes* Pitzias against the Gepids in Pannonia and Sirmium. Pitzias defeated the Gepids and annexed the area for the Ostrogoths. Next year he protected their mercenary ally Mundo against the East Roman army led by Sabinianus and crushed it in the battle at Horreum Margi. See later.

It is unlikely to be a coincidence that the Romans faced similar troubles with their soldiers in the winter of 602 after their armies had achieved a string of great military victories. In both cases the soldiers would have felt they had achieved something great and deserved a break – a winter holiday during which they would be allowed to take their booty back home – a holiday that would last through the entire winter so they could enjoy the rest and their booty. One can imagine that Patricius' men in particular would have demanded this because they had campaigned through the previous winter; it was not usual for armies of antiquity to do that. Unlike in 602, the officers in charge detected the trouble in time and did not attempt to press their case against the unwilling soldiers.[105] Having detected the signs of trouble they wisely allowed the men go to their winter quarters to enjoy their well-earned rest. In 602 the Emperor Maurice was not as wise: he unwisely chose not to follow the wishes of his soldiers and paid the ultimate price for his folly.

The peace negotiated by Celer enabled Anastasius to begin rebuilding the defences immediately, which included the walls at Edessa, Theodosiopolis (Erzurum),[106] Batnae, Amida, Birta/Virta, and Europus.[107] In addition, Anastasius and imperial eunuch Urbicius provided money to those who had suffered. The Emperor also remitted the taxes again. His aim was to ensure that the population would be prepared to fight again if the enemy chose to attack. This was wise in a situation in which Kavadh for some unknown reason refused to ratify the treaty – perhaps he believed he could obtain a better treaty after he had subdued all the revolts he was facing. Perhaps he thought that the Romans had humiliated him to such an extent that he needed to take revenge. The delay, however, was costly to the Roman civilians because the soldiers who were billeted in the cities were behaving rudely towards their hosts. The mass desertion of the troops during the winter was a sign of their state of mind and the civilians were at the receiving end. The officers and officials whose duty it was to discipline the men were either too afraid to do so or took bribes. Ever considerate, Celer sent the men to their winter quarters so that Areobindus, the *magister militum per Orietem*, led his forces to his HQ at Antioch while Patricius led his first praesental army to Melitene, Pharesmanes his second praesental army to Apameia,[108] Theodore his men to Damascus, while Calliopus relocated himself to Hierapolis. The ravages caused by the billeting of the soldiers were not the only ones that the civilians suffered as a result of the war. The large numbers of killed had taught the wild animals to eat humans; once they had tasted human flesh they wanted more. The villagers were forced to form hunting parties to get rid of the danger the wild animals posed to their children, lonely travellers and shepherds.[109]

Some time during the Persian war the Tzani raided Pontus. This event has usually been dated to about 505/6. We do not know the reason for the raid, but it is clear that the measures which had been undertaken by Longinus in about 485 had been insufficient. This time the situation was presumably dealt by the forces of the Armenian *dux* and it probably involved payment of money to some warlords after the raiders had first been punished, but the pacification of the Tzani would prove to be a long process which was finally achieved only in the 520s by Sittas. This raid, however, was a mere nuisance, an example of banditry, and did not affect the negotiations between Rome and Persia.[110]

The delay gave the Arabs of both sides the opportunity to conduct further raids, but this time the leaders of these operations paid the price, because both the Romans and the Persians executed the Arab leaders guilty of this. Nevertheless, the sources make it clear that the raiding had been very profitable to the Arab allies of both.[111]

The fact that Kavadh had not yet signed the peace treaty by the summer 505 resulted in ever more ambitious fortification projects. Anastasius recalled the generals and Celer to Constantinople in the winter of 505/6 to explain why they had not been able to defeat the Persians decisively and conquer Amida and Nisibis. The generals explained that there was no place large enough to shelter a large army close to Nisibis, that there had been no engines of war ready for use, and that there had not been arsenals with enough water and vegetables to support a large army close to the places of operation. These excuses were particularly valid for Areobindus who would like to have used a fortress as his place of refuge when he operated near Nisibis, especially on the first occasion when his superiors had failed to support him. Consequently, the generals persuaded Anastasius to fortify the village of Dara to act as a forward base for any future operations, as Theodosiopolis/Erzurum was for the Armenian front (it was also refortified for the same purpose). The Romans knew that the Persians from Nisibis would attempt to prevent this so Celer made counter-preparations.[112]

Celer returned to the east in the winter of 506 and went to Apameia because his plan was to use Pharesmanes and his forces for the protection of the builders at Dara. The builders and materials were collected throughout the area to begin the operation. After his arrival, Pharesmanes was sent to Edessa from where he would eventually go to Amida to serve as a protection force for the builders at Dara. To secure his loyalty the Emperor had sent a letter at Edessa (undoubtedly thanks to the recommendation of Celer) which appointed him officially the new *magister militum* of the second praesental army. When Pharesmanes then moved from Edessa to Amida, the *dux* Romanus took his place there. Pharesmanes used Amida as his base of operations when he protected the builders at Dara. During these forays, he made great hunting expeditions to capture wild game. Once to demonstrate his manhood he personally killed forty wild boars which he then dispatched to Edessa as a proof. Was this meant as a taunt to his successor Romanus at Edessa?[113]

Romanus was having troubles of his own. According to Joshua (92–4), the Goths billeted at Edessa were particularly violent and greedy towards their hosts so that the people demanded the Goths be relocated to the estates/villages of the rich because these had escaped their ravages[114]. The *hyparch* (Praetorian Prefect of Oriens) agreed to this, but when this was already taking place, the nobles (the rich curiales) pleaded with the *dux* Romanus that he should not let the Goths loot their estates the way they had already looted the poor people. Romanus agreed and put a limit to the amount of hospitality that the soldiers could demand – the nobles probably bribed him. This angered the Goths who then ran to kill the *dux* in the house of the Barsa family where he had been billeted. Romanus heard the noise as they rushed to go up the stairs, put on his armour and equipment, drew his sword, and took a stand at the door with the men who were with him. He prevented the leading Goths from approaching by assuming a fighting stance. They became frightened and stopped while those behind them kept pushing them forward. The stairs collapsed, killing some of the Goths and badly injuring the rest. This gave Romanus the chance he needed to get away. He fled to the roof and from there from one roof to another until he was safe. After this, he was too frightened to do anything, so the soldiers did as they pleased.

When Celer reached Edessa in April, the Persians informed him that the *Astabid* had died and they asked him to wait for the arrival of his replacement at Edessa. The wait lasted five months, which in my opinion should be seen as a proof that Kavadh was indeed in the eastern half of his Empire fighting against the Hephthalite Huns while his other commanders fought the rebels elsewhere. It took a while for the messages to be exchanged and the new *Astabid* appointed. The wait caused so much hardship to the civilians of Edessa and other cities and villages that some brave citizens of Edessa wrote a public complaint against Celer which they posted secretly around the city on paper sheets (*chartes*). This naturally angered Celer, but he had learnt his lesson. He did not punish the culprits because he knew the situation. Instead, he led his forces to Dara and thereby ended the hardship. Then the negotiations began. The new *Astabid* had arrived. The two sides exchanged hostages, because both sides distrusted each other. The Persians brought with them an army which encamped near the negotiating site, while Celer brought his entire massive field army to the site and put it in battle array behind him. Then one of the Roman soldiers noted that their Persian counterparts were wearing armour. He told Pharesmanes and Timostratus who then gave the signal to attack. The Persian negotiators were captured while their men fled headlong to Nisibis. Celer managed to prevent the killing of the Persian negotiators but only with great difficulty. The *Astabid* and his officers were released unharmed. When they noted that their men were no longer at the marching camp, they too went to Nisibis. Now the *Astabid* was too frightened to negotiate without the presence of his soldiers, but they refused to follow him to the site of the negotiations. In this conundrum *Astabid* resorted to a ruse: he called his daughter to Nisibis so that he could marry her himself. This was one of the Persian customs that caused plenty of disgust among the Romans, but since the Romans were aware of the peculiarities of Persian culture the ruse worked so that the *Astabid* was able to postpone the negotiations without causing a diplomatic row.[115]

Finally in November 506, the two men met and made a peace agreement for seven years, because Celer preferred peace over a clear victory at the negotiating table. The terms of this agreement are unknown, but may have included the payment of a large one-time lump sum to Kavadh, as suggested by Geoffrey Greatrex. Kavadh had to sign the peace because he was still fighting against the Huns (Procop. *Wars* 1.9.24; *de Aed.* 2.1.4ff.). Peace even without money would probably have sufficed, but if Celer paid a small sum of money by Roman standards, then this would have definitely sealed the contract because Kavadh was desperately in need of money to pay for his wars. Anastasius had given Celer and Calliopus the authority to decide what to do with the taxes. They decided to remit the taxes for the areas affected and reduced the contributions of Edessa by half. The soldiers were also allowed to go back to their home garrisons and this was undoubtedly the greatest gift of all to those in whose cities they had been billeted.

The East 506–518

According to Zachariah, the building of Dara took two or three years, which would mean that it was finished by about 507/8. According to Zachariah, when Kavadh finally learnt that the Romans were fortifying Dara right next to the city of Nisibis, he sought to prevent it but was unable to do so because the walls had already been completed. According to Procopius, the Persians learnt of the building project when it was taking place but were unable to do anything because they were fighting the Huns. Procopius' version is naturally more likely because the Persians cannot have failed to notice the building project right next to Nisibis. Procopius then notes that when the war against the Huns was over, Kavadh accused the Romans of having broken their previous agreement according to which neither side would build fortifications right next to the border. Anastasius defused the situation with a good cop bad cop routine. He used a combination of threats and gestures of friendship which included the paying of a large sum of money to Kavadh. In short, Anastasius considered the one-time paying of money preferable to having to fight a war as long as the Persians remained at peace and therefore in practice recognized with their inactivity that the refortification of the Roman frontier zone was legally acceptable. At least this would be in keeping with the typical legalistic thinking of the Roman upper classes (they all received legal training) as we shall see in the context of the next Persian war that started under Justin I.[116]

We should possibly connect the ending of the Persian war against the Huns and the fortifying of Dara with the abovementioned raid of al-Mundhir conducted against Roman Arabia and Palestine mentioned by Cyril of Scythopolis. The dating which Cyril gives is remarkably close to the date when the walls of Dara were completed. Cyril dates the raid using two systems which result in either 1 September 508 – 31 August 509 or 8 January 509 – 7 January 510.[117] If we assume that Zachariah misdated the completion by one year or that the war against the Huns ended one year after the completion of the walls, then possibly Kavadh dispatched al-Mundhir against the Roman provinces as his means of putting pressure on the Romans when their mutual treaty had apparently forgotten to include a clause against the use of Arab allies. Whatever the truth, both sides preferred to keep the peace. After all, the war had been very costly to both, especially the Persians.

The achievement of Anastasius and Celer has not received its due merit. Anastasius managed the situation masterfully. He was able to assemble and finance a huge army against the Persians, to rebuild the cities and fortifications, and help the local population. Anastasius' commander Celer achieved far greater successes against the Persians than the much vaunted Belisarius or any other general of Justinian – my intention is not to denigrate Belisarius because he should be seen as one of the greatest commanders of all ages, but it is still clear that his achievements against the Persians were not comparable with those of Celer. In addition, Celer and his superior Anastasius were wise enough not to press their advantage against the Persians too far, but to make a peace treaty which was acceptable to both parties. They did not humiliate the Persians in the same manner as the victors of the First World War did to the Germans. Had Anastasius' successors Justin and Justinian been wiser in their dealings most of the subsequent wars between Rome and Persia could have been avoided. See the next volume for a full analysis of what brought an end to the peace achieved with such great cost under Anastasius.

Some time between 506 and 518 the leader of the Huns (probably the Sabiri) called Ambazouces, who was a friend of the Romans and very old, sent a message to Anastasius that he would be willing to hand over the Caspian Gates in return for a sum of money. Some modern historians date this event to have taken place in 508, but it is impossible to be certain as Procopius does not give us any precise date.[118]

According to Procopius, the importance of the Caspian Gates arose from the fact that if an army went through this pass their horses would arrive fresh and ready for combat, but if they used any other pass they could no longer use the same horses. In the words of Procopius (tr. by Dewing):

But the Emperor Anastasius was incapable of doing anything without careful investigation, nor was it his custom to act thus; reasoning, therefore, that it was impossible for him to support soldiers in a place which was destitute of all good things, and which had nowhere in the neighbourhood a nation subject to the Romans, he expressed deep gratitude to the man for his good-will towards him, but by no means accepted this proposition. So Ambazouces died of disease not long afterwards, and Cabades overpowered his sons and took possession of the Gates.[119]

If the Caspian Gates means the Derbend Pass and not the Darial Pass, then it is probable that the Huns in question had conquered the Derbend Pass from the Persians. This in its turn would mean that the Romans had also managed to ally themselves with the Huns north of the Caucasus range and not only with the Hephthalite Huns of the East. The problematic portion in this is the dating of these events.

It was possibly because of that offer, if it was known to Kavadh, that Anastasius started to pay attention to the Transcaucasus. It was presumably thanks to this that he faced a revolt in Persarmenia in 513/4, which he suppressed, but we do not know whether he had any role in the Sabiri invasion of Roman territories in 515. If he had already won the Caspian Gates from the sons of Ambazouces, then he did, but if he had not conquered the Gates, then Ambazouces' sons would probably have taken Anastasius' refusal as an insult to be avenged. Whatever the truth, the Sabiri invaded Roman Armenia, Cappadocia up to Lycaonia, and Mesopotamia in 515. This invasion caused great damage, in particular to Cappadocia which had not been refortified after the Persian war. It was because of this that Anastasius built walls to protect all the large towns of Cappadocia after the invasion. He also remitted taxes in all of the provinces affected for a period of three years.[120] The obvious reason for the success of this invasion was the simultaneous second revolt of Vitalianus, which required all the manpower Anastasius could muster. That Kavadh did not exploit the Roman difficulties suggests that he had his hands full of troubles of his own and that he had also learnt how destructive Roman counter-attacks could be when Anastasius massed his armies against him.

In the meantime, Anastasius had faced trouble on the southern section of his frontiers, as mentioned by John of Antioch. The Mazices had raided Libya and pillaged Cyrenaica. John of Antioch does not date the event precisely but it seems probable that because the great-grandson of Marinus (in charge of Anastasius' finances) Bassianus was governor of Libya at the time and Marinus became *PPO Orientis* in about 512/5 that he acquired the position after this. Haarer dates this war to 513, which makes it one of Anastasius' worst years, as then he faced the first revolt of Vitalianus. Bassianus and his father who preceeded him in this post lost all the goodwill that the locals had towards Marinus thanks to their corruption and the mess they were clearly responsible for in the area. The raids, however, appear to have been a one-time affair, or at least that is the impression we get – the sources mention no more on the subject.[121]

The West until 518: The Ostrogothic Problem

The Isaurian War, the wars against the Arabs and then the Persian War all meant that Anastasius lacked adequate forces for the defence of the Balkans, not least because he lost 100,000–150,000 soldiers, mostly Isaurian, in the Isaurian War. The neighbours had exploited the absence of troops from the Balkans. The Scythians (Bulgars?) had defeated and killed *magister militum* Julianus in 493. Theoderic was able to conclude a peace with Anastasius in 497. In 498/9 the Bulgars defeated the *magister militum per Illyricum* Aristus and his 15,000 men. In 502[122] thanks to the transferral of forces against the Persians, the Bulgars were able to invade and pillage Thrace completely unopposed.[123]

In the absence of soldiers, Anastasius' first solution for the defence of the Balkans was to build or rebuild fortifications along the lower Danube and build the so-called Long Wall 65 km from Constantinople extending from the Black Sea to Selymbria on the Propontis (Sea of Marmara). The dating of this wall is contested, but I agree with Blockley and Haarer that the likeliest date for the building is 503–504. The building of the wall caused changes in administrative and military organization: Anastasius abolished the vicariate of Thrace and established in its stead two vicars, one of who served under the Praetorian Prefect while the other served under *magister militum per Thracias*. In other words, one vicar was in charge of supplies while the other was in charge of the forces posted there. Archaeological finds have also shown that Anastasius probably fortified or refortified at least Histria, Tomis, Callatis, Stratonis, Tropaeum Traini (Tropaion), Dinogetia, Noviodunum, Ulmetum, Beroe, Sacidava, Ratiana, and Vavova Kale (a ruined fort on Kotel Mountain). Anastasius did not only add walls to these places but also built basilicas and other structures to revive their economic life. He was an Emperor who truly cared for his subjects. The next project of Anastasius was to negotiate with the Bulgars who were apparently pacified with a hefty sum of money to fight on the Roman side by 505. This was highly successful because the barbarian raids deep into the Roman Balkans ended for the rest of his reign.[124] On the basis of the composition of the forces under *Comes Foederatum* Vitalianus in Scythia, I would suggest that Anastasius pacified the Bulgars with land in the province of Scythia so that one or several Bulgarian tribes moved to this area as neighbours of the Huns who had been settled there under Marcian.

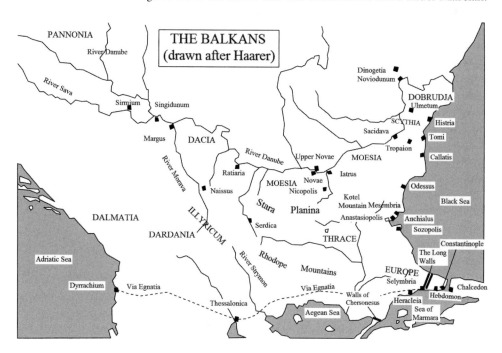

As noted above, Theodoric the Amal exploited the Persian war by sending *Comes* Pitzias against the Gepids in Pannonia and Sirmium in 504. The PLRE2 identifies Pitzias as a native Roman on the basis of his name even if Ennodius (*Pan.* 12) claims he was a Goth – of course it is also possible that Pitzias was a Goth who had taken a Roman name. This readiness to exploit Roman difficulties is not surprising in light of Theodoric's career and it certainly had the backing of the Pope. Ennodius claims that the citizens of Sirmium sent envoys to Theodoric pleading him to help. This formed part of Theodoric's claim to the territory. Pitzias and the other Gothic commander Herduic defeated the Gepids of Tracerius and annexed the area for the Ostrogoths. This annexation was justified with the claims that Pannonia belonged to the Western Empire and that Pannonia belonged to the Ostrogoths because it had been their 'ancestral land' until about 473. The Gepids had conquered it quite unjustly. The fact that the Gepids were on friendly terms with Anastasius was obviously the main reason. Thanks to the Persian war Theodoric could eliminate this Roman ally with a pre–emptive strike before Anastasius could use it against the Ostrogoths, and even claim that he was only restoring a province into the Roman fold. It is probable that it was because of this that the campaign was placed under a Roman commander rather than a Gothic one.

The Ostrogoths had as their ally a man called Mundo, who had fled from the Gepids across the Danube, after which he had formed a mercenary band of warriors consisting of outlaws, ruffians and all sorts of bandits. With this force he captured a 'tower' called Herta and declared himself *rex*. The capture of Herta was unacceptable to Anastasius who dispatched *magister militum per Illyricum* Sabinianus with 10,000 soldiers accompanied by wagons of arms and provisions against Mundo in 505. According to Ennodius (Pan. 12, esp. 12.63ff.), the Romans were accompanied by the Bulgars. This means that the Bulgars had by then concluded a treaty with the Romans. Mundo in his turn asked Theodoric's help and Theodoric obliged by sending Pitzias with 2,000 infantry and 500 cavalry to support him. It is unfortunate that we do not know the size of the force under Mundo or the size of the Roman force because the 10,000 men mentioned by Marcellinus were clearly regulars contrary to the common claim among modern historians who just use the information provided by Ennodius to claim that all of them were Bulgars. This means it is impossible to estimate the comparative sizes of the forces. Sabinianus was on the point of defeating Mundo when Pitzias arrived. According to the version of Ennodius, Pitzias saw the Bulgars from afar, halted his men and encouraged them with a speech. He claims that the subsequent battle was hard fought with the Goths against the Bulgars. Both sides fought with equal determination, and Ennodius even claims that they resembled each other. But finally the Bulgars turned and fled so that the ground shook under the thunder of their hooves. Thanks to their flight they suffered a far greater number of casualties. According to Marcellinus's version, Sabinianus lost thousands of his men killed and drowned in the Margus River together with the wagons in the ensuing battle at Horreum Margi. It is therefore probable that Pitzias surprised Sabinianus. Sabinianus and a few of his followers however were able to flee to a fort called Nato.

It is possible to combine these two versions of the battle. On the basis of Marcellinus' version it is obvious that Sabinianus had placed his Roman army in a separate marching camp (a wagon laager) close to the Margus River while the Bulgars had encamped in a separate camp, as was later instructed in the *Strategikon*.[125] It was not safe to allow the allies into the same camp. The other, more probable, possibility is that the Romans were besieging Mundo at Herta and had deployed the Bulgars as a shielding force. Consequently, when the Goths approached they came face to face with the Bulgars, as described by Ennodius, because for some unknown reason the Bulgars had decided to fight against the Goths without any Roman help. The likely reason for this would of course be that most of the forces under Sabinianus would have consisted of footmen while the Bulgars were unfamiliar with combined arms tactics. Therefore when Pitzias then defeated the Bulgar cavalry, probably with highly disciplined infantry, the Romans were in for trouble. If they were besieging Mundo, they faced an attack from two directions, and if they were just encamped separately along the river, the flight of the Bulgars in plain sight and probably through their lines would have infected the Roman infantry with panic. The fact that the Romans fled into the river does indeed suggest a panic, and so it was that the Romans suffered yet another defeat at Gothic hands.

At the same time as Jordanes mentions the exploits of Pitzias in his *Romana* (356), he also mentions a defeat of Anastasius' nephew Pompeius at Adrianople, but fails to date the event. It has usually been suggested that this refers to the barbarian invasion of the Balkans in 517, but this claim is by no means secure even if it is the most likely. Most importantly, the 517 invasion (Marc. a.517) was clearly a part of Vitalian's revolt because the attackers were Getae/Getic cavalry (i.e. most likely Goths) and not Slavs, Antae, or Bulgars as usually claimed. It is therefore possible that Pompeius engaged the Gothic cavalry and was defeated in 517, but in the absence of a secure dating it is still possible that the defeat actually took place immediately after the defeat of Sabinianus in 505 because at this time the Romans certainly lacked adequate forces to defend Thrace. If the invasion is to be dated to this year, then the identity of the invaders is not known because it is impossible to think that Jordanes would have failed to note if this had been achieved by the Ostrogoths of Theoderic the Amal. In sum, I would still suggest that 517 is the likeliest dating for this war and the reasons for this will be discussed in greater detail in the context of Vitalianus' revolt.[126]

Whatever the truth, it is clear that the transferral of forces from the East back to the Balkans in 506 changed the balance of power in the area so that it was now impossible for any enemy, the Ostrogoths and Bulgars included, to contemplate the invasion of the Balkans without the fear of being completely annihilated by the massive forces posted in the area under their skilled commanders. On top of this, the fortification project of Anastasius had made the besieging of cities, towns and forts ever more dangerous.

It is also likely that East Roman diplomats had been active in Gaul fomenting war between the Ostrogoths of Theoderic and Franks of Clovis. The basis for this is that Theoderic claimed in a letter to Clovis that there was no reason to fight each other and that a third party, 'an alien malignity' (Haarer's tr.), was interfering in their affairs. The immediate reason for the conflict was the flight of some Alamanni after their defeat by Clovis at the battle of Tolbiac into Raetia where Theoderic gave them a place of refuge. In addition, Theoderic sought to prevent a war between the Visigoths of Alaric II, his close ally, and Clovis, whose sister he had married. He dispatched letters to all concerned, which included Alaric II, Clovis, Gundobad and even the kings of the Heruls, Warni and Thuringians, with warnings to maintain peace. This effort proved futile.[127]

Clovis (Chlodovechus) was king of the Salian Franks who had succeeded Childeric on the throne in about 481/2. We have only glimpses of his career and most of the events that I state including the date of his accession are at best only guesses. In about 486/7, he defeated Syagrius and annexed his realm. Soon after this he apparently fought against the Armoricans but was unable to defeat them with the result that the two peoples, the Franks and the Armoricans, were united through marriage.[128] Clovis subjected the Thuringians under his rule in 491. He appears to have concluded a very important marriage alliance with the Burgundians in about 492/4 when he married Chorodechildis better known as Clotilde, who was a Catholic and therefore an important influence over her pagan husband in his subsequent conversion. In 496 Clovis fought against both the Alamanni and Visigoths. He defeated the former but lost territory to the latter. Clovis converted into the Catholic Faith either during this war against the Alamanni or during his subsequent war in 506. The Franks defeated the Visigoths in about 498 and the two sides concluded a temporary peace in about 502. In 500 the Burgundian king Godegisel asked Clovis's help against Gundobad and the latter was more than eager to intervene in Burgundian affairs. Clovis inflicted a severe defeat on Gundobad and the latter was forced to pay a yearly tribute to Clovis. Soon after this Gundobad killed Godegisel, but was still able to maintain peace with Clovis. In 506 Clovis then fought the second of his campaigns against the Alamanni and was in communication with Anastasius. The date 506 is therefore likely for the date of the conversion, but not conclusively so.[129]

Clovis and his Burgundian allies then inflicted a decisive defeat on the Visigoths and killed their king Alaric II at the famous decisive battle of Vouille in 507. Both appear to have done this as allies of Anastasius because Anastasius rewarded Clovis in 508 with the honorary title of Consul while Gundobad minted coins bearing only the head of Anastasius with a monogram on the other side. In other words, Gundobad recognized Anastasius as his Emperor as apparently did Clovis. In addition, there is every reason to believe that Clovis, Gundobad and Anastasius coordinated their military campaigns because we find Anastasius sending a fleet against Italy in 507 obviously with the idea of forcing Theoderic to remain in Italy while Clovis attacked the Visigoths.[130]

According to Marcellinus Comes (1 September 507 – 31 August 508), Anastasius dispatched *Comes Domesticorum* Romanus and *Comes Scholariorum* Rusticus with 100 armed ships and 100 dromons with 8,000 armed soldiers (*militum armatorum*) against the coasts of Italy where they advanced as far as Tarentum. If the ships were of equal size, then each of the ships had 40 men on board drawn from land forces in addition to their regular crews of rowers and seamen, the latter of whom could also be used as fighting men when necessary. In practice the number of men would of course have varied according to the size and type of the ship and it is therefore unfortunate that we do not know the exact numbers for each type of ship together with their vital statistics. Each of the dromons would also have had a complement of marines and it is therefore also unfortunate that we do not know their strength. Regardless, it is clear that this was a major naval effort. In the words of Marcellinus, these forces won Anastasius a shameful victory over the Romans with a piratical attack. The Vandals who were allies of Theoderic failed to intervene in any way. Haarer has noted on the basis of Cassiodorus' letters (*Variae* 1.16, 2.38) that the fleet burnt the crops of Apulia and attacked the population of the town of Sipontum. Theoderic's reaction was to reinforce the walls of Rome and various other cities along the coasts. Consequently, Theoderic was able to march to Gaul to help his kindred only in June 508 at which point it was too late to save the Visigothic kingdom in Gaul.[131]

The unhindered raiding of the Italian coast proves that the Ostrogoths did not possess an effective navy and in the absence of Vandal help were entirely at the mercy of the East

Romans. It is therefore not surprising that Theoderic initiated a project to build a navy of his own, but this did not help him now.

It was then because of this that Theoderic sent an embassy under the *Patricius* Agapitus to Constantinople with the intention of concluding a peace. The reception and result of this embassy is not known. What is known is that Theoderic and Anastasius both continued their diplomatic games in the Balkans while avoiding military confrontation. On the basis of this it is probable that the two rulers concluded some sort of peace agreement or truce, but as stated this did not end their diplomatic games. It is therefore not surprising that Theoderic adopted the king of the Heruls called Rodulf as his son-in-arms to strengthen his position in the Balkans, but this too did not help Theoderic because the Heruls were quite useless as allies.[132]

In about 508, the Heruls, who had subjected all of their neighbours including the Lombards and who had remained at peace for three years, forced Rodulf to attack the Lombards even though the latter had followed their agreement with the Heruls. The reason for this lay in their pagan warrior culture which required the waging of constant warfare so that their youth and adults would be able to prove their manhood in combat, but this time the outnumbered Lombards inflicted a severe defeat on the Heruls and destroyed most of their forces. Rodulf was killed and the Heruls were scattered. Some of them marched to Scandinavia, their ancestral home, while the rest sought a place of refuge in the place where the Rugi had dwelled before they had joined Theoderic the Amal in their march to Italy. They moved on because the land was too barren and could not support their people. In about 509 they migrated close to the Gepids who accepted them as their subjects at first, but then started to abuse them by raping their women and looting their cattle and other property, and then attacked them in force. Then because of this the Heruls crossed the Danube and became *foederati* of Anastasius in about 511/12. Anastasius had received them with great friendliness, but the new arrivals repaid him with lawless behaviour. Anastasius dispatched an army against them, defeating the Heruls and killing most of their men. The remnants begged the generals to spare their lives so that they could serve as allies and slaves of the Emperor. Anastasius was pleased and accepted their plea. Procopius however claims that they were not allies in practice until the reign of Justinian, which is probably an exaggeration even if it is clear that the Heruls were quite barbaric and untrustworthy as allies. It is actually probable that the Heruls proved useful as an outer defensive line where they were settled (presumably around Singidunum).[133]

This was a direct affront to Theoderic who claimed to be the protector of the Heruls. Anastasius countered with diplomatic activities, both among the Romans of Italy and among Theoderic's neighbours. He also received Roman fugitives from Italy and promoted them to high positions thereby gaining an invaluable network of Italian contacts that he could use to promote his goals among the Roman Senate or at least to obtain intelligence of enemy activities. The extant letters of Avitus (ep.83–4) prove that Anastasius' diplomats continued to be very active among the Burgundians who recognized Anastasius as their ruler. It was thanks to this that Gundobad's successor Sigismund sought friendship and submission from both Vitalian and Anastasius in 516 – in the eyes of their subjects the barbarian kings could obtain legitimacy only from the East Roman Emperor. The same was also partially true of the Franks, because they too sought acceptance for their rule from Anastasius to secure their control of the Gallo-

Roman population.[134] This eagerness to seek East Roman recognition among most of the barbarian successor states (Franks, Burgundians, Ostrogoths) can be compared with the modern British Commonwealth in which the member states recognize the Queen/King of Great Britain as their head of state while still being completely independent. The member states of such an artificial structure must think it is somehow in their interest.

The death of Alaric at the battle of Vouille resulted in the division of the Visigothic realm into two competing factions which their enemies, the Franks and Burgundians, were able to exploit. Amalaric, the legitimate underage son of Alaric and the grandson of Theoderic the Amal, was taken to Spain by his guardians while the illegitimate son, Gesalic, who was in his early manhood, took control of one part of the Visigothic army. Gundobad however defeated him with the result that the Visigoths lost Narbonne. Gesalic fled to Barcelona where he stayed for the next four years as one of the Visigothic kings. The city of Arles refused to surrender to the invaders so the Franks and Burgundians besieged it in late 507 or 508. Now thanks to the ending of the East Roman naval raid the Ostrogoths could finally send help to their brethren.[135]

The Ostrogothic forces under Tulum, the Gothic Lord of the Bedchamber, fought a battle against the Franks and Burgundians on 24 June 508 but were unable to cross to the other side of the Rhone, despite the personal bravery of Tulum who was wounded several times. The bridge changed hands several times but ended in Frankish hands. Therefore the Franks and Burgundians were able to maintain a partial blockade of Arles from the other side of the Rhone. Theoderic changed his strategy and sent *dux* Mummo against the Burgundians in 509, but this did not end the siege. Next year, 510, Theoderic dispatched the Gothic *Comes* Ibbas against the united enemy forces at Arles and this time the result was a triumph for the Ostrogoths. The Franks and Burgundians were decisively defeated losing 30,000 killed. They were forced to cede all of Provence and part of the Languedoc which gave the Ostrogoths land access to Spain, and it was along this route that the Ostrogoths marched to put an end to the Visigothic kingdom of Gesalic at Barcelona. Gesalic was forced to flee to the Vandal court, which gave him a place of refuge despite the marriage alliance between the Vandal and Ostrogothic royal houses – Thrasamund was Theoderic's brother-in-law. On top of this, Thrasamund gave Gesalic money and dispatched him back to Gaul. Theoderic upbraided Thrasamund for this and the latter apologized and the matter was left at that. Gesalic marched to Barcelona where he was defeated and killed by Ibbas in about 511/2. From this time onwards Theoderic the Amal ruled in the name of his grandson not only his own domains but also Visigothic Spain and the south of Gaul. The only thorn in his side was the all-too-powerful position of Amalaric's guardian Theudis. This meant that most of the Ostrogothic forces were tied up in Gaul and Spain throughout these years and could not cause any difficulties for the Romans in the Balkans. The Ostrogothic campaigns in Gaul however were not enough to put a stop to Clovis's next object which was the elimination of other Frankish kings and the annexation of the Ripuarian Franks into his realm which finally united all the Franks under a single king. Clovis achieved all of this by the time of his death in about 511. The annexation of the Burgundian realm was left to his sons who achieved this in alliance with the Ostrogoths by first killing Gundobad's successor and son Sigismund in 523 and then his brother in 524.[136]

Anastasius' Religious Policy 491–518[137]

As noted above, Anastasius was by personal conviction a Monophysite (Miaphysite) and had thus been required to sign a declaration of faith by the Patriarch Euphemius before the latter had agreed to enthrone him. In practice however, Anastasius' religious policies vacillated, which is not surprising considering his wife and relatives were Chalcedonians. When Anastasius thought it possible to end the Acacian Schism, he adopted a conciliatory stance towards the Chalcedonians both in the East and West, but when he thought this impossible or when he thought that it was in the interest of the state to please the Monophysites in the East, he either lent his support for the compromise *Henoticon* or gave his support to the extreme Monophysite stance. Haarer has noted that even though it is clear that Anastasius' personal faith was closest to the Monophysite view, this was not his only reason for their support. Most of the frontier regions in the East were in Monophysite hands, and so was Egypt, the breadbasket of the Empire. Consequently it was necessary for Anastasius to retain their support if he wanted to make certain that the Eastern Frontier would be defended against the Persians and Arabs, and that the Egyptians would feed the armies and finance the wars. In short, the compromise doctrine of the *Henoticon* was of the utmost importance for the security of the Empire, as was the occasional direct support for the Monophysites. The *Henoticon* was also of great importance because it implicitly gave the Emperor the right to interfere in matters of religion, as was recognized by the Popes who opposed it because it had been given by the Emperor Zeno alone without any synod. So it is not surprising that Anastasius stubbornly upheld the *Henoticon* compromise throughout his reign.[138]

The most absurd aspect of Anastasius' religious policies was that whereas Euphemius was a staunch supporter of Chalcedon, he was not acceptable to Pope Gelasius because Euphemius refused to acknowledge the Pope as his superior and to abolish the *Henoticon* and remove Acacius from the records. This was a power struggle between the two sees and nothing else and the doctrinal issues were just used as tools in it. They both sought to influence the clergy in their respective areas while the earthly powers, Anastasius and Theoderic, fought for temporal power.

Anastasius consistently sought to coerce the Pope into accepting the *Henoticon* through the pressure he put on Theoderic or the Roman Senate. Theoderic on the other hand was unwilling to do this because it was not really in his interest for the Acacian Schism to end. In fact, as we have seen, the relationship between the churches became worse even after Anastasius had recognized Theoderic as King of Italy. Relations hit rock bottom when Theoderic invaded Pannonia, Anastasius and Pope Symmachus exchanging public insults in letters in 506. The subsequent peace, or at least the avoidance of direct military confrontation between the temporal powers Theoderic and Anastasius in about 508, did not improve the relationship between the two churches, because from this date onwards Anastasius no longer felt it necessary to moderate his religious policies on the grounds that it would have been possible to find a reconciliation with the popes.

Anastasius had deposed his first Constantinopolitan Patriach Euphemius, but he did not find his replacement Macedonius to be any better because gradually, over the years, Macedonius got ever closer to the monks of the capital who were staunchly Chalcedonian. And, while Macedonius approached the Chalcedonians, Anastasius approached the

Monophysite view by adopting the Monophysite interpretation of the *Henoticon* Edict promoted by the bishop Philoxenus and Severus. Anastasius' intention was undoubtedly to unite the Eastern Church behind his view and to stress his temporal powers over the Church. The problem for him was that the Eastern Church was hopelessly divided into supporters of the Monophysite view (Egypt, north-east Syria, Cappadocia), Chalcedonians (Constantinople, Balkans, Jerusalem, monks of Palestina and Syria II) and the moderates represented by Flavian, Bishop of Antioch. In 508/9 Philoxenus and Severus managed to force Flavian to anathematise Chalcedon with the result that Patriarch Macedonius refused to communicate with Flavian. Then Anastasius demanded that Macedonius anathematise Chalcedon, which the latter answered he would do but only at an ecumenical council presided by the Pope. This angered Anastasius because it denied that he possessed the powers implicit in the *Henoticon* and recognized the supremacy of Rome. In response he took away the right of asylum from the Great Church and allowed only the Monophysite churches to have it.[139]

It was then in 511 that the Monophysites added 'who was crucified for us' to the *Trisagion / Trishagion* into the church ceremonies held in the capital, Constantinople, with the result that the Chalcedonian monks drove away the singers of *Trisagion*. After this, the Emperor Anastasius and his supporters among the monks openly attacked and insulted Macedonius with the result that the opposing side incited the largely Chalcedonian monks and people against the Emperor who fled to the Palace, locked the gates and prepared to flee on a ship. He then asked Macedonius to interfere, which he agreed to do. According to Theophanes (AM 6003), when Macedonius marched through the rioters even the *scholae* acclaimed him. Note the importance of the *scholarii* as bodyguards of the Emperor even at this date.[140] When the two men met, Anastasius pretended to agree with Macedonius and accept the Chalcedonian view, so the situation was defused. In truth, he was only planning his counter-attack. Soon after this Anastasius called Macedonius to the Palace where he was accused of being a Nestorian. To prove that this was not the case Anastasius demanded that Macedonius reaffirm his acceptance of the *Henoticon*. Macedonius did this in writing but then withdrew to a monastery where he declared his support for the Council of Chalcedon. Anastasius then demanded that Macedonius hand over the original records of the Council of Chalcedon, which he refused to do, but Anastasius still managed to obtain and destroy them. Severus also advised Anastasius to dispatch Celer with instructions to obtain Macedonius' acceptance to a statement prepared for him, but Macedonius refused to do this. In the end, however, the Emperor and his supporters managed to force Macedonius to renounce Chalcedon in public. When Macedonius once again fled to the monastery, Anastasius decided to get rid of him for good. He removed the subsidies of the monasteries and cut off the water conduits for their baths, allowing them only drinking water (Michael Syrus 9.9). According to Michael Syrus (9.9), Anastasius also secured the support of the military by increasing the money paid to them every five years, because he had learnt that Macedonius was conspiring against him with Macedonius' nephew Vitalianus. He convened a council which denounced Macedonius, after which he assembled the officers on 29 July 511, and the following day bribed the whole army with money. When this happened the clergy abandoned the cause of Macedonius like proverbial rats leaving a sinking ship while the soldiers kept all the monks who could cause any trouble outside the city. On 1 August

511 the soldiers arrested the monk Pascacius who had led the previous riot against the Emperor and the interrogators managed to obtain from him a confession, either false or true (the former more likely), that Macedonius was planning a rebellion. The soldiers confiscated several church documents including the Emperor's profession of faith, after which Anastasius convened a local synod on 6 August in which Macedonius was deposed. On 7 August Celer arrested Macedonius and his remaining supporters from the Great Church and exiled Macedonius to Euchaita. The purge was effective. All supporters of Macedonius were either arrested or fled. It is unsurprising to find Celer in charge of these special operations. As *Magister Officiorum* he was the overall commander of all imperial bodyguards. Bribery of the officers and soldiers was always an effective way to secure their support. The new Patriarch of Constantinople, Timothy, was more prepared to follow the wishes of the Emperor.

The next stage in the power struggle between the Monophysites and moderates/ Chalcedonians was the fight between Flavian and Elias and the Monophysites Philoxenus and Severus. The first attempt by the Monophysites was not successful because they were in the minority at the Synod of Sidon. The Synod was then dissolved either through Eutropius, the representative of Anastasius, or by the victorious Flavian and Elias. Flavian and Elias however wanted to placate the Emperor and confirmed their allegiance to the *Henoticon*. The Monophysites appealed to the Emperor once again, which Flavian sought to counter with still another show of acceptance of the *Henoticon*. The pressure became so intense that Flavian professed the Monophysite view in public, but it was too late. Philoxenus and the Monophysite monks staged a riot and forced Flavian into exile. After this, on 6 November 512, they nominated Severus as the new Patriarch of Antioch. This move appears to have had the full backing of the Emperor because on 4 November 512 he issued an edict which required all churches to add the Monophysite clause 'who was crucified for us' into the *Trisagion/Trishagion*. This resulted in a riot in Constantinople on 6 November.

The supporters of Chalcedon hunted down and killed by fire and sword the supporters of Anastasius who were dressed in monastic garb. Other rioters gathered the keys of all the gates and military standards and brought them to the forum where they had formed a religious camp for the warriors of the religion. When Anastasius passed this place in a procession, the mob shouted that Areobindus should be made Emperor. After this the rioters tore down the statues and images of Anastasius. The Emperor sent Celer and Patricius to hold talks with the rioters, but their response was to stone them and they were forced to flee. After this many of them marched to the Hippodrome and assembled before the throne of Anastasius to sing the Hymn of Trinity without the addition, while demanding that the Emperor hand over Marinus and Plato, accusing them of being instigators of the blasphemy. Anastasius however spoke to the mob and convinced them to disperse. But he had lied and when the rioters realized this they rioted again. This time Anastasius pacified them by assembling a Synod. The Synod, however, exiled Flavian and another like-minded bishop, so it was actually a victory for the Monophysites.[141]

The harsh treatment of the Chalcedonians and moderate supporters of the *Henoticon* led to an Orthodox backlash, as it was called by Haarer. The neo-Chalcedonian movement gained support in Cilicia and among some Arab Federates. Also there were several bishops who simply refused to follow the new Monophysite interpretation of the *Henoticon* which anathematised Chalcedon, so for two reasons the Emperor was obliged to order Asiaticus, *dux* of *Phoenicia Libanensis*, to forcibly eject Cosmas and Severianus from their sees. But this was not the end of the trouble. The Monophysite bishops went ever further in their actions, which only strengthened the resolve of those who opposed them, and even the bishops who were supporters of the *Henoticon*, like the Patriarch of Alexandria, started to lean against the firebrand Monophysite interpretation as expressed by Philoxenus and Severus. The revolt of Vitalian, who professed to protect the Catholic Faith, halted this process because it forced Anastasius to seek reconciliation with the Pope, but the victory over Vitalian at the end of July 516 enabled Anastasius to make a move against the moderate bishop of Jerusalem Elias so that he ordered the governor of Palestine to force Elias either to recognize Severus as bishop or depose him. The monks of Palestine could no longer protect him and Elias was exiled to Aila. His replacement was John, who managed to fool the *dux* Anastasius who was in charge of the nomination to allow the monks to join the ceremony. When about 10,000 monks gathered around John, they all declared their support for Chalcedon. The monks were clearly a powerful military factor in the area. Hypatius, nephew of the Emperor, was at the time in Jerusalem as a pilgrim. He defused the situation by swearing that he supported the Church of Jerusalem after which he bribed the two monk leaders Theodosius and Sabas by giving them 100 lbs of gold each for their monasteries. The monks also asked the Emperor to give his backing for the new Bishop of Jerusalem and to denounce Severus. Anastasius acquiesced, undoubtedly because he feared serious troubles if he would not.

The firebrand Severus was not satisfied with the exile of Elias, and wanted the scalp of the Bishop of Alexandria Dioscorus II, but could not achieve it. In the meantime, large numbers of Orthodox clergymen and monks in the East sent letters to the Pope in which they sought his support. The situation was even worse in the Balkans where the clergymen almost unanimously supported the Pope and Chalcedon. After all it was there that Vitalian stood with his forces after 514. The strong support of Anastasius for the firebrand Monophysites Philoxenus and Severus backfired. It lost him the support of a significant portion of the eastern clergy vis-à-vis the Pope, the support of the populace in the capital Constantinople, and even more importantly the support of significant sections of the military.

The Revolt of Vitalianus (Vitalian) in 513–518

The Beginning of the Revolt in 513

The increasing hostility between the Orthodox who were supported by the Pope and the Monophysites including the supporters of the *Henoticon* was exploited by *Comes Foederatum* Vitalianus, son of Patriciolus, who launched a military revolt/attempted coup against Anastasius in about 513. The immediate reason for the revolt was, however, the refusal to provide the *annona* supplies owed to the *foederati* serving under him in *Scythia*. This decision naturally caused immediate anger among the troops and Vitalianus knew how to channel this anger. It was clearly the principal reason for the success of the revolt, but one cannot exclude the importance of religion because it is clear that Vitalianus exploited this aspect to the hilt by claiming to fight on behalf of Orthodoxy against the heretic ruler. It is therefore not surprising that the sources mention the involvement of the Orthodox clergy in the revolt. It is clear that Vitalianus used the banishment of the Orthodox bishops as an excuse and that the Orthodox clergy specifically asked Vitalianus' support for their cause. It is possible or even probable that there were also very strong personal reasons for Vitalianus' anger and support of the Orthodox cause – Michael Syrus (9.9) claims that Vitalianus was the nephew of the deposed Patriarch Macedonius. The veracity of this claim is usually suspected, but in my opinion the events and Marcellinus' text (1 September 513 – 31 August 514) give strong support for it. The peasants of Thrace were also behind the revolt because Anastasius had not exempted them from the *coemptio* which forced them to sell provisions at a fixed price to the troops when Anastasius had abolished this requirement from every other area of his realm.[142]

Another reason for the initial success of Vitalianus was that he was very popular among the troops and very well connected. As noted above, he appears to have been the nephew of the deposed Orthodox Patriarch Macedonius and he was therefore seen as the champion of the Orthodoxy. According to Zachariah (7.13) and Marcellinus Comes (a. 514, 519 *Vitalianus Scytha*) he was of Gothic descent, son of Comes Foederatum Patriciolus, while on the basis of Michael Syrus he also had Roman blood in his veins. The fact that he had Gothic blood in his veins has been suggested to mean that he cooperated with Theoderic the Amal, but since we do not hear of Theoderic invading the Roman Balkans at this time, I would consider any such cooperation to have been moral in character rather than actual. Regardless, it is clear that Vitalianus was ideally positioned to simultaneously obtain the support of the barbarian troops as their *Comes Foederatum* and the support of the native regulars as Orthodox Roman. He was married and had at least two sons. He was uncle of Ioannes (PLRE3) and related to Stephanus (a military man and *Comes* in 519) and Leontius (a monk in Scythia), and had been born in Lower Moesia where he therefore probably had relatives and contacts. On top of this, the two *magistri militum praesentalis* Patricius and Ioannes (John) son of Valeriana were his friends.[143]

The reason for Anastasius' decision to deny the traditional *annona* from the *foederati* in *Scythia* and the continuing of the *coemptio* in Thrace, in a situation in which the state coffers were full of gold and in which Anastasius was able to reduce taxes everywhere else or even support some regions with money, seems quite strange if not outright foolish. In the notes Haarer (166) has tried to explain this with the situation prevailing in Thrace and Scythia. The reduction of the *annona* and the maintaining of *coemptio* resulted from the same thing, namely that where the area had suffered terribly as a result of barbarian invasions, Thrace simply lacked the means to produce enough *annona* to support the troops without the *coemptio*, and now even this was not enough so Anastasius had to reduce the *annona*. This appears to be the likeliest answer, but it is still clear that it was a foolish or even idiotic thing to do. Anastasius should have done the same as he had done in the East, namely to transport the necessary foodstuffs from somewhere else, for example Egypt or Crimea. The mistake is also unforgivable because the state coffers were full so that Anastasius could easily have used this money to support and bribe the forces in Thrace. Had he done this, the revolt would not have taken place.

However, there are two other possible explanations for the above: 1) that Anastasius and his advisors already considered Vitalianus to be in revolt thanks to the conspirational exchange of messages with Macedonius (Michael Syrus 9.9), so they sought to undermine Vitalianus' position as leader of the *foederati* in *Scythia* by claiming that he was responsible for the reduction; 2) it is possible, or even likely, that Anastasius thought that Vitalianus had already revolted and was therefore attempting to deny the availability of supplies (*annona*) from the enemy so that Vitalianus' forces would lack adequate supplies, because it is clear that the *annona* for the forces posted in *Scythia* would also have come from those regions (Moesia Inferior, Thracia, Haemimontus, Europa, Rhodope) of Thrace which were under loyal troops. I would suggest that this was indeed the case, but it was accompanied by a mistake which was to retain the *coemptio* for the peasants of Thrace so that Anastasius' forces would have adequate supplies to support their own operations against the *foederati* of Vitalianus. The problem with both of these explanations is that according to the consensus view Macedonius was ousted in October 511 and the earliest date for the revolt of Vitalianus in the sources considered reliable is 513, which is also the year which I consider the likeliest contra those who like Haarer consider the revolt to have started in 514.[144] This however does not preclude the above if we think that Anastasius considered Vitalianus already an enemy after October 511, and that from that date onwards he sought to undermine Vitalianus' position while Vitalianus attempted to force Anastasius to reinstall Macedonius back to his see. It is unlikely to be a coincidence that Marcellinus Comes (1 September 513–31 August 514) specifically claims that Vitalianus was fighting on behalf of Macedonius so that he would be reinstalled to the Patriarchate of Constantinople. The situation could be compared with the cold war that existed between Zeno and Illus in 481–4 before the latter revolted openly in 484.[145]

According to John of Antioch (Roberto ed. fr. 311, esp. 311.6–7), *Comes Foederatum* Vitalianus had the support of both the *foederati* and regulars in Scythia and Thrace. The sources give various nationalities for these *foederati*. Malalas (16.6), Theophanes (AM 6006) and Cedrenus (632) say they consisted of Huns and Bulgars while John of Antioch (fr. 214; Roberto ed. fr. 311) and Evagrius (3.43) mention only the Hunnic tribes. Georgius Monachus (619) state that the forces consisted of Goths, Huns and Scythians. In my opinion it is clear that the initial force consisted only of the Huns and Bulgars which were stationed at Scythia, and the inclusion of Gothic *foederati* took place only when Vitalianus had advanced against the forces of the *magister militum per Thracias*. Vitalianus was also able to bolster numbers with the addition of dissatisfied peasants who eagerly joined the rebel ranks, so that according to John of Antioch (Roberto ed. fr. 311.16–18), Vitalianus had 50,000 soldiers and peasants in his army when he moved against Constantinople after he had captured Odessus. According to Marcellinus Comes (a.513–4), he had more than 60,000 Roman cavalry and infantry collected in three days. This figure however refers to the size of the force under Vitalianus when he approached Constantinople (his force was drawn up in battle formation from sea to sea when he approached the Golden Gate) for the first time which presumably implies that he had increased the size of his force during the march, but it is also possible that these two figures represent only the best educated guesses that have found their way into these two sources. The unfortunate point in these references is that it is probable that both figures are based on the estimated number of men under Vitalianus when he reached the capital for the first time and had by then added to his original army the forces of the *dux* Maxentius and *magister militum per Thracias* Hypatius, but it is of course possible that John of Antioch's figure represents the size of Vitalianus' force before the addition of the forces under *magister militum per Thracias* with its Goths (see below) because John of Antioch fails to include the events that took place between the capture of Odessus and the appearance of Vitalianus before the capital.[146]

The fact that Vitalianus commanded only Bulgars and Huns of Scythia as *Comes Foederatum* is important from the point of view of analysis of military organization at this time. It means that the Goths who remained in Thrace, and who had in all probability served under Apskal/Apsical during the Isaurian War 491–8 and under Bessas and Godidisklus during the Persian War 502–6, were in all probability serving under another *Comes Foederatum* whose name is not mentioned in the sources, and who would have been a subordinate of *magister militum per Thracias* Hypatius.

The course of the revolt, especially its beginning stages, and the identity of Hypatius in the sources is contested and the following should therefore be seen only as my best educated guess. Firstly, historians are divided whether we should consider the *magister militum per Thracias* in 513 Hypatius to be identical with the nephew of Anastasius and *magister militum praesentalis* in 514, or as two separate persons.[147] My guess, based mostly on the account of Malalas (16.6) and Evagrius (3.43), is that in both cases Hypatius was the nephew of Anastasius because he was subsequently ransomed. This is therefore my assumption in the following analysis.

The revolt gained rapid success thanks to the skilful preparations of Vitalianus. It started with the assassination of two senior officers, Constantinus and Celerinus/ Celerianus, because they were loyal to the *magister militum per Thracias*. At the same time, he won *dux Moesiae Secundae* Maxentius to his side with a hefty bribe so was able to add his forces to those that he already possessed in Scythia. John of Antioch mentions that Vitalianus also captured Carinus, who was a friend of Hypatius and in charge of finances, with whose help he also captured the city of Odessus (modern Varna) which was the HQ of the *magister militum per Thracias*.[148] However, it is possible that Carinus' involvement in the capture of Odessus took place only later because we find the city in the hands of the imperial forces when Cyrillus was fighting against the rebel, but thanks to the fact that the sources provide us with conflicting information it is impossible to be certain because it is possible that Cyrillus just recaptured Odessus after he had defeated Vitalianus in the first battle. See below.

The above account leaves out the details provided by Malalas (16.6) and Evagrius (3.43) regarding the actions undertaken by Anastasius and Hypatius.[149] After Vitalianus had captured Odessus, he marched as far as Anchialus and it was then, both sources claim, that Anastasius dispatched Hypatius against Vitalianus and the two men then fought a battle in which Hypatius was betrayed by his men and captured by Vitalianus. None of the sources specifically mentions that this Hypatius was the nephew of Anastasius, but in my opinion this remains the most likely alternative. I would suggest that it was now that Vitalianus captured the abovementioned Carinus together with his superior. I would also suggest that Hypatius was betrayed by the Gothic *foederati* of Thrace and that it was because of this that Vitalianus obtained the Goths mentioned by Georgius Monachus. If the figure of 50,000 soldiers and peasants of John of Antioch referred to the size of Vitalianus' forces before this, then it is probable that only the Goths defected, because the figure in Marcellinus for Vitalianus' army appearing before the Golden Gate is more than 60,000. But if both figures refer to the estimated size of Vitalianus' army when it appeared before the capital, then the deserters would also have included the regulars of Hypatius. In my opinion the former is the more likely, even if it is probable that Vitalianus always left men behind to garrison the important cities he had occupied. The march towards the capital had been very profitable in loot, so Vitalianus was able to reward his followers amply.

After this, Vitalianus advanced against Constantinople, formed a base at Hebdomon, and then advanced towards the capital. When the city was in sight, he arrayed his men from sea to sea to frighten the enemy and approached the Golden Gate in person. His demands were justice for the army of Thrace and the reinstatement of Macedonius in office. He also demanded the removal of Hypatius from office to satisfy the angry Thracian forces, and he was in a good position to demand this because Hypatius was his prisoner. Meanwhile Anastasius resorted to a propaganda war of his own. He wanted to demonstrate to all that Vitalianus was not actually fighting on behalf of Orthodoxy but for himself by placing bronze crosses on the city gates and by displaying on the altar of the Great Church a parchment which stated that Vitalianus was seeking the throne for himself. This appears to have worked. As a popular measure he reduced the tax on the import of livestock from Asia Minor by 25 per cent. According to Marcellinus, Anastasius managed to fool Vitalianus with promises conveyed by his envoy Theodore. They included the dismissal of Hypatius from office, who was then duly released in return for a ransom, so that Vitalian withdrew on the eighth day of the siege. But John of Antioch's account actually gives us the key detail which is missing from the former, which is the involvement of Patricius, the benefactor of Vitalianus, in the negotiations. It was undoubtedly because of Patricius' involvement that Vitalianus believed the promises of Anastasius and withdrew.[150]

Anastasius' counter-attack in 514

Anastasius' plan had been from the start to betray his promises to Vitalianus and it was because of this that he appointed Cyrillus/Cyril as *magister militum per Thracias* instead of Hypatius. Cyrillus' only task was to pursue and destroy Vitalianus. We do not know what forces he had but it seems probable that Anastasius had brought reinforcements from the East into which had been added whatever forces were left of the Army of Thrace, including at least some Isaurians settled in Thrace together with some units drawn from the praesental armies. According to Malalas (16.6), Cyrillus defeated Vitalianus in a battle in which many fell on both sides, and then entered Odessus while Vitalianus retreated from the scene of battle. According to Malalas, Cyrillus did not pursue the rebel, but stayed in the city, which is probably the reason why Marcellinus (1 September 513 – 31 August 514) calls him a soft man rather than a hardy *magister militum*, but it is possible that the reason for this characterization rests on the fact that he slept between two concubines at the time of his death – excessive love of the female gender was considered a sign of effeminacy in Rome.[151] John of Antioch (Roberto ed. fr. 311. 43ff.), however, considered him a man not without intellect or military experience. The information we have suggests that Vitalianus then gained entry into Odessus through treachery during the night. According to Malalas, Vitalianus sent some relatives of the gatekeepers to them and they bribed the guards. According to Marcellinus, Cyrillus, between two concubines, rose from the bed when the enemy entered, and Vitalianus killed him with a Gothic knife. According to John of Antioch (Roberto ed. fr.311.123ff.) the killer was a Hunnic leader called Tarrach. It is impossible to know which version is correct.

Evagrius (3.43) gives an entirely different account of what happened. According to him, there was only one battle. He states that the battle was at first evenly balanced so that the forces pursued and retreated in turns until Cyrillus' forces finally gained the upper hand and defeated the enemy. This was followed by the pursuit of Vitalianus' defeated forces who suddenly turned about against their pursuers and defeated them. This is clearly a description of a cavalry battle in which the different successive cavalry lines engage each other in turn. It was then because of this that Vitalianus captured Cyrillus at Odessus. This would imply that Odessus was already in Imperial hands when the fighting took place because it served as the place of refuge for Cyrillus. On the basis of this, it is possible that it was now that the abovementioned Carinus helped Vitalianus to capture the city, but as noted it is also possible that he did that at the very start of the rebellion.

One way to reconcile the sources is to think that they describe different stages of the counter-attack by Cyrillus so that there were at least two battles and that none of the sources describe the events in their entirety. My suggestion is that the counter-attack began with a battle in which Vitalianus was defeated and forced to abandon the city of Odessus to Cyrillus. It was then that Cyrillus made the mistake of not pursuing his defeated foe effectively, which gave Vitalianus the chance to regroup his remaining forces, which would have consisted solely of cavalry, because it is very likely that Vitalianus lost his infantry forces in the first battle. The reason for this conclusion is the description preserved by Evagrius, which implies that both armies consisted of cavalry. This loss of infantry is by no means surprising considering it included large numbers of recently enrolled peasants.

Only after Cyrillus and his men had celebrated victory and enjoyed the carnal pleasures provided by the concubines did they resume their operations against the rebel, but this time they were defeated. Evagrius' description of the troops advancing and retreating in turn should be seen in the light of Procopius's description of the cavalry battle of Satala (*Wars* 1.15.15, tr. by Dewing p.135): 'And both sides kept making advances upon their opponents and retiring quickly, for they were all cavalry.' This sort of fighting could involve the advances of sections of the cavalry line (the *koursores*) in turn to harass the enemy while their defenders (*defensores*) stayed behind, and/or the advance of all of the *koursores* of the first line simultaneously against the enemy which would then have been followed up by their retreat to their *defensores* while the enemy pursued and which would then have been followed up by the advance of the entire first line (consisting of both *koursores* and *defensores*) against the disordered pursuers, and if the enemy then renewed the fight, the entire first line or sections of it would have retreated to the second line, after which they would have renewed the fight and then attacked and pursued the enemy, and then if this had failed then the entire force could try to retreat all the way back to the third line and attempt to resume the fight. On the basis of the ability of Vitalianus' forces to defeat their pursuers, I would suggest that the sequence of combat had resulted at least in the use of the second combat line of Cyrillus against the forces of Vitalianus so that both Cyrillus' first and second lines pursued the retreating enemy force and were defeated when the fugitives turned around. The third line was so small that it is not necessary to think that the forces of Cyrillus would have retreated to it before forcing the forces of Vitalianus to begin their final retreat, but obviously one cannot entirely preclude this because it is possible that Cyrillus' forces had such high morale after their previous victory that even so small a reserve would have been enough to make the two front lines

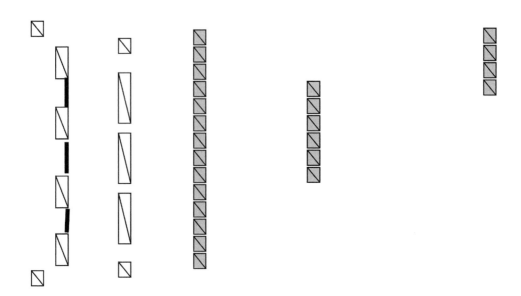

renew their fight so that all three lines started the final pursuit of the enemy that ended in defeat.

It is likely that both sides were roughly evenly matched as far as their numbers are concerned. My best educated guess is that Vitalianus had at least 30,000 men (Huns, Bulgars and Goths) and that Cyrillus had roughly the same number. It is clear that Cyrillus would have used the typical cavalry array as described by the *Strategikon*, but there are two possibilities for the battle formation adopted by Vitalianus. It is possible that he was also using the Roman version of the three-line array, but it is equally possible he was using the Hunnic version which also had three cavalry lines but which was not divided into *koursores* and *defensores* in the Roman manner. In the Hunnic version, all units could act as if they were *koursores* or *defensores* but with the difference that all typically fought using irregular order rather than ordered rank and file. Evagrius' account does not imply any use of ambush which means that the retreating Hunnic forces of Vitalianus simply made an about turn during their retreat when they noted that their pursuers had become disordered, and renewed the fight. The maintaining of order was much more important for Roman type forces than it was for the Hunnic/nomadic style and it was this that enabled the superficially disordered Huns to resume their fight and surround their pursuers. In short, the difference between the forces which decided the cavalry battle in favour of Vitalianus was that his Huns/Bulgars were more prepared to renew the fight even when disordered and in flight than the opposing Roman cavalry forces. It is probable that a significant number of Roman cavalry managed to flee and as we have seen these fugitives included Cyrillus. The accompanying diagram shows one possible way Vitalian could have deployed his army (shown in grey) in Hunnic manner (*Strategikon* 11.2) in which his frontline could have consisted of irregular sized units (not shown in the diagram) with a separate reserve behind (usable as a reserve or ambushing force), with still another third line behind that (usable as a camp guard or extra reserve).

We do not know if Cyrillus was accompanied by infantry at this battle. If he was, then they played no role and either surrendered to the victor or retreated to Odessus. The fact that Vitalianus was subsequently surrounded by infantry forces (Marcellinus a. 1 Sept. 514 – 31 Aug. 515) suggests that Cyrillus' infantry force surrendered to Vitalian who then reinforced them with the remnants of his previous infantry and probably bolstered their numbers also with new peasant recruits. Cyrillus was then forced to seek shelter in Odessus, where Vitalianus surprised him in bed with the two concubines. It is probable that most of the Roman forces that had sought refuge in the city were now killed, because that was the nature of surprise attacks conducted against cities. The fighting between Vitalianus and Cyrillus appears to have lasted until late 514 because this time Vitalianus did not march against Constantinople and I would suggest that Vitalianus rested his army during the winter of 514/15 and reinforced it with new recruits.

In the meantime, in 514 Anastasius had collected a massive army of about 80,000 men which he had placed under his nephew Hypatius. Alathar was appointed as new *magister militum per Thracias*. Alathar was a 'Scythian' (John of Antioch: *Skuthikon genos*), which has sometimes been interpreted to mean a Hun, but I agree with Maenchen-Helfen (423) that it meant Germanic. Theodorus served as their *sacellarius*, which presumably means that he was put in charge of the supplies. This and the subsequent details of a naval battle in front of Constantinople prove that Anastasius still had large numbers of Goths available to him and that he probably intended to use the nationality of this Alathar to cause defections from the enemy.[152]

Hypatius led his forces against the rebel and inflicted a defeat on him which was celebrated in the Great Church in 514, but then things went badly wrong so that Vitalianus' forces were able to capture Julianus, a member of the *scrinium memorialum*. Hypatius then moved his army to a place called Acrae on the Black Sea close to Odessus (modern Varna) and lost in the fighting one of the Imperial Bodyguards[153] called Timotheos/Timotheus ('Timothy') after which he arrayed the wagons as a defensive bulwark for his army. My suggestion is that Timotheus had belonged to the cavalry forces that had protected the marching formation and that Vitalianus had defeated the Imperial cavalry and forced the remnants of the Imperial forces against the sea at Acrae so that Hypatius formed his wagons in a convex formation against the sea, but thanks to the collapse of his protective cavalry line he was unable to complete the building of the rampart before the enemy attacked. After this, the Huns launched a sustained archery attack which together with storm clouds blackened the sun.[154] The arrows killed and wounded the draught oxen with the result that the rampart of wagons was broken and the Huns were able to penetrate the wagon fortress. The fact that the oxen were still attached to the wagons (and they must have been for them to have been able to break up the line of wagons) proves that the Huns had attacked before the Romans had been able to lead the oxen away to the rear out of reach of enemy arrows. It is not known for sure whether the requirement to raise protective screens of heavy cloth behind the wagons to protect the drivers and draught oxen was used at this time or whether the Romans introduced this additional safety measure as a result of this defeat so that it was included in the later *Strategikon*. When the enemy penetrated the laager and sudden darkness fell, presumably as a result of clouds and dust, the Imperial forces panicked and rushed to their deaths in the ravine behind them or were killed by the enemy. According to John of Antioch, the Romans lost 60,000 dead, according to Theophanes 65,000. Hypatius jumped into the sea and attempted to flee, but he was recognised and the Huns took him alive. The Huns also

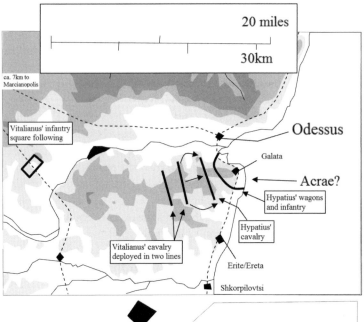

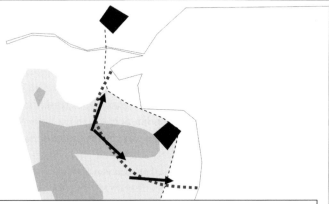

The Battle of Odessus/Acrae in 514
- The exact location of Acrae is not known. All that we know is that it was close to Odessus and that behind it were the ravines and the sea. The above shows my best educated guess based on this description. The area north of Odessus (Varna) is in my opinion unsuitable because it has sandy beaches (The Golden Sands). In this location, just south of Odessus/Varna, there are ravines and the descent onto the sea is steeper. Excluding some of the ravines on the higher ground and next to the beach (not shown in this map which is based on *Barrington Atlas*), the terrain is not forbidding enough to prevent cavalry attack.
- If the battle was fought in this locale, as is likely, then it explains why the Huns were able to break up the cohesion of the wagon laager by shooting at the draught oxen. When the Huns had gained the higher ground shown on the map with the darker grey, they could see precisely from the higher ground where the draught oxen were thanks to the round shape of the wagon laager and target the vulnerable sides of the oxen even if the wagons would have had protective leather curtains behind them, which is a possibility because we find this precaution in the *Strategikon*. See the arrows in the second map, which show the positions from which such attacks could have been launched if the line of wagons was placed in this precise place.

captured Alathar, Eusignius and other officers. Vitalianus ransomed the prisoners from the Huns so that he could keep them as hostages.[155]

Urbicius' *Epitedeuma* (14), which dates roughly from this period, includes an interesting claim. He says it was relatively easy to destroy the barbarian wagon circle with fire if the attacker demonstrated a little ingenuity. Did he have in mind this battle when he referred to the use of fire to destroy wagon laagers? The use of fire darts/arrows in this case should therefore be considered as a distinct possibility even if John of Antioch fails to mention this. It would have been quite easy to shoot arrows/darts and also fire darts/arrows from the higher ground into the vulnerable oxen and wagons, as I have suggested in the accompanying map. In their commentary of Urbicius Geoffrey Greatrex, Hugh Elton and Richard Burgess (p.66, n.14) suspect that Vitalianus may indeed have used fire arrows in this battle, and I agree with them.

What is particularly notable about this battle is that the Roman infantry was not deployed in front of the wagons to protect the cavalry and building of the camp, but was hiding behind the wagons. If we compare this with the infantry force that had been fielded by Anthemius against the Huns at the battle of Serdica in 466, it is as if these forces were from another planet. As such, one cannot use this one instance alone as evidence of any greater problem in the combat performance of the Roman infantry at this time, because a few lazy months with heavy drinking and whoring with no training or discipline at all during the winter, or a complete distrust in the military abilities of the commander, could easily produce an army completely unprepared to face the enemy; at least the latter was undoubtedly true in this case. When one adds to this the descriptions of other battles in which we know that there was infantry present and which ended in defeat, and we also add the descriptions that depict only cavalry combat and also the military treatises of Urbicius which date from this era, it becomes apparent that the overall combat performance of the Roman infantry under Anastasius, and we shall see under Justin and during the first part of Justinian's reign (see *MHLR* 518–565), left a lot to be desired.

One may speculate that this had resulted from a succession of severe defeats in which the Romans had lost not only vast numbers of infantry but also vast numbers of infantry officers that would have been needed to train new recruits. When we remember that the bulk of the Roman infantry forces appear to have consisted of Isaurians after the destruction of the Roman fleet by the Vandals in 468 and that these Isaurians had been mostly killed during the last Isaurian War in 491–8, it becomes quite likely that there had been after this too few experienced infantry officers to train all of the new infantry recruits to the level needed. So Roman generals started to rely more and more on their cavalry forces, which is actually in evidence during all of the wars described to have taken place under Anastasius. This in its turn would have lowered the morale of the infantry, which cannot have been high to begin with thanks to the defeats they had suffered. The evidence of Urbicius of the state of the infantry forces at this time and the drills needed for it are discussed and analysed in the Appendix. The cavalry forces, on the other hand, appear not to have suffered from similar problems largely thanks to two facts: they lost fewer men even in defeat; there was almost always an available supply of foreign tribal cavalry forces for hire.

Vitalianus consigned the captured Hypatius to a pigsty and on one occasion dragged him around the army in the most humiliating manner possible, which Zachariah (7.13) unfortunately fails to describe further. The reason for the treatment, however, is given: Hypatius had apparently captured and raped his wife. Zachariah (7.13, tr. by Hamilton and Brooks) reads as follows: '... carrying him about through the army in the most humiliating fashion, because Hypatius once took the wife of this Vitalian prisoner and treated her insultingly. And in consequence of this Vitalian's indignation against him was very strong. For in the impetuosity of his youth this Hypatius was carnal and wanton in lust after women. And at last he was ransomed by a large sum of gold that was sent for him, and he returned from captivity with Vitalian, possessing the wisdom that results from punishment.' Perhaps it is surprising that Vitalianus only humiliated the rapist and did not kill or torture him to death as many in his position would have done. Vitalianus clearly considered the pros and cons of the situation and considered that Hypatius' value as a hostage outweighed his personal grudge.

The battle at Acrae in 515 was a huge disaster for the Romans. By now they had lost most of the men who had served under Hypatius in 513/4, most of the men who had served under Cyrillus in 514, and now most of the men who had served under Hypatius in 514. The overall number of casualties, both killed and wounded, must have approached 100,000 men. The main culprit for the losses was Hypatius, who was also the main culprit for the losses incurred against the Persians in 503. He lost all of his battles, owing his career entirely to the fact that he was nephew of the Emperor Anastasius and therefore considered a trustworthy commander against Vitalianus. The successive appointments of Hypatius, the destroyer of armies, into high military commands can be considered to have been among the worst decisions Anastasius made during his long reign.

As if the disaster suffered by Hypatius was not enough, the Sabiri Huns had in the meantime exploited the transferral of Imperial forces from the East to serve under Hypatius and possibly the subsequent transfer of additional forces from the East after the defeat at Acrae by crossing into Armenia in 515 from where they then advanced to Cappadocia and marched as far as Lycaonia according to Marcellinus Comes. Theophanes states that the Sabiri advanced through the Caspian Gates, overran Armenia and pillaged Cappadocia, Galatia, and Pontos, almost reaching Euchaita where Macedonius had been exiled. According to John of Antioch, they devastated areas belonging to the *Diocesus* of *Pontica*, which would mean even more widespead devastation, but my guess is that since the areas mentioned by Marcellinus and Theophanes belonged to the diocese in question John actually meant the same areas. Macedonius had reacted to the invasion by fleeing from Euchaita to Gangra, and Theophanes claims that Anastasius then ordered that Macedonius should be kept there after which he sent an assassin to kill him. Macedonius was then buried at Gangra. This has sometimes been doubted by historians, but the killing of Macedonius in a situation in which Vitalianus was supporting him and when Macedonius had attempted to flee could easily have convinced Anastasius of the need to get rid of this potential troublemaker. In response to the Sabir Hun invasion, the Emperor fortified the cities in Cappadocia and remitted taxes for three years.[156]

Vitalianus advances against Constantinople for the second time

When Anastasius heard of the defeat at Acrae in 514, he dispatched Uranius, Polychronius and Martyrius as his envoys with 1,100 lbs of gold to negotiate the ransoming of the prisoners, but they were captured by the rebel forces at Sozopolis. Sozopolis had fallen into rebel hands along with all of the cities and fortresses of Moesia and Scythia. Vitalianus rewarded his followers amply and advanced against Constantinople for a second time, but this time he came better prepared. He had collected a fleet of 200 ships, presumably from the Thracian ports which had undoubtedly been used to support Hypatius' forces. Then Vitalianus dispatched cavalry and these 200 ships as an advance guard while he followed at a more leisurely pace with the infantry. He stopped at a place called variously Sosthenium/Sosthenion/Leosthenion located north of Constantinople and, surrounded by his armed infantry, captured the *palatium*. This implies that the marching formation had been an infantry square. It is not surprising that Anastasius now sought a negotiated peace. He had just lost a very large portion of his available forces and now Vitalianus threatened the capital.[157] According to John of Antioch (Roberto ed. fr. 311.85ff.), there was a riot during the chariot races in Constantinople in which *praefectus vigilum* Geta was killed in 514. Does this mean that there were supporters of Vitalianus among the factions of the capital who supported him by rioting? Whatever the truth, Anastasius dispatched Ioannes/Johannes (John), son of Valeriana and *magister militum praesentalis*, together with several senators to negotiate. This Ioannes was also a friend of Vitalianus and therefore an ideal negotiator just as Patricius had been on the previous occasion. Patricius had obviously lost his credibility in the eyes of Vitalianus after the previous promises had been betrayed. An agreement was reached. Vitalianus was nominated *magister militum per Thracias*, Anastasius promised to convene a synod attended by the Pope at Heraclea, and Hypatius was ransomed with 900 lbs of gold and gifts. Since Vitalianus no longer trusted the promises of Anastasius, he demanded that the treaty be confirmed by the Emperor, the Senate, the commanders of all of the units of the *Scholae* and by the people. This was done, but Anastasius failed to deliver the promised synod because the communication with the Pope failed to produce the desired result. The Pope adopted a stance that Anastasius should demonstrate his submission to him before he would attend the synod. This was naturally unacceptable to the Emperor.[158]

Vitalianus renews his offensive in late 515: The Great Naval Battle off Constantinople

Vitalianus advanced against the capital for the third time at the end of 515. This time he meant business. Unfortunately we do not know whether this happened after or before the appointment of Rufinus as *magister militum per Thracias*. Vitalianus marched to Sycae with the idea of adding the Isaurians and others defending it to his army, but in vain. Anastasius also knew that this was to be a fight to the death and discussed with his Praetorian Prefect Marinus how to deal with the situation. After this, quite probably on the basis of Marinus' advice, Anastasius summoned the Athenian philosopher Proclus/Proklos to advise them on how to defeat the enemy. Proclus told the men to be in good spirits and do as he said. He asked them to provide him with 'elemental/unpurged sulphur resembling powdered antimony', which was to be ground into fine powder. Proclus then prepared this 'elemental sulphur' and advised Marinus to order the men to throw it onto the enemy ships and buildings, all of which would immediately catch fire when exposed to the sunlight. Marinus then asked Anastasius to order one of his *magistri* to take charge of the naval operations. Anastasius ordered the *magistri* Patricius and Ioannes son of Valeriana to take command of the navy assembled for the purpose. Both men refused on the grounds that as former friends of Vitalianus they could be accused of treachery if they lost the naval battle. So Anastasius appointed his Praetorian Prefect Marinus as commander of the fleet.[159]

After everything was ready for combat Marinus assembled all the available forces and ships in Constantinople and arrayed his fleet for combat. The fighters on board included members of the Factions – there exist epigrams commemorating the heroics of the Green charioteer Porphyrius, and it was thanks to this that the Greens regained their former privileges that they had lost at the beginning of Anastasius' reign. Marinus distributed the 'elemental sulphur' among the dromons (the fast ships) and instructed the sailors and soldiers not to bother with other weapons but to throw the sulphur onto the enemy ships when they got close enough and then also throw it on the houses at Sycae. It is unfortunate that the sources fail to specify the exact composition of the 'elemental sulphur' and the exact way it was used. On the basis of the description however, it is likely that it was the same as the boxed naval *pyr automaton*, automatic fire, that had been sometimes used as a form of fire bomb by the Roman navies, and that it was enclosed in pottery hand grenades that the sailors and soldiers then threw onto the ships and at the houses. It is also possible that ballistae and catapults were used, because the Roman fleets certainly knew how to shoot fire bombs from these devices. In fact, I would suggest that the Romans used both the hand grenades and the stone throwers to fire these bombs because it was advantageous to be at a distance from the enemy ships when they caught fire. According to John of Nikiu, when Vitalianus saw the deployed fleet, he posted a large force of Scythian (Hunnic) and Gothic archers on board his ships and ordered them to attack. According to Malalas, Vitalianus manned the ships with fully armed Gothic, Hunnic and Scythian (Bulgar) forces.[160]

According to Evagrius (3.43), the two fleets at first remained stationary, but then after the two sides had made sallies and exchanged missiles, they engaged each other in a fiercely fought naval battle near Bytharia. This Bytharia is not otherwise known. The *Barrington Atlas* has a place called Bythias south of Anaplous, but this is clearly too far north to be the place for the battle. However, it is possible that there was some fighting at this place when the Imperial Fleet pursued the retreating Vitalianus.

In the battle proper, Vitalianus' fleet was completely engulfed and destroyed by fire and plunged to the bottom of the sea. According to John of Antioch, Justin, the *Comes Excubitorum*, distinguished himself by charging ahead of the rest in a fast vessel at a place called Chrysopolis where he then captured an enemy ship with its crew with the result that the rest of the enemy forces fled. This account gives far too important a role to Justin and should be seen as a panegyric of the future Emperor. Regardless, it is clear that he did distinguish himself and that it was one of the reasons for his later fame and ability to rise to the throne. Of note is also the fact that Justin apparently did not use the 'elemental sulphur', which raises the possibility that his heroics actually did not take place during the battle proper but before it during the earlier stage. It is of course possible that Justin did not use the 'elemental sulphur' because he was so close to Chrysopolis or because he was so far ahead of the rest that he did not want to expose the existence of the secret weapon before the main forces had a chance to use it, and it is therefore probably safest to assume that the incident did indeed take place during the main battle and that Justin was responsible for the collapse of Vitalianus' left wing even before Marinus' main

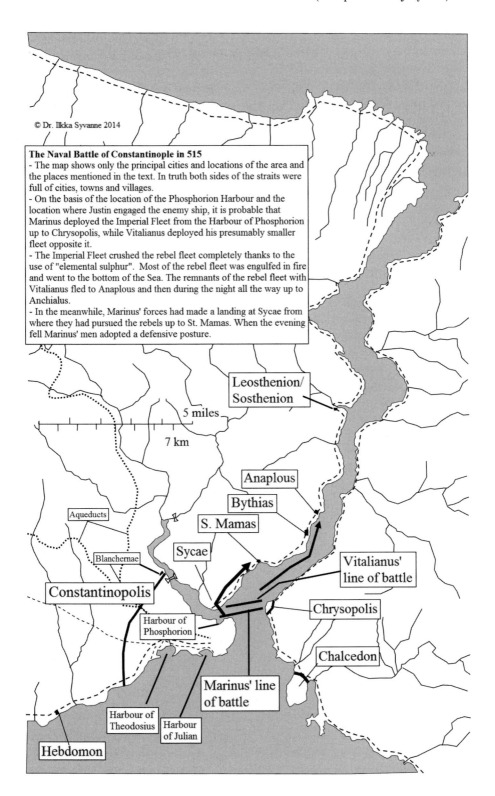

© Dr. Ilkka Syvänne 2014

The Naval Battle of Constantinople in 515
- The map shows only the principal cities and locations of the area and the places mentioned in the text. In truth both sides of the straits were full of cities, towns and villages.
- On the basis of the location of the Phosphorion Harbour and the location where Justin engaged the enemy ship, it is probable that Marinus deployed the Imperial Fleet from the Harbour of Phosphorion up to Chrysopolis, while Vitalianus deployed his presumably smaller fleet opposite it.
- The Imperial Fleet crushed the rebel fleet completely thanks to the use of "elemental sulphur". Most of the rebel fleet was engulfed in fire and went to the bottom of the Sea. The remnants of the rebel fleet with Vitalianus fled to Anaplous and then during the night all the way up to Anchialus.
- In the meanwhile, Marinus' forces had made a landing at Sycae from where they had pursued the rebels up to St. Mamas. When the evening fell Marinus' men adopted a defensive posture.

Leosthenion/
Sosthenion

5 miles

7 km

Anaplous

Bythias

S. Mamas

Aqueducts

Sycae

Blanchernae

Vitalianus'
line of battle

Constantinopolis

Chrysopolis

Harbour of
Phosphorion

Chalcedon

Marinus' line
of battle

Harbour of
Theodosius

Harbour
of Julian

Hebdomon

forces set the rest of the enemy fleet on fire. I would in fact suggest that Justin was in command of the Imperial right wing and led it forward by his personal example, while Marinus commanded the centre and someone else the left wing. I would also suggest that the Imperial battle formation was deployed between Constantinople and Chrysopolis while Vitalianus' fleet was deployed opposite it. The sources do not say anything of the ships placed at the Harbour of Phosporion, but I would suggest that its ships formed the extreme left wing of the Imperial line, while the rest of the ships would have been collected from the harbours of Theodosius and Julian. When Vitalianus and those on the other ships saw that their fleet was ablaze they fled to Anaplous (see the maps). The fact that Vitalianus fled to Anaplous implies that he was on board a ship. Marinus' fleet exploited the victory by making an amphibious landing at Sycae where they used the 'elemental sulphur' once again and killed all Vitalianus' men they could find in the houses or suburbs. Marinus' men pursued the defeated enemy as far as the Church of St. Mamas. It is probable that this was a joint operation in which the men marched on land while the fleet was rowed alongside it up to the same place. When evening fell, Marinus' men assumed a defensive stance at St. Mamas while Vitalianus continued his flight from Anaplous to Anchialus, so he and his forces marched and rowed sixty miles during the night. According to John of Nikiu, the following morning his followers abandoned him, but this is clearly an exaggeration or a mistaken reference to the absence of rebel forces in the Bosporus. When Anastasius then died, Vitalianus was still so powerful that Justin thought it wise to buy him off with concessions and with the nomination to command of one of the praesental armies. Malalas mentions that Vitalianus retreated to Anchialus, where he stayed.[161]

According to John of Nikiu (89.88, tr. by Charles): 'Next the emperor Anastasius ordered that a large sum of gold should be given to the philosopher Proclus. But he refused to take the money and, saluting the emperor, he requested him [*to let him go back to Athens*], saying: "Whoever loves money is not worthy to be a philosopher, and the contempt of the money likewise in those that cultivate philosophy is honourable." And the emperor let him go, and held him in high honour.'[162]

The Last Years of Anastasius 515–518

The defeat of Vitalianus' army meant that there were no significant military threats left even if Anastasius had just lost at least 100,000 men from his side and another 50,000–60,000 *foederati*, regulars and peasants who had served under Vitalianus. This figure represents the initial strength of Vitalianus' force, and does not include the subsequent additions to it to replace men lost or just added to the force. For example it is clear that the fleet of 200 ships had incuded crews which are not in this figure. Therefore, if I say that the Romans had lost altogether a minimum of 160,000 men this is likely to be an underestimation, and we should add to it at least 20,000 sailors and seamen and about 150 ships. It would take years to recruit and train an army of this size, and to replace the lost ships and their crews. However, thanks to the massive amount of money Anastasius had amassed it would have been quite easy to do if the ruler put his will to it. However, as we shall see, the will was lacking because the size of the army subsequently fielded by Justin against the Persians (see *MHLR* Vol.5) was not as large as that of Anastasius had been.

Therefore it is clear that Anastasius' successors Justin and Justinian did not see similar urgency to create mass armies as Anastasius.

There were also other troubles like the personal tragedy of the death of the empress Ariadne in 515, but surprisingly the religious policies were no longer acute problems after the defeat of Vitalianus. The Emperor and his nominees and their religious policies were now secure as long as the aging Emperor lived. However, the fact that Vitalianus and whatever remained of his followers were still on the loose in the Balkans, presumably in Scythia, meant that the rest of the Balkans were open for invasions. The reason for this was that thanks to the massive loss of men Anastasius lacked the means to defend the East and the capital effectively and still at the same time mop up the remnants of Vitalianus' forces. The Sabiri invasion of 515 certainly brought home the need to post a significant number of forces in the East even when the Persians posed no threat.

Marcellinus Comes (1 September 516 – 31 August 517) records the pillaging of both Macedonias and Thessaly, and states that the Gothic cavalry (*Getae equites*) plundered as far as Thermopylae and Epirus Vetus. All modern historians that I have consulted interpret the *Getae equites* to have been barbarian invaders so that the *Getae* have been interpreted to have been either Huns, Bulgars, Slavs or Antae, but in light of the fact that Vitalianus still possessed such large forces as to require pacification by Anastasius' successor Justin it is clear that we should see these 'invaders' as rebel Roman *foederati* who were still fighting on behalf of Vitalianus. Even if we interpret the Getae to have been Huns, Bulgars, Slavs or Antae, it is still likely that they would have been rebel Roman *foederati* serving under Vitalianus.

We should probably connect this 'invasion by the Getic cavalry' with the defeat of Anastasius' nephew Pompeius at Adrianople mentioned by Jordanes in his *Romana* (356) as has usually been done (see e.g. PLRE2). However, contrary to the usual modern interpretation, in my opinion it is clear that we are here dealing with a raid by Vitalianus' *foederati*, which Pompeius failed to stop. This should be seen as still another instance of Anastasius nominating his relatives to high military commands when all of the high ranking regular military commanders were former friends of Vitalianus and therefore either suspect or unwilling to fight against him so that they would not be suspected of treason as happened before the naval battle at Constantinople. And we should not forget that the populace of Constantinople had publicly demanded that Areobindus be made an Emperor in about 511 (Marc. a.511/12). Anastasius was justifiably frightened to place some of the generals in command of large armies. It is unlikely to be a coincidence that even the disgraced Hypatius was still retained as a military commander; he became *magister militum per Orientem* in 518. Hypatius' replacement in the Balkans was his brother Pompeius. Pompeius was also suitable for another reason: he was a Chalcedonian and therefore could be used to undermine Vitalianus' religious claims.

In short, it is probable that Vitalianus invaded Thrace in 516–17 and that his forces were opposed by the forces commanded by Pompeius. The two armies met in combat near Adrianople, and Pompeius suffered a defeat, and thanks to this the 'Getic cavalry' could pillage both Macedonias, Thessaly, Epirus and Greece all the way up to Thermopylae. The destruction of yet another army of Anastasius would have strengthened Vitalianus' position still further even if he no longer possessed the strength to attempt to take Constantinople. Bury (1.452) suggests on the basis of Cyril of Scythopolis that Vitalianus was once again causing trouble during the last months of Anastasius' life in 518. The nephews of Anastasius may have been safe choices as generals because they were unlikely to join Vitalianus, but they were clearly utterly incompetent as generals. On the other hand, it may have been safer for Anastasius to lose these armies in combat rather than face the united armies all under Vitalianus. Regardless, in my opinion he should still have sought out someone loyal, competent and ready to fight against Vitalianus rather than rely on his incompetent nephews.

It is possible that the raiding of Libya and the pillaging of Cyrenaica by Mazices, which is mentioned by John of Antioch, but not dated, took place during this time period, 515–17, and not in 513 as suggested by Haarer. See above. One could use the above military disasters in support of this dating, because in the aftermath of the disasters caused by Hypatius, one could easily think that the Roman government even withdrew forces from Libya and Egypt to make up for the losses further north. This would have given the Mazices their chance to pillage the area. Furthermore, this incident probably took place during the prefecture of Marinus who was *PPO* in 512–516/7,[163] because his great-grandson Bassianus was governor of Libya at the time these raids took place.[164]

The Factional Rioting under Anastasius[165]

As noted at the beginning of this chapter Anastasius was a supporter of the Reds who removed the advantages enjoyed by the Greens under Zeno. It is probable that Anastasius did the same to the other major Faction, the Blues. This resulted in rioting. Not unnaturally, the Greens having lost their privileged position, they were the principal rioters. Factional riots became more common during the reign of Anastasius than they had been before. As noted, the first of the riots resulted from the restrictions placed on the theatrical shows by Julian in 491 and were probably connected with the Isaurian aspirations. Anastasius' response was typical for him. The riot was crushed with soldiers. In 493 there was another riot in Constantinople. And still another riot of the Greens followed in 498 because Anastasius refused to release its members who had been arrested by the City Prefect for stone throwing. Anastasius again responded by sending in the army, but this resulted only in inflaming the rioters so that they attacked Anastasius when he was in attendance at the Hippodrome. The rioters also resorted to arson, destroying a part of the Hippodrome together with a section of the Mesê as far as the Forum of Constantine. The culprits were punished, but at the same time Anastasius replaced the City Prefect with Plato, a supporter of the Greens. The greatest number of casualties resulted from the riot that took place during the Brytae Festival in 501 when the stage where the dance and mime performance took place collapsed. More than 3,000 lost their lives as a result of this, or from thrown stones, or being cut to pieces by the soldiers. The casualties included the bastard son of Anastasius.

After this there was a long period of peace, which suggests that the Emperor's harsh measures to restore peace had worked. The rioting started again in 512 as a result of the abovementioned *Trishagion/Trisagion* incident, but this time it resulted from Anastasius' religious policies and not from some other civil disturbance. This time it was the bigoted monks who fanned the flames of religious fervour among the Factions and populace.

Anastasius disarmed the rioters by appearing in the Hippodrome without his diadem with the promise to resign if they so wished. The last of the known major riots of Anastasius' reign involving the factions of Constantinople took place in 514. This riot resulted from the cancellation of the chariot races by Anastasius, which he did as a punishment for the earlier rioting during which the rioters had killed the City Prefect Geta. However, as noted above, it is possible that there was some unknown connection between these riots and the rebel Vitalianus.

There were similar riots in the provinces. The first took place at Antioch in 491 and it was instigated by the Greens as a result of the removal of their privileges. The Greens attacked *Comes Orientis* Calliopus. Anastasius was dissatisfied and replaced him with another man who was instructed to pacify the Greens. In 507 there was another worse riot in Antioch. This time it was anti-Semitic. The charioteer Calliopas led the rioters against the Jews. They plundered and torched the Synagogue at Daphne and killed the Jews inside. Anastasius' response was to appoint Procopius of Antioch as *Comes Orientis* and Menas of Byzantion as *Praefectus Vigilum* with the task of punishing the anti-Semites. The Greens, however, destroyed a large part of the city and killed Menas. Anastasius' response was harsh. He sent Eirenaios Pentadiastes as new *Comes Orientis*, and he exacted vengeance on the Greens and 'brought fear into the city'. The last of the provincial riots of which we have knowledge took place in Alexandria in 515/6. It was caused by a shortage of oil and resulted in the murder of the *augustalios* Theodosius. Anastasius' response was again harsh and the culprits were punished.

The above has shown that Anastasius' response to all civil disturbances was to punish the culprits. In addition, he sought to limit the opportunities to riot only to the hippodrome by forbidding the wild beast shows in 499 and the pantomimes after the Brytae incident in 502. Haarer has also noted that Anastasius used the charioteer Porphyrius to diminish the eagerness of his supporters to riot by having him drive the chariots of both the Greens and Blues. The Greens were pacified by the end of Anastasius' reign.

The Death of Anastasius on 8–9 July 518

Many sources record dreams and omens for the year 518 preceding the death of Anastasius. It is even claimed that Anastasius himself saw such dreams and that the philosopher Proclus told him that they meant he would die soon. The Empress Ariadne had died in 515. Anastasius' death finally came on 9 July 518 at the age of 88 or 90. The sources are not unanimous about his age, but all agree he was very old. After his death there followed a power struggle, as almost always happened when the Emperor died.

Each of the nephews Hypatius, Pompeius and Probus might have expected to succeed, but if so they were wrong, because Anastasius had failed to nominate a successor. Hypatius, the eldest, was anyway too far away from the scene as *magister militum per Orientem* to influence the outcome. When the Emperor had died, the *silentiarii* informed Celer and Justin. Celer assembled the *candidati* and *scholarii* while Justin assembled the *excubitores*. Both told their men that they now had to choose an Emperor who would be pleasing to God and useful to the Empire.[166]

On the morning of 9 July, the high officials, the Senate, the Patriarch and the highest ranking military officers assembled at the Great Hall of the Palace known as Triklinos of the Nineteen Akkubita. The *demes* (the people, meaning the factions Blues, Whites, Greens, and Reds, which also served as paramilitary forces of Constantinople) assembled next to it in the Hippodrome with some of the soldiers belonging to the *scholarii* and *excubitores*. The *demes* (as representatives of the people) then acclaimed the Senate and demanded that the Senate would give them the Emperor, given by God for the army and the world. The high and mighty then deliberated, but were unable to reach a consensus with the result that Celer demanded that they nominate an Emperor while this was still possible because if they failed to make their decision quickly the army and / or the *demes* would take the initiative.

With the officials and officers still unable to reach a consensus, the soldiers and *demes* saw an opportunity and grasped it just as Celer feared. The *excubitores* in the Hippodrome were first to act. They shouted Justin's friend John (the later bishop of Heraclea) as Emperor and raised him on a shield (I would suggest that Justin was behind this). This was opposed by the Blues who threw stones and in the resulting chaos some were killed. Then the *scholarii* nominated *magister militum praesentalis* and *patricius* Patricius as Emperor and took him to the hall of the Palace and raised him on a table with the intention of crowning him (I would suggest that Celer was behind this). But this was prevented by the *excubitores* who dragged Patricius from the table and would have killed him had not Justinian (the future Emperor), who was a *candidatus*, prevented this. Justinian transferred Patricius to the quarters of the *excubitores* officially for his own safety, but in practice to prevent his nomination. We should consider Justinian, the nephew of Justin, to have acted as an undercover operative among the *scholarii* for his uncle at this time, such that he had informed the *excubitores* of the attempt to raise Patricius so that they were conveniently close by to prevent the nomination of Patricius. The fact that Justinian moved Patricius to the quarters of the *excubitores* shows how he now probably joined their ranks for his own safety. The excited *excubitores* now asked Justinian to take power, but he declined – after all, it is likely that he was seeking to have his 66 or 68-year-old uncle Justin nominated. He could expect to succeed him. The fact that the Excubitores were located between the Scholae and the Triklinos of the Nineteen Akkubita enabled Justin and Justinian to take control of the situation. For a detailed map of the Palace, see Ilkka Syvänne's academia.edu website.

It was then, according to the version presented by *De cerimoniis*, that the Senate forced Justin to become Emperor. However, before this happened another important development had taken place. According to a number of sources, the *praepositus sacri cubiculi* Amantius, who was a staunch Monophysite, gave Justin money to bribe the *excubitores* to back up the candidacy of Theocritus, the *Comes Domesticorum*, who was also a staunch Monophysite. Depending on the timing of this move, the wily Justin either bribed the *excubitores* to back the candidacy of the abovementioned John, or his own candidacy. Whatever the timing, Justin had clearly given the money in his own name so that the *excubitores* followed up his wishes. The candidacy of *Comes Domesticorum* Theocritus appears to have been a rather far-fetched personal attempt by Amantius because, as we have seen, the *domestici* and *scholarii* backed Patricius.[167] When the *excubitores* then managed to confine the candidate of the *scholae* to the quarters of the *excubitores*, the only candidate left was the *Comes Excubitorum* Justin. The *scholarii* opposed the nomination and attacked Justin in the presence of the Senate so that Justin suffered a bloodied lip, but the *scholarii* were too late to prevent the *fait accompli*, because Justin had in the meantime managed to gather the support of the *demes* and the army.[168] Justin's *excubitores*, who seem to have stayed in the Hippodrome after their first candidate John had failed to gather the necessary support, had undoubtedly made a number of promises to the heads of the *demes* to obtain their support. We do not know what Justin did to obtain the support of the army, but it is clear that he had managed to bring praesental forces into the capital to back up his claim because a member of the *Lanciarii* was present in the coronation. Money must have changed hands, because the regular donation of money (five *nomismata* and a pound of silver) for the soldiers could have been expected from all candidates.

Justin was then brought before the *demes*. They acclaimed him and Imperial robes were ordered. Then Justin, entering the Imperial Box in the company of the Patriarch and high officials, was lifted on a shield and a *campiductor* called Godila from the *Lanciarii* placed a chain on his head. The *labara* and other standards were raised after which Justin changed clothes underneath the *testudo* formed for him. The Patriarch then placed a crown on his head and Justin took a lance and shield. The text of the imperial address, Justin's manifesto to the people, was read by a *magister a libellis*, because Celer, whose duty it was to read this, excused himself on the grounds of gout. This was just an excuse. He had lost the power struggle and did not want to appear on the scene. Justin and Justinian had outmanoeuvred Celer, Patricus and Amantius so that the only candidate left for the Senate to proclaim had been the illiterate son of a peasant and this was too great a humiliation for the learned Celer to bear. The rest of the story can be found in the next volume.

Anastasius as Emperor

An accurate evaluation of the reign of Anastasius is difficult, because he was highly successful in certain areas of his rule while in other areas he can at best be called a disaster. My overall assessment of his reign however, is that he should be included among the best emperors Rome ever had, regardless of his failings. The reason for this is that under Anastasius the administration probably worked better than at any time during the late Empire. Corruption was kept to a minimum so that the taxpayers were protected from the abuse of the rich while the powerful and the rich were forced to pay their fair share of the taxes as required by the law. It is another question whether the share of the burden for the rich was fair, but at least under Anastasius the rich paid what the law required. Most importantly, when possible Anastasius prevented the rich from stealing from the poor or middle classes, which improved the ability of the latter to pay their taxes. This meant that Anastasius could actually lower the taxes for the middle class at the same time as he filled up the state coffers, and even paid the great costs resulting from a number of badly managed wars. One should also include among Anastasius' achievements the ending of the Isaurian problem for good, and, at least equally importantly, he reinstated Roman naval supremacy on the Red Sea so that commerce between Rome, Africa and India flourished under him and brought a windfall of customs duties to the state coffers.

Anastasius nominated a string of very able civil servants who were known for their learning, ability and experience, so it is not a surprise that the civilian administration worked well to support the state apparatus and its military forces.

However, Anastasius' nominations to high military posts were not quite so successful. Even if he nominated a large number of very able (the civilian Celer and Marinus, and the military men John the Scythian, John the Huncback, Romanus, and Vitalianus) or competent (Patricius, Patriciolus, Areobindus) generals, he also nominated quite a few commanders who were not up to their task or were unable to cooperate with each other as happened during 503. On the other hand, as soon as he saw the inability of his commanders to cooperate in 503, he rectified the situation immediately. The commanders who were probably incompetent included Hypatius, Pompeius, and Aristus, but there are possible vindications for these appointments. Anastasius sacked his nephew Hypatius in 503 when it became apparent that he was the principal culprit for the defeat, which means that he did pay attention to the performance of his officers. It is probable that he felt compelled to appoint Hypatius and Pompeius to high military commands during the revolt of Vitalianus only because the other commanders could not be trusted or refused to fight against Vitalianus. This meant that Anastasius had had no choice in the matter, just as he had no choice but to appoint the *PPO* Marinus in charge of the naval combat against Vitalianus when the *magistri* refused. The appointment of Vitalianus as *Comes Foederatum* can of course also be considered to have been a grave mistake, but this is actually an understandable mistake because Vitalianus was certainly an able commander and had important backers in the military, including his father Patriciolus. Therefore it is clear that the top brass, especially Patricius, had supported Vitalianus' nomination and Anastasius had just followed their advice. Therefore this mistake is understandable and forgivable, even if it proved disastrous.

Anastasius' greatest mistake was perhaps the support he gave to the Monophysite/Miaphysite interpretation of the *Henoticon* of Zeno and the exiling of the Patriarch Macedonius, because these were used by his enemies against him. He was not compelled to do these things because his early reign shows that he could have followed a more moderate course. These mistakes probably resulted from Anastasius' personal religious beliefs. The second and third of his major mistakes were the denial of *annona* to the *foederati* in the Balkans and the keeping of *coemptio* in effect in the Balkans. It was this combination of three grievances that Vitalianus used to raise his forces and the regulars in the Balkans together with the peasants behind his rebel flag. The naval defeat at Constantinople meant that after 515 Vitalianus could no longer pose a serious threat against the capital, but he could do so by other means, and the appointment of Pompeius in charge of the defence of the Balkans against Vitalianus ensured that this remained so.

Anastasius left the Empire in much better condition than he received it. The economy flourished, the cases of corruption were minimal in comparison with earlier reigns, and the administration and tax gathering functioned well. In fact, Anastasius demonstrated by his actions what could be achieved by a good Emperor. The end result was that the state coffers were now full. Anastasius left his successor 320,000 lbs of gold. The only problem that remained was Vitalianus with his *foederati* rebels, but he was easily convinced to end his revolt by Anastasius' successor Justin who changed Imperial policy to follow the Chalcedonian faith. It was largely thanks to the money gathered by Anastasius that his successors were in a position to revive Roman fortunes.

Chapter Thirteen

Appendix: Urbicius and the State of the Roman Armies under Anastasius

Introduction

The two treatises of Urbicius, the *Tacticon* and the *Epitedeuma*, and his two epigrams, which date from the reign of Anastasius, are of the greatest importance for the analysis of Roman combat doctrine, tactics and fighting power, and are therefore summarized and analyzed here.[1]

Urbicius has sometimes been claimed to have composed the *Strategikon* of Maurice or its infantry section (Book 12) or its hunting section (12.D, the *Cyneticus*) and a fragment on river crossings, but I agree with the latest commentators of the *Epitedeuma*, Greatrex, Elton, and Burgess that this is very unlikely for the reasons that they state in their analyses. It is just possible that Urbicius composed the infantry portion of Book 12 (12.B), but even this is unlikely. I therefore agree with the suggestions made by Greatrex, Elton and Burgess that it is possible or even likely that some version of the epigrams preceded the *Tacticon* and that the *Epitedeuma* followed after the *Tacticon* so that the Epigram, *Tacticon* and *Epitedeuma* made up one book originally. The epigrams clearly appear as sort of prefaces to the *Tacticon* while the *Epitedeuma* (1) referred to the combat formations of the ancients just presented, in other words to the *Tacticon*. The *Tacticon* is an epitome of Arrian's *Tacticon* (2nd c. AD) while the *Epitedeuma* presents the author's invention that could be used to protect the infantry against enemy cavalry.[2]

The author

The only absolutely secure information that we have of the author Urbicius comes from his own texts, but we also have some later evidence to shed further light on his career. According to his own texts, he lacked personal military experience and wrote in deferential terms of the Emperor. The later evidence consists of two epigrams from the reign of Leo VI and a reference in the *Patria Constantinoupoleos*.

One of these epigrams has been translated by Greatrex, Elton, and Burgess as follows: 'Urbicius travelled through his life always with this [*book*], expounding to all in the company of mighty princes; he bade the images of ancient wars be revived, a skilful imitation of battles for the bronze-covered hosts.'[3] This suggests the possibility that Urbicius sought to revive the Macedonian style phalanx he referred to in the *Tacticon*, but in my opinion this is taking the evidence too far. It is probable that this statement meant only that Urbicius sought to revive the proper training of infantry so that they could be used to fight effectively in the various phalanx arrays described or implied in the *Tacticon*, because as far as tactics and organization were concerned the Roman and

Macedonian systems were similar. The only real difference was that the Macedonians used the longer *sarissa*-pike.

The reference in the *Patria Constantinoupoleos* claims that Urbicius built the Church of the Theotokos, was known by the nickname Barbatus (bearded), wrote *strategika*, and had been *magister militum per Orientem* and *patricius* under Anastasius.[4] Of note here is the reference to Urbicius being bearded, which would presumably have been a noteworthy fact when the Emperor was shaved – most of his courtiers would have followed his example; and also the reference to the writing of the *strategika*, which may imply that he authored other works too, even if this means merely the *Epigram/Tacticon/Epitedeuma*.

The above information has been accepted by the PLRE2, but has not been accepted by Greatrex, Elton and Burgess. Their argument is that the author of the *Patria* has just made educated guesses on the basis of Urbicius' own texts. They claim that Urbicius cannot have been the *magister militum per Orientem* because he referred to his own lack of practical military experience. As evidence against the appointment of commander without military experience they point out that this would have been entirely out of place after the Persian War in 504/5. Furthermore, they point out that none of the period sources mention Urbicius as *magister militum per Orientem*. Consequently, they suggest that this Urbicius may have been the *praepositus sacri cubiculi* Urbicius (see the Persian War) who certainly lacked military experience, or even more likely some unknown Urbicius.[5]

None of these arguments is convincing. The first rests on the assumption that the information presented by the author must be wrong. They actually prove their second argument (the Emperor could not have appointed an inexperienced man in charge of the Eastern Field Army) incorrect themselves by referring to the inexperience of the commanders Patricius, Hypatius and Areobindus at the time of their appointment to high positions in the war against Persia (pp. 36–7). One can add to this list of inexperienced commanders Celer, Marinus and Pompeius. Therefore, there is no reason to think that Anastasius could not have appointed Urbicius as *magister militum per Orientem* even when he lacked practical military experience. It is unlikely to be a coincidence that the sources stress the learning of Celer who must have learnt his military trade from books just like Urbicius. There is every reason to suspect that Anastasius appointed his highest ranking officers on the basis of their literary knowledge of military treatises, just as he appointed his highest ranking civil servants on the basis of their literary learning. The only exceptions to this may have been the appointments of the nephews, but it is entirely possible that they had also demonstrated their book knowledge before their appointments. It is unlikely to be a coincidence that we find the philosopher Proclus advising both Anastasius and Marinus before the naval battle. In light of all of this, it is entirely plausible that Urbicius obtained his appointment as *magister militum per Orientem* as a result of his military treatise, which sought to correct the problems of his own day.

The Tactical Treatise of Urbicius: Epigram, Tacticon and Epitedeuma[6]

The epigram can be used to date the other two treatises. It mentions the Emperor Anastasius just like the two other texts, but in addition he mentions as enemies the western men (Hesperian men, the Ostrogoths), Persians, Saracens, Isaurians and the Huns. This dates the treatise to the period after the Persian War and the War against the Ostrogoths, which means that it dates from the period after 505. The *Epitedeuma* (2) states that Anastasius had at the time launched a campaign with all his forces to avenge Roman affairs, which in combination with the reference in the epigram to the times of Trajanus under Anastasius (the last two lines, with the name emended) should probably be taken to refer to the war in the Balkans against Vitalianus.

In short, it is probable that Urbicius wrote the *Tacticon* and *Epitedeuma* to correct the problems he had witnessed at a time when Anastasius was fighting against Vitalianus. The *Tacticon* portion suggested that the Emperor should train the infantry very thoroughly in the traditional manner so that it could perform all of the manoeuvres that he listed, and since he knew that at the moment the infantry consisted mostly of green recruits he suggested the precautionary measure of using protective devices invented by him around the infantry against the possibility that the green recruits would just run away when the enemy cavalry attacked instead of performing the manoeuvres described in the *Tacticon*.

The *Tacticon*, which is an epitome of Arrian's *Tacticon*, enumerates the traditional units and their officers. The 16,384 heavy infantry hoplites were under the following commanders (I have added some clarifications to this list): *lochagos* (a *lochos* of 16 men), *dilochitês* (with 32 men), *tetrarchês* (with 64 men), *taxiarchês* (128) also called as *hekatontarchês*, *syntagmatarchês* (256) also called as *xenagos*. Each *syntagma* of 256 men had five supernumeraries: a standard-bearer, a file-closer, a trumpeter, an aide and a herald. After this followed: *pentekosiarchês* (with 512 men), *chiliarchês* (1,024), *merarchês* (2,048) also known as *telarchês*, *falaggarchês* (4,096) also called as *stratêgos* by some, *difalaggarchês* (8,192 men known by some as *keras*/wing), and finally *tetrafalaggarchês* (16,384 men).

The unit orders that Urbicius (2) lists are the *pyknosis* (shields rim-to-rim) and *synaspismos* (shields interlocked). According to him, the Romans made out of these two orders another order called *chelône* (tortoise, *testudo*) which could be either square or round in shape. This is indeed an accurate description of the reality. The rim-to-rim order (either square or oblong) was used when the front rank kneeled and the men behind placed their shields on top of those in front. This was the standard way to receive a cavalry charge. The other order, shields rim-to-boss, was tighter and used by men standing usually against infantry but could also be used against cavalry either by standing or by kneeling. It was presumably the latter tortoise that could withstand the stones and wagons drawn from the example of Arrian. The third chapter describes requirements for file-leaders and file-closers, which were naturally required to consist of the better fighters.

The fourth chapter lists the light-armed *psiloi*. There were to be 8,192 light-armed so that each heavy infantry file of 16 men had 8 light-armed behind it. The commanders were: *syntagmatarchês* (commanded 32 men), *pentêkontarchês* (64), and *hekatontarchês* (128). Each *hekatontarchy* of 128 men had five supernumeraries: a standard-bearer, a file-closer, a trumpeter, an aide and a herald. The rest of the officers were: *psilarchês* (256), *xenagos* (512), *systremmatarchês* (1,024), *epixenagos* (2,048), two *epixenagiai* were a *stifos* (4,096 men, Arrian/Urbicius fails to mention the title of the commander *stifarchês*), and finally *epitagmatarchês* in command of all *psiloi* (8,192).

The fifth chapter lists the 4,096 cavalry for the army as expected in a treatise based on Macedonian concepts. Please note, however, that these basic concepts were retained throughout the period, even if they were adapted and modified according to the availability of each type of force so that there could also be considerably more cavalry. We should not forget that in practice the Macedonians varied the proportion of each type of force according to availability, so they did not follow the theory slavishly. However, it is still clear that by presenting these traditional figures Urbicius was expressing his opinion that one should place greater trust in infantry. The cavalry was not to be arrayed in eight ranks but four. One wonders whether this was also meant as a criticism of practices followed during the sixth century, because we find the cavalry deployed from 5 to 10 ranks according to the quality of the unit in the *Strategikon*. The cavalry officers mentioned by Urbicius were: *ilarchês* (in command of 64 horsemen), *epilarchês* (128), *tarantinarchês* (256), *hipparchês* (512), *efipparchês* (1,024), *telarchês* (2,048), and finally the *syntagmatarchês* (4,096).

Urbicius lists unit manoeuvres in Chapter 6. These included: *klisis* (each soldier turning either right spearward *epi doru klisis*, or left shieldward *epi aspida klisis*), *metabolê* (about-face), *epistrofê* (quarter-turn/wheeling), *anastrofê* (to wheel back to the original position), *perispasmos* (half-turn/wheeling), *ekperispasmos* (three-quarter-turn/wheeling), *stoichein* (to file = to stand in file), *zygein* (to rank = to stand in rank).

Urbicius lists the countermarches and other combat formations in Chapter 7. The countermarches consisted of three: Macedonian (phalanx moves to occupy the ground in front), Lakonian (phalanx moves to occupy the ground behind), and Chorios (the phalanx holds the same ground), the last of which was also called the Persian or Cretan. Other manoeuvres were: *displasiasmos* (doubling of number of soldiers or area), *parembolê* (insertion of the same type of soldiers, e.g. hoplites besides hoplites), *prostaxis* (one *stifos* of 4,096 men of light-armed men placed forward on each of the flanks of the phalanx), *entaxis* (insertion of light-armed between the files of hoplites called by Asclepiodotus as *parentaxis*), and *hypotaxis* (the light-armed placed behind the flanks of the phalanx; Arrian's original text likened it to the *epikampios* = *epikampios opisthia*).

Chapter 8 lists the voice, visual and trumpet signals used to direct the cavalry and infantry. Chapters 9–10 give a list of commands. Chapter 11 shows how the baggage train, the *touldon/skeuoforoi*, was to be arrayed in different situations. If it was expected that the enemy would be in front, the baggage train was to be placed behind the army. If it was expected that the enemy was to the right, then the baggage train was to be on the left, and *vice versa*. If the enemy was suspected of threatening all sides, then the baggage train was to be placed inside (i.e. inside a hollow square/oblong or double phalanx).

Urbicius ended his *Tacticon* with the words (tr. by Greatrex, Elton, and Burgess p.60. n.1), 'Tactics of such a kind are instructive, providing safety for those who use them, but defeat for those inexperienced in such things.' I agree with Greatrex and Elton that this probably introduced what followed in the *Epitedeuma* 1–2 (tr. by Greatrex, Elton and Burgess): 'The aforementioned formations are the inventions of the ancients, to be set forth to the soldiers who are trained to receive attacks of the enemy. Because of this instruction it was easy for them to change their formations to deceive the enemy. But our gloriously triumphant and most pious lord, impelled by God, has now embarked upon a campaign with all his forces to avenge Roman affairs, and it has come about that the veterans are lost through old age and the new recruits gain their experience of the enemy amidst the dangers of actual combat, with the result that those who are hard-pressed in battle suffer discouragement and fear as well. For these reasons, I have been so bold as to present a particular formation that will preserve the soldier unharmed and overpower the enemy. It was not mentioned by the ancients, but has been invented by me, ... The advantage of this formation will be of particular benefit to the infantry when fighting against cavalry.'

Greatrex, Elton and Burgess are quite correct to point out that Urbicius foresaw problems resulting from the lack of training that needed to be addressed. Urbicius clearly thought that green infantry forces would be unable to resist an enemy cavalry charge, and if they used the tactics implicit in the manoeuvres of the *Tacticon*, they caused troubles only to themselves. Urbicius' solution was that the infantry was to use only one combat formation, the hollow square, which was also to be used during marching and encamping. This minimized the manoeuvres that the infantry had to make and gave every soldier the illusion of safety because his rear and flanks were always protected.[7]

Urbicius' solution to the problem posed by the first cavalry charge (the *impetus*) in the minds of the soldiers was to build an encircling fence (the new invention built according to his instructions) outside the infantry square at such a distance that enemy arrows would be unable to reach the soldiers, while arraying ballistae in movable wagons (*carroballistae, ballistroforoi hamaxai*) on the outer edges of the square to shoot at the attacking enemy horses. According to Urbicius, the ballistae could shoot three times as far as the bows so this worked well. Urbicius expected the Roman arrows would destroy the foremost barbarians (presumably their front rank consisting of their better equipped 'noblemen') just in front of the fence so that the horses and men would pile up while some of the fallen horses would become stuck on the nails of the fence. Those following the front rank would ride into their fallen comrades trampling them. If the enemy dismounted and attempted to dig up the poles of the fence, the soldiers were to kill them with their spears if the ballistae did not do it for them. Urbicius expected that the sight of their front ranks falling would demoralize the enemy so that they would flee, after which the Romans could pick up the fence, place it back on the pack animals, then pursue the enemy and repeat the above if the enemy appeared.[8]

Unfortunately we do not possess illustrations of the device Urbicius invented. All we have to go on are that each *decuria* of soldiers[9] took three poles fitted with nails from a pack animal carrying thirty such poles for a group of ten *decuriae* and drove these into the ground outside the range of bowshot when they learnt of the approach of the enemy. The end result was likened to a fence in which there were nails protruding presumably from the ground because the fallen horses are claimed to have become stuck on them. Urbicius (14) considered this device far better than the barbarian manner of using a circle of wagons for protection because it was easy to destroy by fire if the attackers showed some initiative.[10] This last portion of the text can actually be used to date the text to the period following the defeat of Hypatius at Acrae in 514 if it involved the use of fire arrows against the wagons and oxen.

I have below included one possible version of the device invented by Urbicius. Note that this version could also have plates with nails at the bottom of each pole in the manner I have described in the second alternative even if I have not included such plates with nails in this variant. It is unfortunate that we do not know if the device was ever used; none of the extant texts refer to it in any context. It is possible that the device was used for example by Pompeius in 516/7, but as said we have no evidence. If it was, then the defeat certainly sealed its destiny. On the other hand there are strong grounds to believe that the device, whatever it looked like, was found useful, because the *Epitedeuma* has survived to this day and was included among the military treatises of later generations.

The likeliest structure if the barrier
had sharp end towards the enemy.

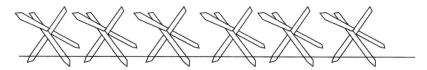

My suggestion for
the likeliest structure
with the nails

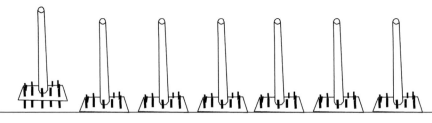

Solution suggested
by Rigaltius in 1599

Bibliography

Primary Sources:
Most of the primary sources (e.g. Jordanes, Cassiodorus, Paulus Diaconus, Priscus, Malchus, Nonnosus, Zonaras, Cedrenus/Kedrenos, various Armenian sources etc) are now available on the web either as old editions (e.g. FGH, MGH AA, PL, PG etc.) and translations or as html documents. Good places to start seeking them are Robert Bedrosian's Armenian Resources, the Internet Archive, Google Books, and the Tertullian Project. Whenever possible I have used Loeb or Budé editions and translations, excepting when I have been writing in places where I have had access to my books or library. The following list (Select Primary Sources) refers only to those modern editions/translations that I have cited in the text or notes.

Select Primary Sources and Translations
al-Biruni, The *Chronology of Ancient Nations*, ed. and tr. by C.E. Sachau, London 1879.
Arrian, *Tactica, Flavius Arrianus, techne taktika (Tactical Handbook) and ektaxis kata alanon (The Expedition Against the Alans)*, tr. and ed. J.G. DeVoto, Chicago (1993).
Balami, *Chronique de Abou-Djafar-Mohammed-ben-Djarir-ben-Yezid Tabari traduite sur la version persane d'Abou-Ali Mo'hammed Bel'ami*, vol.2. French tr. by M. Hermann Zotenberg. Paris 1869.
Blockley R.C. (tr. and com.), *The Fragmentary Classicising Historians of the Later Roman Empire Eunapius, Olympiodorus, Priscus and Malchus*. 2 Vols. Liverpoool 1983. A very useful collection of sources with comments.
Candidus, see Blockley.
Chronica Minora, see *Monumenta*
Codex Justinianus, ed. P. Krueger, Berlin 1877.
Ennodius, Opera MGH AA 7, ed. Vogel, Berlin 1885 (includes Panegyric of Theoderic and Vita Epiphanius); English tr. of The Panegyric of Theoderic: *Ennodius' Panegyric to Theoderic the Great. A Translation and Commentary, Master's Thesis*, University of Ottawa, Barbara S. Haase, Ottawa, Canada, 1991.
Evagrius, *Ecclesiastical History*, ed. J. Bidez and L. Parmenties London 1898; The *Ecclesiastical History of Evagrius Scholasticus*, tr. M. Whitby, Liverpool 2000.
FRMG = *From Roman to Merovingian Gaul*, ed. and tr. by A.C. Murray. UTP 2008 (very useful collection of translated sources).
Gallic Chronicle, see Chronica Minora and FRMG.
Gordon C.D., *The Age of Attila*. New York (1960). A very useful collection of translated sources (Candidus, Olympiodorus, Priscus, Malchus, Ioannes Antiochenus/John of Antioch) with commentary.
Gregory of Tours, *The History of the Franks*, tr. by Lewis Thorpe. London 1974.
Hydatius, *The Chronicle of Hydatius and the Consularia Constantinopolitana*, ed. and tr. by R.W. Burgess. Oxford (1993).
John of Antioch, *Ioannis Antiocheni Fragmenta ex Historia chronica*, ed. U. Roberto. Berlin and New York (2005). Partial English tr. in Gordon.
John of Lydus, *see Lydus.*

John of Nikiu, *The Chronicle of John, Bishop of Nikiu*, tr. of the Ethiopic text by R.H. Charles. Oxford (1916).

Joshua the Stylite, *The Chronicle of Joshua the Stylite*, tr. by William Wright. Cambridge (1882); *The Chronicle of Pseudo-Joshua the Stylite*, tr. F.R. Trombley and J.W. Watt. Liverpool (2000)

Kedrenos/Cedrenus, *Georgii Cedreni Historiarum Compedium*, ed. I. Bekker, CSHB. Bonn (1838) and in PG (fragments also translated in Zonaras/Banich).

Lazar P'arpets'i,/Ghazar Parpetzi, Bedrosian, New York (1985)/ *www.rbedrosian.com*.

Lydus, John, *De magistratibus, Ioannes Lydus On Powers or The Magistracies of the Roman State*, ed. and tr. by A.C. Bandy. Philadelphia (1983).

Malchus, see Blockley.

Marcellinus Comes, *The Chronicle of Marcellinus*, ed. (Mommsen's text) and tr. by Brian Croke. Sydney (1995).

Michael the Syrian, *Chronicle*, several versions available from Robert Bedrosian's Armenian Resources. Most importantly, Bedrosian has not only translated two Armenian versions of the text, but has also included either links or articles dealing with the text and has also provided links to Langlois' French translation of the composite of Armenian versions and to Chabot's French translation of the Syriac text (the most complete version).

Monumenta Historia Germaniae, several volumes

Monumenta Historia Germaniae Auctores Antiquitissimonum Fontibus Tomus IX (*MGH AA IX, Chronica Minora Volumen I*), (includes: *Anonymi Valesiani pars posterior* which I have also used from the Loeb ed.; *Fasti Vindobones priores and posteriores; Paschale Campanum; Prosperi continuation Havniensis* which is also known as *Auctarium Prosperi Hauniensis* sited either as *ordo prior* or *ordo posterior*; Agnellus).

Moses Khorenatsi, *History of the Armenians*, tr. R.W. Thomson. Cambridge and London (1978).

Nonnosus, fragments in ed. C. Müller, *FGH 4*, 178–81.

Olympiodorus, see Blockley

Paul the Deacon, see Paulus

Paulus Diaconus, *Historia Romana* (available online e.g. from Internet Archive).

Priscian of Caesarea (Prisc. *Pan.*), *De Laude Anastasii Imperatoris*, ed., tr. and com. A. Chauvot, *Procope de Gaza, Priscien de Cèsarée, Panègyriques de läempereur Anastase 1er*, Bonn (1986); ed., tr. and com. P. Coyne, *Priscian of Caesarea's De Laude Anastasii Imperatoris*. Lewsiton/ Queenston/Lampeter (1991).

Priscus of Pannium, see Blockley.

Procopius of Caesarea, *Wars, Buildings, Anecdota/Secret History*, ed. and tr. H.B. Dewing, 7vols. Loeb, London 1914–1940.

Procopius of Gaza, (Proc. Pan.), *Panegyricus in imperatorem Anastasium*, ed., tr. and com. A. Chauvot, *Procope de Gaza, Priscien de Cèsarée, Panègyriques de läempereur Anastase 1er*, Bonn (1986);

REF2 = *The Roman Eastern Frontier and the Persian Wars. Part II AD 363–630*. Eds. G. Greatrex and S.N.C. Lieu. London and New York (2002). A useful collection of sources.

Sidonius Apollinaris, *Poems and Letters*. 2 vols., tr. and ed. W.B. Anderson. Loeb ed. Harvard (1936/1965).

Strategikon, *Das Strategikon des Maurikios*, ed. G.T. Dennis, German tr. by E. Gamillscheg. Vienna 1981; *Maurice's Strategikon*, tr. by G.T. Dennis. Philadelphia (1984).

Suda/Suidas a.3970, tr. by Jennifer Benedict, vetted by David Whitehead, William Hutton, Catharine Roth at www.stoa.org.

Tabari, *The History of al-Tabari. Vol. V. The Sasanids, the Byzantines, the Lakhmids, and Yemen*. tr. by C.E. Bosworth. New York (1999).

Theophanes, *Chronographia* ed. C. de Boor (Leipzig 1883) and PG version both available online; *The Chronicle of Theophanes Confessor*, tr. by Cyril Mango and Roger Scott with the assistance of Geoffrey Greatrex. Oxford (1997).

Zachariah of Mitylene, *The Syriac Chronicle known as that of Zachariah of Mitylene*, tr. by F.J. Hamilton and E.W. Brooks, London 1899.
—— *The Chronicle of Pseudo-Zachariah Rhetor*, ed. Geoffrey Greatrex, tr. by R.R. Phenix and C.B. Horn with contribtions by S.P. Brock and W. Witakowski. Liverpool (2011).

Secondary Sources
Alföldy, Geza. *Noricum*. London and Boston (1974).
Anderson, W.B., see Sidonius
Aquileia. Città di frontiera. Fondazione Aquileia (a fragment available as a PDF on the web).
Arabs and Empires before Islam (2015), ed. G. Fisher. Oxford.
Ariño B.D., 'Las murallas romanas de Cartagena en la segunda mitad del siglo I a.e.', (available from academia.edu).
Audin (1949), 'Le Tracé colonial de Lugdunum', *Revue de géographie jointe au Bulletin de la Société de géographie de Lyon et de la région lyonnaise 24*, 51–58.
Barbera G. (1999), 'La valle dei Templi: il mandorlo e il 'Museo vivente', in *ANGKN 26*, 177ff.
Barrington Atlas of the Greek and Roman World (2000). Ed. R.J.A. Talbert. Princeton.
Bernardes P. & Martins M., 'Computer Graphics and Urban Archaeology. Bracara Augusta's case study.' (available at academia.edu), highly recommended for its nice computer graphics of the city.
Blockley R.C. (tr. and com.), *The Fragmentary Classicising Historians of the Later Roman Empire Eunapius, Olympiodorus, Priscus and Malchus*. 2 Vols. Liverpool 1983.
Blockley R.C. (1992), *East Roman Foreign Policy. Formation and Conduct from Diocletian to Anastasius*. Leeds.
Brulet R. (1995), 'La sépulture du roi Childéric à Tournai et le site funéraire', in *La noblesse romaine et les chefs barbares du IIIe au VIIe siècle*, ed. by F. Vallet and M. Kazanski, 309–326
Bury J.B. (1923) *History of the Later Roman Empire*. 2. vols. London.
Ciglenecki S. (2011), *Iulian Alps*, Power Point presentation 2011 (available at academia.edu).
Edwell Peter, with contributions from Greg Fisher, Geoffrey Greatrex, Conor Whately, and Philip Wood, 'Arabs in the Conflict between Rome and Persia, AD 491–630', *Arabs and Empires*, 214–275.
Escher K. *Les Burgondes Ier-Vie siècles apr. J.-C.* Paris.
Filippo R. de, 'Nouvelle définition de l'enceinte romaine de Toulouse', *Gallia 50*, 181–204.
Fisher, Greg, *see Arabs and Empires*.
Geneviève V., Chuniaud K., Raux S., and Simon L. (2011), Monnaies et mobiliers associés d'un ensemble clos de la fin du IVe s. apr. J.-C. sur le site de l'auditorium de Bordeaux (Gironde, France), in JAN 1, 141–216.
Gray J.A. (1954), *The Walls of Verona*. Venice and New York (can be accessed from the web).
Greatrex G. (1996), 'Flavius Hypatius, quem vidit validum parthus sensitque timendum, An investigation of his career,' in *Byzantion* 66, 120–142.
Greatrex G., Elton H., and Burgess R. (2005), 'Urbicius' Epitedeuma: an edition, translation and commentary', in *BZ* 98, 35–74.
Greatrex G. and Bardill J. (1996), 'Antiochus the Praepositus: A Persian Eunuch at the Court of Theodosius II', in *DOP* 50, 171–197.
Haarer, F.K. (2006), *Anastasius I. Politics and Empire in the Late Roman World*. Cambridge.
Haase, Barbara S., see Ennodius.
Heather P. (1996), *The Goths*. Oxford.
Hendy M.F. (1985), *Studies in the Byzantine Monetary Economy c.300–1450*. Cambridge.
Hippone, see Laporte.
Hodgkin T. (1892), *Italy and Her Invaders Vol. 2*. Oxford.
Hughes I. (2015), *Patricians and Emperors*. Barnsley.
italicapress.com (webpage).

Jakobsen T.C. (2012), *A History of the Vandals*. Yardley.

James Edward (1988), *The Franks*. Oxford.

Jones A.H.M. (1964/1986), *The Later Roman Empire 284–602*. Oxford.

Lebedynsky I. (2001), *Armes et guerriers barbares au temps des grandes invasions*. Paris.

MacGeorge P. (2002), *Late Roman Warlords*. Oxford.

Maenchen-Helfen O.J. (1973), *The World of Huns*. Berkeley.

Murray, see FRMG.

Petrikovits von H. (1971), 'Fortifications in the North-Western Roman Empire from the Third to the Fifth Centuries AD', in *JRS* 61, 178–218.

PLRE1, (1971/2006), *The Prosopography of the Later Roman Empire*, A.H.M. Jones, J.R. Martindale & J. Morris. Volume 1 A.D. 260–395. Cambridge.

PLRE2, (1980/2011), *The Prosopography of the Later Roman Empire*, J.R. Martindale. Cambridge.

Ribeiro J.M.P. (2010), *Arquitectura romana em Bracara Augusta*.

Richmond L. A. (1931), 'Five Town Walls in Hispania Citerior', *JRS* 21, 86–100.

Rouche M. (1996), *Clovis*. Fayard.

Shahid I. BAFIC (1989, 2006), *Byzantium and the Arabs in the Fifth Century*. Washington.

—— BASIC (1995–2010), *Byzantium and the Arabs in the Sixth Century*. Washington.

Syvänne (Syvänne/Syvaenne) I, - *A Military History of Late Rome Vol. 6 518–565*, Pen & Sword, forthcoming 2020.

—— *A Military History of Late Rome Vol.4 425–457*, Pen & Sword, Barnsley 2020.

—— *A Military History of Late Rome Vol.3 395–425*, Pen & Sword, Barnsley 2020.

—— *Britain in the Age of Arthur*, Pen & Sword, Barnsley 2019.

—— 'East Roman Naval Warfare and Military Treatises,' forthcoming in 2020.

—— *The Reign of Emperor Gallienus. The Apogee of Roman Cavalry*. Pen & Sword, Barnsley 2019.

—— *A Military History of Late Rome Vol. 2 361–395*, Pen & Sword, Barnsley 2018.

—— *Caracalla: A Military Biography*, Pen & Sword, Barnsley 2017.

—— *A Military History of Late Rome 284–361*, Pen & Sword, Barnsley 2015.

—— 'Scutarii' in the Wiley-Blackwell's *Encyclopedia of the Roman Army*, edited by Yann Le Bohec, 2015

—— 'Excubitores' in the Wiley-Blackwell's *Encyclopedia of the Roman Army*, edited by Yann Le Bohec, 2015

—— (2004), *The Age of Hippotoxotai*. Tampere.

Syvänne, Ilkka and Maksymiuk, Katarzyna, *A Military History of Fifth Century Iran*. Forthcoming Siedlce 2020.

Szuppe M. (2002/2012), 'Herat iv. Topography and Urbanism', in *Encyclopaedia Iranica* available at iranicaonline.org.

Tarraco, Archaeological Visual Guide (available e.g. from academia.edu).

Trombley F.R. and Watt J.W. (2000), *The Chronicle of Pseudo-Joshua the Stylite*. Liverpool.

Vasiliev, A.A. (1950), *Justin the First*. Cambridge.

Wagner P. (2002), *Pictish Warrior AD 297–841*. Oxford.

Whitby, M., *see Evagrius*

Wolfram H., (1990), *History of the Goths*. Berkeley, Los Angeles, London.

Notes

Chapter 1

1. This chapter gives only the bare outline of these topics and follows sometimes word-by-word the introduction of volume 4. Readers are advised to consult the previous volumes (esp. vol.3) in the book series if they seek a more detailed discussion. I will include in the following text only the skeleton version of the administrative and military matters into which I will add new fifth century material.

Chapter 3

1. Most of the sources mentioned in this chapter can be found under the names of the persons mentioned in the PLRE2 and/or in the *MGH AA Chron. Min. 1–2* (these include several chronicles which are organized annalistically and are therefore quite easy to check up). I include a reference to the original source only when I think this adds something new to the discussion or is otherwise interesting for readers, but I have always included references to the secondary literature if I have used them.
2. For a fuller discussion of Aegidius's background and career, see MacGeorge. Note, however, that my views differ from hers in many places even if my account is still heavily indebted to her analysis.
3. Based on Greg. 2.11 and Fredegar 3.11. I have here accepted that these two accounts are based on real events, but I have not accepted Fredegar's account in its entirety.
4. According to Anderson (tr. of Sidonius, p.94).
5. The sources are listed under the individuals named in the PLRE2. I have included direct references to them only when I think it is necessary for the case or otherwise informative, but I have always included references to the secondary literature if I have used them.
6. As I will demonstrate below, Majorian was in charge of operations in Italy, which means that the campaign against the Ostrogoths in the Balkans continued through most of 458 as well.
7. He cannot have been Ricimer, because Ricimer stayed in Italy in 458/9 when the unknown *MVM* accompanied Majorian to Lyons.
8. This approximate date is given by Sidonius in his Panegyric of Majorian. However if he has for some reason made a mistake in the dating of the peace between Majorian and Visigoths (5.476), it is possible that Majorian actually advanced first to Lyon to obtain reinforcements before marching south to Vienne (Valence of Arles) where Aegidius was besieged, and then crushed the Visigoths in very early 459. This version receives support from the order in which Hydatius's text is organized (peace between the Visigoths and Romans as last date) and from the dates and locations of Majorian's *novellae* (Majorian attested to be at Arles in: NMaj. 9 on 17 April 459; NMaj. 10 lost; NMaj. 11 on March 460). However, since Sidonius is supposed to have delivered the Panegyric when Majorian reached Lyon in the early winter of 459, I have opted to accept his version.
9. I.e. I do not accept MacGeorge's reasoning for placing the Campanian campaign to the year 457 under some general. Sidonius states in no uncertain terms that the campaign took place after Majorian was declared Augustus on 27 December 457 (Pan. Maj. 5.385–392) and implies that Majorian had been in charge of the ops. in question (5.489). Furthermore, I do not accept Ian Hughes' (2015, 69) view that it was Ricimer as Majorian's *MVM* in 458.

10. The locations and dates of Majorian's novellae: NMaj. 1 at Ravenna on 11 Jan 458; NMaj. 2 at Ravenna on 11 March 458; NMaj. 3 at Ravenna on 8 May 458; NMaj. 4 at Ravenna on 11 July 458; NMaj. 5 at Ravenna on 4 Sept. 458; NMaj. 6 at Ravenna on 26 Oct. 458; NMaj. 7 at Ravenna on 6 Nov. 458; NMaj. 8 The Restoration of the Right to Use Weapons, text lost; NMaj. 9 at Arles on 17 April 459; NMaj. 10 lost; NMaj. 11 at Arles on March 460; NMaj. 12 text lost.

11. In other words, I follow Sidonius' text more closely than Ian Hughes (2015, 69) who places Ricimer in Campania. In my opinion it is preferable to follow Sidonius' text in this case. The above list of novellae which places Majorian at Ravenna throughout the year contains such long periods of time between them that it would have been quite easy for him to march south to defeat the Vandals and then back for example between 11 July and 4 September; even shorter periods of time would have sufficed for the travel.

12. Priscus Blockley ed. frgs 31.1–2; John of Antioch Roberto ed. fr.295; Hyd. a.460; Marius a.460; Ian Hughes (2015, 90–91).

13. I do not believe that Majorian would have been attempting to reach Rome on the double in an effort to influence the powerplay among the major players there as suggested by MacGeorge. It is quite believable that Ricimer could have kept Majorian in the dark if he controlled the information flow from Italy to Gaul as appears likely.

Chapter 4

1. The sources are listed under the individuals named in the PLRE2. I have included direct references to them only when I think that it is necessary for the case or otherwise informative, but I have always included references to the secondary literature if I have used them.

2. Priscus, Blockley ed. frg. 38.1–2, 39.1.

3. Analysis of the possibility that Epirus may have been ruled by Marcellinus in MacGeorge, 42ff.

4. Sources in the PLRE2 Marcellinus 6.

5. E.g. Priscus Blockley frgs. 38.1–2, 39.1, 41.1–2

6. Hydatius actually places the battle in the province of Armorica.

7. Marius uses the word *inter* to denote location between the Loire and Loiret, which could of course mean that the armies would have been deployed along an east–west line or that Aegidius's army would have been deployed further to the west without any possibility of withdrawal across the Loire via the bridge to Orleans. I have opted against these two interpretations because of three objections: 1) if Aegidius's army had been deployed along an east–west line (and would therefore have been small-to-medium sized contrary to what the sources state) it is difficult to see how the Visigoths could have failed to encircle them on their right flank; 2) if Aegidius's army had been deployed further west between the rivers, his army would have been small-to-medium sized contrary to what the sources state and in that case it would be difficult to comprehend why the Visigoths would have attacked Aegidius rather than defeating him through hunger; 3) since Procopius's text makes it clear that in the sixth century one third of the Frankish realm was able to send armies of 100,000 men to Italy, it is difficult to imagine that Aegidius would have had fewer men at his disposal with the regular units, Armoricans, Salian Franks and Alans included. My estimates are actually quite conservative and probably on the low side. As I have repeatedly noted, the city of Bourges alone was able to put to the field a levy of 15,000 men for expeditionary purposes.

8. MacGeorge, 228–31.

9. The chapter is based on Alföldy Chapter 12 and Life of St. Severinus. Readers should note that my version of events differs from Alföldy's reconstruction in that I include material he has left out. This causes changes to the overall picture and to the dating of the events. Regardless, this chapter is heavily indebted to Alföldy's groundbreaking research.

10. For photos, maps and illustrations, see the research paper of Slavcko Ciglenecki available from academia.edu.
11. The sources are listed under the individuals named in the PLRE2. I have included direct references to them only when I think that it is necessary or otherwise informative, but I have always included references to the secondary literature if I have used them.
12. Procop., *Wars* 3.3.22–25.
13. Jord., *Get.* 272–273.

Chapter 5

1. Hughes, 2015, 120–122; PLRE2; Reigns of Majorian and Leo in this book.
2. Hodgkin 3.136 after a letter of Pope Gelasius to the bishops of Dardania in Migne PL 59.74; PLRE2 Severus 19.
3. Hughes, 2015, 122.
4. Hydatius a.466–7; Hughes, 2015, 124.
5. Hydatius a.467; Nestorius, *The Bazaar of Heracleides*, 379; Victor of Vita 1.51; Procop, *Wars* 3.5.22ff.; Hughes, 2015, 123; Syvänne, *Britain in the Age of Arthur*. See also the reign of Leo.
6. Isidorus of Seville 34; Hyd. a.468
7. The following account is based on my analysis of this event in *Britain in the Age of Arthur*, but in such a manner that I have left out those sections which refer to King Arthur. The principal sources are: Jordanes (Get. 237–8); Gregory of Tours (2.18–19), usually thought to be based on lost *Annals of Angers*); sources mentioned in the PLRE2.
8. On the basis of Sidonius's letter to Riothamus (Ep. 3.9) it has been suggested that Riothamus was actually one of the kings of Armorica. This is unlikely because it is contradicted by Jordanes' text. Ian Hughes (2015, 142–3) and others who choose to ignore Jordanes' reference to the sailing are therefore simply ill-informed and their quite obvious intention is just to demonstrate their learning by claiming that the source must be wrong because it is at odds with their preconceived idea of what must have been, which is that Britain cannot have had a loyal Roman commander at this time because that would prove correct those who accept the existence of King Arthur.
9. I analyze this letter and the other letter of Sidonius to Riothamus in detail in my *Britain in the Age of Arthur*.
10. The sources for these events are collected in the PLRE2 with the addition of Theophanes AM 5964.
11. Ian Hughes (2015, 146–7) also includes the other alternative, that it was actually an illness, which Anthemius only suspected to be an attempted poisoning. In my opinion this was needless caution because Romanus would not have dared to attempt the poisoning of Anthemius without the backing of Ricimer. It is unlikely to be a coincidence that Ricimer's enemy Marcellinus died at the hands of an assassin in 468 and that Anthemius was probably poisoned in 470. The only person who could benefit from this was him and nobody else.
12. Armatus was an important East Roman commander. See later.
13. The following discussion of the end of Noricum is based on Alföldy Chapter 12.

Chapter 6

1. The dating of events in the GC 511 is problematic. It (652) dates this even after Ricimer and Gundobad had advanced against Anthemius (650) and after *Comes Gothorum* Gauterit had conquered Pamplona and Zaragosa (651). The problem with this is that on the basis of Isidore it is likely that Pamplona and Zaragosa were already taken in 468, but it is of course possible that the siege of both lasted until ca. 472/3. It is also usual for historians to date Vincentius' campaign in Italy (653) to 473 (e.g. PLRE2 and Hughes, 2015, 167–8), but I would suggest that Helfredus and Vincentius operated in Spain in 473 and that Vincentius'

campaign in Italy should be dated to 474 so that its results would explain why Euric was prepared to negotiate with Nepos.

2. The sources are usefully collected in the FRMG, 233ff.

Chapter 7

1. References to the sources collected in PLRE2 Glycerius, Gundobadus, Nepos.
2. E.g. the PLRE Vidimer 2 dates the invasion of Italy to 473/4.
3. This is an educated guess based on the fact that sources refer only to barbarian troops in Italy when the troops are named.
4. See FRMG, 233ff.
5. The analysis of the loss of Noricum is based on Alföldy chapter 12.

Chapter 8

1. See PLRE2 for the sources.
2. Zachariah 4.1–5.
3. The Arian *Cartadon* are otherwise unknown. One possibility is that they were Vandal captives from Carthage, but that is only a guess of mine.
4. Zachariah 4.1–3; PLRE2 Dionysius. I base the division of the army into two factions on the fact that Zachariah continuously calls the soldiers Romans who were fighting against the people/citizens of Alexandria and that he states that the Romans were also divided into two parties.
5. Zachariah 4.3–9.
6. Zachariah 4.9. Theophanes AM 5951–2.
7. Gordon, p.117ff.; Blockley 1992, 72.
8. See before with Gordon, p.117ff.; Blockley 1992, 72.
9. Priscus (Blockley frgs 40.1–2, 47); Blockley, 1992, 73; Maenchen-helfen, 436–7.
10. If the pillage of Illyricum has been placed in the wrong year by the relatively poor source called *Prosper, Addimenta 4, Auctarium Epitomae Vaticanea 3.11 (MGH AA, Chron. Min. 2, p.492)*, it is possible that it took place now.
11. Priscus, Blockley frgs. 45–48.1; Theophanes AM 5956 and 5961; other sources mentioned in PLRE2 Marcellinus and Severus, and in the chapters that deal with western matters.
12. Sources mentioned in PLRE2 Marcellinus and Severus, and in the chapters that deal with western matters.
13. Priscus, Blockley frgs. 45–48.1.
14. Priscus, Blockley fr.56; John of Antioch fr. 206.2/Roberto fr. 298.7ff. See above.
15. Priscus, Blockley frgs. 45–48.1.
16. Priscus Blockley frgs 42, 48.2 (Evagrius 2.14).
17. See PLRE2 with the text that follows.
18. This is proven by the fact that the emperor Leo was *comes et tribunus* of the Mattiarii and *domesticus* of Aspar before his rise to the throne, and the sources state that Mattiarii were in charge of the Selymbrian Gate of Constantinople with headquarters at Selymbria/Eudoxiopolis. See PLRE2 for the sources.
19. This is the likely alternative. It is probable that Anthemius was indeed in command of these as praesental *MVM* of eastern forces while Aspar was praesental *MVM* of the western forces. Leo appears to have dispatched these eastern contingents with Anthemius to the west when he appointed Anthemius emperor of west. See my *Britain in the Age of Arthur*. There is plenty of circumstantial evidence to support the veracity of the account preserved by Geoffrrey of Monmouth regarding the eastern units in the west.
20. According to the *Strategikon* 12.2.13, the cavalry was to be deployed ten deep when it was deployed with heavy infantry and had over 12,000 horsemen. If there were fewer, then the depth was five. For further details, see Syvänne, 2004.

21. Anthemius was probably praesental MVM and therefore began his journey at Constantinople.
22. The other possibility is that Aspar was in charge of the entire operation and that his name has been carelessly deleted from the extant text at the time he and his sons were killed so that the censor or Priscus himself did not note all of the references to Aspar in the text. However, in light of the other evidence which clearly states that it was Basiliscus who achieved great successes against the Scythians in Thrace at this stage, I would still suggest that the original meaning of the text was the *strategos* of Aspar's forces, Ostrys, under whom served the *hypostrategos* Chelchal.
23. According to Theophanes, Chrysaphius had been responsible for the death of his father and it was because of this that Pulcheria handed Chrysaphius to Jordanes in 450 so that he could avenge his father's death. However, other sources claim that it was Arnegisclus who killed John so that one may assume that it was actually the clique led by Aspar that was behind the murder. In this context it is of note that Anagast/Anagastes is claimed to have started his rebellion in 469 because Jordanes was given the consulship for 470 and that he had been incited to revolt by Ardaburius son of Aspar. It had been Arnegisclus, father of Anagastes, that had killed John, father of Jordanes, and as said, one may suspect that this had been done on behalf of the clique led by Aspar, but it is also possible that both Aspar and Chrysaphius had conspired together and that it was only the latter that was made a scapecoat by Pulcheria in 450 in a situation in which she needed Aspar's support. For the sources, see PLRE2.
24. John Lydus (De Admin. 1.16); Vita St. Daniel Stylites (55); PLRE2 Ardabur, Ioannes the Vandal 13, Iordanes, Zeno.
25. Priscus 41.1–3; Elishe (Thomson ed./tr.) 242–3; al-Biruni 215ff.; Blockley, 1992, 74–5.
26. Chron. Pasch AD 465.'; Blockley, 1992, 74–5 with references to sources.
27. Priscus Blockley frgs.40.1–2, 47; Elishe 242.
28. Priscus Blockley fr. 51.1–2.
29. Sources in PLRE2.
30. For the sources, see Theophanes AM 5963–4; PLRE2 Basiliscus, Heraclius 4. Note however that I interpret the campaign of Heraclius differently so that he would have actually led two campaigns to Tripolitana, the first with a fleet from Constantinople in 468 and the second with land forces together with Marsus/Marsos from Alexandria in 471.
31. Note that I do not agree with the dating given by the PLRE2 for the different military offices held by Zeno and Anagastes from 467 until 470, but follow the dating given by Marcellinus Comes, *Chronicon Paschale* and Theophanes AM 5962. According to Marcellinus Comes, the head of Denzic son of Attila was brought to Constantinople during the consulship of Zeno and Marcian (1 Sept. 468–31 Aug. 469) while according to *Chronicon Paschale* (468), Anagastes, *magister militum per Thraciam*, killed Dinzerich son of Attila, and that his head was brought to Constantinople.
32. Jord. *Get.* 273–4; PLRE2 Marcellinus; Alföldy, *Noricum*, 213ff.; Further references in the western section of this book.
33. Jord, *Get.* 277–79.
34. In other words, I do not date the revolt of Theoderic Strabo to 473 as does Blockley (1982, 78), but rather see it as a continuation of the actions of Ostrys and the reason for the hostility of the Amal Ostrogoths in 473.
35. Sources collected in the PLRE2.
36. Tr. by Blockley, 1982, p.369.
37. The possible barbarian troubles demanding Zeno's appointment include: 1) The Ostrogoths fought against the Suevi in 468/9; 2) The wars of the Ostrogoths against the Sciri, Sarmatians and Suevi if these are to be dated to 469 rather than 471.
38. Priscus Blockley fr. 56–57; Theophanes AM 5962); Vita Daniel St. Stylite 65. The sources are once again collected in the PLRE2. However, contrary to what is stated in the PLRE2 I do not connect the nomination of Zeno as *MVM per Thracias* with the exploit of Anagast

against Dengizich but with the revolt of Anagast, because it is clear that the latter took place in 468 while the revolt took place at the same time as Zeno was nominated to this position.

39. Priscus Blockley fr. 56–57; Theophanes AM 5962); Vita Daniel St. Stylite 65. The sources are once again collected in the PLRE2.

40. The existence of the plot against Leo has needlessly been doubted because it is quite clear that there really existed a power struggle between the Germanic bloc led by the Alan Aspar and the Roman-Isaurian bloc led by Leo and Zeno.

41. This part of the text includes a misleading reference to the Vandal campaign so that Basiliscus would have arrived from that campaign in time to save the capital. In this case Theophanes must have confused the accounts with each other when condensing the material.

42. Theophanes AM 5963–4; other sources in PLRE2. Most of the sources claim that Patricius was killed at the same time as his father, but I am inclined to follow Candidus and Nicephorus Callistus that he survived and was allowed to live. Note that Heraclius conducted two separate campaigns against the Vandals, the first of which was the amphibious landing in Tripolitania in 468 and the second a land campaign from Egypt in 470. As far as I know, the existence of two separate campaigns has not been noted by modern research, which see both to refer to the campaign of 468.

43. The following account of Ostrys and Theoderic Strabo is based on: Malchus Blockley fr. 2; Theophanes AM 5963–4; *Chronicon Paschale* 467; Malalas 14.40–41.

44. PLRE2 Armatus.

45. Note that Blockley does not include in its entirety the fragment 8 of Malchus in his edition of Malchus, because he does not accept the authorship.

46. The sources for these events are collected in the PLRE2 with the addition of Theophanes AM 5964. See also the Western section.

47. References to the sources collected in PLRE2 Glycerius, Gundobadus, Nepos.

48. The location of the island of Iotabe on the 'mouth of the Red Sea' is not known. Many locations have been suggested and some have even suggested that it was not an island at all. See e.g. the indexes in Haarer, Shahid BAFIC, and Arabs and Empires.

Chapter 9

1. Malchus Blockley ed. fr. 8.

2. Procopius, Wars 1.3.8, 12; Joshua the Stylite 9–10; *Chron. Seert* 2.5, Blockley 1992 215 n.30.

3. Does this imply bisexual behaviour in public?

4. Malchus, Blockley ed. frs.5, 6.1, 15; Theophanes AM5970; John of Antioch fr.210, Roberto ed. fr.302.1ff.; ; Blockley, 1992, 79, 213.

5. Negotiations between Zeno and Theoderic in 476 when he was at Novae: Malchus Blockley ed. fr. 15; Ennodius, Pan. 12; Anon. Val. 42/9.42. Wolfram (1990, 270) suggests that Theoderic the Amal moved his Ostrogoths from Macedonia to Lower Moesia on his own initiative in 474–6 and waited for the Roman government to react positively to this by forwarding payments.

6. Malchus Blockley fr. 6.1–2. This Heraclius had previously been in charge of expeditions to Lazica in about 463/4 and to Tripolitana in 468 and 471 so he was not entirely without military abilities. Regardless, it is clear on the basis of Malchus' text that he behaved recklessly in 474 and was therefore probably ambushed.

7. The extant text of John of Antioch actually claims that it was Illus who convinced Basiliscus to revolt, but Roberto's translation of the relevant section (p.511) follows the emendation of Bury (1.391 n.1) that it was Basiliscus who convinced Illus.

8. John of Antioch fr.210, Roberto ed. fr. 302.1ff.

9. Theophanes AM 5967; Chron. Pasch. a.477; Malalas 15.1–3. Bury (1.390–391) has accepted this version of events. he also suggests that Basiliscus was living in retirement at Heraclea, but in my opinion this seems improbable in light of John of Antioch's text.

10. Blockley does not accept Malchus as author of this fragment.

Chapter 10

1. Sources for his reign are collected in the PLRE2. Translations of some of these can be found in Blockley 1983 and Gordon.
2. This is not the famous Hagia Sophia built by Justinian.
3. Does this again imply something about the sex life of the emperor? Was he a gay? And, was it because of this that his young wife Zenonis was so in love with Armatus? Considering the paucity of evidence, it is perhaps best to leave this question unanswered.
4. Life of Daniel the Stylite 70–85; Footnotes and comments of Whitby in Evagrius/Whitby, 137ff.
5. On the basis of this text it has usually been suggested that this Pyrrhus refers to the son of Achilles or to the red colour of the hair, but in my opinion it is inherently more likely that the Pyrrhus' shout was meant as an insult by the populace and referred to the previous battles that Armatus had fought against Theoderic during the reign of Leo. He had clearly obtained Gothic prisoners and had cut off the food supply from the enemy, but had similarly been unable to defeat the Goths decisively.
6. See the previous chapters; Evagrius/Whitby, 142–43.
7. Malchus Blockley ed. fr. 15; Ennodius, Pan. 12; Anon. Val. 42/9.42.
8. It is of course still possible that Trocundes had actually taken the city and imprisoned the bishop, but did not do anything else before the arrival of Zeno's order.
9. Krautschick has suggested that Basiliscus, Verina and Armatus were all related to Onulf and Odoacer on the grounds that a fragment of John of Antioch can on philological grounds be interpreted so that Onulf, Odoacer and Armatus were brothers. If Armatus was Arian, then this would support the claim. However, I am inclined to follow the opinion that does not accept this interpretation because it rests solely on the philological interpretation of the text of John. It would be strange if all of the extant sources failed to point out the barbarian origin of Armatus, Basiliscus and Verina when they point out so many hostile things about their life – one needs to ask this question when one makes such interpretations: why would it have been more suitable for Aspar to enthrone Basiliscus as emperor than his son Patricius in 468? The obvious answer would be that Basiliscus as a Roman was more suitable as a puppet emperor and that it was because of this knowledge that Basiliscus could think Aspar's promise to make him emperor believable. Therefore it is likely that Armatus was actually a Greek pagan possibly from Thessaly, the place of origin of Achilles and his Myrmidons, with the implication that Basiliscus and Verina would also have originated from Thessaly.
10. Nicaea was en route to Pylai where Zeno embarked his forces in ships so it is clear that Malalas has made a mistake.
11. According to a variant version preserved by Evagrius 3.8, Basiliscus and his family were already killed at Cucusus en route to Cappadocia.

Chapter 11

1. Additional sources not specifically mentioned here for all persons and events in the PLRE2.
2. Malchus Blockley ed. fr 15.
3. *Ibid*. fr 15–16.
4. Sources in PLRE2 and Blockley 1992, 80–81. See also the western section.
5. Hodgkin 2.130; Hughes 2015, 201–2; PLRE2.
6. For the sources, see PLRE2. See also the discussion in the western section. For a fuller analysis of Syagrius, see esp. MacGeorge, 111ff. In my opinion one should also include the Briton/British successor state among the Roman successor states that were ruled by Romans, but just as it is with the Kingdom of Soissons, they lacked the means to influence affairs in the south of Gaul or in Italy. Furthermore, they were not considered to be part of the legitimate Roman Empire as envisaged from Constantinople. Therefore I have left a discussion of their political and military history out of this book. For a fuller analysis of the

problem, see my monograph *Britain in the Age of Arthur* in which I argue for the existence of this great man and also for the existence of his successors named in the sources not usually accepted as reliable. I analyze the reliability and problems associated with these sources in detail in the study in question and argue that we should accept those as relatively accurate descriptions of reality because the information in them corresponds with that provided by other sources.

7. Evagrius 3.8–11 with comments of Evagrius/Whitby 143–146 (with further references therein).
8. I have analyzed this in detail in a separate study dealing with Persia.
9. Blockley (1992, 83, 215 n.33) thinks it is probable that the Armenians and Romans supported the Persarmenian revolt on the basis of the name of Hipparchos in Lazar, but this is a mistake. The Hipparchos in question is the Greek title of Hazarabed and not a Roman title. Lazar's account makes it quite clear that at no point in time did the rebels receive help from the Romans side. Towards the end of the revolt they were actually on their way to cross the border in an attempt to obtain it, but in the end did not do so. A fuller analysis can be found in my forthcoming study of the Persarmenian revolt.
10. A fuller discussion of these can be found in my forthcoming analyses of the revolt of Vahan Mamikonean and biography of Peroz.
11. Malchus Blockley ed. fr. 4; Suda/Suidas a.3968; Candidus Blockley fr. 1. 60ff.; and PLRE2 Armatus, Onoulphus for further sources. Onulf had a colourful career. According to one version he was a brother of Odovacar and son of Edeco which means he was a Hun, while another version claims that he was the son of a Thuringian father and a Scirian mother. In the 460s Onulf and Edeco led a group of Sciri against the Pannonian Ostrogoths but were defeated (see above). After this Onulf sought service in Constantinople, where he lived in poverty until Armatus took him in as a protégé. Armatus had him appointed first as *comes* presumably in his own forces and then as *MVM per Illyricum* in about 477. Onulf served in this capacity at least until 479 after which he became probably *magister militum vacans*. Then he went to Italy where he served as commander of his brother Odovacar's army when they defeated the Rugians in 488. When his brother was then murdered in 493, he fled to a church but was killed anyway.
12. Sources in PLRE2. In my opinion the references to the Pyrrhus son of Achilles or to the reddish colour of the beard mentioned in the sources are less likely than the double meaning implying Pyrrhic victories.
13. Malchus Blockley ed. fr. 17 with the PLRE2.
14. John of Antioch fr.211, Roberto ed. 303.1ff. with the sources mentioned in the PLRE2.
15. Malchus frg. 18.1–2.
16. John of Antioch fr.211.1–2, Roberto ed. 303.6ff.
17. Malchus Blockley ed. frg. 18.2, 18.3.32ff.
18. *Ibid*. frg. 18.2.1–11.
19. *Ibid*. frg 18.2, frg.20.164ff.
20. *Ibid*. frg 18.2–3.
21. *Ibid*. frg 18.2–3; Anon. Val. 9.42.
22. Malchus Blockley ed. frg. 18.3.
23. Plural of the Greek *nomisma*, the Greek equivalent of the Latin *solidus* (gold coin).
24. Malchus Blockley ed. frg. 18.3–4. In military theory the *moira* meant a unit of 2,000–3,000 men, but it is uncertain whether this was meant in this case.
25. Malchus Blockley ed. fr. 18.4. Note that the pay and food for 13,000 men is unlikely to mean the entire armed strength of Strabo. Rather it is likely that these 13,000 men were Strabo's personal retinue and that most if not all of them would also have had squires that should be added to the armed strength. Furthermore, since we speak of tribal forces with families, it is clear that there were also other men who are not included in the figure.

26. Malchus Blockley ed. fr. 20.1–19.
27. *Ibid*. fr. 20.20–62.
28. *Ibid*. fr. 20.63–120.
29. *Ibid*. fr. 20.121–157 with Blockley comment on p.461.
30. *Ibid*. fr. 20.137–157.
31. *Ibid*. frg. 20.158–257.
32. *Ibid*. frg. 20.258–274.
33. The principal sources are: Candidus (Blockley ed. 1.96ff.), John of Antioch fr.211.3–4 (Roberto ed.303.48ff.); Evagrius 3.26; Theophanes AM 5971–5972 together with Gordon (p.149–150). The PLRE 2 Fl. Marcianus 17 lists these and other sources and summarises his career. See also PLRE Anthemius Procopius 9 and Romulus.
34. The location has been identified differently by different historians. Some place it just north of the Palace while others place it just north of the Circus.
35. John of Antioch fr.211.4 Roberto ed. 303.65ff.; Sources collected in PLRE2 Aetius4, Dionysius 10, Epinicus, Marcianus17, Thraustila2, Trocundes. Dionysius was in office after May but was no longer in office in December 480.
36. John of Antioch fr. 211.4, (Roberto ed. 303.58ff.; Gordon 149ff.,); Marcellinus 479–81.
37. John of Antioch fr. 211.4–5, fr. 213 (Roberto ed. 303.58ff., 305; Gordon 149ff., 180ff.); Evagrius 3.25; Theophanes AM5970.
38. The location is not known to the *Barrington Atlas*, but according to Heather (156, 163) it is located between Philippi and Maximianopolis in Macedonia.
39. John of Antioch fr. 211.5; Jodanes Rom. 346; Evagrius 3.25; Theophanes AM5970; Marcellinus 480/1. Sources are once again collected in PLRE2 Theodericus 5; Recitach.
40. Sources for the murder of Nepos collected in PLRE2 Glycerius, Nepos, Ovida, Odoacer, Viator. The various alternatives in the following narrative result from the differences in the sources. The evidence is very poor and sometimes contradictory.
41. John of Antioch fr. 211.4, fr. 213 (Roberto ed. 303.58ff., 305; Gordon 149ff.); Marcellinus 479–481; PLRE2 Sabinianus Magnus, Iohannes Scytha 34, Moschianus1.
42. John of Antioch fr. 213 (Roberto ed. 305); Marcellinus 481/2.
43. Theophanes AM5972; Evagrius 3.27; Malalas 15.13; Joshua the Stylite 13. For other sources, see also PLRE2.
44. If this *spatharius* belonged to the Palace *cubicularii* then one might assume that Zeno was actually playing on both sides of the fence so that he prevented the actual murder while still claiming to condone it to his wife, but this is not as likely as the other version mentioned in the text.
45. For a fuller analysis of the *scholarii*, see Frank, Syvänne (esp. *MHLR* vol.1, 2015) and Jones. For the *spatharii*, see Frank and Jones. For the *bucellarii*, see Syvänne (2004) with Jones.
46. Marcellinus 482/3; Jord. Get. 289; John of Antioch fr.214.3 (Roberto ed. 30619ff.); Lazar p.234; Gordon p.181. For other sources, see PLRE2 Theodericus 7; Recitach.
47. The principal sources for this chapter are: John of Antioch fr.214 (Roberto ed. fr. 303); Joshua the Stylite 14–17; Theophanes AM 5972–76; Evagrius 3.16, 27. Other sources collected in PLRE2 Conon 4, Illus1, Leontius 17 and under other names mentioned in this chapter. There are some contradictions in the sources, the most important of which is the nature of Leontius' usurpation and connection with Illus. In the following discussion I have adopted the standard consensus interpretation which is that Leontius was dispatched by Zeno against Illus and that Illus just corrupted the man with promises.
48. See e.g. Bury 1.396–399.
49. Zachariah 5.6–7; Evagrius 3.12–13; Evagrius/Whitby, 145–6.
50. Zachariah 5.6–7; Evagrius 3.12–16; Evagrius/Whitby146–150.
51. Zachariah 5.6–7; Evagrius 3.12–16; Evagrius/Whitby146–150; Hodgkin 2.143–145.
52. Zachariah 5.10–12, 6.1; Evagrius 3.16–18; Evagrius/Whitby 150–54.

53. Evagrius 3.18; Evagrius/Whitby, 153–4.
54. Evagrius 3.3.19–21; Evagrius/Whitby, 154–59; Hodgkin 2.143–146.
55. The PLRE2 dates the demand to release Longinus to 483, but other historians (e.g. Gordon, p.152) date it to 484. The former date is likely in light of the date of the death of Peroz.
56. For other variants of this name, see PLRE2 Lilingis.
57. In addition to the names in the PLRE2 and sources given above, see PLRE2 Conon, Lilingis, Leontius 17.
58. See e.g. Bury 1.398–9.
59. Gordon's translation on page 181 of the relevant fragment is incorrect. This John was a commander who had fought against Basiliscus (*Iôannes ho kata Basiliskon* or *Iôannes ton kata Basiliskon*) who is likely to be the usurper. See PLRE2 Ioannes 33 with Roberto ed. and tr.
60. *Sacellarius* was the Keeper of the Privy Purse. This office appears for the first time under Zeno. See Jones, 567–8. See also PLRE 2 Ioannes 33, Paulus 25. This John is not to be confused with John the Scythian who was in charge of land operations.
61. Joshua the Stylite 15–17 with the comments of Trombley and Watt 14–15; PLRE2 Leontius 17.
62. Or that the two men were sent as envoys to Zeno by Illus as suggested by the PLRE2.
63. For the sources, see the lists in the PLRE2.
64. For the siege, see in particular John of Antioch fr.214.5–12, Roberto ed. fr.304.25ff.; Theophanes AM5976–5980; Marcellinus 484/485–488; Malalas 15.13–14. For the different men named Longinus in the sources, see PLRE2.
65. Sources listed in PLRE2 Longinus 5.
66. Shahid, 115–119.
67. Zachariah 6.2–4; Evagrius 3.22; Evagrius/Whitby, 157–8.
68. Zachariah 6.4–7; Evagrius 3.23; Evagrius/Whitby, 158–160.
69. Ennodius Pan. 19–22; Marcellinus 486/487; Malalas 15.9; John of Antioch fr. 214.7–8 (Gordon, 181–82) Roberto ed. 306.54ff.; Jordanes *Get.* 290; Anon. Val. 2.48; Eustathius fr. 4 with other sources mentioned in PLRE2.
70. It is of course possible that John of Antioch has confused the evidence completely so that it was actually the Rugians who were planning to ally themselves with Theoderic and that Odoacer really performed a favour for Zeno when he destroyed the Rugians. A subsequent alliance between Fredericus and Theoderic could be taken as evidence of this, but there is no concrete evidence for this. Therefore, I have here given the version as presented by the sources.
71. These same events are detailed in many previous works of history, the most recent of which is probably that by Ian Hughes (2015, 208). For references to other sources than mentioned in the text, see Hughes and PLRE2.
72. This and the following are based on the reconstructions of Hughes (2015, 212–13), Wolfram (1990, 278–9), PLRE2 and the original sources mentioned therein.
73. Wolfram (1990, 279); Heather (164); Hodgkin 182–3; Haase (71) collects the various views. The suggestion of Pallmann has the advantage of being closest to the other figures given in the ancient sources.
74. Syvänne, *MHLR* Vol.1, 232.
75. It is clear that all of the retainers had servants/squires to take care of their extra horses, but I have here made the educated guess that only a third of those would have been used for combat duty.
76. The traditional way to interpret the evidence in Procopius is to dismiss all of the larger figures in his text by proving them false with the smaller armies in his text. As is obvious, this is ridiculous. The source is either reliable or it is not. However, the principal points against this way of interpreting the evidence are actually the following: The besieging of Rome with its very long walls required a huge army to be effective; Belisarius' army was actually not as

small as it appears at first sight in Procopius because in truth it also included marines and local citizen militia and not only his field army carried on ships; Procopius was an eyewitness to the events; fourthly, it is ridiculous to attempt to prove the references to the use of sizable field armies false on the basis of the references to smaller armies because in truth armies have always fielded forces of various sizes from squads and companies all the way up to large army corps and armies. See also *MHLR* Vol.6 (518–565).

77. The principal sources for this are: *MGH AA IX* (*Chronica Minora Volumen I*), pp.316–22 (includes *Anonymi Valesiani pars posterior; Fasti Vindobones priores; Paschale Campanum; Prosperi continuation Havniensis* which is also known as *Auctarium Prosperi Hauniensis* sited either as *ordo prior* or *ordo posterior*; Agnellus); Ennodius, *Panegyric of Theoderic* and *Vita Epiphanius; Annales Ravennates*, Paulus Diaconus, *Historia Romana* 15.13ff.; John of Antioch fr. 214; Jordanes, *Rom.* and *Get.* For earlier or later careers of Odoacer and Theoderic see also *MGH AA IX* (*Chronica Minora Volumen I*), pp.305–16 and 322ff. For other sources, see the PLRE2. The core events are well known and have been reconstructed quite adequately by several historians which include many others besides the following examples: Hodgkin 3.177ff.; Wolfram (1990, 278ff.); Heather (216ff.); Hughes (2015, 212ff.); Haase, 41ff. (a commentary of the Panegyric which summarises the evidence and different interpretations adopted by modern historians). The following account is in most of its details the same as their account because we all use the same meagre sources. Consequently I will include specific references to the sources or to the maps only when I attempt to go beyond what is found in them or when I feel that this would be otherwise beneficial. This concerns in particular the battles and their locales, which I have tried to reconstruct in as much detail as possible.

78. See the earlier discussion of the likely composition of these tribes in this volume and in *MHLR* volume 3. It is also likely that most of the Heruls under Odoacer consisted of both East and West Heruls because the West Romans had access to both. Among the West Heruls the role of infantry appears to have been greater on the basis of the fact that the Romans had infantry units drawn from the Heruls (e.g. *auxilia palatina Heruli seniores* and *iuniores*) and used Herulian infantry swords (for this, see, Syvänne 2004). It is probable that Odoacer had brought at least some of these Herulian *foederati* (and possibly also 'regular' *auxilia palatina* units) from Gaul when he fought there as a mercenary adventurer and then added to their strength the East Heruls together with the Sciri, Torcilingi and Rugians when he was in Noricum where he met St. Severinus in about 469/70. It is possible that his units included some remnants of the Saxons with whom he had previously fought in Gaul.

79. Note the numbers of men maintained in republican-era Rome, the vast numbers of tribal warriors settled in Italy by the emperors during the third and fourth centuries, the numbers of regulars in the *Notitia Dignitatum*, and the large numbers of citizen soldiers (militias) maintained by the Italian city states before the introduction of the *condottieri* system. The evidence for the ability of Italy to maintain vast numbers of *foederati* on their soil is overwhelming.

80. In the siege of Rome, the Ostrogoths were deployed in separate camps all around the city so that each separate army consisted of far fewer men than when the entire nation was deployed for combat as it was under Theoderic.

81. See the Appendix and reign of Anastasius for an analysis of Urbicius' military treatises.

82. The other alternative is that Theoderic posted his first cavalry line in front of the wagon laager as he had done at the battle of River Ulca, but in this case I think it is preferable to interpret the legions of Ennodius literally so that Theoderic had posted his infantry in front of the camp.

83. The Burgundian invasion: Paulus Diaconus, *Historia Romana* 15.17; Ennodius, *Pan.* 54, *Vita Epiph.* 138–178; Hodgkin 3.201; Haase, 81.

84. This is my theory, not included in the sources mentioned.

85. See Hodgkin 3.203–4; Haase, 77–8.
86. English translations of John of Antioch by Hodgkin 3.212.
87. For other sources, see PLRE2 Theodorus 33.

Chapter 12

1. The following analysis of the reign of Anastasius I is largely based on the excellent biography of him by F.K. Haarer who also includes a valuable discussion of the sources in the Appendix A–B. However, I have enlarged Haarer's material with specifically military material and in these places I have referred solely to the sources. This concerns in particular the analysis of the military tactics and Urbicius' *Taktikon* and *Epitedeuma*, which Haarer fails to analyze, and with the analysis of tactical details of various battles. Sources for Anastasius I and others can once again be found in the PLRE2, but this list is enlarged by Haarer, and also by me with the discussion of Urbicius.

2. Haarer (1ff.) provides an analysis of the circumstances and ceremonies associated with the nomination based on Constantinus Prophyrogenitus (*de Cer.* 1.92) and other sources, and this discussion is based on it but does not follow slavishly Haarer's analysis. The sources can be found in Haarer or the PLRE2.

3. It is possible that Flavius Strategius, who is known to have occupied this position in 497, was already in this office, but this is not known. I would also identify the PLRE2 Strategius 8 and 9 with each other so that he would have subsequently been promoted to become a consul and honorary *MVM* under Anastasius and *patricius* under Justin I. Strategius was a native of Oxyrhynchus in Egypt and a member of the Apion family. This is important for another reason which is that it is known that Anastasius had visited Egypt either as a result of a shipwreck (Theophanes AM 5984) or being exiled there by Zeno (John of Nikiu 89.2–17), and had struck a friendship with the bishop John the Tabennesiote at some point (Victor Tonnensis a.494). See PLRE2 Anastasius 4. This suggests a possibility that Anastasius had formed a friendship with this Egyptian and that this played a role in what followed, but that is of course merely a speculation on my part.

4. Here we have another Egyptian promoted by Anastasius, which does lend support for the above speculation of mine that Anastasius had formed really good relationships with a number of Egyptians and that these connections played a part in the events.

5. John of Antioch 214b (Roberto ed. fr. 308); Malalas 15.3; Theophanes AM 5984–5985; PLRE2 for the individuals and sources; Haarer 23–4.

6. My analysis of the riot differs from that adopted by Haarer.

7. In my opinion Haarer has needlessly given the alternative that the Isaurians left of their own free will from Constantinople in a situation in which they could expect to be punished. Some may have done that but at the same time it is clear on the basis of confiscations of property that the intention was from the start to expel all Isaurians and to confiscate their property so that it could be used to bribe/reward Anastasius' supporters and finance the war against the Isaurians. Theophanes AM 5984–5 divides the expulsion of the Isaurians into two years. Firstly, he states that Longinus brother of Zeno attempted to usurp power immediately after Anastasius had been nominated in 491 and was then exiled to Egypt, and that he also exiled the *magister* Longinus at the same. Theophanes then claims that next year in 492 Anastasius expelled all Isaurians from Constantinople, because of their outrages. When they reached Isauria, the *ex-magister* Longinus assembled them and other barbarians and bandits. However, the other alternative in which Conon and Lilingis began the revolt immediately in Isauria after which all of the Isaurians were expelled from Constantinople, appears likelier.

8. The PLRE2 Iustinus 4 suggests that Justin joined the *Excubitores* during the reign of Leo and served as *comes rei militaris* during Isaurian war of 492–8. I would rather suggest that he was appointed *Comes Excubitorum* in 491.

9. Haarer, 213–16.
10. John of Antioch 214b (Roberto ed. fr. 308); Malalas 16.3; Theophanes AM 5985–8; Jord. *Rom*. 355; Theod. Lect. 449ff.; Marcellinus a.492; Evagrius 3.35; Prisc. Pan. 52–60, 103–117; Zonaras 14.3.22 (PG 1215–6).
11. The PLRE2 and Haarer (24) both suggest that John the Scythian would have held the position of *MVM per Orientem*, but in light of the fact that the army was drawn from the Balkans, I would suggest that he was actually *MVM per Thracias* or *MVM praesentalis*. There is actually still another possibility, which is that he was *MVM per Illyricum*, because Anastasius addressed a law to Ioannes who had this title. The PLRE2 Ioannes 40 claims that he is not to be identified with either Ioannes Scytha 34 or Ionnes Gibbus 93, but possibly rather with Ioannes 60 (*MVM Praesentalis* in 514–5). However, I am not quite as certain about this. The sources do sometimes use Illyricum and Thrace interchangeably so that in my opinion it is possible that John the Scythian could actually have been *MVM per Illyricum*, but I would still suggest that in this case he was *MVM per Thracias* or *MVM praesentalis* on the basis of what the sources state.
12. The Battle of Cotyaeum in 492: Malalas 16.3; Marcellinus a.492; John of Antioch fr. 214b (Roberto ed. fr.308.40ff.); Theophanes AM 5985; Theod. Lect. 449; Evagrius 3.35; Jord. Rom. 355 Procopius, *Anecdota* 5.38.4ff. Theophanes calls Diogenianus with the name Diogenes, which to me makes it possible that we should actually identify him with the PLRE2 Diogenes 7. He was subsequently appointed *MVM per Orientem* by Justin I in about 518–520, but after this Isaurian war he was exiled by Anastasius for unknown reasons. The Huns would have consisted of those who had been settled in Scythia during the reign of Marcian, while the Goths consisted of those who had remained behind in Thrace somewhere near the capital when Theoderic the Amal marched to Italy in 488.
13. For these later instances, see Syvänne, *Excubitores*.
14. The figures are calculated so that each cavalry *vexillatio* in the ND is estimated at 500 men, each legion as 2,000 men and each *auxilia palatina* as 1,000 men.
15. See the problems in dating in Haarer, 25.
16. Marcellinus a.491–2; Malalas 16.3.
17. The PLRE2 notes that Malalas calls him such in the context of the Isaurian War, but the date and circumstances when he received him are not known. The PLRE2 suggests that it was actually after his recall from exile (Anastasius exiled him, Apion, and Philoxenus at some unknown point in time) that he received the title.
18. Malalas 16.3; Theophanes AM 5986.
19. [Pseudo-]Joshua the Stylite (20–24) with the comments of Trombley & Watt; Haarer, 31, 42; Shahid, BAFIC 120;
20. Theophanes AM 5987; Theod Lect. 449 PG p.187; Evagrius 3.35.
21. Haarer 25, 136–8.
22. It should be noted that it is possible that one of the Athenodori was called Theodorus.
23. Leo, *Naumachia* (10th century) 19.57; Syrianus Magister, *Naumachica* 12 (6th century). For the naval battle between Constantine the Great and Licinius see *MHLR* Vol.1. See also Syvänne, *East Roman Naval Warfare and Military Treatises*, forthcoming in 2020.
24. Evagrius 3.35; Prisc. Pan. 171–3; Haarer 26–7. This is precisely the same strategy that was later adopted by none other than Joseph Stalin to subdue any opposition to his rule, namely the massed deportations of people in conjunction with the use of violence and terror to subdue any pockets of resistance. The basic principle is the same as was also followed by the British during the Boer Wars, namely the elimination of support provided by civilians to the guerrillas. In South Africa the civilians were isolated in concentration camps, while in Isauria or the modern day Soviet Union civilians were deported to new lands. Both methods removed the civilian support from the picture. See Syvänne, 2004.
25. See above with Haarer, 80–2.

26. See above with Haarer, 89–90, 130–31.
27. See Haarer, 73–91, 131–35.
28. Haarer, 202–206.
29. Haarer, 194–199.
30. Haarer, 185–222.
31. Haarer, 190–193.
32. Cyril of Scythopolis, *Vita Abrahamii* 1; Joshua the Stylite 20ff.; Shahid BAFIC 120; Haarer, 31.
33. The Persarmenian revolt must have taken place after the Isaurians had revolted against Anastasius I because Kavadh made his demand of tribute payments after he had heard of it (Joshua 23).
34. I would suggest that we should identify this Eugenius (PLRE2 Eugenius 5 with the title of dux *Euphratensis*) with the commander of the Armenian forces in 502 also called Eugenius as is suggested by the PLRE2 (PLRE2 Eugenius 6, *dux utriusque Armeniae*) rather than consider them separate persons. If this Eugenius was the *dux utriusque Armeniae* already in 498 then he would have advanced from Armenia to the scene of operations, but it is of course possible that he had merely been transferred to the Armenian command after the events of 498 or after the fall of Theodosiopolis, and in fact if Bithrapsa is to be identified as Resafa/Rusafa/Sergiopolis, then it is actually preferable to think that he commanded forces in Euphratesia.
35. For a fuller discussion of the various alternatives of identifying the different Arabic chieftains mentioned above, see Edwell et al., 219ff.
36. Analysis provided in the following pages.
37. For a fuller discussion of the various alternatives of identifying the different Arabic chieftains mentioned above, see Edwell et al., 219ff. , Haarer (33ff.), and Greatrex (1998, 78).
38. Haarer 33ff.; Shahid BAFIC 120ff.; Rubin et al. 219ff.
39. Haarer, 42–47.
40. Haarer, 40–42; Rubin, 2015, 147, 155–6.
41. For earlies examples, see my *Caracalla*, *MHLR* vols. 1–3 and *Bahram V Gur*. I have also discussed this in research papers at ASMEA and Annapolis, which I will upload online at academia.edu at some point in the future.
42. This war has been studied in great detail by Greatrex (1998, 79ff.) and the following is based on this outstanding study, but it should still be noted that I depart from his conclusions in several places. References to the original sources can be found in it and in the PLRE2. See also Rubin et al. 219ff.; Haarer, 47ff.; Shahid BAFIC 120ff. I will add references to the original sources with additional analysis only if it is at variance with these (and in many places it is) or if I think that it adds something new and valuable or just 'drama' to the discussion or analysis. The principal original sources for this war are: Joshua the Stylite; Zachariah of Mitylene; Procopius (*Wars* and *de Aedificiis*); Theophanes. The REF2 has also collected a significant portion of these as translations.
43. The identification of these tribes is not secure, but it is usually thought that the Kadishaye/Cadusii/Kadisenoi occupied places by Singara and Thebatha near Dara while the Tamuraye were an Iranian mountain tribe. The Cadusii/Kadisenoi may actually have lived in several places because some of them almost certainly lived on the south-west coast of the Caspian Sea.
44. Joshua the Stylite 50 with the comments of Trombley and Watt.
45. See above his exploits as *dux* of Euphratesia or as *dux* of the Armenias in 498. He was one of the best commanders of his age, but his services clearly went unappreciated by the Emperor despite the high praises preserved e.g. by Theophanes. According to Joshua 51, Eugenius had brought his forces down presumably from Armenia to the scene of operations, but it is possible that he had remained in the area after 498 if he had not been *dux* of Euphratesia but the *dux* of the Armenias as I have already suggested. In other words, it is possible that he

had all along been in command of the Armenian forces at least from 498 onwards and that he had been posted in the Euphratesia/Mesopotamia region because of the threat posed by the Arabs. After all, we should not forget that the forces of Arethas had raided the Palestines in 501 and that Anastasius had concluded his treaty with Arethas in 502, the same year as the Persian invasion. It is easy to see why Eugenius could have been deployed further south in such a situation and why Roman Armenia then lacked adequate forces to protect Theodosiopolis/Erzurum.

46. The inclusion of the origin of the archimandrite/hegumen was meant to imply possible guilt but none of the sources actually claim that he was the culprit. Joshua the Stylite (53) mentions the accusation, but clearly did not believe it.

47. Hamilton & Brooks in their translation suggest an aqueduct, but Trombley & Watt and Greatrex are surely correct to say that this was a stream as stated by Procopius. It is therefore possible that Trombley & Watt (p.60–61) are correct to state that the stream through the wall was a sewer, but one still cannot entirely preclude the possibility that the underground stream could have been an aqueduct because aqueducts were also built underground.

48. Procopius (*Wars* 1.7.20ff.) provides a slightly different version, but I would suggest that Zachariah's more detailed account is to be preferred in this case. According to Procopius, one of the Persians had found the underground opening for the stream close to one of the towers and brought the ruler with a few men and ladders to the scene on the following night. The monks guarding the tower were all fast asleep as they had celebrated some annual religious festival with wine and food. When the Persians entered the passage and found all the monks asleep, they killed the lot and informed Kavadh who then brought the ladders against the wall. It was now already day and this was observed by those in charge of the nearest tower. They sounded the alarm and ran to the scene.

49. Zachariah 7.4; Procop. *Wars* 1.7.20ff.; Greatrex, 1998, 91–2.

50. Does this imply that he was a retired war veteran or was he just a militiaman with enough money to buy armour? On the basis of the information provided by Zachariah, Joshua and Procopius, he would seem to belong to the latter category, but one cannot entirely rule out the other alternative.

51. Zachariah 7.4; Procop. *Wars* 1.7.20ff.; Greatrex, 1998, 91–2.

52. Procopius, Wars 1.7.33 claims a garrison of 1,000 but the figure of Zachariah is more likely.

53. Greatrex 1998, 93 with the sources mentioned before.

54. According to Trombley & Watt, a presbyter who supervised churches in the *territorius* of a city.

55. Joshua 54.

56. See e.g. the discussion of Mango & Scott in their commentary of Theophanes, p.148.

57. The title in Trombley & Watt, p.77. n.367.

58. Regardless, it is still clear that Areobindus should no longer be considered to have been a mere barbarian Goth as is noted by Mango & Scott in their commentary of Theophanes on p.147. Areobindus was the great-grandson of Aspar (consul 434), grandson of Areobindus (consul 434) and Ardaburius (consul 447), and son of Dagalaiphos (consul 461). He was married to Anicia Julian, daughter of the emperor Olybrius. His son was Olybrius (consul in 491 ahead of his father). He was clearly a member of the Constantinopolitan aristocracy at this time despite his Gothic descent.

59. E.g. PLRE2 Patriciolus; Trombley & Watt (64–5). For the career of Hypatius, see Greatrex, 1996.

60. See Joshua 54ff. with the comments of Trombley & Watt.

61. E.g. Trombley & Watt, p.65 n.310.

62. He was the gifted commander who had previously captured Iotabe as *dux Palestinae*.

63. Joshua 55–6; Theophanes AM 5997; Zachariah 7.5.

64. See also the comments of Trombley & Watt in their translation of Joshua the Stylite 56. Zachariah 7.5 places this event after the battle of Opadna/Apadna, but this is clearly a mistake unless it refers to the general activities of Pharesmanes.
65. Note however that my reconstruction differs from that adopted by Greatrex (1998, 99–100) in that I include from Zachariah also the raiding of Arzanene by Patricius and Nisibis by Hypatius and Areobindus.
66. Distance by Trombley & Watt in their commentary of Joshua 57.
67. Malalas 16.9 claims that in the battle between the Romans and Persians many died on both sides, but this is clearly a mistake unless it refers to this war in general and is not included in the discussion.
68. According to Trombley & Watt, the fortress was also called Sifrios or Isfrios, but that its location is unknown. However, Greatrex (1995, 95) on the basis of Procopius identifies it with the place from which Patricius and Hypatius had advanced into the battle of Apadna and places it north-west of Apadna.
69. PLRE 2 Apion 2, Hypatius 6; Theophanes AM5998; Malalas 16.9.
70. Joshua 58 with the notes of Trombley & Watt (esp. n.341). The swelling of al-Numan's head has a logical explanation. He had previously been hit in the head, which had clearly weakened some vein which burst when al-Numan became enraged, but this was certainly a story that strengthened the Christian faith in the area. It is not known how the change in the tribal leadership affected the combat performance of the Lakhmids. What is certain is that morale cannot have been as high as it would have been under al-Numan or under another member of the dynasty.
71. Contantina/Constantia/Tella would have been the HQ of *dux* of Mesopotamia Olympius (see above) as is noted by Greatrex (1998, 101), which in my opinion probably means that he was accompanying one of the field armies that had been defeated, or that he had united his forces with some other *dux* for the purpose of protecting some other sector of the frontier, or alternatively that he had already been dispatched as an envoy to negotiate with the Persians. The Persians did not allow him to return after his mission so he became a hostage, but he died of illness before the Roman captives were returned. See later.
72. Joshua 59.
73. Joshua 59–60; Greatrex, 1998, 104; Trombley & Watt, 76.
74. Joshua 61.
75. I agree with Greatrex (1998, 106) that it would seem very doubtful that none of the defenders died. However, stranger things have happened in history so I guess we just have to accept the statement as accurate.
76. Joshua 64–5.
77. For the sources, see PLRE2.
78. Joshua 64.
79. Greatrex, 1998, 107. Trombley & Watt (p.102, n.502) date this raid to 509 on the basis of the dating in the source Cyril of Scythopolis (dates it to 1 Sept. 508–31 Aug. 509 and 8 Jan. 509 – 7 Jan. 510), which is therefore quite possible. This would mean that al-Mundhir would have broken the subsequent seven year peace with this raid. However, I have here included this raid in this location as suggested by Greatrex because Cyril's datings are not certain. However, I have included it in the later discussion because Cyril's dating may coincide with the information provided by Procopius of the events after the conclusion of the peace in 506.
80. Joshua 66 with the comments of Trombley & Watt.
81. This same question is also analyzed in the book dealing with fifth century Persia by Katarzyna Maksyiuk and Ilkka Syvänne.
82. Joshua 66 with the comments of Trombley & Watt. Joshua's account leaves out details, as is noted by Trombley & Watt, but it is quite easy to reconstruct them from the place names and details that he provides. Furthermore, it is clear that he did not abandon the siege of Amida

when he advanced against the Persian supply column because the forces he used against the convoy clearly consisted of cavalry.

83. Joshua 67–8 with comments of Trombley & Watt. For cynical uses of religious miracles, see my *MHLR* vol.1 and research paper dealing with Holy War presented at ASMEA in 2016.
84. See *MHLR* Vol.1 for a detailed map of this mountain.
85. Greatrex, 1998, 110–11.
86. Joshua 69; Greatrex, 1998, 110–11.
87. See the comments of Trombley & Watt who note that Ald was a *comes/tribounos* of one of the provincial *numeri* serving under Timostratus, which means that this event took place after the arrival of Celer.
88. Or actually like most Western militaries, including the Finnish one.
89. Joshua 71 with the comments of Trombley & Watt.
90. Joshua 73ff.
91. Joshua 74–5.
92. Joshua 75 with the comments of Trombley & Watt.
93. I analyze the circumstances of this defection in greater detail in a separate study dealing with Vahan Mamikonean, but here it suffices to say that it is probable that Mushleg defected because he had not been chosen as successor of Vahan as *marzban* of Armenia. The Persians had nominated his brother as *marzban*.
94. Joshua 75 with the comments of Trombley & Watt.
95. At a later time, the Mamikoneans also possessed domains inside Roman territory, but it is uncertain whether this was already the case. However, it is certain that Mushleg was given lands now.
96. See *MHLR* Vol.3.
97. Theophanes (AM 5998); Greatrex, 1998, 113.
98. For additional details of his career and sources, see PLRE2 Celer2.
99. Zachariah's source was none other than this fellow himself. Procopius *Wars* 1.9.5ff. has a different version according to which the general who ambushed Glon was Patricius, but in this case it seems preferable to accept Zachariah's version because it came from the eyewitness. It is of course possible that Zachariah could have invented this detail and that his source could have confused matters or exaggerated the number of enemies killed and so forth, but it is still clear that with the exception of the enlarged role of Pharesmanes in the events Zachariah's details are more believable than those of Procopius. However, I still include Procopius' version here because one cannot be certain. According to Procopius (*Wars* 1.7.33), Glon had only 1,000 men to act as his garrison (even with servants/squires clearly too small a figure for Amida). He claims that a Roman hunter suggested to Patricius that he could deliver Glones with 200 men into his hands. Patricius accepted the suggestion so the man approached Glones as if he was a victim of Roman violence. He claimed that there was some wild game nearby that the Persians could capture. Glones agreed to his suggestion, and to his suggestion that a hunter would first reconnoitre the situation. The hunter then approached Patricius who sent him with two of his bodyguards and 1,000 men (one could think that one of these was Pharesmanes with 500 men) which were concealed in a village called Thilasamon 40 stades from Amida. After this the hunter went back to Glon and said that everything was ready. So the Persians went out and were ambused by the Romans. When the son of Glones then learnt of this, he torched the sanctuary of Symeon. In short, it appears more likely that Zachariah's account is more accurate in particular because Pharesmanes was subsequently promoted as the second *magister militum praesentalis* in 505. The office was left unfilled after the sacking of Hypatius presumably because he had lost so many men and it took time to fill up the ranks as is suggested by Trombley & Watt (p.108). As a foreigner Pharesmanes must have performed some outstanding feats to achieve this promotion.
100. Joshua 76; Zachariah 7.5.

101. This account is based on Joshua, Zachariah, Theophanes and Greatrex, 1998, 114ff. Further references to the sources can be found in Greatrex and PLRE2.
102. Joshua 80 with the comments of Trombley & Watt; Greatrex, 1998, 114–5.
103. *Ibid*. If Celer had ordered Nonnosus away because of superstitious beliefs the whole thing was extremely silly because a good commander should have been able to give his oath and then betray it if it served his interest just as for example Caracalla did. However, I would suggest that in this case it is very unlikely that Celer would have been forced to resort to such ingenious trickery because he feared to break his oath. Rather, since he was known for his intellect and learning, he just wanted to maintain the public pretence that he had not gone back on his word.
104. Joshua 81; Zachariah 7.5; Greatrex, 1998, 115ff.
105. See e.g. the comments of Theophanes AM 5998 who praises this decision. It was cheaper to pay the Persians than face a revolt. For the revolt of 602 see my *The Age of Hipptoxotai* with the *MHLR* Vol.7.
106. It is probable that the rebuilding and building of walls had started immediately after it had been recaptured.
107. Located between Zeugma and Hierapolis (i.e. not the famous Dura-Europos).
108. Joshua 88 places the appointment of Pharesmanes after his stay at Apameia, but it is clear that he had at least the de facto command of the remnants of Hypatius' force after he had been recalled even if it is possible that he received the official title only after having commanded these forces for almost two years. See the comments of Trombley & Watt, pp. 105–6 and 108.
109. Joshua 84–6; Greatrex, 1998, 115ff.
110. Theodore Lector 2.19 (pp.193–4); Procop. *Wars* 1.15.21–25, de Aed. 3.6.1ff. (describes the methods used by the Tzani and Romans up to the time when Sittas fought there in the 520s); Haarer 70; Greatrex 1998, 129–30.
111. Joshua 88; Greatrex, 1998, 116.
112. Zachariah 7.6 with Greatrex 1998, 116ff.
113. Joshua 88–93.
114. This situation resulted from the fact that the wealthier classes were usually in a position to avoid having to pay taxes. In this case the local magnates distributed the soldiers into the houses of the poorer classes. On an empire-wide level this meant that the poorer classes and the Roman emperors usually financed the wars out of their own pockets. This was very problematic in a situation in which wealth was concentrated in the hands of very few rich people, the most important of which were the senators. Only the most ruthless emperors, Caracalla and Gallienus for example, were prepared to make the senators and other wealthy people pay their fair share of the costs of defence or wars. This is why both of these emperors received bad press from pro-senatorial historians. As I noted in the context of West Rome, this ability of the rich to avoid having to contribute their fair share of the costs of the defence of the Empire was certainly one of the main reasons for the fall of West Rome. The rich refused to pay for the upkeep of the native army while they also refused to pay the protection money required by the barbarians. This was a combination which resulted in their own downfall.
115. Joshua 95ff. with the comments of Trombley & Watt; Greatrex 1998, 117–8. Marriage between father and daughter was allowed in Sassanian society.
116. Zachariah 7.6; Procopius, *Wars* 1.10.13ff.
117. Greatrex, 1998, 107. Trombley & Watt (p.102, n.502).
118. Greatrex 1998, 129–30.
119. Procop. Wars 1.10.1–12.
120. Marcellinus a.515; Malalas 16.17; John of Antioch fr. 214e (Roberto ed. 311.104ff.); Cedrenus 633; Haarer, 70.
121. John of Antioch fr. 216 (Roberto ed. 313); Haarer, 70; PLRE2.

122. Marcellinus' dating 1 Sept. 501 – 31 Aug 502 would of course allow the dating to 501, but his reference to the complete absence of forces proves that this invasion must have taken place in 502.
123. Marcellinus a. 493, 499, 502.
124. Marc. 493, 499, 502; Blockley, 1992, 87, 94; Haarer, 106–114.
125. See Syvänne, 2004.
126. Sources for this and above can be found in the PLRE2.
127. Hodgkin 3.353ff.; Haarer, 94ff.; Rouche with the letters, translations and comments.
128. The Armorican incident is mentioned by James after Procopius *Wars* 5.12.13ff. The reason for the inability of the Franks to defeat the Armoricans was obviously that they were still part of the Briton-Roman Empire, the fate of which I have described in the monograph *Britain in the Age of Arthur*. The collapse of the Briton Empire started when Keredic succeeded Malgo/Maglocune on the British throne in about 508. The collapse was due mainly to internal divisions at a time when the Saxon invaders raided the island.
129. For the career of Clovis, see James, 78ff.; Haarer, 94–5; PLRE2; and esp. Rouche who has also collected a very significant portion of the extant evidence at the end of the book together with an analysis and French translation.
130. Haarer, 94ff.; James, 86ff.; Hodgkin, 3.353ff.
131. Haarer, 97; James, 78ff., Rouche, 307ff.; PLRE2.
132. Haarer, 98–100; James, 87–8; Hodgkin, 3.399ff.
133. The accounts of the war between the Heruls and Lombards are slightly different in Procopius (Wars 6.14–15) and Paulus Diaconus (*Hist. Lang.* 1.20). The former says that the war started because the Heruls detested peace and is in this case more reliable as a period author who had access to reliable witnesses. Furthermore, this information coincides with what we know of their habits. See the above text of Procopius with the information of their habits drawn from Procopius in *MHLR* vol.1. The latter claims that the reason for the war was the murder of Rodulf's brother by Lombard king Tato's daughter Rumetruda while it hides the submission of the Lombards to the Heruls. If one were to try to reconcile these two, then it could be possible that the murder contributed to the situation, but was not the decisive factor. The date comes from Marcellinus a.511–12.
134. Haarer, 98–100; James, 87–8; Hodgkin, 3.399ff.
135. Hodgkin, 3.353ff.
136. *Ibid.*
137. Based on Haarer Chapter 5.
138. Haarer, 115ff.
139. The right of asylum meant that a person who fled to the church was safe from authorities, at least officially.
140. Their continued role as Imperial bodyguards will be discussed in greater detail in the context of the Nika Revolt in *MHLR* vol. 6.
141. Marcellinus a.511–12. I have here adopted a different dating based on Haarer.
142. John of Antioch (Roberto ed. fr. 311); Malalas, 16.16; Theophanes, AM 6005; Haarer, 164–6.
143. PLRE2; Haarer, 164–5.
144. Victor Tonnensis places the revolt to the year 510, but he is obviously not as reliable as Marcellinus. Haarer places the revolt to have taken place in 514 and not in 513 as Theophanes claims because as a sixth century author Marcellinus Comes is to be considered more reliable, but we should not forget that in actuality Marcellinus' dating always includes two years because it is based on indictions, which in this case covered the period 1 Sept. 513 – 31 Aug. 514. Therefore the two sources are actually in agreement regarding the date 513.
145. In the same manner as had happened during the reigns of Leo and Zeno with Theoderic Strabo and Theoderic the Amal and Illus after 481.

146. See Haarer, 166–9; PLRE2 Hypatius 5–6 and Vitalianus 2; and the sources mentioned in the text above.
147. See Haarer, 167ff.; PLRE2 Hypatius 5–6 and Vitalianus.
148. John of Antioch (Roberto ed. fr. 311.9ff.) with the PLRE2 and Haarer (167).
149. Haarer (167–8) does not accept their account, but in my opinion this is a mistake because their account actually explains how Vitalianus obtained the support of the Goths and the varying details concerning the ransoming of Hypatius.
150. John of Antioch, (Roberto ed. 311.19ff.), Marcellinus a.513–4 and John of Nikiu 79.72–77 with the other sources and analysis in the PLRE2 and Haarer 167–9.
151. It was probably because of this that the hardy warrior Emperor Gallienus was called effeminate. See my biography of him. This was kindly suggested by someone on the Facebook discussion and I thank him for this comment.
152. John of Antioch (Roberto ed. fr. 311.48ff.); Haarer (170) with the PLRE2 and sources therein.
153. 'tinos tôn en tois sômatofulaxi tetagmenôn tou Basileôs' in John of Antioch, which Haarer interprets as one of the protectores while Roberto interprets as one of the excubitores.
154. John of Antioch claims that the darkness was caused by the magical arts of the Huns, but a more prosaic version would be that the arrows shadowed the sun or simply that storm clouds created darkness.
155. John of Antioch (Roberto ed. fr. 311.67ff.); Theophanes AM 6005; Haarer, 170–71. For the information regarding the oxen and Strategikon, see Syvänne, 2004, 196, which also refers to this battle.
156. Marcellinus a.514–15; John of Antioch (Roberto ed. fr.311.103ff.); Malalas, 16.17.
157. Haarer connects this invasion with Vitalianus' third attack against Constantinople, but in my opinion this is not the case because John of Antioch places it between those.
158. Haarer, 173–75 with the sources mentioned therein.
159. Malalas, 16.6; John of Nikiu 79.78ff.; Syvänne, 2004, 509–10, PLRE2; Haarer, 176.
160. Malalas, 16.6; John of Nikiu 79.78ff.; Syvänne, 2004, 509–10; PLRE2; Haarer, 176ff.
161. John of Antioch Roberto ed. fr. 311.109ff.; Malalas, 16.6; Evagrius, 3.43; John of Nikiu, 79.78ff.; Syvänne, 2004, 509–510; PLRE2; Haarer, 176ff.
162. The same is also mentioned by Malalas (16.6) who adds that Proclus died soon after he reached Athens.
163. He was no longer in office after 1 April 517, because Sergius is attested as PPO in 1 April 517. Marinus was nominated again by Justin to this position in 519.
164. John of Antioch fr. 216 (Roberto ed. 313); Haarer, 70; PLRE2.
165. This is entirely based on Haarer, 223–9.
166. The principal original source is Constantine Porphyrogenitus' De cerimoniis 1.93, which has been borrowed from Peter the Patrician. For the Amantius/Theocritus affair, see the sources listed in Bury (2.16) and PLRE2. This and the following discussion of the process of electing the new Emperor is based on Constantine Porphyrogenitus' De cerimoniis 1.93, and on the secondary studies Vasiliev (68–82), Bury (2.16–20); PLRE2 and Greatrex (1996, 126), but does not follow their version.
167. Bury (2.16ff.) interprets this differently so that he considers Theocritus to have been a domesticus of Amantius.
168. Bury (2.18) suggests an alternative in which Justin purposely sought the support of the Senate from the start for himself by first having his men nominate John who would have been unacceptable to the Senate so that in the pressure of time the Senate would be forced to nominate none other than Justin. In my opinion, this is incorrect because it does not take into account the actions of Celer and the scholarii, even if it is still a better theory than the version of Vasiliev which just follows the account of Constantine/Peter the Patrician without any further analysis.

Chapter 13

1. The latest edition, translation and analysis of the *Epitedeuma* is by Geoffrey Greatrex and Hugh Elton (hereafter *Epiteudeuma* when referring to the source and Greatrex & Elton when referring to comments). The latest edition of the *Tacticon* and two of the epigrams (p. 150, 162) are by Förster.
2. See Greatrex & Elton.
3. Greatrex & Elton, 40.
4. *Ibid*, 41.
5. *Ibid*, 41–2.
6. I will produce an edition, translation and commentary of these when I have enough time and the necessary funding for it.
7. Urbicius 3ff. with the comments and analysis of Greatrex & Elton.
8. *Ibid*.
9. *Decuria, dekania* and *dekarchia* all imply a unit of ten men, but in truth it was the same unit as the eight-man *contubernium* (tent-group) because the ten men included the eight men plus one recruit and one servant who were usually left inside the marching camp during combat.
10. Greatrex & Elton, 50ff.

Index

Arnegisclus, Ornigisclus, father of Anagastes
  East Roman *MVM*, 64, 90, 267
Arsenius, general, 145
Artemidoros, *bucellarius* of Trocundes, 142, 144
Arthur, King, Ambrosius Aurelius /
  Aurelianus, Utherpendragon, Riothamus,
  Dux Bellorum, High-King and *Augustus*, 28,
  32, 39–40, 42, 119, 262, 265–6, 270, 281
  see also Riothamus; Syvänne, *Britain in the
    Age of Arthur*
Artillery, stone-thrower, onager, mangonel,
  trebuchet, ballista, carroballista, scorpion, 3,
  69, 82, 186, 211, 244, 257
  see also Fortifications, Sieges, Wagon Laager
Arvandus, *PPG*, 40
Arverni, Arvenia, Arverna, ix, 42, 51, 54
  see also Auvergne, Clermont-Ferrand
Arzamon / Arzamena area and river, 194, 201
  see also Apadna
Arzanene, Arzoun, 79, 191–3, 208–209,
  211–15, 278
Ascanius, traitor, 22
Asclepiades, *Dux Palestinae*, 143
Asclepiodotus, military writer, 256
Ashparin, fort, 193, 197
Asiaticus, general, 232
Asouades, phylarch, 190
Aspalius, brother of Illus, 118
Aspar, son of Ardabur Sr., East Roman *MVM*
  (c.424–71), 1, 39, 45, 57–60, 63, 68, 74–6,
  79, 82–4, 86, 89–95, 97–100, 140, 266–9,
  277
  see also Syvänne, MHLR Vols. 3–4
Assassin, Assassins, Assassination, murder,
  killer, 10, 15, 21, 32, 34–5, 39, 45, 47–8, 63,
  86, 92–4, 97–9, 102, 104–105, 116–20, 131,
  133–6, 146, 162, 172, 203, 235, 242, 249,
  265, 267, 270–1, 281
  see also Agentes in Rebus, Diplomacy, Poison,
    Stratagems
Astabid (spahbad/spahbod, presumably
  meaning Eran-Spahbad / Eiran-Spahbad),
  Persian commander, 199, 216–17, 219–20
Astat, *comes*, 95
Asteria, wife of rebel Illus, 144
Asthiane, 182
Astura (Zeiselmaur), 34
Asturica, city, 9
Astyrius, West Roman *MVM*, 50
Asuristan-Babylonia, 205
Athanasius, Bishop of Alexandria under Zeno
  and Anastasius, 145

Atesis [Athesis, mod. Adige], river, 153, 158
Athenodorus, Isaurian senator and rebel,
  167–8, 172–3, 275
Athenodorus, Isaurian rebel, 168, 173, 275
Attila, High-King of the Huns, 2, 7, 55, 62–4,
  67, 78, 87, 89, 259, 267
  see also Syvänne, *MHLR Vol.4 (425-457)*
Augsburg, city of, vii
Augustulus, Romulus, *see* Romulus
Augustus, Augusta, titles, 2, 9, 12–13, 25, 55,
  63–4, 104, 106, 108, 144, 174, 217, 263
Auragenses, 21, 23
Aureliani, *see* Orleans
Auvergne, 42, 51, 53–5
  see also Arverni, Clermond-Ferrand
Auxilia / Auxiliaries, 16, 273, 275
  see also Allies, *Comitatenses*, Federates,
    Palace, *Bucellarii, Limitanei*
Auxilia Palatina, see Auxilia
Avars, nomads, 62
Avitus, West Roman *MVM* and emperor (455-
  6), 9–10, 13, 20, 24, 44, 49
  see also Syvänne, *MHLR Vol.4 (425-457)*
Avitus, bishop, 227
Azerbaijan, 208
Azov, Sea of, 62

Babai, Sarmatian king, 88, 90
Bacaudae / Bagaudae of Armorica, 1
  see also Armorica, Tarraconensis
Badicharimos, brother of Ogaros, 180
Baelo Claudia, 20
Baetica, 15, 18, 20–1, 23, 25
Bahram V Gur, Ruler of Persia (420-38), 7, 276
Balas / Valash, ruler of Persia, 80
Balearic Islands, 148
Balkans, ix–x, xv, 15, 35, 62, 65, 68, 74, 76, 78,
  86–7, 90–1, 97–8, 109, 112, 114, 146, 163,
  174–5, 217, 222–3, 225, 227–8, 230, 232–3,
  247, 252, 255, 263, 275
Bar-hadad, bishop, 198
Bardones, a tribe, 64
Barsa family, 219
Barsauma of Nisibis, 144
Basil, Basilius, *comes*, 202, 217
Basiliscus, Fl., brother of Verina, emperor
  (475-6), v, 39, 47, 63–4, 68–9, 74–7, 81–6,
  92–3, 99, 104–12, 116, 129, 267–9, 272
Basiliscus, son of Armatus, *Caesar*, 110, 112,
  116
Basilius of Aix, bishop, 54
Basilius, *PPI*, 137

Mummo, Ostrogothic general, 228
Mundhir, al-, Arab sheik, 197, 206, 221, 278
Mundo, warlord, 217, 224–5
    see also Syvänne, *MHLR Vol.6 (518-565)*
Mushleg the Armenian / Mushleg
    Mamikonean, 212, 279
Myrmidons, 269
Mysia, 73, 118
    see also Moesia

Naaman (Numan?), phylarch, 178, 180
    see also Numan
Naissus, mod. Niš, 95, 169
Namatius, friend of Sidonius, 50
Napoleonic after Napoleon I, emperor of
    France, 2
Narbonne / Narbo, 25, 54, 228
Nato, fort, 224
Naval Tactics, *see* Fleets
Navy, *see* Fleets
Neapolis in Samaria (not to be confused with
    modern Naples), 143
Nedao, river and battle, 149, 151
Negbath, village, 203
Nephalius, messenger, 145
Nepos, Julius, nephew of Marcellinus, *MVM*,
    emperor (474-5/474-80), v–vi, viii, 26, 44,
    48, 52–6, 95, 97–9, 108, 113–14, 124, 126,
    133–4, 266, 268, 271
Nepotianus, father of Nepos, general, 13–14,
    20, 22–5
Nestor, Nestorians, 77, 144, 163, 172, 230, 265
    see also Christians, Monophysites
Neuri/ Neurians, a tribe, 17, 21
Nicaea, city of, 110, 269
Nicomedia, city of, 140
Nicopolis, city of, 102
Nicostratus / Nikostratos, general, 175
Niketas, officer?, 129
Nisibis, city of, 144, 172, 178, 182, 190–3, 209,
    212, 214, 219–20, 278
Nobatae, Nobatai, Nobatia, *see* Nubians
Nobles, *see* Senators
Nonnosus, general, 217, 280
Noricum, Nori, 17, 31, 33, 41–2, 46, 56, 87–8,
    146, 148, 261, 265–7, 273
Novae, city of, 103, 110, 146, 268
Noviodunum, city of, 223
Nubians, Nobatae, 8, 83
    see also Blemmyes
Nuceria, 175
Numan, al-, sheik, 180, 193, 197, 201, 206, 278
Nymphius, river, 208–209

Odessus, (mod. Varna) city, x, 234–9
Odoacer, Odovacar, Odovacrius, Adovaricus,
    father was Edeco the Hun and mother
    probably either a Sciri or Goth, warlord or
    king of the Saxons, *patricius* and King of
    Rome (476–493), vi, 27–8, 32, 40, 42, 45–6,
    55–6, 113–14, 124, 133–4, 137–9, 145–8,
    151–61, 163, 173–4, 269, 270–3
Ogaros, son of Arethas, son of Thalabene,
    179–80
Olba, 105
Olisipo (or Ulixippona, mod. Lisbon), 10
Olybrius, Anicius, emperor in 472, v, 26–7,
    35, 37, 44–6, 48, 53, 60, 83, 94–5, 117, 121,
    188, 277
Olympius, general, 185, 217, 278
Onoguri, nomads, 62
Onulf (Onoulphus / Hunuulf), brother of
    Odoacer, 45, 55, 89, 113, 116–17, 124, 133,
    146, 161, 269–70
Opadna/Apadna/Apadana (mod. Tell
    Harzem), *see Apadna*
Orestes, *Patricius* and *MVM* (475-6), v, 52,
    54–6, 108, 113
Orleans, Aureliani, ix, 11, 27–8, 30–1, 35, 264
Osiris, tomb of, 58
Ostrogoths, ix, 7, 17, 19, 21, 35, 46, 50, 52–3,
    56, 61–5, 67, 73–6, 80, 86, 88–9, 93, 95,
    97–9, 103, 105, 117, 119–21, 123–4, 126,
    131, 134–5, 138, 142–3, 145, 147–50, 156,
    161, 173, 217, 222, 224–6, 228, 255, 263,
    267–8, 270, 273
    see also Goths, Visigoths, Theoderic
Ostrys, general, 68, 74–6, 92, 267–8
Ovida, *comes*, 133–4, 271
Ourba (Olba, mod. Ura), 105
Oxyrhynchus, 274

Pagan, pagans, Hellene, god, gods, goddess,
    10, 13, 37, 46, 110, 118, 136, 142, 180, 197,
    226–7, 236, 269
Pagarch, tax official, 177
Palace, *Palatina, Palatini,* Palatine, "of Palace",
    xiii, 2, 19, 45, 76, 92, 101, 104–105, 107,
    109–11, 118, 129–30, 135, 161–2, 165–6,
    174, 230, 243, 249–50, 271, 273, 275
Palchus, astrologer, 140
Palentia/Palencia, city, 10
Palestine, 58, 73, 143, 178–81, 197, 201, 206,
    221, 230, 232, 277–8
Palogorius the Gallaecian, envoy, 30
Pamphylia, 73